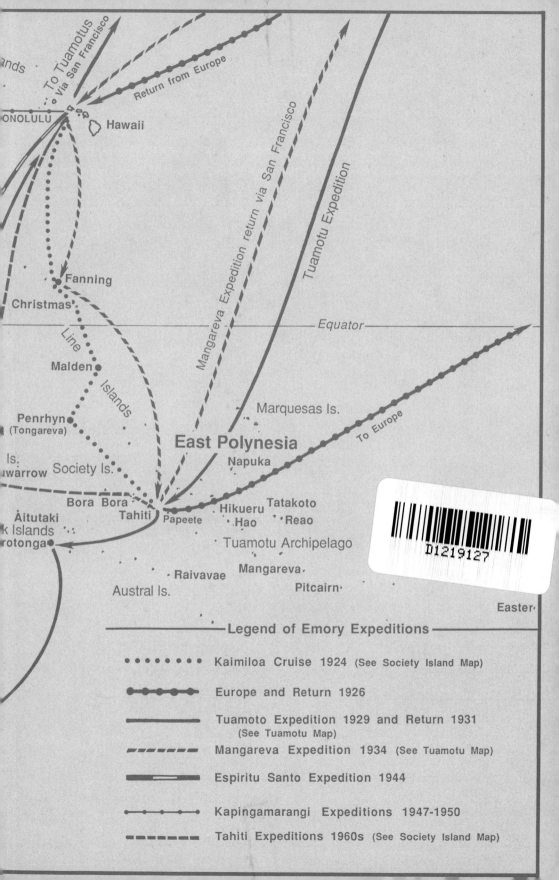

To Tuamotus
via San Francisco

Return from Europe

ONOLULU

Hawaii

Tuamotu Expedition

Mangareva Expedition return via San Francisco

Fanning

Christmas

Line

Equator

Malden

Islands

Penrhyn
(Tongareva)

Marquesas Is.

To Europe

Is.

uwarrow

Society Is.

East Polynesia

Napuka

Bora Bora

Tahiti

Papeete

Hikueru   Tatakoto

Aitutaki

Hao   Reao

k Islands

rotonga

Tuamotu Archipelago

Raivavae

Mangareva

Austral Is.

Pitcairn

D1219127

Easter

Legend of Emory Expeditions

• • • • • • • • Kaimiloa Cruise 1924 (See Society Island Map)

●━●━●━●━● Europe and Return 1926

──────── Tuamoto Expedition 1929 and Return 1931
              (See Tuamotu Map)

- - - - - - Mangareva Expedition 1934 (See Tuamotu Map)

━━━━━━━ Espiritu Santo Expedition 1944

•━•━•━•━• Kapingamarangi Expeditions 1947-1950

- - - - - - Tahiti Expeditions 1960s (See Society Island Map)

Keneti

Keneti
South Seas Adventures of Kenneth Emory

Bob Krauss

A Kolowalu Book
University of Hawaii Press • Honolulu

93 92 91 90 89 88   5 4 3 2 1

Library of Congress Cataloging-in-Publication Data

Krauss, Bob.
  Keneti : South Seas adventures of Kenneth Emory / Bob Krauss.
    p.   cm. — (A Kolowalu book)
  Includes index.
  ISBN 0-8248-1153-4 :
  1. Oceania—Description and travel. 2. Emory, Kenneth Pike, 1897-
—Homes and haunts—Oceania. 3. Anthropologists—United States—
Biography. I. Title.
DU22.K776   1988
919'.04'0924—dc19   88-10693
[B]   CIP

Contents

Prologue

On July 9, 1930, on the South Pacific atoll of Vahitahi, deep in the remote Tuamotu Archipelago, the high priest Tangi called forth the people of the island. He stood before them under the arching coconut palms and recited the ancient chants used when hauling canoes over the reef to shore. There is no pass into the lagoon at Vahitahi and canoes had to be dragged from the sea to safety. Tangi drilled the people to be sure they remembered correctly the old Polynesian sea chanties.

A thirty-two-year-old white man, deeply tanned, hovered on the fringes of this activity. The natives called him Keneti, for Kenneth. He had set up a hand-cranked motion picture camera on a heavy tripod at the edge of the reef. Keneti was not from Hollywood, although South Sea movies had become money-makers. This slender, broad-shouldered man was a scientist who had come to Vahitahi to advance the cause of anthropological research among Polynesians.

Nineteen thirty was a good year for the advancement of a lot of things. The first airline stewardess pioneered her profession for a new company called United Airlines. General Motors introduced the 16-cylinder Cadillac. Henry R. Luce founded *Fortune* magazine and the *Time-Life* empire. King Features started a new comic strip called *Blondie*. Frozen foods came on the market. Also sliced bread. And French's Worchestershire Sauce. The first supermarket opened for business.

The natives of Vahitahi were unaware of these milestones because their only contact with the outside world was an occasional trading schooner and the tiny missionary cutter of Père Paul Maze. The only modern-age miracle they had seen was Keneti's little battery-powered radio transmitting set on which he tapped out signals in Morse code and sometimes raised the operator in Tahiti. The Tuamotuans did not look upon Keneti as a scientist but as a friendly visitor who spoke their language and was interested in such things as chants and string figures. They were happy to haul his canoe onshore.

Keneti's salt-stained craft was some twenty-eight feet long, a cutter built in Tahiti for scientific cruising among the tricky currents and dangerous reefs of the Tuamotus. The vessel had one mast and a balky engine. She was called *Mahina-i-te-Pua*, which means "moonlight on the bow wave." A current had swept her so far off course on the approach to Vahitahi that the captain spent half a day finding the low streak of dark green that marked the island. Then the *Mahina* sailed back and forth around the atoll for nine and half days because there was no anchorage. One night a storm blew her far off station. The advancement of anthropology required that she be hauled to safety.

Every man, woman, and child on Vahitahi gathered on the reef to participate in this marvelous event. The rope was made fast and the crowd grabbed hold. Tangi took up the chant and the heaving began. The *Mahina* wallowed up on the reef as Keneti cranked the movie camera, recording a scene that had never been put on film. The men from the past strained on the rope that drew the benefits of science to their atoll.

In this case, science proved reluctant. The *Mahina* weighed far more than a graceful canoe, even more than a double-hulled voyaging canoe. She inched forward on the reef and stuck. Now the chanting became more spirited. Tangi implored the gods to infuse strength into the arms of the people of Vahitahi. They strained mightily, shouting the chanties in full-throated unison. The *Mahina* stirred a few times and then stubbornly refused to be disturbed further.

A cold wind came up and it began to rain. The people of Vahitahi sensibly returned to their homes, leaving the *Mahina* high and dry and reasonably safe on the reef. Keneti also ran for shelter to protect his movie camera. The failure to beach the *Mahina* really didn't disappoint him too much. But the old Polynesian sea chanties, those voices from across the centuries, had stirred him deeply. To record such elusive scraps of human experience he endured seasickness, sunburn, loneliness, and bad water. For this he risked his life, slept on the floor, suffered pain, and worked like a stevedore.

The man South Sea islanders called Keneti became the father of archaeology in the Pacific and the premier authority about a romantic island race called Polynesians. To him travel in the South Seas was an adventure dignified by the opportunity to assist fragile human beings in their understanding of one another. He did not write with the skill of Herman Melville or Robert Louis Stevenson or other authors who created images of the South Seas. Yet he etched a picture of the people who called him Keneti with a realism that is in many ways more intriguing.

And he was, like Melville, a pioneer. As a boy he sailed with Jack London. As a young man he worked with another beginning scientist, Margaret Mead. As an adult he encouraged a French naval cadet for whom he predicted a brilliant future, Jacques Cousteau. The important moments of his life were spent in tropical valleys and arid atolls so remote that even today most travelers don't know how to get to them. His life was so full of South Sea adventures there isn't room here to include them all, although the major portion of this book describes from his vivid and detailed journals eight strenuous expeditions to exotic corners of the Pacific.

Like most pioneers, he did not conform. That makes it difficult, sometimes, to separate the anthropologist from his sense of humor and lack of pretension. He could have been taken for a sailor, a schoolteacher, a newspaper reporter, a photographer, a handyman, a janitor, a filing clerk, or the next-door neighbor. In fact, he was all of these things.

The following pages will explain how he did it, and why.

PART ONE
A DREAM OF THE SOUTH SEAS

Chapter One

A Paradox
of Origin

During the past two hundred years a great many normally staid and sensible mortals have felt an implausible urge to go adventuring among the South Sea islands. One of the principal attractions there is a race of handsome, hospitable people called Polynesians, who inhabited this latitude of perpetual summer long before Europeans first sailed into the Pacific.

It is not uncommon that adolescent dreams of sailing to far-away places eventually give way to mature reality. But continuing reports of the tropical, palm-shaded paradise and the exotic inhabitants of the South Seas have made the islands desirable, even to rational adults. Long before travel commercials sailors before the mast swore by the beauty of Polynesian women. Philosophers who had never set foot on a Pacific island discovered there the noble savage. As soon as steamships and airlines and hotels were put in place, tourists flocked to see the hula girls and suntanned surfers.

It was inevitable that scientists should eventually enter the field. These sober-sided debunkers of pleasant myths for once forgot to be cynical. They found in the South Seas the most romantic of scientific mysteries. A hint of this came in 1778 when Captain James Cook, who put Polynesia on the map, discovered to his surprise that the Hawaiians understood a language he had learned more than 2,000 nautical miles to the south in Tahiti. The Maoris of New Zealand, some 1,800 miles southwest of Tahiti, spoke another dialect of the same language. Yet New Zealand is 4,000 miles from Hawaii.

How could this be? The Hawaiians, Tahitians, and Maoris, as well as the inhabitants of widely scattered islands in between, apparently all belong to one race and share a common origin. By what wild stretch of probability could Stone Age people have populated these vast reaches of the Pacific long before the white man came to teach them the principles of navigation? Where did they come from and how did they get there? Museums around the world are filled with research reports about the origin and exploits of the enigmatic Polynesians.

About 125 of these reports were written by Kenneth Pike Emory, known to South Sea islanders as Keneti and, at the height of his career, regarded by his colleagues as the most distinguished archaeologist of the Pacific. Emory achieved a position as a scientist at the Bishop Museum in Honolulu in 1920 when anthropology in Polynesia was still a guessing game. He discovered temple ruins that no one knew existed and recorded the last surviving oral literature from the age of island mythology.

No sailor or beachcomber poked around so many remote and exotic corners of the Pacific nor spent more time living with Polynesians. He spoke three dialects of their language. During World War II he taught more than a quarter of a million American fighting men how to survive on desert islands.

At the age of fifty, when his pioneering days should have been over, he revolutionized archaeology in Oceania by digging in the ground in spite of the accepted dogma that held there was nothing to find on islands. His carbon date from a shelter cave on Oahu inspired museums from Europe, the Americas, and Asia to dig in the Pacific.

It is fitting, therefore, that the story of Kenneth Pike Emory, like that of the mysterious islanders he studied, should begin with his origin. But here we run hard against a mystery as profound as that of the Polynesians themselves. For he did not originate amid palm trees and the sound of the surf. He was born in a winter-bound, missionary-oriented, factory-infested place called Fitchburg, Massachusetts.

Let us now explore this paradox.

A few tantalizing glimpses into the past hint at a streak of panache in the Emorys, a spark of rebellion that might prefer coconut palms to mass production. For one thing, Walter L. Emory, Kenneth's father, was born with the photogenic features of a matinee idol, a gift of persuasion and a passion for collecting postage stamps. Walter took up, of all things, amateur acting. And that wasn't the worst. Instead of enrolling at the Massachusetts Institute of Technology and making something of himself, he signed on a schooner and sailed off to the Azores. A report reached his family that the ship went down in a storm. Fortunately, it was the wrong ship. Walter returned to Fitchburg safe and sunburned. He found work tending machinery in a cotton mill while continuing his stamp business and dramatic career.

Apparently he was good enough to make guest appearances, for it was in Boston that a highly eligible young lady named Winifred Pike attended one of his performances. She had come to Boston with her

father, a prosperous New Hampshire merchant and manufacturer of whetstones, who had founded the village of Pike where his factory was located. They were in town for a commercial fair where Pike whetstones were on prominent display, each stamped with a regal letter "P" and the sign of the fish that shared its name with the manufacturer.

Winifred later told her daughter-in-law that she "greatly admired" Walter Emory from across the footlights. The phrase does not express today the emotion it conveyed then. Winifred was, after all, a properly bred young woman of the early 1890s. She dressed beautifully and did her hair in the elegant fashion of the time. She read books and wrote poetry and knew how to manage a household. She was a devout Congregationalist, but was not prudish. There was nothing she liked better than a party, which, to her, meant having guests to dinner or tea.

Father Pike made no objection when his beautiful daughter fell in love with a man who worked in a cotton mill. Walter Emory did not behave like a factory worker. He recited Shakespeare and told fascinating stories about his adventures at sea. He also published two issues of a journal for postage stamp collectors for which he sold advertising. Clearly, Winifred saw in Walter more than the cotton mill, even though he was an Episcopalian. To prove her love, she joined his church and agreed to be married in Fitchburg by an Episcopalian minister. The couple moved in with the Emory family on High Street. There was plenty of room in the big, three-story, white house flanked by chimneys on either end and with columns ranging along the front porch. That was in 1893.

Walter did not join his father in the family meat market as expected. He couldn't settle on a career even after the birth of a son, Closson, in 1894. Walter's dreams outstripped his means while his gift of persuasion made the dreams sound plausible—at least to a wealthy Fitchburg resident named Crocker. Walter persuaded this gentleman that there was a great deal of money to be made planting coffee in a Pacific archipelago called Hawaii. The two of them would therefore travel at Mr. Crocker's expense to Hawaii to investigate this attractive proposition.

Winifred remained behind with their year-old baby in 1895 while her husband, the coffee expert, escorted his client 15,000 miles around Cape Horn on a journey that parted Mr. Crocker from some of his money and finally provided Walter with a goal in life. He returned to Fitchburg determined to live in Hawaii, a proposition even more impractical than his speculation in coffee because he had no visible prospects there for supporting his wife and son.

Yet his dream did not fade even after a second son arrived on November 23, 1897, in the same room where Walter himself had been born. Family tradition failed to make it a promising birth. Kenneth Pike Emory weighed only four-and-one-half pounds. He remained frail and caught every childhood disease there was to catch. Winifred had been ill during the pregnancy. She took the blame for little Kenneth's poor beginning and tried to make up for it by coddling him. The child got what he wanted by pointing. By age two, he had not yet learned to form words. Winifred worried and fussed over him. But he would not talk. He only pointed.

Meanwhile, the remote Hawaiian Islands moved closer to New England. There had always been an umbilical cord of Protestant missionary activity that linked Fitchburg and Honolulu. Now, on July 7, 1898, President William McKinley signed a resolution passed in the House of Representatives that annexed Hawaii to the United States. Walter didn't miss the headlines. Every time he passed a book stall there were more titles about America's new, exotic islands. The books reminded Walter of what he had been saying all along; here was a land of new opportunity, perpetual summer, and reasonably reliable plumbing.

Kenneth, the youngest son, had started his third year when his father decided to make the move to Hawaii. Walter was twenty-seven. We do not know where the money came from. What we do know is that Walter went ahead alone to find work and a place to live. Winifred could only wait and hope it would turn out all right.

Chapter Two

I Can be Coaxed but not Driven

Walter Emory arrived at Honolulu February 28, 1900, on board the SS *Alameda* in the middle of a bubonic plague epidemic. The disease had broken out the previous December in crowded Chinatown. In a few weeks it had spread alarmingly. On January 20 a fire set to destroy contaminated houses burned down thirty-eight acres of tenements. It was the worst fire in Honolulu's history. About seven thousand homeless Chinese, Japanese, and Hawaiians had to be segregated as well as sheltered because they were exposed to the plague. The entire island was under quarantine.

Having arrived amidst pestilence and disaster, Walter looked for a job. He went about this task with commendable singleness of purpose. No coffee speculations this time. No stamp collectors' journals or amateur theatricals. He found work as a bookkeeper for a part-Hawaiian building contractor, William Mutch. How he talked Mr. Mutch into giving him such an assignment must remain a mystery because nobody in the family can explain it.

One reason may have been a demand in the construction industry for bright, literate, and employable young men. Since annexation, new houses had been going up all over town: Manoa Valley, Palolo Valley, Kalihi, Makiki. Hawaii's first resort hotel, the Moana, was on the drawing board at Waikiki Beach. Plans were coming together for an even larger hotel-office complex downtown, the Alexander Young. At six stories it would be Honolulu's tallest building.

On May 1, 1900, the *Pacific Commercial Advertiser* proclaimed in a banner headline, "Plague Pilikia Pau Loa," which means "the trouble with the plague is over at last." Now Walter could send for his family. The journey required five days and nights by train to San Francisco via Chicago, then another week by steamer to Honolulu. There is no family tradition that Winifred made any protest. With Closson, six, and Kenneth, two and one-half, she set out to join her husband.

By the time they reached California in June, the whole state was under quarantine because of the plague. Passengers leaving on trains had to show health certificates in order to cross the border into other states. However, the restriction did not apply to travelers going overseas because they posed no threat to fellow Americans except in the new Territory of Hawaii, which was already infested.

Honolulu appeared harmless enough the first time Winifred saw it. As the SS *China* rounded the grim bulk of Diamond Head Crater on June 29, she got her first glimpse of Waikiki, a fringe of white sand beach separating the vivid blue of the ocean and the vivid green shore. Cottages and a few larger buildings nestled in the vegetation against a magnificent backdrop of rugged, jungle-robed mountains.

Close up, the city of Honolulu looked like an American town at a costume party. The business district appeared familiar, if a trifle tawdry. Drays and carriages plodded along the streets as in San Francisco although not in the same numbers. The same brands of merchandise on display in the stores had been on display in Fitchburg. But hack drivers in San Francisco did not wear floral wreaths as hatbands. Clerks in Fitchburg did not babble in foreign tongues. There were no Chinese in pigtails nor petite Japanese women tripping along in kimonos. For Winifred, the contrast was even more marked in residential neighborhoods where the houses were smothered in flowering trees, and gardens erupted with tropical vitality.

Walter had found a cottage to rent on Emma Street—above Vineyard Street and below Punchbowl Crater. A bachelor friend from Fitchburg, Charles Merriam, soon took a room, which helped pay expenses. The house was within easy walking distance to downtown offices and shops and to St. Andrew's Episcopal Cathedral down the street. Farther down and around the corner on Beretania Street lived Queen Liliuokalani, Hawaii's deposed monarch, in a charming white house called Washington Place. All in all, the location was convenient and sufficiently respectable until Walter made enough money to buy a home of their own.

It didn't take him long to figure out how to accomplish this. The books Walter Emory kept for Mr. Mutch must have taught him there was money to be made in the construction business. He began bringing home texts on civil engineering and architecture. Years later, his son remembered, "Father began studying as soon as we moved to Hawaii. He was always reading and he was very bright. Learning came easily to him."

The 1905 city directory listed Walter Emory as a contractor, not as Mutch's bookkeeper. Then he linked up with a neighbor on Emma Street, Marshall H. Webb, who had been promoted from draftsman in the city Department of Public Works to oversee the U.S. Engineering Office in Honolulu. Webb designed the houses that Emory sold and built. "Father was good at getting contracts," said his son.

"He could talk anybody into anything." But Emory was not content as a contractor. He kept studying. By 1911, Emory and Webb had opened offices as architects upstairs at 925 Fort Street. No doubt about it, Walter had settled down.

There is every indication that Winifred fell in love with Honolulu on sight. She kept a scrapbook that she called "Primer on Hawaii Nei." In it she pasted her own poems and verses by others written in the flowery sentimentality of the time. Winifred had promised to love and honor her husband and she did that, although the standard of living he provided in the beginning could not have matched that of her father. Maids were common in *haole* (meaning foreign, particularly Caucasian), white families but Winifred did her own housekeeping. The lack of labor-saving appliances was partially offset by other conveniences. The markets delivered groceries ordered by telephone. A milk wagon appeared at the back door every morning. Chinese peddlers toured the neighborhood with pushcarts, hawking fresh fruits and vegetables. There is not much doubt that Winifred spoke her mind at home. Among the mementos pasted into her scrapbook was a greeting card she received from her father. The illustration shows a seated bulldog with a caption, "I can be coaxed but not driven." This probably describes her relationship with Walter Emory.

The favorite form of entertainment in Honolulu took place in the home: birthday parties, anniversaries, school graduations, parties for friends leaving on trips, surprise parties, weddings, receptions for new residents, and so forth. "Father made friends easily," said their son. "There was nothing Mother liked better than giving a tea or dinner party. She was always having people over; cooking, putting out the silver and the heirloom china."

Winifred and Walter moved in the elite *haole* society but were also welcome in a number of Hawaiian homes. Walter's part-Hawaiian employer became so close to the family that Winifred acted as chaperone for teenage Maria Mutch on her first trip to the mainland of the United States. The Emorys made other Hawaiian friends including a branch of the prominent Cleghorn clan. "Father liked Hawaiian music," explained Kenneth later. "There was always a ukulele in the house."

It was not a politically involved family. Walter voted Republican, as did his business associates, but there are indications that he did not discuss with his Hawaiian friends issues like the revolution of 1893, which aroused bitterness. Winifred, who felt strongly about sin and morality, must have read with dismay the newspaper accounts of violence on sugar plantations, where police broke up strikes by immigrant Japanese over grievances that the newspapers seldom explained clearly.

None of these concerns loomed as large to Winifred and Walter as work and home and family. They enrolled Closson at Punahou School, which was established by Protestant missionaries in the 1840s and had an academic standing as high as any school in New England. Winifred became deeply involved in church activities and Walter tended to his blossoming career.

Chapter Three

A Dunk in the Lily Pond

Kenneth was four years old before he began to talk in a weak voice that squeezed out of his throat. He was still small and slight but no longer frail. Wiry described him better. His problem was not lack of energy but too much of it. Winifred, still protective, insisted on mothering her "precious darling." Kenneth hated that.

At an early age he displayed an inquiring turn of mind, especially about matches. His afternoon naps had become particularly trying. To relieve the boredom of lying awake he sneaked a box of matches into bed. Striking one, he threw the flame into the mosquito net above his crib and set the mosquito net on fire. His mother rushed in from her own nap, grabbed Kenneth, and inadvertently ignited her nightgown. Mura, the cook, slapped out the fire. Kenneth emerged with singed eyelashes but still fascinated by matches. He next experimented by lighting a fire under the house. A neighbor spotted the smoke in time to extinguish the blaze before it burned the place down. This time Kenneth got a licking, which satisfied his curiosity about matches.

The Emory boys were as unlike as two brothers can be. Closson, older and bigger, had his father's confident way with people. He made friends with no effort. Kenneth, small and shy, kept to himself. He invented his own games. One day he sat in the front yard in the little rocking chair his parents had brought for him from Fitchburg. The driveway was covered with black ash from Punchbowl Crater, a commonly used paving material at the time. When a pedestrian passed by, Kenneth picked up a handful of ash and pretended to eat it. The attention he received and the laughter his deception produced delighted him.

He was a little older when he made a careful observation of the newsboy on a downtown street corner. Honolulu's newsboys were a picturesque lot of ragamuffins: small Hawaiians, Chinese, Portuguese, and Caucasians in cloth caps and ragged pants and bare feet. Kenneth noticed that every time the newsboy gave someone a newspaper, he received a nickel in return. Kenneth's father subscribed to the newspaper. Kenneth found a back issue, ran outside, and sold it to the first passerby. The expression on the man's face when he opened the newspaper told Kenneth something had gone awry in his plan, so he took to his heels and, thereafter, gave up the newsvending business.

At the proper time, Kenneth's parents sent him to school. His experimental approach to learning and his high-energy lifestyle had not prepared him for the classroom. He flunked the first grade. The teacher explained diplomatically that she loved Kenneth so much she was keeping him for another year. This did not bolster his fragile ego. He became more shy and less confident.

One of his favorite adventures at age seven was a family excursion to Waikiki by tram behind two trotting mules. The route passed by patches of taro with graceful stalks and broad, regal leaves. Marvelous, mosquito-infested fish ponds with mirror tops reflected the soaring, spidery trunks of coconut palms and their ragged explosion of fronds.

The destination for these trips was Ainahau, one of Honolulu's botanical showplaces and famous as the former home of Hawaii's most romantic figure, the beautiful Princess Kaiulani, daughter of King Kalakaua's sister and a Scottish businessman named Cleghorn. A dirt drive off Kalakaua Avenue just beyond the Moana Hotel led between rows of ornamental palms into a jungle of exotic vegetation to a sprawling wood house that had once been the scene of royal receptions. In 1905 it was occupied by a new architect in town, Oliver G. Traphagen, and his family. A business relationship between Walter Emory and Oliver Traphagen had led to a family friendship. Young Kenneth loved to explore the Ainahau jungle but he was ambivalent about his female playmate, little Geraldine Traphagen. On one trip he pushed her into the lily pond.

In 1907 Walter Emory bought the house he had been promising his wife. The new address was Bates Street, located at the bottom of Nuuanu Valley—Honolulu's most fashionable residential district. The handsome stone bungalow stood on a hill with a view of Honolulu from the front windows. The laundry room, garage, and storage areas occupied the slope underneath. Winifred sat right down and wrote a poem about it:

Among ferns, kiawe, bananas and palms
  On picturesque rocks our little home stands.
Blue glimpses of ocean in storm and in calm,
  With its harbor of ships and its coral sands,
Brings song to the lips and joy to the eye
  As we gaze through the trees from our little *lanai*.

Walter's father and mother came to live with the family soon after the move to Bates Street. Grandfather Emory sent the furniture, china, and family heirlooms by sailing ship around Cape Horn while he and Grandmother Emory rode the train. However, the vessel foundered and all of the elder Emory's possessions sank to the bottom of the sea. Grandfather Emory consoled himself by tending plants in the yard. He also did the marketing, especially for meat, being by far the best-qualified member of the family for the task.

Kenneth unabashedly loved his grandfather and could not wait for summer to come when he and his brother would stay with the gentle old man in a whitewashed shack on Kaneohe Bay. This major adventure of the year began by a carriage ride up forested Nuuanu Valley on the path of an old Hawaiian foot trail that led to the Pali, a wind-buffeted pass over the Koolau Range. On the windward side of the pass, the road twisted upon itself as it hugged the cliff. At one switchback, the Emory boys liked to jump out and scramble down a ridge to meet the buggy as it rounded the turn below. Then it was on down the mountain and across the flat through mango and banana groves to the shore of Kaneohe Bay, a broad lagoon with a fringing reef. There Walter Emory had rented a shack where his boys spent their summers in the care of Grandfather Emory. Winifred, Walter, and Grandmother Emory drove over on weekends.

It was like living in the South Seas. A path led right to the lagoon. The shack had no electricity. Kerosene for lanterns came from Kaneohe Store, operated by a Hawaiian family, almost a mile away. There you could find anything you desired: candy, fishhooks, gloves, bread, slippers, poi. Every morning, Kenneth, who was about ten years old at the time, walked to the store with a pail to fetch milk. He had to make his way through taro patches where gray water buffalos with huge horns stood in the cool water chewing their cuds. The beasts terrified the boy but he did not tell his grandfather. One day Kenneth fell out of a papaya tree. Instead of scolding him, the old man rigged up a sling for his arm and made him feel like a hero.

His only playmates beside his brother were the children of a Hawaiian woman who had married a deaf Swede. They lived next door in a wooden house. A grass-thatched house also stood on the property. It was cool and dim inside. The adults took naps there. Kenneth learned that the Swede was deaf because his father had boxed his ears, which was why he ran away from home and went to sea. His playmates all had Biblical names: Abraham, Isaac, Rebecca, and Mary. They spoke Hawaiian to their mother and pidgin English to Kenneth. He felt comfortable with them.

The Hawaiian children took their shy *haole* playmate with them when they swam in the bay or went fishing. They also taught him Hawaiian superstitions. One day as they paddled out in a canoe, Kenneth said he was glad they were going fishing. The Hawaiian children turned the canoe around and paddled back. It was bad luck to mention fishing to a fisherman on his way to work.

Bates Street was quite an affluent neighborhood. Tour drivers pointed out the estate of James Campbell, sugar magnate and land baron, on Nuuanu Avenue at Bates. Across Nuuanu Avenue from Campbell's tropical showplace stood the mansion of W. O. Smith, attorney, politician, and financier. The Emory's lived farther in on Bates Street, flanked on one side by Judge W. J. Robinson and on the other by Lorrin A. Thurston, a newspaper publisher. Robinson was a circuit judge appointed in 1902 and again in 1906 by President Teddy Roosevelt. Thurston owned the *Pacific Commercial Advertiser*, Honolulu's morning newspaper, in which he supported the sugar industry, boosted tourism, and acted as Hawaii's self-appointed ambassador to the world.

The Thurstons and Emorys became friends as well as neighbors. Winifred Emory and Harriet Thurston shared an interest in church work. Their children played together, and so Kenneth had the run of the Thurston house. This added to his education because the publisher, heavyset and hearty, had all sorts of strange friends.

One morning in 1907 Kenneth found Thurston at the breakfast table with author Jack London, who had recently arrived in his yacht, the *Snark*. London, in animated conversation, sat slouched in a chair with his feet on the table. The author had become the talk of the town, especially among ten-year-old boys who had read *The Call of the Wild*. Kenneth listened to the conversation in a state of hero worship, yet he could not help but feel that London had the manners of a peasant.

Publisher Thurston was always bouncing off on one expedition or another. Once he invited Walter Emory and the boys along on a trip to the island of Hawaii where his passion was Kilauea Volcano. He was leading a campaign to establish a national park there. On this trip, Kenneth was amazed and envious to discover that Thurston could speak Hawaiian to natives along the road. He did so fluently and with obvious pleasure.

The Thurstons had two children near Kenneth's age, Margaret and Lorrin Potter. Little Lorrin became Kenneth's playmate. Although two years younger than Kenneth, he was big and muscular like his father. Smaller and slighter, Kenneth seldom won their wrestling matches although he did manage once to spit on Lorrin's head as an accolade of victory. The boys attended Punahou, some-times riding together on the new electric trolley or taking their bicy-cles.

The image of Kenneth Emory that comes down from this period is not that of a Tom Sawyer or of a Horatio Alger hero. He was too sen-sitive, too insecure. He was also undersize. The things that stimu-lated his active imagination did not interest other boys. So he spent much of his time alone. His weak voice added to the isolation. Lor-rin recalled later, "Kenneth was a loner. He didn't have anything to say in particular. And when he did, he said it to the side so you couldn't hear him."

Family photos show him dressed as his mother insisted he be for church: polished shoes, black stockings, woolen knickers with matching jacket of stylish cut, high collar, and an enormous, floppy, black, Little Lord Fauntleroy bow tie. He gazes out of the photos with an expression of resignation and bewilderment. For play he wore overalls and went barefooted.

Chapter Four

The Stamp Business

At Punahou School, Kenneth Emory's favorite subjects were English, the natural sciences, and geography. By applying himself he got Bs and Cs. But the activities that unleashed his restless energy and ultimately shaped his career took place outside of school. His friend Lorrin Thurston was a letterman in football for four years, captain of the swimming team, a member of the dramatic club, and First Lieutenant, Company A, Punahou Cadets. Kenneth played tennis but participated on no athletic team. He was too shy for the dramatic club, although his brother Closson held starring roles. His major contribution to campus activity outside the classroom was a three-year stint on the school yearbook.

Lorrin said later, "He was not a big man on campus. He was rather unknown, neither an athlete nor socially prominent. The other students weren't aware of him. I never heard Kenneth make a speech or head a meeting. He was just one of those present."

So he made his way alone pursuing interests of which his classmates were hardly aware. These interests ranged so widely that it is difficult to reconstruct their development. The best starting place is probably postage stamps. Closson inherited his father's acting ability. Kenneth inherited his stamp collection. At Punahou quite a few students collected stamps, although it didn't rival the swimming team as an image builder. Then it turned out that attorney W. O. Smith down the street collected stamps. So did newspaper publisher Lorrin A. Thurston next door. Kenneth made this discovery about the time he entered the seventh grade.

Determined to excel as a stamp collector, which did not require brawn nor a loud voice, he cast about for a way to enlarge his collection. His father's business mail and that of Uncle Charles produced mostly common, garden-variety stamps. Kenneth made a strike at the post office on Bethel Street when he noticed that Portuguese immigrants tossed envelopes into the wastebasket in their hurry to read letters from the old country. He dived into the litter and rescued the foreign stamps. But mail from Madeira didn't arrive very often and some of the Portuguese were not even considerate enough to throw away their envelopes. Clearly, he needed to find a better source.

One solution soon presented itself. Publisher Thurston collected not only postage stamps but also shells, both seashells and land shells. Thurston amassed shells like Midas did gold. Every weekend he tramped into the mountains to look for land shells as faithfully as he went to church. He took young Lorrin along to climb trees in the search for arboreal shells. Kenneth appeared to be a promising recruit, so Thurston offered an inducement he could not possibly refuse. For every land shell Kenneth added to Thurston's collection, he would receive a postage stamp.

The boy did not know he had begun his scientific education when the publisher showed him boxes of shells, each box carefully labeled as to genus, species, variety, the place where the shell was found, and by whom and when. This method of classification, after all, was little different from the way Kenneth kept track of his stamps: by country, year of issue, denomination, color, condition, number of perforations, and so forth. He could see that it was important to classify the land shells because they came in mind-boggling variety. There were more than 350 species of the genus *Achatinella* alone, divided into terrestrial and arboreal shells, plus more than 100 additional varieties.

It was easy enough to identify them all. The shells found in Manoa Valley tended to green. Those from Pauoa Valley were more yellowish. Shells picked up around Wahiawa in the middle of the island were rose colored while those from the Waianae Coast came in gray and brown. This rainbow of colors had startled early scientists. Captain George Dixon of London had in 1786 traded at Honolulu for a native necklace made of *Achatinella lugubris*, a purple-black shell found at Waialua, Oahu. Scientists in England were so eager to possess this novelty that they gave thirty to forty dollars for a single shell. Johann Hieronymus Chemnitz, the resident authority, mistook it for a marine shell and named it *Turbo lugubris*.

Thirty-five years passed before zoologists began to appreciate the evolutionary miracle of Hawaiian land shells. Arriving somehow on these isolated islands, two thousand miles from the nearest land mass, the little animals in protective shells had made their homes in forested valleys. Each small colony of shells was so able to adapt to its environment that it developed a species of its own within one valley, while another species evolved in another valley only a few miles away across the ridge. Such a proliferation of species on a single, small island made the discoveries by Charles Darwin on the Galapagos Islands seem modest in comparison. By 1850, "land shell fever" had swept the Hawaiian Islands. Thurston represented merely one generation of amateur scientists who collected land shells.

Thurston, Lorrin, and Kenneth explored the Koolau Range like prospectors in the Klondike. Land shells were found on the ground and in trees, mostly on *kukui* trees and *ohia ai*, the mountain apple tree, in knots where the branches had fallen off or under leaves where the animals fed on little things nobody else was interested in. Kenneth and Lorrin shinnied up the trees while publisher Thurston shouted directions from below or scouted new territory. Since climbing out on a limb without falling off required the application of both hands and both feet, and pockets were hard to reach, Kenneth often descended with a mouthful of his slimy captives. The expeditions ended around the Thurston dining-room table where Kenneth helped the publisher remove the animals from their shells. There is no record of what Mrs. Thurston said about this.

Having begun his scientific career as a commercial venture in the form of barter—land shells for postage stamps—Kenneth now went in search of investment capital. This is how he got into the mouse-foot business. Mousefoot is a ground pine which then grew in some profusion in the deep grass in undeveloped tracts of Nuuanu Valley. It resembles holly, which does not grow in Hawaii. Mousefoot, therefore, became a saleable substitute. On the morning of the two weekends before Christmas, Father Emory transported his son and Lorrin to mousefoot territory above the water reservoir, where he would return for them in the evening. They picked until they had enough mousefoot to fill the orders for Christmas wreaths they solicited by going door to door in the neighborhood. The mousefoot remained fresh in a little taro-patch stream that ran by the house. On the day before Christmas the boys delivered the wreaths, after washing off the mud deposited by the stream, for twenty-five cents each or five for one dollar. One year they made eighteen dollars.

Backed by venture capital Kenneth became a stamp dealer, buying and selling as well as trading with land shells. It is not clear how his next enterprise, the printing press, fit in. Printing may have begun as an entirely separate enthusiasm or merely as a necessary skill to advertise his stamps. Kenneth doesn't remember. Publisher Thurston probably exposed him to printers at the *Advertiser* who taught him the art, and his father bought him a five-by-eight-inch Kelsey hand press as well as several fonts of handset type. He was the only high-school freshman in Honolulu with such a hobby.

Kenneth installed his new press below the house next to the laundry room. He printed stamp price lists and approval sheets that he took to school and passed out to clients at recess. They carried the stamps home for inspection, chose those they wanted to buy, and brought the money to school. As his printing skills improved, Kenneth branched out into business cards and letterheads that he sold to friends of his father. Every year he printed the family Christmas cards, which went out with one of his mother's poems. He printed Punahou dance cards and programs for the Morning Music Club. All the profits went into his stamp business. But that was not the only reason he did it. "I was fascinated with that press," he said later.

Photography formed a natural adjunct to printing. Like other boys his age, he snapped photos with a Kodak Brownie camera. Unlike other boys, he developed his own pictures. Nobody taught him how to do this. He found some directions, read them carefully, and then went out and bought some equipment and started practicing. Asked why he did it, he answered, "I wanted to." He did not enter his photos in contests or have them published in the school yearbook. The darkroom he built under the house next to his printshop and postage stamp headquarters was a private sanctuary few of his friends knew about. He was still a loner very busy satisfying an immense curiosity.

The steel guitar came later, probably about 1915, and the pattern is clearer. Hawaiian music had become so popular that it was an export commodity. At least half a dozen Hawaiian musical groups had toured the mainland of the United States by this time. The Emory family owned a windup Victrola with a horn and Walter brought home all the latest recordings. Kenneth's favorites were by Ernest K. Kaai, who featured a new instrument called the steel guitar. This instrument produced a plaintive, gliding tone that is now synonymous with Hawaiian music. "I loved the sound of that steel guitar," Kenneth said later.

One day on the corner of Fort and Hotel streets Kenneth saw a Hawaiian boy sitting on the curb with a guitar held flat across his legs. The boy picked the strings with his right hand while running a steel bar made from a file up and down the neck of the guitar with his left hand. Kenneth recognized the sound of a steel guitar. More important, he saw how it was played. He had strummed a ukulele as long as he could remember. Now he had to master this new instrument as he had the printing press and photo developing.

He got hold of a guitar and made his steel bar out of an old file. Picks for the fingers of his right hand he cut from a tin can. Then he took a few lessons from a Hawaiian steel guitar teacher named Eddie Hutchinson who taught him how to tune the strings in slack key and the rudiments of manipulating the steel bar. From that point, Kenneth taught himself by listening to the Hawaiian records. To develop his vibrato, he took the steel bar along to school and practiced making it quiver on his leg while riding the trolley. In time, he could imitate Kaai's rendition of "Ua Like No A Like" and "Hilo March" to perfection, vibrato and all.

Kenneth Emory was probably the first *haole* to play the steel guitar, but his friends were unaware of it because he never performed in public while he was in Closson's shadow. He sometimes played the ukulele with friends at parties where he felt comfortable, but he never gave a solo performance. He seemed to have accepted his older brother, who acted in plays and was a cheerleader, as the performer. There are indications that Closson did not encourage Kenneth to overcome his shyness. Lorrin remembered that "Closson raised hell in the family. He had several girls on the string. He took a drink, too. That didn't earn him any kudos at Punahou where few of the students drank. And he had a temper. Kenneth was sort of a nonentity. Closson made more noise than Kenneth but he didn't have much to make noise about."

It is difficult to assess Kenneth's reaction to Closson's close resemblance to their handsome, facile, socially adept and business-oriented father, while Kenneth himself had to be content with sharing mutual interests in stamps and Hawaiian music. Could this factor account for the boy's preoccupation with these hobbies as well as his school-boy attempts to prove himself a businessman? For whatever reason, he had already developed in his teens perseverance and the capacity for self-motivation, traits that would stay with him for the rest of his life.

One activity, at least, brought him into contact with others and taught him to compete on equal terms with his peers. This activity was surfing. The old Hawaiian sport had declined in the face of criticism by early missionaries who called it a waste of time and associated it with nudity. But missionary descendants helped revive surfing in the 1890s. By the time Kenneth entered Punahou, it had again become a popular activity.

Students shaped boards from redwood planks. They could see from Punahou hill when the surf came up at Waikiki below, and the exodus from classroom to beach began after school if not before. But there were problems. The solid-wood boards were too long and too heavy to take on the trolley or even to carry very far. Only boys who had friends in Waikiki could leave surfboards there. The Steeres, longtime friends of the Emorys, lived on Kalia Road down the shore from the Moana Hotel. Kenneth often swam near the Steeres' residence, yet most boys were not so fortunate. To make matters worse almost all of Waikiki fronted on private homes, and residents had built seawalls to protect against high surf. One result was that the ocean currents changed and washed away the sand. Water came right up to the seawalls all along the ocean front except for a short stretch of sand in front of the Moana and Seaside hotels. In short, there was no public beach where boys could launch their surfboards.

To remedy this injustice, an energetic former journalist named Alexander Hume Ford mounted a campaign to establish a beach club for local residents between the Moana and Seaside. Local business-men supported this plan. In 1908, when Kenneth was in the fifth grade, the Outrigger Canoe Club came into existence. A grass-thatched hut served as a locker for surfboards while another was put to use as a dressing room. A spreading *hau* tree provided shade for picnics.

Kenneth insists that he was an original member of the Outrigger Club and that he changed into his swimming suit behind the *hau* thicket. Children payed a five dollar initiation fee and five dollars in annual dues. As a grade schooler, Kenneth probably spent his time paddling in the small shore break called Cornucopia. The indica-tions are that he was mostly alone because Lorrin doesn't remember being with him at Waikiki.

As usual he was very attentive to the scene around him, watching closely the overhand stroke and powerful kick of a young Hawaiian called Duke Kahanamoku on whom he modeled his stroke. The Kahanamoku clan lived farther down Kalia Road in an enclave of Hawaiian residences. In 1912, when Kenneth was a freshman in high school, Duke Kahanamoku broke world records in the 50-yard, 100-yard, and 100-meter freestyle swimming events in the Olympic Games held in Stockholm, Sweden. By that time Kenneth had also become an accomplished, self-taught swimmer and surfer.

Surfing is a highly individualistic sport. Once the surfer paddles from shore, he must make his own decisions. He must deal directly with the ocean on its own terms. Whether or not he catches a ride depends on his skill in reading the incoming swells before they hit the reef. Once on a wave, he becomes part of its rhythm and power. Sliding across the steep, glassy slope of a roaring comber is an exhil-arating experience. Kenneth said he will never forget the first time he caught the curl. At the same time, surfing builds a physique that female tourists have always admired in males: lean hips, flat belly, and powerful shoulders developed by paddling the board. The power is not in bulging muscles but in suppleness. It was during his surfing period that Kenneth began to grow. By the time he graduated from high school he stood five-feet, ten-and-one-half inches tall and weighed 125 pounds. He also had the shoulders of a surfer.

But he was still undersize in the summer of 1913 when a Punahou classmate, Gerard Baldwin, invited him to spend a month at his home on the island of Maui about one hundred miles southeast of Oahu. It was Kenneth's first trip by himself away from Honolulu. Gerard's father, Harry Baldwin, a descendent of a medical missionary, owned a major portion of Maui including a ranch on the slope of the ten-thousand-foot-high dormant volcano, Haleakala. In a high-altitude setting of giant *koa* and gnarled *ohia* trees, of lava chasms and spectacular vistas of the tropical island sweeping into the ocean below, Hawaiian and Portuguese cowboys roped and branded cattle. These men were friendly, and seemingly impervious to physical hardship and pain. Kenneth's host and the manager of Haleakala Ranch was Louis Von Tempsky, who was more colorful than his cowboys. Von Tempsky had come from New Zealand and was a veteran of the Maori wars. For Kenneth, it was an adventure out of a Zane Grey novel.

A diary Kenneth kept on ranch stationary reveals not only his inability to spell but also the excitement of a tough and durable fifteen-year-old determined to master the skills of a cowboy:

Diary, July 8th, Tuesday

Got up at half-past three o'clock in the morning and saddled our horses by candle light; after a hasty breakfast of coffee (cold), oranges and bread and butter, went to the roundup. . . . We were delayed considerably and did not get into the drive until about six o'clock.

It is a great sight!!! [sic] to see hundreds of cattle comming [sic] down through the passes and over the rolling plains. The cattle often broke and that was where part of the fun came in. I roped a small calf who broke and another man helped me bring it back.

We reached the pen about 8 o'clock and it took several hours to rest the cattle, count them, and separate the unbranded from the branded. While this was going on I changed to a fresh horse. Here's where the real fun came in. Roping and landing the cattle.

When I first got into the pen I got all mixed up with the laso [sic] and it was a long time before I got into the real business. I was kind of bashful for there was quite a large audience and they all expected me to take a spill and they expected to have a lot of fun watching me. But they were mistaken.

The first two throws I missed but the third one landed fair and square and I was off in no time making for the branding irons. The first thing I did was get all mixed up in the ropes and forgot to twist the rope around the pommel of the saddle. I finally came out all right and after a little fight threw the calf all by myself. After this I got four calves softly landed.

One bull began charging. He came for me and gave my horse a little lift. Then he charged a man on the ground throwing him over and breaking one of his teeth. Two of the horses set up a lively time. One of the men was thrown and broke his thumb. I had another small bull chase me but he had hardly any horns and did not do any damage.

There were about six cowboys roping including ourselves. The cattle made an awfull [sic] amound [sic] of noise and the cracking of whips, yelling of the men, bawling of calves, clouds of dust, made it seem just like a wild west show.

We had a late lunch and I changed horses again and got back just in time to rope two more calves before the end. After driving the cattle out and to a new place we returned home. I am tired out with blisters all over my hand but have had a wonderful good time. Clear day. Kind of hot. The end.

Back on Oahu it was during this year that Kenneth had his only brush with the law. He and Lorrin went out on Halloween with "dynamite caps" to enliven the neighborhood. These caps contained just enough explosive to make a loud noise. They were sold in stores to Chinese celebrating the lunar New Year and to boys like Lorrin and Kenneth on July 4. The caps were commonly exploded by attaching one to the end of a cane and tapping it on pavement.

Kenneth and Lorrin, however, found a way the caps could scare a lot more people with much less effort. After dark they put the dynamite caps on the street car tracks in Nuuanu Valley. When the trolley came along and passed over the caps, placed some six feet apart, it sounded like the battle of San Juan Hill and made the street car passengers furious. "I had the area from Bates Street halfway to town and Kenneth took the street car tracks up to the cemetery," said Lorrin later. "When the street car came down; bang, bang, bang. I was busy putting caps on the tracks when somebody grabbed me by the nape of the neck and said, 'You son of a bitch, we finally got you.' It was the cops."

Kenneth escaped by jumping over a ditch, sliding down a palm tree and scrambling under a bridge where the police couldn't see him. Lorrin got hauled to the station where, after about three hours, the irate officers discovered he was the son of the newspaper publisher and let him go. He walked home at 3 A.M. and sneaked in the back door.

Chapter Five

Kamakahiki's Fight with a Shark

One day a teacher at Punahou, accustomed to students who approached the library with the same reluctance they displayed toward homework, watched Kenneth Emory prowl the stacks. He seemed as intent and discriminating as a shopper in pursuit of a bargain. Yet he was not known as a brilliant scholar. Curious, she asked what he was looking for.

"Something on the South Seas," he answered.

She was not the only one surprised by this interest. Lorrin later said, "I never knew he was into that so deep." Neither did his other friends. How it happened even he cannot explain. Maybe it was a reflection of his mother's love for the islands. Perhaps it was because his now thoroughly domesticated father still harbored one last dream of sailing to a faraway place, the Fly River in New Guinea. "We'll go there together," Walter Emory promised his younger son.

Kenneth read everything he could get his hands on about the South Seas: the logs of Captain Cook, books by Robert Louis Stevenson and Joseph Conrad and Herman Melville, the short stories of Jack London about Hawaii, missionary accounts, and the *Journal of William Ellis.* He pored over the illustrated pages of *Mid-Pacific Magazine*, a monthly edited in Honolulu by the tireless Alexander Hume Ford. The publication projected Ford's vision of Pacific island peoples joined in happy association before the world as an example of peace and harmony. Ford's enthusiasm had infected government officials and normally levelheaded businessmen to the extent that they paid him a small salary as executive director of the Pan Pacific Union headquartered in Honolulu. *Mid-Pacific Magazine* was Ford's propaganda weapon, a smorgasbord of travel articles, anthropological accounts, yachting adventures, natural science essays, economic reviews, bare-breasted natives, grass-thatched houses, picturesque outrigger canoes, and waving palm trees—all of which fed Kenneth Emory's voracious appetite for the South Seas.

Lorrin said, "We were a damn sight more interested in football and swimming." As a result, Kenneth did not tell his friends about this new interest nor the idea that it spawned. He got into his head the idea that he should learn Hawaiian, a language as useless on campus as an overcoat. So he confided in adults. "Uncle" Charles, the register of deeds, was the most helpful. There were several young Hawaiians in the office who translated old documents from Hawaiian into English. Uncle Charles arranged an introduction to Thomas Maunupau from Kona. He agreed to become Kenneth's Hawaiian tutor.

They met once a week at the Emory home on Bates Street during Kenneth's senior year at Punahou. Kenneth wasn't a natural linguist but he applied himself with tenacity, and his eagerness to learn encouraged Maunupau to teach him a lot more about Hawaiians than their grammar. The two became close friends. Rather than study from a textbook, Kenneth subscribed to *Kuokoa*, a Hawaiian-language newspaper published by Thurston.

It was a busy year. Kenneth moved up from manager of the *Junior Oahuan* to manager of the *Oahuan*, Punahou's yearbook. The post was not a literary one. Kenneth's job was to go out and hustle advertising. As a businessman in his own right, he bought space in the *Oahuan* beneath E. W. Quinn, the plumber, and right beside Nunes' Ukulele Company. Kenneth's advertisement read, "K. P. Emory, Expert on all Philatelic Subjects, Postage Stamps, Bought, Sold and Exchanged, Splendid line of Postage Stamps always on hand—especially from the South Seas."

During his senior year Kenneth also achieved a smattering of notoriety on campus because he had shared an adventure with Jack London and his wife on the island of Molokai during summer vacation. London had gone over to the leper settlement at Kalaupapa to gather material for one of his short stories. Publisher Thurston, accompanied by Kenneth, followed in a chartered sampan to pick up the author and his wife for a cruise to one of Molokai's remote valleys accessible only by boat. The voyage aroused in Kenneth a latent urge to write. He spent his senior year struggling to commit the trip to words. Here's how he described his arrival at Molokai in 1915:

> We could see the surf beating fountains of spray as it dashed and foamed against the cliffs on the windward side of the island—honeycombed cliffs, overtopped by brown, scraggly grass and sickly shrubs. . .
>
> Before us lay a beautiful village with a church, store house, post office, etc. in neat red and green, canopied with the spreading limbs of trees which extended down to the wide coral beach. A place where "every prospect pleases and only man is vile." Kalaupapa [the leper colony] is isolated from our world by the sea on three sides, and an enormous pali or precipice effectually walls up the remaining side.

> A little boat was dropped over the side and propelled ashore by a sweeper. . . . Returning the boat brought the author and authoress, Jack London and his wife, who were to accompany us from here.

Readers who expect to hear more about the literary celebrity of the party must remain disappointed. Kenneth Emory disposed of Jack London with that single mention. He was more interested in the stunted palm trees on tiny Mokapu islet since they, "it is believed, thrive nowhere else in the world with the exception perhaps of Necker Island." Kenneth captured the lonely isolation of the village at Pelekunu Valley on their arrival with a description of a dog hurrying up the cliff path and children running behind.

He also gave readers a word picture of the precarious landing. Passengers jumped from the boat to a sea shelf in the cliff, then scrambled to safety on the stoney beach or were hoisted in a basket by hand winch to the cliff path above. Kenneth described this procedure, making Mrs. London the star:

> By the time we were all ashore, bag and baggage, a kindly native of fifty years and seven little children were peering down from the derrick above. They let down a huge basket for us to come up in. Mrs. London was the only one to accept the offer. While the basket soared and swayed in mid air, I expected the frail bottom to fall out, or the rusty cable to break, or the ten-year-old native children to get "rattled" and let go the cable, but fortunately for Mrs. London, none of these horrible things happened just then. . .
>
> The cliff trail wound down to the village, nine rather dilapidated old-fashioned and crudely-built houses. . . . Every inhabitant who could walk was there to greet us with all the hospitality of the native race. . . . There were no roads, stores, shops, or any of those comforts or discomforts that we are accustomed to associate with the word "town" or "village"—only houses and people with the bare comforts of civilization such as kerosene lamps, tin and iron ware, matches, etc.

This was not Kenneth's only literary effort of 1916. As a senior, he was required to submit a composition for the annual school contest. He wrote a piece of fiction, a short story entitled "Kamakahiki's Fight With A Shark." The scene was set in ancient Hawaii as Kamakahiki, a fisherman, paddled out to replenish his larder. The canoe was overturned by a *nuihi*, the most ferocious of all sharks. Kamakahiki floated as if lifeless for "a move would have been fatal." The shark attacked. Kamakahiki jammed the broken paddle into the mouth of the shark as it bit down. The jagged ends of the paddle drove through the roof of the shark's mouth and the jaw below. That night in the village of Kaaawa there was a *luau*—a feast—of shark's meat.

To Kenneth's astonishment, his story won the prize. He had never won anything before in his life. His astonishment turned to terror when the class voted that he should be valedictorian and recite his composition at the graduation ceremony. He was so shy it took all his courage to raise his hand to go to the bathroom. Somebody, probably his mother, decided he had better have some lessons in elocution.

We assume the suggestion came from his mother because Winifred Emory had previous experience with her son's inability to perform before an audience. As a child he had once recited a little verse for her morning club. Kenneth became so disoriented that, after reciting the verse, he started over again and kept going like a broken record until his mortified mother shooed him off the stage. This time a voice teacher took him in hand to teach him to project from the diaphragm, and to smile and make gestures with which to dramatize his recital. It was all pure agony.

Meanwhile, he had to prepare for college. Kenneth was weak in Latin, a subject that didn't interest him. His parents hired a tutor to help him cram for entrance exams to Dartmouth College. The Latin tutor had no more success than the speech teacher. Kenneth was staying with the Thurstons at the time in their home on the heights of Tantalus above Punahou. He walked to school. Instead of studying Latin on the way, he carried his Hawaiian-English dictionary and tried to memorize the Hawaiian words for things he saw by the roadside: bird, leaf, cloud, flower, horse, and so forth.

It is doubtful who was most relieved, Kenneth or his Latin tutor, when she discovered that proficiency in Latin was not required at Dartmouth. What's more, his recital of "Kamakahiki's Fight With A Shark" went off without a stammer. All in all, it turned out much better than his parents had reason to hope.

Chapter Six

Crackers An

Dartmouth College, located in a town called Hanover on the New Hampshire side of the Connecticut River, was a long way around to the Pacific islands and atolls in Kenneth Emory's future. But it was a necessary detour. The truth is, he hadn't settled on a career when, bound for college, he sailed with his mother on June 28, 1916, to San Francisco in the SS *Matsonia*. Winifred wrote in her diary on Saturday, July 1, "Kenneth much taken with Thelma Boyum." An entry on Monday written after the captain's dinner read, "Kenneth much in love." Apparently, he had discovered girls. Anthropology would have to wait.

The shipboard romance ended in San Francisco and Kenneth traveled on to get his education. While his mother visited relatives and renewed friendships in her hometown of Pike, New Hampshire, Kenneth spent the summer swimming and canoeing before arriving bag and baggage and steel guitar at Dartmouth on Monday, September 18. He was assigned a dormitory room in Fairweather Hall with Ray Youman, a student who spoke with a Yiddish accent and came from New York.

Ten days after the semester began, Winifred and assorted relatives drove thirty miles downstate from Pike to check on the new college student. Her diary entry for that day reads, "We all went to Hanover and found Kenneth comfortable and happy." He certainly had no trouble making the transition to Dartmouth where the enrollment numbered only a few hundred more than Punahou's total enrollment of 712. The campus wasn't much larger; an elm-shaded green enclosed by a rectangle of academic buildings and dormitories. Webster Hall, the dining room, stood across the green from Hanover Inn where parents stayed when they came to visit and where young ladies registered during the Winter Carnival. A short walk from the green brought students to the little college town of Hanover.

The leaves began to turn soon after Kenneth arrived. He loved this autumn symphony of rusts and ambers and golds. A range of foothills called the White Mountains rose in the distance. They were domed and rounded with gentle contours unlike the jagged

Koolau Range. The trees were also different: graceful birches and spreading maples and tall, stately pines. Often in the morning a mist lay on the campus. All this was new and exciting. And the snow! It turned the whole outdoors into a fairyland.

The first time his new roommate lit a cigarette, Kenneth jerked it from his mouth and threw it out the window in Puritan indignation. Fortunately, their friendship survived the test. Kenneth soon found himself involved in campus activities. This Kenneth Emory was so different from the shy student at Punahou that the change requires some explanation. For one thing, the Dartmouth freshman was no longer undersize. He towered over his roommate. Also, Kenneth no longer walked in the shadow of his brother. Closson had flunked out of the school in New York to which his parents had sent him, and had enlisted in the army. Most important, probably, Kenneth was one-of-a-kind at Dartmouth. He came from the never-never land of Hawaii.

His steel guitar emerged from the closet and became his passport to celebrity status. The Theta Delta Chi fraternity rushed the freshman steel guitar player. Kenneth became a member. He couldn't afford to live at the fraternity house but he played sensuous Hawaiian melodies at house parties while his fraternity brothers engaged themselves as romantically as possible with their female guests. Kenneth was still too shy for that sort of thing.

There was at Dartmouth a prestigious musical organization called the Mandolin Club. Members were divided into first mandolin, second mandolin, third mandolin, guitar, violin, cello, clarinet, and traps. Each member had to take a test in sight-reading music to ensure a high level of competence. In the spring, the Dartmouth Glee Club and the Mandolin Club made a concert tour through New York and Boston and as far west as Cleveland, Ohio.

It did not take long before impresarios of the Mandolin Club, planning their next concert tour, recognized the drawing power of Kenneth's steel guitar. They insisted he join the club. He explained that he couldn't read music. Nevertheless he was given an audition. "They put a sheet of music in front of me," Kenneth recalled later. "I played the songs I knew. I didn't pay any attention to the music because I couldn't read it anyway. They said, 'You pass.' "

The eyes of his Punahou classmates would have popped had they seen him in his debut on the tour. He performed in a starring role near the end of the concert just after a rousing "Football Medley" by the Glee Club and before the Mandolin Club strummed "Serenade D'Amour." "They had me in a little play," Kenneth explained. "In this play, the emperor, he was there. He ordered his slave brought out. At the summons, I came on stage in a leopard skin with my steel guitar. There was a big audience. I played the Hawaiian songs I knew with the accompaniment of regular guitars. You could hear a pin drop. The steel guitar was new to them."

If the Mandolin Club made Kenneth Emory a minor celebrity at Dartmouth, the Dartmouth Outing Club established his credentials as "one of the lads," imbued him with the Dartmouth spirit, and almost taught him to smoke a pipe. The Outing Club had been started in 1909 by fresh-air enthusiasts and had become one of the chief attractions of the college. By the time Kenneth joined, the club had built a ski jump near the campus, had blazed an eighty-two-and-one-half mile trail to the White Mountains, had opened a network of shorter trails that led out of Hanover, and had built a chain of seven cabins for overnight hikes. The club also put on Dartmouth's Winter Carnival, the highlight of the campus social season.

For Kenneth, skiing took the place of surfing and trail hikes replaced forays into the Koolaus for land shells. The Outing Club introduced him to other students who shared his love for the outdoors. One of his best friends, Lyndon Frederick Small, established in 1918 a club record by hiking 533½ miles on the trails that year. Kenneth came in third with 432 miles. Small's record fell the following year to W. P. Fowler who hiked 681½ miles. Kenneth logged only 217 miles that year, but his efforts to post the trails earned him the chairmanship for outdoor events of the Winter Carnival.

In January of 1919 he began keeping a line-a-day diary to document his involvement in the big event. He planned the preliminary ski competition and worked out routes for race courses. When warm weather thawed the slopes and caused two cancellations of the preliminary meet, he went to a Douglas Fairbanks movie and read Stevenson's *In The South Seas*. His diary entry for February 7 read, "Ran off the cross country race for one of the preliminary events. Read Jack London's *Chun Ah Chun* about the Ah Fong family."

With the carnival three days away, he "worked on carting of snow for the ski jump. Heard Professor Irving Fisher of Yale speak on League of Nations." On Thursday, February 13, he wrote, "I doubt if I ever worked harder in my life. All set for the Carnival. The girls streamed in today." Kenneth reported that the final meet was a perfect success. His adopted aunt, Frances Dickerman, came down from Pike to visit him. That night he and three cronies "watched the girls at the ball for a while, then came up to the room for eats." His shipboard romance notwithstanding, Kenneth was still too shy to make a date for the Winter Carnival.

The diary describes his social life. On Thursday, February 27, he cut a geology exam in favor of a long weekend hike to the Franconia Range. The following Saturday he heard Alden Clark from India describe the life of a missionary, then played his steel guitar in Home Talent Night. After a round of exams he hiked to Happy Hill Cabin with his three best friends. They talked until midnight about astronomy. In April, he read Herman Melville's *Omoo*, broke in a new baseball mitt, and finished an article on skiing and surfing for *Mid-Pacific Magazine*. On Saturday, May 10, he was back at Happy Hill with his friends. "There was half a foot of raspberry shortcake apiece. How it did floor us. Six freshmen showed up before dark. Rain."

Kenneth and his friends formed a quartet consisting of Kenneth himself, Edward "Bug" Blaine, Faber Lyndon "Shorty" Southworth, and "Kauku" Small. They called themselves the "Crackers An" group. After dinner in Webster Hall, they hit the books in their dormitories until about 9 P.M. when the least studious that night came outside and went from window to window shouting, "Crackers An." That was the signal for the other three to come down and walk to Hanover for crackers and milk at Scotty's, a hole-in-the-wall cafe, before going to bed.

Kenneth had come to Dartmouth with the notion that he'd like to be a writer like Jack London. Kenneth's article about Molokai appeared in *Mid-Pacific Magazine* in 1917, spurring this ambition. His English teacher dashed these hopes at the end of his freshman year by flunking him because he misspelled so many words. This convinced Kenneth that he had no future in the literary world.

As a sophomore he got another idea. While he didn't know exactly *what* he wanted to be, he knew very well *where* he wanted to be. That place was the South Seas. He was aware that besides writers, missionaries went there. He did not drink or smoke. Perhaps, with a little practice, he could become a missionary. With this end in view, he joined the Dartmouth Christian Association and remained a member into his senior year.

But the more he learned about being a missionary, the less he liked it. The whole idea was to teach the natives how to speak English, put on clothes, and, generally, turn them into dark-skinned white people. This was not what Kenneth had in mind at all. He liked natives the way they were. That's what made them so interesting.

During his junior year he took a course in classical archaeology. There was no awakening of slumbering potential, no recognition of his future life's work. The class spent most of its time learning to identify motifs on Greek columns. Professor Johnson was a funny little fellow who started his lectures by reciting, "We're all here, we're all here, so do thyself no harm." Kenneth could never figure out what that meant. The only indication that he had begun to grope toward his career was a class paper entitled, "Values in Clothing." In the paper he defended the scanty attire of Polynesians on Pacific islands as not only decent but healthy and natural. He got a good grade in this course.

Kenneth finally chose biology as his major. He liked the field trips. On one class excursion around the campus in winter, the professor explained how to identify leafless trees by the tiny scars left by leaves when they fell off. Kenneth became an absolute whiz-bang at leaf scar identification. His proficiency earned him an extra 10 percent in grade points on tests. Probably more significant than the major he chose was the one he did not—business. "I had my business career in high school," he said. "I enjoyed it but it tied me down and kept me indoors." Now he was cutting himself loose from his father and was trying to find his own way.

Kenneth did not spend his summer vacations at home in Hawaii. Instead he went to Pike where his Uncle Bertram had taken over the family whetstone business after the death of Grandfather Edwin Pike in 1908. Uncle Bertram also got into tourism by developing the Tarleton Club on five thousand scenic acres of pine, spruce, and hardwood four and one-half miles south of Pike.

The Pike property included three lakes: Tarleton, Armington, and Katherine, the last named after Kenneth's aunt. Uncle Bertram's four-story, colonnaded clubhouse on Lake Tarleton fronted on a golf course and gardens and offered superb views of the White Mountains. An orchestra played for evening dances. Wealthy guests had a choice of staying in the clubhouse or in lake-side cottages. These bungalows ran to three and five bedrooms with one or two baths. There were stables for horses and special quarters for private servants and chauffeurs. Jews and Irish were not allowed. The Pike family kept its own two-story cottage, called Happy Thought, on Lake Tarleton, and Kenneth had the run of the place.

Uncle Bertram also felt obliged to share his magnificent real estate with youth. He permitted a member of the Gulick family, a missionary clan from Hawaii, to operate three camps for girls on the lakes. These resorts were called Aloha Camps out of respect for Gulick's Hawaiian background. The girls ranged in age from ten to twenty years and came from fairly affluent families. They spent the summers in healthful exercise: learning to swim, hiking, canoeing, riding, tennis, dancing, and so forth.

Kenneth worked as a handyman and groundskeeper at the exclusive Tarleton Club. Later he also became a swimming instructor at the Aloha Camps, a job his classmates must have envied for it rounded out his education in a subject not taught at Dartmouth, girls. Even Kenneth's mother was impressed during her stay at Pike while getting Kenneth settled in school. She had written in her diary, "Big camp meet at Tarleton. Six hundred fifty girls in bloomers."

Most of his swimming students were rather young for a Dartmouth scholar. But those aged nineteen and twenty looked pretty good. Kenneth had already met a young lady named Margaret Manning, whose parents belonged to the Tarleton Club. Her father was a judge in Manchester. Then, in the summer of 1919, Betty and Dorothea Whitney checked in. On July 9, a Wednesday, their swimming instructor took them to Wrights Hill for a picnic supper, then to Woodsville for movies. They played tennis and swam the following Sunday. By Monday Kenneth was favoring Betty, who wore her stockings rolled below the knee. He took her out in his canoe. They played tennis in the afternoon and danced in the evening. An entry in Kenneth's diary for Sunday, July 20, read, "Out on the lake in the evening with Betty and the steel guitar."

All things must come to an end. On Friday, August 1, Kenneth wrote, "Fred, Dot, Betty and I swam before breakfast. The Whitneys left at 10 A.M. Sad day for me." On his last day at Happy Thought he cleaned the rooms "while fog hung heavy among the red maples on the shore of the lake. Wrote several long letters [to the young ladies] and packed all my possessions." Then, to get himself in the mood for college, he read an article on astronomy. Dartmouth, he wrote on arrival, was a welcome sight.

Chapter Seven

What is an Ethnologist?

Kenneth celebrated the Christmas holiday of 1919 at Pike, as usual. But it turned out to be a most unusual vacation. Closson delivered a letter that contained unbelievably good news. The letter came from an old family friend, Dr. C. Montague Cooke, in Hawaii. Cooke was the scientist in charge of the shell collection at the Bishop Museum in Honolulu. He had written the letter as an introduction for Kenneth to Professor Herbert E. Gregory at Yale. Gregory had just been named as new director of the Bishop Museum.

This letter of introduction was a typical island gesture. Kenneth's father had built a house for Cooke. Cooke also went shelling with publisher Lorrin Thurston. From both Thurston and Walter Emory, Cooke had heard about Kenneth's fierce interest in the South Seas. Cooke knew that the museum's new director wanted to expand the staff and that expeditions would soon be going to the South Pacific. Kenneth would graduate in June. Why not give this deserving lad a chance to work for the museum?

Dr. Cooke's letter introduced Kenneth Emory to Dr. Gregory as an "island boy" interested in the Hawaiian language and folklore and ready for the "Great Idea," a code phrase for Gregory's ambitious plan for scientific investigation of the Pacific. It is not clear if Kenneth even knew such a plan was afoot. But he understood that scientists went to the South Seas and he was eager to grasp the opportunity. The next day he composed a breathless, rambling request for an interview:

> . . . I want to see you right away. . . When and where can an appointment be made. . . ?
>
> I am free to follow my one aim in life, which is simply to undertake some work I am interested in enough to follow for its own sake and, having satisfied my conscience that it is a work worth while as a benefit to mankind, to pursue that work with all my energies. Any work connected with obtaining or preserving records of the South Sea peoples, or information valuable to the economic development of the islands, or the solving of present day natives' problems, has been in the back of my mind the ideal work for me.

Gregory answered promptly. Kenneth had returned to Dartmouth for only a few days before he was off again on January 9 for Yale on the afternoon train. Lorrin, now a star on the Yale swimming team, met him at the station and took Kenneth to his room for the night. Another student named Peterson from Hawaii came over. He and Kenneth played guitars. Then Lorrin took his guest to his fraternity house.

The next morning Kenneth went to the campus to see Dr. Gregory in his office. We can assume that our job applicant wore a suit and tie and that his shock of brown hair was carefully brushed. The young man who sat before the geology professor-museum director shifted frequently in his chair, not out of nervousness but because of excess energy. He was lean and muscular and had broad shoulders. His sharp nose and prominent jaw added intensity to an already penetrating gaze. He smiled easily and laughed often with quick humor. Emotions passed across his face like rapid cloud shadows.

Gregory, also an outdoor man, proved easy to talk with. He was scholarly but approachable, decisive and thoughtful at the same time. He apparently liked what he saw because only a few minutes passed before Kenneth felt he had won him over. Kenneth's shyness disappeared in the pleasure of being taken seriously about things that seemed frivolous to other people. They talked for hour and a half.

"When you get through at Dartmouth, when you come to Honolulu, go to the museum," the scientist said at the close of the interview. "I'll put you on the staff as assistant ethnologist at $75 a month. If it doesn't work out, it will come out in the wash."

Kenneth walked out of Gregory's office in a state of euphoria complicated by bewilderment. Apparently he was being hired to do important and useful work connected with Polynesians. But what in the world was an ethnologist? He hurried to Lorrin's room and looked up the word in a dictionary. It meant a person who studies the divisions of mankind into races, their origin, distribution, relations, and peculiarities. Kenneth didn't have the courage to use his new title that night when he wrote in his diary, "I am going to the islands in July! [sic] for scientific work and study."

Back at Dartmouth he received a businesslike letter from Gregory restating their conversation and its result. Kenneth answered, then started to study Hawaiian grammar again. He read *White Shadows in the South Seas* by Frederick O'Brien, a few chapters of Matthew Arnold, and "History" and "Compensation" from Ralph Waldo Emerson's *Essays*. A letter arrived from Betty Whitney saying she might be able to accept his invitation to the Winter Carnival. Then another letter arrived saying she couldn't come after all. So Kenneth and his Crackers An gang skied to Happy Hill Cabin where Kauku prepared a fifteen-egg omelet with jelly and french fried potatoes.

Now Kenneth studied Hawaiian almost every day. On February 13 he discovered a new enthusiasm, ski jumping. Two days later he went over the Dartmouth jump ten times. Both Kauku and Bug tried it and fell. The next day Kenneth jumped all afternoon. His best effort was fifty-five feet. On February 19 he fell twice out of four jumps and another student was knocked unconscious. On February 21 Kenneth broke one of his skis. Yet he went to Woodstock, Vermont, the following Monday and entered a ski jump contest with six other Dartmouth students. On Thursday, February 26, he made his longest jump, seventy feet, on fast snow.

During his senior year, in addition to all his other activities, Kenneth learned as a member of a National Guard unit to make simple plane table surveys and to draw maps. His diary on Monday, March 22, read, "Warm, quiet, bright skiing day. Snow balls flying. The morning mail brought news of my appointment. Wrote home in the afternoon. Read some Bret Harte." He received a letter several days later from Margaret Manning. She promised to come to his commencement. By this time he was reading *Mystery of Easter Island.* The snow began to melt. Kenneth picked up ten broken ski tips while strolling alone at the ski jump.

Graduation approached, life had taken on new purpose and meaning, and the world was full of miracles, great and small. On May 20, 1920, Kenneth listened for the first time to a wireless telephone. He heard an operator talking from a ship at sea. Six days later, he and Bug Blaine lay under the leafing elm trees outside their dormitory on a fresh spring afternoon and "gazed into a perfect blue heaven." The days grew warmer. A full moon flooded the campus on the night of Friday, May 28. Kenneth brought his guitar to the dormitory window and strummed softly to the stars. Then he plunged into exams.

The best news that spring came from his father. Walter Emory, who seldom traveled anymore, would make the journey all the way from Hawaii to see his son graduate. There was no better evidence that Kenneth had made his father proud. Walter arrived in Pike on June 14 while Kenneth was taking his last exam. The next day Kenneth went to Pike. Walter Emory had become distinguished with silver, wavy hair and a well-tended mustache. His handsome face was fully fleshed and he had a comfortable paunch. Uncle Bertram loaned them his super-six for driving around to visit relatives.

They all went to Dartmouth for the baccalaureate service on June 20. Margaret Manning and her mother arrived in time for class day exercises the next afternoon. Kenneth divided his time between his father, Margaret and her mother, and Frances Dickerman until graduation on Wednesday, June 23. He and Margaret stayed at the ball past midnight. Then Kenneth and his father drove to Fitchburg and Barnstable, Massachusetts to visit relatives there.

One more experience rounded out Kenneth's days at Dartmouth. On July 1 Kenneth attended the annual reopening of the Tarleton Club for the summer. The beautiful Whitney sisters were there. Kenneth took them swimming and dancing. Late in the night of July 3 he wrote in his diary, "Moonlight on the lake with Betty." His last entry on July 5, before departing for Hawaii, was both exultant and enigmatic. It read, "Cloudy, cold, then clear with north wind . . . Swam! One of the happiest days of my life because? . . ."

PART TWO

STONES, BONES, AND CINDER CONES

Chapter Eight

Are You a Divinity Student?

Kenneth Emory began his professional career as a scientist at age twenty-two on Thursday, July 22, 1920, when he climbed on a street car and clattered out past the taro patches on King Street to the Bishop Museum. He must have felt as he had at age five on his first visit to Pike when his grandfather taught him to swim by dunking him from a rowboat into the lake.

Kenneth didn't know much about the museum except its location on the outskirts of town in the direction of Ewa (west). From the street car he could see the handsome, stone structure on a knoll in a scatter of other buildings in an open space like a cattle pasture. The other buildings belonged to the Kamehameha Schools for Hawaiian boys and girls. Kenneth was not alone in confusing the museum with the schools—many people did. In fact, Charles Reed Bishop had originally intended his museum to be an appendage to the schools. It might have become so had he not hired at a salary of $2,500 a year a tireless, hotheaded, dictatorial botanist-geologist named William Tufts Brigham as the museum's first director. Brigham bulldozed Bishop into establishing a scientific institution instead of what he called a "mere curiosity show, to amuse the idle hour." That was in the late 1880s.

Now, thirty years later, Kenneth had to walk among classrooms and student dormitories and teachers' cottages and children playing games in order to approach the museum. The approach did not contribute toward the museum's stature as a scientific institution, and Kenneth would have to learn that neither did the financial relationship between Bishop Museum and the schools, which were supported by the Bishop Estate. None of the considerable income from the extensive Bishop Estate lands was available to the struggling museum, which had an endowment of thirty thousand dollars. Kenneth, however, was much too agog by his first day on the job to worry about the museum's financial matters. That was a problem the trustees hoped that Herbert Gregory would solve.

A Hawaiian woman sat inside the arched stone doorway. She greeted him with the courtesy and poise she had acquired as a lady-in-waiting at the court of King David Kalakaua. Her name was Lahi-lahi Webb, and she acted as museum receptionist and guide. She directed him to one of two buildings in the rear where Gregory had his office on the second floor. Kenneth walked back through a crooked tunnel that resembled a passageway in a dungeon, past a little garden, and up the stairs.

The anticipation and intense excitement that greeted his arrival would have flattered a scientist with an international reputation. But the excitement was not aimed at Kenneth. Everybody was in a flutter to get ready for the first Pan-Pacific Scientific Congress, which was scheduled to open in a week and a half. It would be the most important event at the museum since the doors first opened. There was hardly time to shake Kenneth's hand. He felt like a new in-law at his first family reunion.

Gregory had accomplished the impossible since he had replaced Brigham as museum director. First he had talked Yale University into keeping him on the payroll as Silliman professor of geology while he served as director of Bishop Museum six months of each year, from May to October. Yale even granted Bishop Museum two fellowships for research in anthropology, botany, geology, zoology, and geography of the Pacific. Then Gregory had obtained a grant of forty thousand dollars from a former Yale student, New York banker Bayard Dominick, to be used for sending expeditions to the South Seas to research the origin and migrations of Polynesians.

That wasn't all. Gregory had recently become chairman of the Committee on Pacific Investigations of the National Research Council. The council had organized itself during World War I when scientists volunteered and the government accepted their services as a clearing house for scientific questions. After the war it seemed a shame to break up so valuable a group, so the scientists continued their work. Their purpose was to coordinate scientific activity around the world without overlap. With the help of this influential body, Gregory had put together a Pan-Pacific Scientific Congress, the first of its kind. Scientists from around the Pacific would gather in Hawaii to formulate a plan to investigate this great ocean about which so little was known. Bishop's curiosity show was about to become a museum of international stature.

The new keeper of insects, young Ed Bryan, who was fresh out of the University of Hawaii, scurried around trying to get an insect exhibit ready. Slow and careful John F. G. Stokes, curator from New Zealand, did the same for artifacts. Staff members pored over papers they would present before the most prestigious gathering of scientists ever to assemble in the Pacific. Yale University fellows in all sizes ran underfoot. Dr. Clark Wissler, head of the bureau of anthropology at the American Museum of Natural History in New York, was at the museum in the capacity of consultant.

Kenneth's new bachelor's degree caused hardly a ripple among the ten doctor's degrees and four master's degrees now on the small fulltime and the swollen associate staff. He was not so much awed as envious, especially of the scientists participating in the Bayard Dominick expeditions to the South Seas. Edward S. Handy, Ph.D. and instructor at Harvard, was in charge of the Marquesas expedition. His partner, Ralph Linton, a master of arts at the University of Pennsylvania, had taken part in five field expeditions and had served as ethnologist for the State of Illinois. Edward W. Gifford had been to the Revillagigedo and Galapagos Islands, had been assistant curator at the department of anthropology at the University of California, and had published papers on Indian tribes. He was presently in Tonga with William C. McKern, instructor in sociology at the University of Washington.

Then there was Kenneth Emory who had been to Molokai. Director Gregory listed the qualifications of his assistant ethnologist as follows: "Mr. Emory is familiar with survey and field methods and his residence in Hawaii has given him an interest in Polynesian problems." Kenneth was not assigned to any expeditions. Instead, Gregory put him to work as tour guide and errand boy for the visiting scientists.

There is no evidence that Kenneth felt discouraged. His diary on the following Monday read, "Saw Mr. J. R. Galt for work on entertaining guests to the conference." On Tuesday he wrote, "Worked all day for the committee looking out for scientists." This committee needed all the help it could get because its members were dealing with a rigorous discipline called Polynesian hospitality. Kenneth would be as busy as a mother of the bride at her daughter's wedding.

The University Club had offered its rooms as a social headquarters downtown. The Pacific Club was planning a chowder dinner at the Waikiki Beach home of John Guild. There was to be an outing at Nanakuli and a trip around the island to visit sugar plantations. Governor Charles J. McCarthy would host a dinner, the Japanese Chamber of Commerce a reception, and the Trail and Mountain Club a picnic. Kenneth went to work on Wednesday when he met a group of scientists arriving on the SS *Manoa*.

The Congress opened Monday, August 2, in the Throne Room of Iolani Palace with more than one hundred delegates in attendance from the United States, Japan, the Philippines, Australia, and New Zealand. They represented the most advanced knowledge in 1920 about the Pacific. When welcoming speeches gave way on Tuesday to discussion and debate, Kenneth found himself in exactly the right place at exactly the right time to learn about the state of anthropology in the Pacific, as well as its goals and problems and the methods being used to meet those goals and arrive at solutions to the problems. Even more exciting, he heard Gregory tell the assembly, "The one thing that research needs is capable young men."

The state of anthropology in the Pacific, it turned out, had not advanced very far. A primary goal was to solve the riddle of where Pacific Islanders came from, how they got there, and when. Were Polynesians related to American Indians? Had they come from somewhere in Asia? Were they survivors of a sunken Pacific continent? Crusty Dr. Brigham said he had heard at least five theories. Nobody knew for sure. Over and over, America's leading anthropologists said the same thing in different words. Alfred Tozzer, professor of anthropology at Harvard, called the question of Polynesian origins "the most popular, the most difficult and the most nebulous of scientific subjects."

Another goal was to collect the evidence before it got lost. Brigham lamented the passing of *kahunas* (priests) of the past generation who had taken with them knowledge of the old religion. Gregory stated flatly, ". . . the opportunities for obtaining information are rapidly disappearing." Again and again, scientists complained that island cultures were dying out. Gerald Fowke of the bureau of ethnology at the Smithsonian Institution in Washington, D.C., called the preservation of Polynesian ruins a "vast future work."

The wide-ranging lectures gave Kenneth plenty of opportunity to see that his goal to study South Pacific islanders could benefit from the study of insects, mammals, snails, ocean currents, geological formations, and other disciplines. We can picture him between errands attending the speakers as intently as he had attended the fingering technique of a Hawaiian boy picking a steel guitar. William E. Safford lectured on plants and language as clues in tracing the origin and migrations of Polynesians. Safford was an economic botanist with the U.S. Department of Agriculture. He had been a naval officer and governor of Guam during World War I.

"How does it happen that Hawaii, a Pacific island so far removed from New Zealand and South America, has some forms of life similar to those found in those countries?" Safford ask his fellow scientists. He said the answer lies in dispersal. For example, breadfruit, yams, taro, paper mulberry, and other plants were probably carried to the islands by man. Safford added that language also requires dispersal. "The natives of such widely separated groups as Hawaii,

New Zealand and Easter Island, together with the intervening groups of Tahiti and Samoa, all speak a language . . . clearly allied," he said. He added that in his opinion both plants and animals on these islands reflect a common source of human dispersal, the Polynesians.

But other scientists, Safford explained, had other theories. He said, "It was long supposed, on account of the wonderful hieroglyphics on Easter Island, that the earliest inhabitants were not Polynesians. However, a study of the language on that island shows not a trace of anything but Polynesian."

Having presented evidence for two conflicting theories, Safford must now reconcile them with a Polynesian explanation for the Egyptian-looking hieroglyphics from Easter Island found on wooden tablets. He said, "It is probable that [they] were genealogical records more or less mythical, beginning, as in the case of the pedigree of the Hawaiian kings, with the marriage of earth and light."

This must have been heady stuff for the Bishop Museum's new assistant ethnologist. And there was more to come. Safford drew on the pioneering research in language conducted by William Churchill of the Carnegie Institution of Washington. Churchill had also acted as consulting ethnologist for the Bishop Museum.

"Languages develop very much like plants or animals," added Safford. He explained that languages have a tendency to vary from one another when isolated on different islands. This divergence increases with the length of isolation. The same tendency to diverge in isolation occurs in plants and animals, he said. "Dialects may be compared to varieties (of plants or animals); distinct languages to species, and language groups to zoological families," he went on.

The importance of such divergence in the study of Polynesians, Safford explained, is that it provides a tool for measuring the time spent in isolation. How long had the Polynesians been isolated on their widely scattered islands? Judging from the similarity of their dialects Safford estimated that "the Polynesian dispersal took place not more than one thousand years ago."

Then he got down to the great question, where did the Polynesians come from? "More interesting still," he said, "is the fact that cultivated plants bearing similar names . . . point back to the Malay archipelago. There can be no question but that the Polynesians are descended from the primitive inhabitants of the Malay archipelago or the Malay peninsula."

That was all well and good. But one thing Kenneth Emory learned by listening to the leading scientists of his day was that they frequently did not agree. On August 6 a mind-boggling array of disciplines entered the lists, all aimed at supporting or demolishing the theory that Pacific islanders walked to their destinations in the dim, distant past over land bridges that at one time connected the islands to continents.

Henry S. Washington, geologist with the Carnegie Institution, had staked out his position before the conference began. In polite terms he called the land bridge theory poppycock. He said the Hawaiian Islands are entirely volcanic in origin and have no connection with any continent.

Yet how did volcanoes explain the fact that some insects found in Hawaii came all the way from America or, say, India? F. Muir, entomologist with the experiment station staff at the Hawaii Sugar Planters' Association, admitted that there was a lot of conflicting evidence and opinion. Nevertheless he came down firmly on the side of Washington. As an expert on insects, he made the following points: Just because a few of the insects found in Hawaii come from America or India does not mean they walked from there over land bridges. The evidence of insects not found in Hawaii is much more conclusive. By and large, the insects living in Hawaii upon the arrival of man were those who could travel by means of wind and water. Those not found were insects that had to travel over land.

For example, Muir said, a little leaf hopper that could have been carried by the wind is found in sixty species in the islands. He added that larvae of other insects capable of floating on logs are also found in Hawaii. But the tide beetle, which does not care for logs and is too heavy to fly very far, never made it to the islands. Thus Muir concluded as diplomatically as possible that a land connection with a submerged Pacific continent was a fairy tale.

Dr. Forest B. Brown, botanist at the Bishop Museum, introduced a new element into the discussion, begonias, which muddied the waters even further. He said begonias are found in primitive form in Hawaii and other Pacific islands. His theory about begonias was quite ambitious. Brown believed that because they are native to South America, begonias were swept through Central America some time in the past on an Atlantic equatorial current and out into the Pacific. The problem was that begonias are also found in the Philippines, East India, and Southeast Asia. How did they get so far from South America? Brown surmised that begonias traveled by land bridge over Siberia during warmer climes. He added helpfully that fossils of the tropical breadfruit tree had been found in Greenland.

The submerged continent theory found an advocate in Dr. W. A. Bryan, listed as a scientist at the University of Hawaii, who had just returned from a visit to Easter Island and San Juan Fernandez Island off the coast of Chile. He stated categorically, "I am as satisfied that that island went down in a vast submergence as if I had stood there and watched. But we need more data. I feel there is a submarine ridge connecting these islands. The feeling is in my soul that when we get to the bottom of the affair we will find a general submergence of the whole region."

The discussion became quite lively. Dr. H. A. Pilsbury, conchologist and curator of the department of mollusca of the Philadelphia Academy of Sciences, spoke for snails and a land bridge connecting Pacific islands and Asia. Obviously, snails do not walk on water. Pilsbury said the distribution of snails from Asia throughout Polynesia indicated a continuation of a land mass from New Guinea as far into the Pacific as Tahiti.

Dr. Safford, the economic botanist, stood up to disagree. He asked pointedly if Pilsbury might inform him about the distribution in Polynesia of mammals as well as snails. Pilsbury admitted that Polynesia had no native mammals. Safford nodded vigorously to prove his point. There never had been a land bridge that mammals could walk across.

Getting back to snails, Alfred G. Mayor, biologist with the Carnegie Institution, offered a theory of how they could have reached the Pacific islands even though they can't swim. He said scientists who have not had experience with island natives fail to understand what tremendous sailors they were and what part they played in distributing plants and animals around the Pacific. Mayor said a good example is a snail called *Partula hyalina.* "This snail commonly feeds on the taro and banana plant," he said. "The Polynesian natives are daring navigators. They make voyages as long as three weeks in length. Before putting to sea they load their canoes with food including taro wrapped in taro and banana leaves."

Mayor said the snails arrived at their island destinations as stowaways. He added, "This particular snail [*Partula hyalina*] is common in Tahiti. It is not found on Moorea, twelve miles away. This indicates that the native navigators brought it to Tahiti, which was a long voyage, but did not take it to Moorea because they did not need a stock of food for so short a trip [thus leaving the snails behind in Tahiti]."

The conference also introduced Kenneth to the scientific attitude, a skeptic's distrust of the marvelous. Gerald Fowke of the Smithsonian was so careful that he refused to answer reporters' questions about the origin of Polynesians because he was an archaeologist, not an anthropologist, and therefore did not deal in the subject. He would only say with certainty that his research in Hawaii with skeletons and artifacts indicated there had been no race in the islands before the Hawaiians.

News stories in Honolulu about the conference aroused plenty of interest among laymen with firm if not too well-informed opinions about where Polynesians came from. The *Honolulu Star-Bulletin* on August 9 published a long letter from D. M. M'Allister who insisted that the "Polynesian race were, most likely, a white people, and probably of the Shemitic [sic] or Israelitish tribes." M'Allister explained that an oracle of God had led these people to America, from whence they migrated to Polynesia. This was revealed in the Book of Mormon. Another letter in the same issue from George Graham in Auckland, New Zealand, argued that "there can be little doubt the Polynesian people emigrated from the west and that it is to India and still farther west the cradle of their race is to be found."

It must have become more and more clear to Kenneth Emory that nobody really knew very much for sure about the Pacific. There was a great deal of work to be done and not much time to do it. Why couldn't he be part of this? His diary indicates he caught fire on August 6. He wrote, "Listened to a splendid discussion on anthropology."

On that day Gregory told the group, "The big vanishing problem of the Pacific is the Polynesian race. The influenza epidemic [of 1919] removed half of the Polynesian inhabitants. That means we must go to work. I have been told of four islands in the Pacific where the last words of the native dialect have been spoken. That part of the race is gone. There are three men on Tahiti whose death, if they had been overcome by the influenza, would have decreased ethnological work fifty per cent."

Louis Sullivan, physical anthropologist with the American Museum of Natural History, spoke as bluntly. "In all fairness to those who have worked in this part of the world," he said, "this may still be considered to be a virgin field. Probably the history of no similar group of mankind has been so much speculated upon and maltreated as that of the Polynesians. Voyagers, missionaries, legislators and students of all subjects who have traveled in Polynesia, or have talked with somebody who has, or who have seen photographs of the natives, have been generous in their contributions to the theories and speculations in vogue; nor have they been backward in adding new theories of their own to the manufacture. It is easy to find authority for including them [Polynesians] or excluding them from all the races of mankind. I do not exaggerate."

Kenneth must have listened very closely when Sullivan went on with superb self-confidence to promote his own discipline as that which would find the key: "Physical anthropology can accurately define and describe the Polynesian groups. It can prove beyond reasonable doubt the racial origin of the Polynesians. . . . It can point out the probable types with which the Polynesians have come in contact and intermixed during their migrations in recent times."

If there had been any doubt in Kenneth's mind about what he wanted to do with his life it evaporated during a lecture by the American Museum of Natural History's Clark Wissler. The scientist gave a scholarly dissertation on races. The talk ended like this: "What we seek in Polynesia is to interpret man's distribution in terms of time and space as the outline for an investigation of his evolution. If anything is to be done with the Polynesian problem, it must be done now."

A number of delegates to the first Pan-Pacific Scientific Congress noticed and approved of their eager and energetic errand boy. After all, several of the speakers had stressed the need to interest young men in the cause. One of them, Dr. A. L. Kroeber, professor of anthropology at the University of California at Berkeley, had apparently overlooked this important phase of the conference. Kroeber bumped into Kenneth at a Bishop Museum reception. The scientist tried to classify the young man who stood in his way.

"Are you a divinity student?" he asked.

Kenneth explained that he was the Bishop Museum's new assistant ethnologist although, at the moment, somewhat inexperienced and without an ethnologist to assist. His infectious enthusiasm so impressed the professor that Kroeber offered Kenneth a position the following semester as his teaching assistant. In return for collecting papers and checking attendance, he could monitor courses that would give him a beginning background in anthropology.

That was on the morning of Monday, August 9. In the afternoon Kenneth told Gregory about the offer and found him agreeable. Kenneth wrote in his diary the next day, "Called up Kroeber [to accept]." On Wednesday, August 11, he wrote, "Saw Dr. Kroeber off." In less than three weeks he had taken his first step upward in the world of science.

Hawaiian Islands

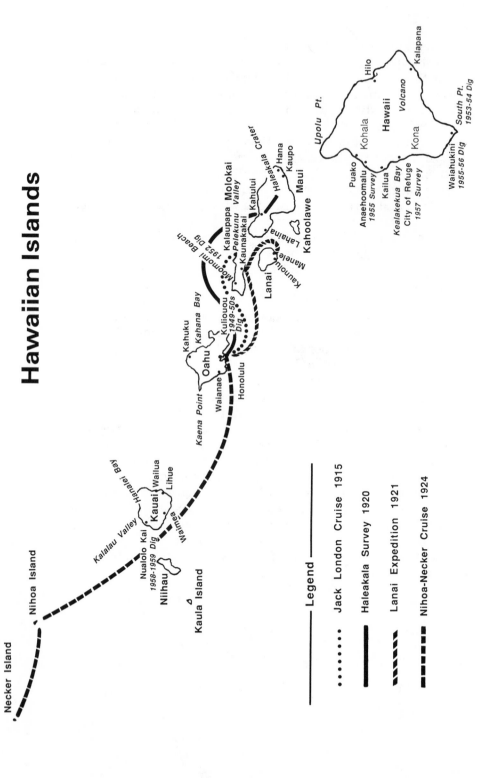

Necker Island

Nihoa Island

Kauai
Hanalei Bay
Kalalau Valley
Wailua
Lihue
Waimea
Nualolo Kai
1958-1959 Dig

Niihau

Kaula Island

Kauai

Kaena Point
Kahuku
Kahana Bay
Oahu
Waianae
Honolulu
Kuliouou
1949-50s
Dig
Moomomi Beach
1952 Dig
Kalaupapa
Molokai
Pelekunu
Valley
Kaunakakai

Lanai
Manele
Kaunolu

Kahoolawe

Lahaina

Kahului
Haleakala Crater
Hana
Kaupo
Maui

Upolu Pt.
Hilo
Kalapana
Kohala
Hawaii
Volcano
Puako
Anaehoomalu
1955 Survey
Kailua
Kona
Kealakekua Bay
City of Refuge
1957 Survey
South Pt.
1953-54 Dig
Waiahukini
1955-56 Dig

—— Legend ——

•••••• Jack London Cruise 1915

▬▬▬ Haleakala Survey 1920

⧷⧷⧷ Lanai Expedition 1921

▬ ▬ ▬ Nihoa-Necker Cruise 1924

Chapter Nine

This is
my World

It did not take Gregory long to find a task at the museum better suited to the abilities of his new assistant ethnologist than running errands for visiting scientists. The museum director was prodding Stokes, who did not like to be prodded, to finish his report on *heiau*s because Stokes was due to leave soon for the Austral Islands. He and Robert T. Aitken, assistant in the department of anthropology at the Milwaukee Public Museum, would form a third team of the Bayard Dominick expeditions. Gregory wanted Stokes to finish with the *heiau*s report before the boat sailed. But there was still a map to draw. At this point Gregory remembered that Kenneth Emory had said he could draw maps. Why not let him prove it?

This was the reason that after seeing Kroeber off, Kenneth went back to the museum. At a large table in Stokes' office he mapped the monumental stone structures of the City of Refuge at Honaunau on the island of Hawaii. Gregory kept him at it all week. Meanwhile he got to know Bob Aitken, who proved to be not at all awesome at close range—even though he was a real archaeologist. Only a few years older than Kenneth, he had been a foreman in steel construction at Hog Island Shipyard during World War I before getting his degree at Columbia University.

Kenneth had almost completed the map when publisher Thurston called Gregory about a sighting of undiscovered Hawaiian ruins on the island of Maui. Armine Von Tempsky, the oldest daughter of the manager of Haleakala Ranch, had spotted stone terraces while exploring inside the enormous cinder cones that dot the floor of Haleakala Crater. She had tipped off Thurston. This information came on the heels of another report with a photograph taken by territorial forester C. S. Judd of a walled enclosure on the floor of the crater. Von Tempsky said the ruins looked to her like burials. Thurston urged Gregory to investigate before artifact hunters heard about them and looted the graves.

Nobody at the museum had suspected the existence of man-made ruins in so unlikely a location. There were many Hawaiian legends about the ten-thousand-foot-high crater of Haleakala volcano where the demigod Maui had lassoed the sun. But it was a cold, arid, and inhospitable place for humans. Here was an opportunity to conduct at home the kind of research other Bayard Dominick expeditions were carrying out in the South Seas. There was just time for archaeologist Aitken to make a brief survey before he sailed to the Australs. On August 23, 1920, Gregory told Kenneth he could go along for the experience and to take photographs.

The most remarkable thing about Kenneth Emory's approach to the first scientific expedition of his career is the assured way he went about it. His first move was to spend an evening with Thurston to learn as much as he could about Haleakala. Kenneth had been in the crater as an apprentice cowboy at age fifteen. Thurston had gone in with Jack London in 1907. Now Kenneth checked his memory against Thurston's. Where were the best places to camp? Where were the water sources?

At the museum, Kenneth cleaned out the darkroom and limbered up an old five-by-seven view camera, which was smaller than a bread box—but not much. The camera perched on a heavy wooden tripod. To focus it, the photographer draped a black cloth over his head and peered through a frosted glass while moving the lens back and forth along its track until the image in the glass became sharp. The cameraman guessed at exposure settings. Camera and tripod weighed between seven and eight pounds. This bulky, sharp-edged machinery, together with film packs, would be carried on the photographer's back.

In a wilderness like Haleakala, the expedition must come fully equipped but not overloaded. This called for careful selection of equipment: canteen, knapsacks, hunting knife, field glasses, measuring tape, notebooks, toilet paper, boots, warm clothing, eating and cooking utensils, rifle, and tent. Then there was the plane table survey board, which required a tripod. The scientists would buy food supplies on Maui. Kenneth finished the map of Honaunau on Friday, August 27, in time to sail with Aitken at 10 P.M. on the interisland steamer *Claudine.*

Kenneth's value to the expedition soared when they arrived at Kahului. Henry A. Baldwin, his former host, provided horses, pack mules, and the help of two cowboys for two weeks at minimum cost to the museum. From a little settlement called Olinda, they started up the mountain the next morning in darkness; four men on horseback leading a train of pack mules through dry grass that hid stones and cracks in the lava. The starlight chill bit through Kenneth's jacket as they paused on the rim of the crater to watch the sunrise and let the horses blow.

On the rim they were above the clouds and surrounded by silence.

Haleakala Crater lay in gloomy shadow, an enormous pit covering fifteen square miles spread out one thousand to three thousand feet below. A fiery orange ball peeped over the opposite rim. Soft, subdued light invaded the crater and brought gradually alive its great swirls of burnt red, gray, purple, orange, black, and yellow. The soaring sweep of craggy crater walls came into focus, and the vast field of cinder cones cast long shadows in the strengthening light. The cones reminded Kenneth of a herd of red and gray elephants.

For Kenneth it was a religious experience. He sat in the saddle absorbed in the unfolding panorama and the singing silence. A conviction came to him with startling clarity that he had found his life's work. He gazed out over the wilderness where the mysteries of old Polynesia lay hidden, and said to himself, "this is my world."

A twisting path along the crater rim led to Sliding Sands Trail, which zigzagged across rust-colored cinders to the bare crater floor below. The horses plodded through sand to a sheltered spot at the base of the crater wall near a spring. There the cowboys set up camp while Aitken and Emory rode on to a gray cinder cone called Puu Naue in the center of the crater.

From above the cinder cones had appeared in miniature. But Puu Naue towered 250 feet high from its base. Aitken and Emory slogged on foot up the soft cinder slope. They peered down into the rounded hollow inside. There, partially covered but clearly outlined in the gray sand, were three flat stone structures. Kenneth raced Aitken down the inside slope to explore the ruins.

It is logical to assume that he learned from Aitken as they worked. Field procedure, for example. The job of an archaeologist in the field is to obtain information about past human activities through the study of ruins and artifacts. He does this by disciplined observation. Aitken began by taking careful measurements of the ruins and jotting down what he could learn by a search for clues. He took photographs of the ruins. The plane table survey provided data for a map that would show the ruins in proportion and relation to one another. Each scrap of information went into his notebook as raw data from which conclusions could later be drawn.

Kenneth insists that he really did not learn much from Aitken. He said he already knew how to measure and describe and survey and photograph. It was as if he emerged, like a butterfly from its cocoon, as a full-blown archaeologist. Perhaps it would be more accurate to compare him at this time to a maturing puppy, bursting with energy, strong and quick and eager for the hunt. It is certain that Aitken did not resent Kenneth's help, but rather welcomed it because the job proved bigger than either had anticipated.

They kept finding more stone ruins. There were some in the twin black cinder cones of Halalii, more in a little pocket between Mamani and Kumu hills, and there were *ahus* (cairns) in many locations. At Halalii, Aitken picked up two water-worn pebbles that must have been carried there from the seashore or a streambed. The archaeologist pronounced them sling stones used in hunting or warfare.

Some of the stone structures were platforms, others terraces, still others cairns. For what purpose had these remote structures been built? And when? Unfortunately Kenneth broke off his diary during the expedition. He left no record of the campfire conversations he and Aitken must have had about the mysterious platforms and terraces.

One indication of the excitement they felt came from I. A. Dangerfield, head of the Weather Bureau in Hawaii, who visited the expedition site while on a trip through the crater. Later he talked to a newspaper editor in Wailuku, the capital of Maui. The *Maui News* reported:

> Inside some of the cones, under the hanging walls, man, in some past day has built up terraces of large stones surfaced with small stones and made practically level. They range from three to five or more feet in height and some extend back a dozen feet or more. Dangerfield was with the party for three nights and two days. . . . He said the terraces, though much smaller, were weirdly reminiscent of the cliff dwellings of Arizona and New Mexico. Whether the terraces were used as a base for dwellings of some primitive people or whether they were used for ceremonial purposes is a question the scientists have not yet answered.

Publisher Thurston could not resist joining the expedition for which he felt responsible. He arrived with Armine Von Tempsky in tow. They spent one night in Haleakala. Armine turned out to be the kind of visitor every young, male archaeologist in the field is happy to welcome into camp. She was dark-haired, pretty, feminine and athletic at the same time, well-read, and a stimulating conversationalist. But it didn't do Kenneth much good. Armine had eyes only for his slender, handsome partner, who was more mature and also married. Aitken took her on a tour of the ruins while Kenneth snapped pictures.

Thurston and Armine departed the next morning for Kaupo, a fishing village on the leeward shore of Haleakala. At the mention of Kaupo, Kenneth asked permission to go along. If anyone would know how the ruins inside Haleakala Crater got there it would be the Hawaiians of Kaupo, because they had lived in the shadow of the mountain for centuries. Aitken stayed in camp because he didn't speak Hawaiian.

The dramatic descent through Kaupo Gap and down the nearly two-mile-high slope of Haleakala led from a sterile environment of high-altitude desert through stunted *ohia* and fern into a belt of luxurious forest, down into rolling meadows, and finally to the hot, parched, lava-bound shore. Here a cluster of frame cottages marked the village of Kaupo with its dogs and outrigger canoes and drying fish nets. When they were not fishing, the men of Kaupo worked cattle. They were equally at home on horseback or in a canoe.

Kenneth made the acquaintance of a Kaupo native, Leonard Poouahi, who ticked off the Hawaiian names of cinder cones, trails, caves, cliffs, and springs in the crater with easy familiarity. Poouahi said his grandparents had gone into Haleakala to hunt the seabird called *uwau* because it was good eating. Morning and evening the birds flew through a narrow place in the crater rim. There the old people strung nets to catch the birds. Poouahi knew nothing about the platforms and terraces in the cinder cones. But Kenneth urged him to visit the camp. His knowledge of place names alone would add to the museum's store of information.

Poouahi could not go back with Kenneth. But he turned up in camp a few days later with his son. He carried a bag of sweet potatoes for provisions. The Hawaiian took Kenneth to a pit called Na Piko Haua, ten feet deep and fifteen feet in diameter, where Kaupo parents came to tuck the umbilical cords of their newborn children into crevices. Poouahi's own umbilical cord was stored there. Some of the cords were wrapped in the hair of the child's mother, others were preserved in small glass bottles, testifying to the perpetuation of this Hawaiian custom. Poouahi asked Kenneth with genuine interest where his umbilical cord was buried. Nonplussed, Kenneth blurted, "Fitchburg."

It appeared that Hawaiians in ancient times had traveled through Haleakala Crater with regularity. Kenneth's guide told him about a trail he said had been built by Kihapiilani, a chief from Makawao on Maui, brother-in-law of a very early chief on Hawaii named Umi. This trail was supposed to lead to a pond called Wai Ale on the outside slope of Haleakala where Kihapiilani had built a dam to store water. Later, Kenneth found traces of this trail paved with lava blocks.

Not all of Poouahi's information appeared to be accurate, however. The old man pointed out a stone structure nine feet long and five feet wide near a cinder cone called Pa Puaa o Pele. Poouahi said it was the grave of a man and a woman who in recent times had "scratched the sacred sands" in violation of a *kapu*. In consequence, they had become lost in a fog and perished. If this structure was of recent vintage, perhaps the others were also. But Kenneth became suspicious of Poouahi's tale when he found a sling stone in a crevice of the platform. The Hawaiians had not used sling stones since the arrival of firearms. The only way to discover if this or any of the other stone structures marked burials would be to excavate for skeletons.

By the time Aitken and Emory came out of the crater they had raised as many questions as they had answered. Nevertheless, they were in a mood to celebrate and Armine Von Tempsky's invitation to dinner came as a welcome end to the expedition. Armine, it developed, was determined to put Bob Aitken in a romantic mood. She fixed him a very strong drink. But the glasses got mixed up and Kenneth, who asked for something nonalcoholic, received the drink intended for Aitken. Kenneth didn't know the difference because he had never tasted whiskey. He had no idea why the room spun and he babbled without making sense. The truth eventually dawned on Armine who took Kenneth to a bedroom to sleep it off.

Back at the museum, Aitken reported to Gregory that the mysterious ruins in Haleakala must be excavated to determine whether or not they were burials. Publicity about the ruins would soon draw artifact hunters, so the work should be done immediately. Aitken recommended that Kenneth be sent back because he knew the crater and was capable. The fact is, there was nobody else available. Kenneth's diary reveals how badly he wanted to go.

Tuesday, September 21, 1920—Used the typewriter at the museum to write letters to Mr. Baldwin concerning arrangements for another trip. At museum all day. Home in evening. Reading *The Napoleon of the Pacific.*

Wednesday, September 22, 1920—Museum. Sullivan [the physical anthropologist] came back from Hawaii, stirred him up on the need of going back to Haleakala. Bob [Aitken] and I moonlight swim, party.

Friday, September 23, 1920—The trustees appropriated $500 for Haleakala. I go!

It meant double work because Kenneth helped Aitken and Stokes pack for the Australs while he prepared to return to Haleakala. Meanwhile, Aitken and Emory worked on a preliminary Haleakala report. They finished it the day before Aitken sailed with Stokes on Wednesday, September 29. On Friday, Kenneth set out once more for Haleakala. He was equipped to stay a month.

This time he carried a typewriter and kept a journal. As a result.

we know that he hired three cowboys as helpers: Antone Gouveia, Joe Silva, and Ben Franco. They pitched camp two-and-one-half miles from the nearest spring, having found that the previous campsite, near water, was too wet and rainy. Every day someone walked the two-and-one-half miles to fetch seven or eight gallons of water. They lived on wild goat meat. Goat hunting took up almost as much energy as hunting for ruins.

On Tuesday, October 7, Kenneth wrote, "Franco and Silva killed eleven goats and brought home the six best. These ought to keep us in fresh provisions for five days. Meat will not keep longer than that. We eat one whole goat a day, stewed with rice, potatoes, onions, macaroni, and tomatoes."

The cowboys brought back a captured black nanny goat from one of their hunts. She gave birth to a kid in camp. Kenneth wrote, "In a few days, we can have fresh milk for our coffee. We have quite a ranch with the billy captured Sunday. The practical outcome of maintaining it is that goats are attracted to within rifle shot of our camp so we do not have to search far for our daily meat."

Excavation of terraces in Puu Naue cinder cone began the first day and digging at various sites continued to the end. Kenneth's journal describes a typical day:

Monday, October, Mamani Camp—It was an extremely cold, still, moonlight night and in the morning the ground was heavily frosted. Hanakauhi Valley appeared as if covered with snow . . .

We trenched an area in front of the north wall [of a terrace] in the hopes of finding some evidence in the nature of shells or stone implements . . . I took two pictures of the men at work . . . one showing the south platform restored.

Our lunch consisted of two crackers, a fig bar and a drink of water apiece. I set up the camera for a view of the camp with Hanakauhi looming over it but, as often happened, the clouds suddenly enveloped what would have made an ideal picture.

I had in mind the *ahu* [cairn] in Kamoa o Pele [cinder cone] as an afternoon job. . . . We took down the stones . . . in such a manner as to be able to restore them. . . . A shovel full of sand brought up pieces of rotten wood and bone . . .

Brushing down the sand six to eight inches brought into relief the remains of a body placed face downward, the right arm extended the length of the right side, the left arm bent back at the elbow over the back. Two sticks of wood three inches in diameter and longer than the remains lay immediately above and to each side. These must have served as a stretcher for carrying the body . . .

Twenty-five minutes were taken in returning to camp. By spreading out in skirmish formation . . . we found three more pebbles [sling stones]. There were several lying on the sand a hundred yards from Mamani Camp. In the scarcity of water for boiling tonight we had to fry our goat meat.

The cairn in Kamoa o Pele cinder cone, then, marked a burial. But the excavations in Puu Naue revealed nothing. In hunting for goats, Kenneth found hundreds of stone shelters apparently used as windbreaks by travelers. On the highest part of the crater rim he found a stone platform fifty-seven feet long and thirty-six feet wide built on two levels. It was so imposing he called it a *heiau*. He and his men dug below the platform that Poouahi from Kaupo had called a burial. But there were no skeletons. Kenneth wrote, "I believe that this story, that . . . natives perished in the crater and were buried here not long ago, has become attached to the platform in an attempt to explain it."

By the time Kenneth returned to Honolulu, he and his cowboy helpers had revealed the existence of forty-eight stone terraces and platforms, most of them unknown before. They had found nine groupings or camps of stone shelters, which Kenneth estimated could accommodate two hundred travelers. In addition, the team had recorded several hundred *ahu*s and a section of ancient paved trail. Kenneth had made a plane table survey of the three most important archaeological sites. He and his men had picked up 101 sling stones, which he suggested might have been used for hunting for plover, a migratory bird. He had added many new place names to the museum's scientific vocabulary. His team had excavated and then restored five platforms, ten terraces, and three *ahu*s. He had pried open a new window to old Polynesia that scientists had not known existed.

But the terraces and platforms refused to give up their secret. For what purpose had they been constructed in the bone-chilling cold of Haleakala Crater? It was easier to determine what they were not than to determine what they were. Kenneth wrote in his final report, "I gained the impression that the facts are opposed to the view that the terraces and platforms are either house foundations [no post holes], fortifications [no walls], places for hiding things [no hidden objects] or burial sites [no skeletons]. The only feature which these mysterious structures seem to have in common is a square or rectangular paved flat surface, from one to six feet above the ground, from three to twenty feet wide and from four to forty feet long. . . . If a flat surface was the result desired, they may have been used for a single purpose as altars . . ."

Chapter Ten

$125 a Month

The average age of scientists working out of the Bishop Museum in 1920 did not fit the image its first director, Brigham, had projected of a gray-haired scholar with spectacles on the end of his nose. Ed Bryan and Ken Emory were just out of college. Most of the members of the Bayard Dominick expeditions were in their twenties and thirties. Louis Sullivan, in spite of his reputation, had not reached middle age. Consequently the museum was a congenial and stimulating place for young Kenneth Emory.

Sullivan had come to Hawaii from New York to measure racial types. His goal was to obtain a physical description of the Polynesians; once he had decided on their physical characteristics it would be a simple matter to trace these characteristics back to the source. Physical anthropologists like Sullivan believed this discipline would bring order out of the chaos of races if only measurements could be taken of enough people. Hawaii's multiracial population made it an excellent place to work. By enlisting the cooperation of schools, Sullivan planned to measure students of pure Hawaiian, Chinese, Japanese, and Caucasian ancestry.

This project was about to get underway when Kenneth returned from Maui loaded down with notes, photographs, rocks, and the skeleton he had uncovered. Because one area of Sullivan's expertise was bones, it was only natural that he go over the material Kenneth showed him. So the busy assistant ethnologist found himself in the middle of another new and exciting discipline.

He listened in fascination while Sullivan read the story of the skeleton from the crater of Kamoa o Pele. It was that of a female adult. She had been about four feet, eleven inches in height, judging from the leg bones and spine, and thirty-five years of age, based on an examination of the skull. The skeleton's teeth were slightly decayed and showed advanced pyorrhea, or inflammation of the sockets, in the molar region. Most interesting of all, there was a shattered place about the size of a silver dollar on top of the skull. Sullivan said this represented a concussion from a blow on the head, which probably caused her death. But not immediately. Some knitting of the fracture indicated the woman had lived for a while after the injury.

With this tantalizing introduction to physical anthropology it did not take much persuasion by Sullivan to recruit Kenneth as his assistant in the measuring project. They began on Tuesday, November 16, by taking the names and histories of children attending Royal School. On Friday they started measuring: dimensions of heads, shoulders, height standing, sitting height, weight. By Monday, they were taking the pulses of students.

Kenneth respected Sullivan's single-minded devotion to measuring, but indications are he had already made up his mind to take a broader approach to the study of his fellow humans. He stubbornly disagreed when Sullivan told him it was not important that an anthropologist know how to take a plane table survey. At times, Kenneth surprised Sullivan with some expertise of his own.

"This one is Chinese," he commented while they were measuring a young male.

"How do you know?" asked Sullivan.

"By his jade anklet. It's as common among Chinese as bound feet."

The limitations of physical anthropology became clearly evident to Kenneth one day when Sullivan announced that he was getting dramatic variations in the pulse rates of girls. It turned out that the pulse rates of some of the teenage girls registered abnormally high while Kenneth held their wrists.

He and Sullivan spent the rest of November and the first of December taking measurements of students. Kenneth enjoyed it. On December 6 he wrote in his diary, "Normal School. Began measuring cadets. Very interesting and full of fun." Sullivan took advantage of this enthusiasm by teaching Kenneth how to measure and photograph the skulls he wanted to include in his report. He demonstrated how to set up the skull, a complicated and precise procedure. Sullivan explained that the orientation was exactly the same all over the world for purposes of comparing one skull with another. Without precision and correct orientation, the photographs would be useless. Kenneth photographed the skulls and developed the photos. They were finished in time for Christmas.

Four days later, on December 29, 1920, Kenneth sailed for the University of California at Berkeley and directly into another love affair. He had intended to devote his energies exclusively to anthropology. However, a young lady named Isabelle Hill met the ship and took him in tow. Isabelle was related to the Thurstons, and the Hills had hosted Winifred Emory and her brood on their trips to the East.

But Kenneth was not prepared for the startling transformation in Isabelle. She had matured into a pretty, exuberant, if somewhat scatterbrained, young woman.

Isabelle, it appears, also approved of what the years had done to Kenneth. The day after he arrived, she drove him around the city and helped him find a room near the campus at Mrs. Smart's establishment at 2017 Parker Street. The room and two meals a day rented for ten dollars per week. That evening, Kenneth and Isabelle went to a movie and then dancing. It is difficult to tell from his diary whether he was the pursuer or the pursued. That weekend, she drove him around Oakland and into the countryside. They went out in the evening for dinner and dancing.

And they talked. Isabelle confided that she was not doing very well in school. In fact, she might flunk out if her grades did not improve. In addition she did not know what to do about George, a fraternity man who wanted to marry her. Kenneth analyzed the situation. To him the problem was obvious. Isabelle was seeing too much of George.

On the Berkeley campus Dr. Kroeber advised Kenneth about the choice of his electives. He registered on Monday, January 10, as a graduate student. The next day he went to a meeting of anthropology assistants and learned from Kroeber that his chances for a teaching fellowship had plummeted along with a drop in enrollment in introductory anthropology, because its reputation had changed last semester from an easy course to a difficult one. However, Kenneth would receive a small stipend to help defray his expenses and he would not be charged tuition.

Kenneth plunged into anthropology, the science of man, a field so new that the first major department of anthropology had been established at Columbia University less than twenty-five years before. Its founder, Franz Boas, was training students to conduct intensive, eyewitness studies of individual cultures, the model for Bishop Museum's pioneering Bayard Dominick expeditions on Polynesian islands. American Indians had already come under scrutiny and Kroeber was an authority.

Anthropology is such a broad field that students were already electing to specialize in one of its branches. There was physical anthropology, which dealt with fossil remains, skeletons, brain size, blood types, skin colors, and hereditary diseases. Archaeologists studied objects left behind by earlier peoples: tools, buildings, clothing, canoes, pottery, ornaments, and idols. Linguistic anthropologists analyzed the languages of different societies as tools for understanding their inner relationships and to trace their wanderings.

Some anthropologists specialized in ethnology, the social and cultural aspects of a society, including religion, family structure, social status, art, and music. Kenneth embraced all of this like a starving man unable to distinguish between salad and dessert.

At Berkeley, Kenneth found the contact with anthropology professors and other anthropology students as stimulating as the courses. From Kroeber he learned about the American Indian. Ruth Greiner, a classmate with a hunchback, was interested in primitive art. Kenneth talked in class on February 14 on the Malayo-Polynesian language and began writing a report on canoes. Kroeber encouraged him to take a civil service exam for a position in the National Museum in Washington, D.C., because his test score would give him an idea of how he rated nationally with other applicants.

Meanwhile, Isabelle took a lot of his time. She was still trying to decide about George who had taken a severe disliking to Kenneth who did his best to protect her from George. Kenneth took a "big brother" attitude toward Isabelle. He encouraged her to study with him in the library, thus keeping her out of George's clutches and improving her grades at the same time. But it wasn't all study and brotherly advice. On Friday, March 4, he wrote, "Went to all but one class today. Alpha Delta Phi dance. Took Isabelle. Home 2:30."

The semester was over almost before it had begun. Kenneth finished his canoe paper on April 26 and took his final exam the next day. On May 11 he rode with Ruth Greiner and another male student on a street car to the post office in San Francisco to sit for the civil service exam advertised by the National Museum.

Two days later Kenneth set out with Isabelle in her Dodge to spend his last weekend in California. Hope Clark, Isabelle's friend, went along. They drove on Friday to Monterey and stayed overnight, then journeyed on to Carmel gazing at each other and the scenery and beaches along the way. On Saturday they drove home. The next day, after a tennis match, Hope skipped off intentionally so the lovers could be alone. Kenneth wrote in his diary, "A never to be forgotten evening."

He boarded the SS *Matsonia* on Wednesday, May 18, 1921, and returned to Honolulu where he displayed amazing powers of recuperation from his tragic parting with Isabelle. Within a few weeks he was dating a young lady named Margaret Andrade. He took her to dinner, swimming at Kawela Bay and Nanakuli, horseback riding, dancing at the Halekulani Hotel, and to a Punahou night entertainment.

His professional life proceeded at the same pace. Gregory put him to work helping the new curator, Stanley Ball, catalogue a collection recently donated by S. M. Damon of Honolulu. While measuring the artifacts, writing their histories and descriptions, and tagging them, Kenneth received a crash course in the material culture of Polynesia. "I had to learn everything fast," he said later. He became familiar with fishhooks, poi pounders, adz heads, stone lamps, *ulumaika* [bowling] stones, *tapa* beaters, and hammer stones, all manufactured and used by the people of old. Kenneth never tired of handling these objects. He treated them reverently and with unflagging curiosity. And he continued to read. One young lady who knew him at this time said later, "He was always studying, studying."

A cable arrived in June from the National Museum. The director offered Kenneth the position of aide at $125 per month, fifty dollars more than he was making as an assistant ethnologist. His test score had put him among the top anthropology students in the nation. But he wasn't sure he wanted to work in Washington, D.C.

Kenneth went to Gregory for advice. The director glanced at the cable and grumbled, "They offered you $125? I guess we'll have to pay you that much." On June 20 Kenneth cabled the National Museum, "Unable to accept position of aide." Then he went home sick with the flu. The next day Margaret Andrade came calling with a jar of jam, a bouquet of honeysuckle, and her photo.

Chapter Eleven

The Stone Man

The relationship between Herbert Gregory and Kenneth Emory was somewhat like that of a college athletic coach and an unrecruited player who performed like a star. First, the young man with no formal training in archaeology had brought back from the crater of Haleakala proof that there were still important archaeological discoveries to be made in the Hawaiian Islands. Then, after four months of study in anthropology, he had brought back from Berkeley a job offer from the National Museum. Gregory was much too astute a museum politician not to take advantage of this increase in credibility. For the first time in public, he began talking about a fourth arm of the Bayard Dominick expeditions.

This newly discovered, Hawaii-based team consisted of Louis Sullivan, the American Museum of History physical anthropologist, and Kenneth Emory, the Bishop Museum's assistant ethnologist who had nobody to assist because there was nobody else in his department. At the moment, this distinguished Bayard Dominick scientist was moving *tapa* beaters out of drawers in Stokes' office to the basement. He was too busy in the basement to share in the glamour of a dockside greeting for the returning Tongan expedition. On June 15 he wrote wistfully in his diary, "Gifford and McKern came out to the museum today."

Kenneth did not remain long in the basement because Gregory had no intention of leaving him there. It occurred to the director that his assistant ethnologist had an uncanny way of conducting research in the field without spending money. He thrived by living off the land. Everybody Kenneth dealt with seemed to be either an old school chum, a family friend, or was related to somebody in both categories, and they all enjoyed helping him. H. A. Baldwin had been delighted with results of the Haleakala expedition. We can assume these considerations loomed large in Gregory's decision to send Kenneth to Lanai.

There were other considerations, of course. Although less than one hundred miles away on the map, the island of Lanai was nearly as unspoiled by civilization as an island in the South Seas. Sullivan, while taking measurements there, had found an enclave of pure Hawaiians. Lanai had never been explored by an archaeologist. Reports about untouched ruins had reached Gregory from George C. Munro, manager of the Lanai Ranch Company and a museum associate in ornithology (which meant he worked as an unpaid volunteer collecting birds). If Lanai turned out to be half as interesting archaeologically as Haleakala Crater, it would be the perfect place to keep Kenneth Emory busy and add another Hawaii dimension to the Bayard Dominick researches.

Still, the best reason for sending Kenneth to Lanai was that it would cost the museum practically nothing. H. A. Baldwin owned the Lanai Ranch Company. A letter arrived from ranch manager Munro extending an invitation for Kenneth to headquarter at the ranch where he could eat and sleep and be provided with horses to ride in the field. The letter also gave instructions how to reach the island by motor launch from Lahaina, Maui. Lanai was so remote that steamers touched there only to pick up cargos of cattle and honey.

On Tuesday, July 12, 1921, Kenneth's father drove him to the pier where he boarded the interisland steamer *Mikahala* with two duffle bags, a suitcase, the five-by-seven view camera, and his guitar. It was no coincidence that Margaret Andrade boarded the same ship because they had purchased tickets together: Margaret for Kaunaka-kai, Molokai, where she would visit friends, and Kenneth for Lahaina, Maui. They stood on the stern to watch the sunset as the vessel steamed past Diamond Head.

While conducive to romance, the stern also shuddered and shook, being just above the propellers, and heaved around a lot. One by one the other passengers retreated to their cabins to throw up in private. Kenneth wrote in his journal of the expedition, "I felt surely as if I was going to be sick but Margaret wasn't. We moved to the middle of the boat protected from spray and the shake of the stern." He forgot about his queasy stomach when one of the Hawaiian deck passengers, Mrs. Williams from Pukoo, Molokai, began strumming a ukulele and singing. Then the moon came out to silhouette Molokai, Maui, and Lanai against the stars. Kenneth and Margaret stayed up all the way to Kaunakakai where she disembarked at 11 P.M. on the half-mile wharf and rode the mule-drawn flatcar to shore.

Kenneth turned into his bunk and awakened in time to strike up an acquaintance with fellow passenger Mrs. Mary K. Fitzsimmons, a pure Hawaiian who taught school on Lanai. She told Kenneth she would have sixteen children when school opened in September and that he should feel free to stay at the schoolhouse and use the cooking utensils there.

Kenneth landed in a whaleboat with his baggage and Mrs. Fitzsimmons on the wharf at Lahaina. She introduced him to the waiting Munros. They were both New Zealanders, friendly and informal. Munro, a small man with a scholarly accent, said the launch would be leaving for Lanai in an hour. Kenneth strolled into Lahaina, a sleepy village of false-fronted frame stores, and had breakfast at a Chinese restaurant on Front Street.

He returned to the wharf in plenty of time because the motor launch, used by the ranch to carry mail and supplies from Lahaina, didn't get off until 11 A.M. By then the weatherbeaten little craft was loaded down with seven Hawaiians, two Munros, one Emory, baggage, and assorted freight. They chugged across Lahaina Roadstead under a brassy sun for two-and-one-half hours and landed in the afternoon heat at Manele Beach. Then it was eight miles up the slope over a dirt road through parched grassland in a Model T Ford to ranch headquarters on a cool plateau in the center of the island.

The Munros lived in a sprawling ranch house fronting on a comfortable *lanai*. Kenneth found himself in the midst of a warm, close-knit, and self-sufficient family. Two daughters, Georgina and Ruth, both in their late teens or early twenties, greeted him with demure interest that soon turned into friendly familiarity. There was also a nephew, Hector Munro, who helped his uncle. He was a little older than Kenneth and was built like a football player, yet his manner was gentle and conscientious.

Books were as much a part of the house as furniture. A Victrola, a piano, and a parrot occupied prominent places. The ranch manager's extensive collection of Hawaiian artifacts filled one room. Hector helped Kenneth settle into a guest cottage where there was plenty of room to spread out archaeological rubbish and a table for working on maps.

The next day, Munro drove Kenneth on a scouting expedition in the Model T. Kenneth returned with a new respect for Lanai. From offshore the island—only seventeen miles long and twelve miles wide—appeared deceptively smooth and barren, shaped like a whale with the tail pointing northwest. But on the ground the terrain was gashed and contorted into ravines, gulches, cliffs, and weirdly eroded sandstone sculptures. The population numbered 185, according to the census of 1920, 102 of whom were Hawaiian or part-Hawaiian. Exploring Haleakala had been easy compared to the task of surveying the ruins on Lanai. First he had to find them.

He began the next day with an assault on a ruin pointed out to him on arrival at Manele. A crumbling pillar of lava rose from the water in the middle of the bay. From the top of a cliff behind the bay, one could look down on this natural rock formation. Visible atop the column of lava was a rectangular platform made of stones. Lanai Hawaiians, the Munros told him, called this place Puupehe, after a girl of that name who had drowned in a sea cave nearby. Her lover, Makakehau, had wrapped her in *tapa* and carried her to the top of the sea tower where he covered her body with the rocks, forming a platform, then leaped to his death.

Kenneth and Hector drove to Manele in the Ford. Like two school boys on an outing, they stripped to their bathing suits and swam to the rock island in the bay. The sea tower appeared to be sixty to eighty feet high. Gripping with fingers and toes, they pulled themselves up the crumbly pillar. Three-quarters of the way up, they got stuck and had to climb back down.

The inaccessible ruin atop Puupehe became for Kenneth the first of many puzzles on the isolated island. Lawrence Gay, another land owner on Lanai, told him there was an ancient fortification on a ridge above Maunalei Gulch. The valley had been a population center in prehistoric times because a stream from the wet upland provided the most dependable water source on the island. The only way to find out if the fortification existed would be to investigate.

On Wednesday, July 20, Kenneth set off on foot into the upcountry toward the head of the gulch, climbing through underbrush with the bulky camera and tripod riding on his back. He emerged on the brink of a cliff that plunged straight down for one thousand feet into the gorge. Far below, the stream meandered between towering cliff walls to the sea. The gorge opened upon the channel, foaming with whitecaps kicked up by the wind that tugged at Kenneth's clothing. Maui and Molokai rose dreamlike on the horizon.

A thin spur of ridge jutted from the head of the gulch. On the spur ridge he saw the mysterious fortifications, or at least he saw what Gay had described—three notches in the ridge. Buffeted by the wind, Kenneth set up his clumsy tripod on the cliff edge and mounted the camera. His hat went sailing into space. The black rubber focusing cloth kept pulling out of his hands as he held it over his head. It was like trying to take a photograph on a high wire in a hurricane. He took one double exposure and several overexposures before getting a clear image for museum records.

According to Gay, the ridge was the scene of a great battle in 1778 when an army from Hawaii attacked Lanai. The Lanai warriors had defended themselves in the notches cut for the purpose. Was this a true story or a marvelous tale invented to explain an unusual natural formation? He would not know until he climbed out on the ridge. But the afternoon was almost gone. Reluctantly, he packed up his camera and headed for home.

Lanai, he found, did not give up her secrets easily. He located a *heiau*, shown on an old map, at a place called Hii. The temple ruins were buried under a leafy tangle of stout guava bushes. He crawled through the intertwined branches for a close look. The ruin was barren of interest except for pieces of coral scattered through the stone work. But it had to be measured and photographed, an impossible task until the guava was cleared away. Kenneth hacked with a machete until he had raised two blisters. The next day he was up at 5:30 A.M. for an early start. By 11:30 A.M. he had cleared the *heiau*, but the sun went under a cloud. He had to wait an hour before he could take a photograph. Then he sketched the ruin.

That afternoon, mail arrived from Honolulu. According to Kenneth's journal the Munro girls received "a lot of new pieces for the piano and performed all evening." These family entertainments made his museum work difficult. One night he wrote in the journal, "In the living room this evening there was a cheery fire of *naio* or false sandalwood so I found it hard to tear away and come to the cottage to write Dr. Gregory. I tried to write Dad back in the living room but with a card game going and the Victrola playing I had to make the letter short."

On Monday, July 25, he strapped the view camera and tripod to his back and hiked again to the head of Maunalei Gulch, taking his direction from landmarks because there was no path to follow. By the time he reached the ridge he was waist deep in *ieie* vine and staghorn fern. At 1 P.M. he came out on the spur ridge where the notches were located. There he settled himself in a soft bed of fern and opened his lunch, a *lau lau* wrapped in *ti* leaf of steamed pork, butterfish, and taro top.

Then he made his way along the ridge to the notches; his excitement mounted as he examined the first. It was not a natural formation. The notch had been cut into the ridge, as was the next, and the next. He took out his tape. The notches measured about twenty feet wide and eight feet deep. Against the ridge near the first notch he found five tiers of neatly stacked boulders, each the size of a man's head. Kenneth rolled a stone over the cliff. There was a long pause. Then the rock landed with a report like a cannon in the canyon below. He found waterworn pebbles, used as sling stones, scattered about.

There could be no doubt that the ridge had been used as a fortification. Defenders took shelter in the notches and rolled rocks down

on invaders below. Gay had told him the Lanai warriors were beaten because the invaders sent sling men to the tops of the ridges opposite. The notches, within range of the slings, became traps as the deadly stones shot home. For Kenneth the story was no longer legend but reality.

Yet for every scrap of understanding he wrestled from the silent past, several more mysteries rose to confront him. The next day he found crude human figures chipped or scratched into great, black boulders at the mouth of a gully in Miki Basin. Farther up the slope were more of the images, ten to one boulder. He recognized the carvings as petroglyphs, but little was known about this primitive art form. On the following morning he investigated a report of rock carvings at a place called Luahiva. Here the mystery deepened. He wrote in his journal:

> I found a veritable playground for the natives' crude art of stone-picture carving. On ten boulders were altogether more than fifty petroglyphs. There were a fish, a canoe, a few unrecognizable symbols, and one of the conventional figure seated on a horse! Certainly the art was not practiced by a prehistoric race. Maybe old Kilohananui will have a clue as to the real purpose of those who did this work. If the problem of these petroglyphs could be answered here, it would settle the discussion concerning them for the whole Hawaiian group.

Kenneth returned to Miki Basin to photograph the petroglyphs. A new dilemma arose. The petroglyphs were located in a bull paddock. The bulls found Kenneth as fascinating as he did the petroglyphs. He ate his lunch in a monkeypod tree. Beset by rain and bulls, it took him six hours to snap a dozen photographs.

The news of his interest in ruins and stones and petroglyphs circulated among the Hawaiians of Lanai. One afternoon a local resident brought around a small collection of stones for *ulumaika* (the Hawaiian game of bowling) he had found at Kaa, a red, windblown hill to the north. On August 6, a pleasant Saturday afternoon, Kenneth, with nothing else to do, saddled a horse and rode out to Kaa to try his luck as an artifact prospector. He came to a tableland of eroded red dirt a thousand feet above the shining sea. An abundance of *opihi*, or limpet shells, cowry shells, and waterworn pebbles brought him out of his saddle. All of these items had been carried to this arid place from the seashore.

He looked about in disbelief. Stones were everywhere on the bare, red dirt, like the litter of an abandoned campsite. Kenneth knew this area had once been grassland, but the grazing of sheep and goats had destroyed the ground cover. Wind had done the rest. Now all that was left were stones, each resting on a little pedestal of red dirt like a golf tee shaped by the wind. He stooped to pick up a beautifully rounded bowling stone. It lay toppled on its side where it had come to rest a hundred years before, after the force of its roll was spent. He found a stone ground into the shape of a doorknob with a hole in one side. Could it be the handle for a drill? His journal describes the excitement he felt:

> I soon had my trouser pockets, my shirt pockets and my camera bag filled with stones. I could not have been happier if I had been picking up golden eggs. I had never dreamed that such a thing could be; the specimens that I had been handling so religiously at the museum were here as thick as berries to be had for the picking. In two hours I had more of an archaeological collection than I had expected to gather in a whole year in the field. With the coming lateness, I left the treasure ground reluctantly.

Kenneth hiked back the next day. This time he carefully went over ten acres of ground. Besides stone implements, he found a level stretch of smooth, hard dirt a hundred yards long that had been the *ulumaika* course for rolling the bowling stones. Along the track he found twenty *ulumaika* stones, some broken "probably in the third part of the game when they are rolled against each other by opponents." The ground was strewn with hundreds of sharpening and polishing stones, of which Kenneth picked up only the best samples.

That night in the guest cottage he counted 126 artifacts and tried to determine their use. It was like browsing in a Stone Age hardware store. He identified twenty-two coral files, four sharpening stones, part of a lamp, coral and lava bath rubbers, forty-four bowling stones, nineteen adzes in the rough, a stone that might have been used as a spindle for a top, the stone shaped like a drill handle, and a stone that Mr. Munro said was a bird trap holder.

By this time Kenneth knew that his original plan to spend a few weeks on Lanai was hopelessly inadequate. In addition to the whole north end of the island to explore, there was the east coast where many of the Hawaiians lived. He was especially anxious to prowl among the ruins of Kaunalu, a place described to him by Munro as a deserted village accessible only by foot or horseback. For this he needed his camping equipment in Honolulu and much more time.

Gregory had no objection to a longer stay since the museum was paying for little more than the cost of notebooks and film. He gave permission for Kenneth to return to Honolulu and pick up his wilderness gear. On August 9 Kenneth packed his precious group of stones for shipment to the museum. The next day he rode the motor launch to Lahaina where he boarded a steamer for Honolulu.

His two-week stay proved to be a busman's holiday because he spent most of his time on petroglyphs. He wrote in his diary, "Dr. Gregory was pleased with the petroglyph pictures." Over the weekend he visited a petroglyph field above Nuuanu Stream near his home. Ralph Linton had brought back sketches of petroglyphs from the Marquesas. Kenneth pored over the sketches, comparing them with the stick figures he had discovered. Meanwhile he recruited Uncle Charles' son just back from Dartmouth, Ted Merriam, as a volunteer assistant for a two week camp-out at Kaunalu.

They boarded the SS *Mikahala* on Tuesday, August 23, with a group of Honolulu children enroute for an annual visit with their parents at the leper settlment of Kalaupapa on Molokai. "The children on this trip were all girls, natives," Kenneth wrote in his journal. "They curled up on mattresses on deck like a brood of puppies to try to fall asleep but most of them were terribly sick. It was too rough for Ted Merriam. But I kept my sickness away with my guitar."

At the Munro's ranch house Kenneth awoke at 6:30 A.M. on Friday, August 26, to the sound of Mr. Munro giving instructions for the Kaunalu expedition. What a morning to oversleep! Kenneth struggled into his pants, threw on a shirt, and hurried outside to participate in the crucial conversation. Two Hawaiian cowboys, Pohano and Kuwelo, were taking instructions from Munro. They were to saddle three horses, and two mules with pack saddles, and lead them as the crow flies to the head of the Kaunalu trail, then wait. The cowboys nodded. They mounted and rode away leaving behind the tangy smell of horse manure in the crisp morning air.

Still sleepy, Ted Merriam dressed in time for a substantial ranch breakfast washed down with strong coffee. Kenneth was too excited to eat much, too eager to begin this adventure, too busy going over in his mind the list of things he must not forget. The ranch manager was himself going as a guide, an indication of his interest in the expedition. Yet he made only one addition to the pile of equipment in the back of the Ford, a brace of fishing spears.

They climbed into the Model T and bumped over dusty dirt roads heading south by southwest. Pohano and Kuwelo were waiting at the end of the road where a fishermen's trail led into a desolate wilderness of parched grass and burnt lava. There, at 8:30 A.M., the expedition set out on horseback, the camping equipment riding on the pack mules. They stopped at a cattle watering trough to fill canteens and water bags, then made their way eight miles farther down the sunburned slope to the beach.

Kenneth had never seen such a desolate spot. Why would anyone choose to live here? Yet widely scattered stone ruins showed above the grass on both sides of a dry gulch that debouched upon a rocky beach. A grim, black *heiau* brooded on a commanding knoll. Here was a complete village; temple, house sites, platforms, terraces, stone inclosures, and *ahu*s, all undisturbed since the site had been abandoned.

Why had the people of old selected this forbidding place as a settlement? Mr. Munro provided the answer as Kenneth and Ted Merriam pitched their tent on a house platform near the *heiau*. Their host trotted to the beach with a fish spear. When he came back with his catch, he explained that Kaunalu was noted for its fishing. Currents eddying around the point carried nutrients that attracted fish and, consequently, fishermen. A famous fish god had once stood below the *heiau*. Munro showed Kenneth the location of an old brackish water well, now dry, that contained seepage when rains made the gully flow. After lunch the rancher saw his guests comfortably settled, then returned up the slope with the horses and mules.

Ted Merriam wandered down to the beach. Alone among the silent ruins Kenneth became conscious of the majestic serenity of the place. The sky arched overhead, a canopy of pristine blue. A carpet of cobalt ocean extended to the horizon. A warm wind breathed on his cheek and the musical boom of the surf drummed faintly in his ears. The fortress-like *heiau* commanded a superb vista of cliff coastline: great, black buttresses rising one thousand feet from the ocean in an uncompromising wall. Seabirds soared above the cliffs. Below, the surf surged and exploded in plumes of spray. Kenneth followed his friend to the boulder-strewn beach. There were shadowed sea caves and limpid tide pools below the cliffs. The two men splashed in and lolled there, defying the furnace heat in delicious, wave-washed indolence. Here was another good reason for living at Kaunalu.

Hector and the Munro girls visited over the weekend. The routine of work began on Monday with a careful investigation of the ruins. Two house sites yielded six squid hook sinkers for the museum's collection, half a dozen hammer stones, excellent grinding stones, files, shells, and stone platters so large they could hardly be lifted. Most of what Kenneth did was less exciting than his finds. Kaunalu became an oven after the morning coolness burned off. There was no shade except for a thicket of *kiawe* at the beach and in the gully. All day Kenneth measured stone ruins that radiated heat. It was an endless task because he counted forty-nine separate sites, each with numerous features to be measured and described. There were fireplaces and pens and walls and niches and pits.

Every two days they hiked to the nearest water trough two miles away. Each man carried back five gallons of water weighing about forty pounds. The campers did their own cooking and tried, without much success, to catch fish. They bedded on piles of *pili* grass. One night as Ted was about to turn in he heard a movement in the grass. He switched on his flashlight and found a twelve-inch centipede in his mattress. That night he and Kenneth slept on the beach.

The first week passed before it had begun. There would not be time to photograph and survey. There never seemed to be enough time. So Kenneth explored the cliff coastline. He and Ted hiked six miles to Manele. "There is no trail, not a fence or a tree," Kenneth wrote in his journal. "It is like one vast rock heap over which we had to pick our way slowly so as not to loosen the stones. The six miles looked easy on the map but we forgot to reckon with the gulches which were invisible until we reached their brink." Ted lost the sole of one shoe. But there were petroglyphs on both sides of the gulch below Mamaki. Kenneth also found house platforms there and a few in the next two gulches.

Hector and the Munro girls turned up in camp on the last weekend to help pack out. Kenneth decided it was a good time to test a famous legend about the place. Seaward of the *heiau* was a niche in the cliff that provided a natural ramp for jumping off. This place, which Kenneth estimated to be about fifty feet above the surf, was known as Kahakili's Leap. Kahakili, a Maui chief during the period of Hawaii's discovery by Captain Cook, had ruled Lanai, Molokai, and Oahu as well as Maui. He had been a noted jumper-off of cliffs, a daredevil sport by which chiefs demonstrated their courage. This leap had been one of his favorites.

If the chiefs could do it, Kenneth saw no reason why he could not also. He changed into his swimsuit and sent Hector to the foot of the cliff to rescue him if something went wrong. The Munro girls found him pacing back and forth to screw up his courage. They demanded he abandon this foolhardy stunt. Chastened, he gave up the attempt. That night he explained apologetically in his journal, "If I had landed a little *kapakahi* [crooked] in the water it might have knocked me unconscious and occasioned some trouble for the Munros."

Perhaps to atone for scolding him, Georgie Munro drove Kenneth a few days later to the home of an old Hawaiian named Kilohananui whose family came from Kaunalu. The old man talked about the leaps that Kahakili had made from the cliff before the time of Kame-hameha, and gave Kenneth some Kaunalu place names. He said his brother, at the request of Kamehameha V, had hidden the stone fish god that had stood at the foot of the bluff. Kenneth went home with the feeling that there was a lot about Lanai he didn't know.

On September 7, shortly after his return from Kaunalu, Kenneth set out on foot alone along the uninhabited north shore, a seacoast of endless, windswept beaches littered with driftwood. He carried forty pounds in his knapsack, slept in old shelters, and cooked over a campfire. His journal sketches glimpses of this three-day expedition:

Slept very comfortably until 5. From where I lay, I spied two crabs sneaking into the grub. A yell sent them head-over-heels. As I touched the water bag to pour, I nearly put my hand on an eight-inch centipede. . . . But overhead it was sublime; an opal cloud bank stretched over Kamakou Peak on Molokai. . . . The coming sun instantly painted the whole cloud a fiery red. . . . At 7 I finished crackers and jam and two bowls of coffee. Out on the northeastern point [of the island], Lae Wahie, there is a fish *heiau* which I excavated, finding the bones of offerings all through the structure.

My grub supplies are lasting well. I am a little short on implements but an *opihi* [limpet] shell makes a good spoon and a coconut shell a good sugar bowl. . . . Dinner went badly tonight. The wind kept me ten minutes lighting matches, then the rice was too salty. I use ocean water. . . . Before dinner I stripped for a run along the beach and a dip in the waves. I dared not go out into the unknown water for it was dark. The sun had set gloriously. Turtles are numerous here. I watched two play about noon time.

The fishing shrines guarding the coast stirred questions in his mind. Where had these fishermen lived? Were they the same people who had camped and played games on the nearby plateau at Kaa? Very likely. But he had heard no report of a village in this area. On Monday, September 12, after returning to the ranch, he borrowed a horse and rode back to Kaa for another look. This time he picked up sixty pounds of stone artifacts including adzes, bowling stones, coral polishers, files, shell spoons, fishhook sinkers, and grind-stones. What pleased him more were the ruins he found by taking another way home. His journal describes them:

Along the bluffs which bound the plateau on the *mauka* [inland] side, I counted thirty-one house sites as I came home. Here certainly is where the natives lived. Allowing for twenty more house sites marked with stone divisions, and fifty grass houses at least . . . and allowing five natives to a house, this sheltered spot could have and probably did hold a population in ancient times of about five hundred.

Another week flew by in mapmaking, sketching, and packing the stones for shipment to the museum. Then Kenneth was ready for an extended stay at Keomuku, the home of a colony of Hawaiian families. He sent a mattress, stove, lamp, and blankets ahead with the cowboys and followed on horseback with a new schoolteacher at the ranch, Mrs. Handy, who wanted to see the island. The trail meandered seven miles from the upper plateau to a quiet shore where thorny, lacy-leaved *kiawe* trees grew along lonely, hardpacked beaches. Shallow water extended far out to the channel, flat and languid in contrast to the boisterous waves that churned along the north shore.

Late in the afternoon, a light appeared through the *kiawe* branches. It was the schoolhouse. Mrs. Mary Fitzsimmons, the warmhearted Hawaiian schoolteacher Kenneth had met on the steamer, invited them in for a chicken and *poi* supper. That night he slept in the barn because the room he was to occupy in an abandoned ranch house hadn't been cleared of junk. Mrs. Handy bedded down in the schoolhouse during her short visit.

In Keomuku shades of the past haunted the living. Mrs. Fitzsimmons' third husband had died recently in Lahaina. Now his ghost rode the mill route to the ranch at night. No Hawaiian resident of Keomuku would go alone over this trail after dark. This end of the island had once been planted to sugarcane but the plantation had gone bankrupt. The Hawaiians told Kenneth the plantation failed because rocks from sacred *heiau*s had been used to build the mill. He recorded it all in his journal.

Two very shy Hawaiian girls helped Mrs. Fitzsimmons with the cooking and housework. They were so in awe of Kenneth it made him uncomfortable. The first time they invited him to eat in the kitchen, he wrote:

> I was rather pleased to be treated thus informally. I minded only the raw fish which was hanging over my head. Seeing that I was not partaking of the raw mullet, Hanna Makahanaloa fried me some goat and onions which went well with the *poi* . . .
>
> The wind blew along the *lanai* of the old ranch house keeping it cool and free of mosquitoes so I slept fairly well although the doors rattled in the empty house. I told the girls I would be off early and when I stepped into the school house breakfast was getting cold. They had started it at 5:30 and it was [now] 7. Going along the road, every native child took off

his hat and said good morning. Several boys followed me to the barn, caught and saddled my horse, and in other ways were eager to help me.

A few hours later Kenneth found four large ruins, including two *heiau*s, at the old village site of Lopaa. The next day he visited the only inhabitants of Maunalei Gulch, a Hawaiian couple named Kauhane who lived in a shack. Mrs. Kauhane was weaving a *lauhala* mat. She called out to Kenneth to tie his horse to the doorpost and come in. He did so. Inside he found her meek-looking husband making a fishnet. For the next hour they talked about place names, fish *heiau*s, burial places, and Lanai people. The following days were equally productive—new ruins, more artifacts, many place names, and random scraps of information that began to reveal the shape of the past.

Kenneth promised to take a picture of Mrs. Fitzsimmons' school children in gratitude for their hospitality. It turned out to be an important event. On the appointed morning, the children arrived in their best clothing, even shoes. Several of the boys wore coats so large they must have belonged to their fathers. Each carried a necktie in his pocket to be put on at the proper time. Kenneth lined them up on the school steps. He was about to snap the photograph when a mother came running along the dusty road with her first grader.

"Hurry," called the children, "or you will miss the *paa kii* [picture taking]."

The students had to be lined up all over again and cautioned not to wiggle. Kenneth had taken the photograph and one of Mrs. Fitzsimmons alone when they realized that one of the students, Hana Makahanaloa, was missing. The search began. They found her hiding because she had no stockings to wear with her new shoes. To Hana's intense embarrassment, Kenneth stood her and pretty, twelve-year-old Makaleka Nakihei against a coconut tree and took a picture anyway.

A map Kenneth was compiling of Lanai, showing the location of *heiau*s and villages, became an object of great curiosity to residents of Keomuku. That afternoon Mrs. Fitzsimmons brought Mrs. Joe Makahanaloa forward to see it. They chatted in Hawaiian. Later Kenneth wrote in his journal:

> Soon I was getting new place names by the dozen, with their meaning and now and then a story with them. Moreover, Mrs. Makahanaloa knew the use of the stone implements I had collected on this side. She explained the use of the hammer for the first time; to strike a flint. I was told the location of the *heiau* Kalulu and of an ancient prison on the top

lands. After she had gone, I compared her information with the Kauhane's. So far as the ground was the same, there was not one mistake.

At the end of September he came home from measuring a *heiau* to find Grandma Makahanaloa sitting on a mat in front of the schoolhouse smoking a pipe while half a dozen Hawaiian women worked in the kitchen. They were preparing a *luau* (feast) for Mrs. Fitzsimmons who was leaving to teach in Lahaina. That night Kenneth saw the *hula kui*, or naughty hula. He wrote in his journal, "There was no *okolehau* [*ti*-root whiskey] or swipes about but there was no lack of good fun." Most of the jokes were at the expense of the *haole*s who did not understand Hawaiian. The party lasted until midnight. A few days later, Mrs. Roland Gay took Mrs. Fitzsimmons place. Now Kenneth had to do his own cooking.

On October 5 he went to Lahaina for supplies. It was like returning to civilization and he wasn't sure he liked it. For the first time he saw a full-page spread in the *Sunday Advertiser* feature section about his petroglyph discoveries. What he read came as a shock. Reporter A. P. Taylor wrote enthusiastically:

Where lies the Rosetta Stone in the Hawaiian Islands that will . . . unfold a narrative of a grander history than has been written by modern chroniclers of the Pacific, and rend the veil that may reveal a hitherto unknown civilization buried underneath recurrent flows of lava from Hawaii's burning mountains?

Beneath all that has been discovered, an older and probably very remarkable civilization, a civilization of finer texture and more advanced, far different from that which the early white man found may be discovered. . . . It is so with the pictographs.

The pictographs may reveal something of the origin of the Hawaiians. They may tell something of the arrival and merging of *haole*s with the native race hundreds of years before Captain Cook discovered the islands. They may tell of towns and cities that were wiped out by the belchings from the volcanoes, and of a newer race inhabiting the islands.

Kenneth didn't know whether to be flattered or embarrassed by the praise heaped upon him for his work with the petroglyphs and archaeological ruins on Lanai. He read:

Dr. Gregory asserts that the scientists of today are all Christopher Columbus who have voyaged across the waters and are discovering Hawaiian anew. . . . The real, vast resources of ruined temples, their exact form and use, are but now being newly discovered, for out of the chaos of volcanic destruction, more ruins are being revealed . . .

> The researches of Kenneth Emory on Lanai have proved a pleasurable surprise to the scientists, for it has opened again the field of exploration and research to them with newer examples of activities of the ancient Hawaiians . . .

The part about finding new ruins and petroglyphs was true. But where had Taylor gotten the information about lost civilizations buried under lava flows? Kenneth learned from the article that the Hawaiians were not the only people capable of inventing marvelous tales. He returned to Lanai determined not to read into his discoveries meanings that weren't there.

October flowed into November and still he was not satisfied. There was so much to learn on this deceptively uncomplicated island. Always he felt a sense of urgency. One night he wrote in his journal:

> The museum is in the nick of time. Some house sites are more striking in appearance and larger than some of the *heiau*s on Lanai. Without native help it is impossible to tell with certainty which are house sites, until a thorough study has been made, then there is [still] room for much doubt. There are about five natives to whom I can go in the extremities who know, at least, the location of all the ruins of the temples.

New dilemmas constantly confronted him. He spent the best part of three days clearing a *heiau* of brush and rubbish so he could photograph it. Here's how he described the work:

> I was delayed at the bone pit. It is eight feet square and seven feet deep and, as it seems to have come down intact from another time and was reeking with the victims from off the *lele* or altar, I was anxious to have a good picture of it. . . . In clearing the weeds from the dirt bottom I unearthed some teeth. They may be those of a cow which fell in here but as likely they are those of a goat or dog or pig. I'll have to catch one of the pigs that sleep under my house at night and in the heat of the day, and make a study of its teeth.

Often his information came from unexpected sources. He took a weekend off to attend the Maui County Fair, getting up 3:30 A.M. for an early start in the launch. With him were Mr. and Mrs. Nakihei, who rode with Kenneth on top of the cabin. Mrs. Nakihei, who weighed 230 pounds, sat on one side until her husband told her to get in the middle so the boat wouldn't list. That put her beside Kenneth. He described the trip in his journal:

It was a beautiful night. While I watched phosphorescence and the reflection of the stars in the oily water, my curiosity was stirred. . . . Would this native woman, who even among the natives would be considered of the lowest class, know any of the stars by name? [I ask] *"Aue o nana i ka Makilii maluna, ua kea oia?"* "Do you notice how clearly the Pleiades are shining above us?" She answered, *"Ae, pu me Huihui me Iona."* "Yes, and also Huihui and Iona." She pointed out the Pleiades, then swept her finger westward to Aldeberan [sic] in Taurus, then Orion. Then in turn I asked the name of the Dog Stars. She said there was a native name but she had forgotten it. The Morning Star, Old Lucifer, was scintillating gloriously over the rim of Haleakala. *"Oia no, Kahokulua,"* she said. "That is the Great Star."

I had another surprise. To pass the several hours before daylight, I [brought out] my steel guitar and played a native piece. . . . Mrs. Nakihei began to sing. . . . I laid down my guitar and told her to keep singing while I took down the words. [When she was finished] She pointed out a peak on West Maui which lifted itself above the clouds, and told me it was Laihau. This song was entirely about this same mountain.

The schoolchildren at Keomuku loved to crowd around outside his windows or the door, which had come off its hinges, and watch him at the typewriter. They never interrupted and always spoke in whispers. Because he was always bringing home rocks, they called him The Stone Man. One day he took his guitar to the Makahanaloa house. His journal describes what happened:

I found the women delegates to the Church of Reasonable Service all there with their children. One of them from Molokai suggested that I sing certain songs. I don't think she dreamed that I knew these for she surely looked surprised when I sang every one.

Mrs. Makahanaloa beamed over his accomplishment. He took advantage of these friendships when the mail brought a clipping from the Hawaiian-language newspaper, *Nupepe Kukoa*, about a lecture Dr. Gregory had given on the disappearing Hawaiian. Kenneth ask the Lanai natives how they felt about the decrease in their population. He reported the answers in his journal:

Over here they have given little thought to it. They do not seem to be fully aware that they are disappearing and they appear indifferent to it. In fact, on all issues that go beyond their immediate comfort they rarely occupy their minds. They are utterly without ambition. Not that they haven't the capacity for it. But it is simply not stimulated by what is held forth to them and their children by the white man. It is now much easier [for them] to live and [at the same time] much harder to gain success than in the old strenuous days when famine and war were never far off.

One more challenge remained before Christmas vacation. This was the inaccessible stone platform atop the sea tower in Manele Bay. Kenneth and Hector made another assault on Saturday, December 10. "This time we were prepared for the worst," Kenneth wrote in his journal. "We brought ladders, block and tackle, rope, picks, a lot of lumber, a carpenter, two [more] men to draw on if necessary, in fact everything but a coffin or two." The launch was supposed to transport this cargo from shore to the base of the sea tower.

No launch had appeared when Kawano, the carpenter, and his Japanese helpers went to work constructing a derrick like those erected over oil wells. This machine, in four portable sections to fit one upon another, was to extend as high as the sea tower. Kawano was only half finished when it became obvious that the derrick would not be high enough. Work came to a halt. It didn't matter because the launch never arrived to carry the derrick out to the island anyway.

Determined not to give up, Kenneth pointed out a ledge not too far from the top of the sea tower. Maybe they could climb by ladder that far. Once on the ledge, they might be able to make it to the top. "Into a little box we put a pocket camera, a tape measure, a bottle of coconut oil [for suntan lotion], a hand pick, a pencil and paper," Kenneth wrote. "We floated this on the ladder as a raft."

On the island, they positioned the ladder. Kawano went up like a monkey. "He tested the rock with a hammer," Kenneth wrote. "He pronounced it okay. I went up and the first piece of rock I grabbed came down on the back of Hector's head. . . . This was not too encouraging." Nevertheless, Hector came up and they reached the ledge, teetering there while they tried to find a way to the top. A desperate climb got them into exactly the same dead end in which they had found themselves the first time. It was the wiry Japanese who scaled an impossible place and reached the top. Kenneth followed, refusing to be outdone. They lowered a rope to Hector who was hopelessly stuck.

The afternoon had slipped away. In less than an hour the sun would sink below the horizon. Kenneth made a hurried excavation in the platform. It was six feet wide, twenty-one feet long, and three feet high, constructed of the loose rock scattered about the top of the sea tower. Bird bones mingled with rock in the platform. But there were no human bones. The top of the tower was littered with bird bones and egg shells.

That night Kenneth wrote in his journal, "There were bird bones in the structure just as there are fish bones in structures erected for offerings to the fish god. Natives climbed this island . . . the platform tells us that. Did they come for birds? And is this an altar to the Bird God?" At least he knew now the platform was not a burial. Beyond that, he didn't know much. Would these silent, ancient structures ever yield their secrets to him?

After Christmas he went back to Lanai for another month of frantic photographing and mapping. The *heiau*s had to be sketched because photographs did not reveal their architectural features. He went back to Kaunalu for more surveying to make sure his map would be accurate. Then he went to work photographing every petroglyph on the island: one day he photographed fourteen, the next day thirty-five, and the day following seventy-four. On January 6 he set a record by photographing 130 petroglyphs.

By this time he had collected many clues about these cryptic rock carvings. An aged Hawaiian had told him he'd carved a few himself. *"Pa'ani wale no,"* the old man had explained. "They are just for play." But some petroglyphs did not appear playful. At Kaunalu there were stick figures with bird heads. These carvings, Kenneth learned, depicted Halulu, the mythical "thunder" bird who dwelt in the sea cliffs.

He was still recording place names when the expedition ended on January 27, 1922. And he was still unsatisfied. In a preliminary report to the museum trustees he suggested that a description of Kaupo village on Maui be added to his description of Kaunalu village on Lanai. "It would be an invaluable comparison with our new Marquesan, Tongan, and Austral material to have a complete and accurate description of the various elements and organization of Hawaiian villages," he wrote.

Little by little, he was fitting pieces into the jigsaw puzzle of old Polynesia.

Chapter Twelve

What is
Your Source?

Kenneth's Lanai expedition drew praise from Dr. Clark Wissler, the museum's consultant from the American Museum of Natural History in New York. He wrote, "There is every reason to believe that his story of the Polynesian on Lanai will be a cross-section of his career elsewhere." By that time, Kenneth's dreams had soared far beyond Lanai. His next step must be a master's degree. Then he could hope for an expedition to the South Seas. Unfortunately, Lanai would not go away. Gregory was firm about his policy on reports; always write up one expedition before starting another.

Kenneth plunged into it, aghast at the formidable pile of notes and sketches and photographs he had brought back. Tom Maunupau and L. A. Thurston helped him with place names. Interruptions made it slow going. Kenneth had scarcely begun to draw a map of Kaunalu when word arrived of exposed sand burials on the west end of Molokai. He caught the next steamer, hired an old Buick at Kaunakakai, and happily kicked up dust all the way to a magnificent stretch of tawny beach where he collected twenty skulls.

Monday, March 6, 1922, found him back at the museum dutifully drawing the map. He was not unhappy when Miss Stone of the *Honolulu Star-Bulletin* showed up the next day to interview him. On Wednesday he finished the map and was sorting out his notes to begin writing when a shipment of artifacts arrived from Guam in Micronesia. These had to be unpacked, then examined.

Then Kenneth and Tom Maunupau made a trip to Kaupo on Maui to compare the physical features of the inhabited Hawaiian village with the abandoned one on Lanai. Maunupau proved to be an invaluable assistant because the Kaupo Hawaiians accepted him as one of the family and the informants amazed Kenneth by the extent of their knowledge. They recited myths and chants and told him about fish shrines and sorcery and canoe-making—things that had never been written down.

Meanwhile, he was trying to decide where to take his master's degree in anthropology. It was not like enrolling in business or education or engineering. Only a few schools offered advanced courses in the field. Fewer still specialized in the Pacific. Both Gregory and Kroeber, Kenneth's former professor at Berkeley, advised him to study under Franz Boas, the pioneer anthropologist at Columbia University in New York. Kenneth wrote to Boas and received a courteous reply. But younger anthropologists gave him different advice. His friend Louis Sullivan wrote from the American Museum of Natural History:

> I should say Harvard was the only logical place for a man to go if he expected to work in Polynesia. Aside from having the benefit of Dr. [Roland B.] Dixon, who has specialized for years in Polynesia, you have the advantage of a well-trained department. . . . Boas, of course, is our leading anthropologist but is handicapped by having no assistance. Of course, if you are interested in linguistics he will give it to you in large doses. His critical attitude and interest in technique and method are valuable, too.

Edward S. Handy, now back from the Marquesas and on the museum staff, was a Harvard graduate. He urged Kenneth to go there. So did Ralph Linton, now at the Field Museum in Chicago. A diary entry on Tuesday, April 25, read, "Dr. and Mrs. Gregory up to dinner. . . . I know I am going East and to Harvard." He made the choice because Dr. Dixon was the only anthropologist in the United States who specialized in Polynesia.

The Lanai report continued to be slow going, partly because Kenneth had other things on his mind. On Saturday, May 13, he played his steel guitar over Honolulu's new wireless telephone station, KGU, owned by publisher Thurston. Three days later he took a driving lesson. His diary states on May 17, "Got my chauffeur's license today."

Kenneth inherited the family's black Model T Ford flivver. But it is doubtful that he fully understood the relationships between brake and clutch, high and low gear, or the outside lane and left turns. The first time he got behind the wheel he crumpled a front fender against a stone wall. His father, another victim of this casual attitude toward automobile technology, after loaning Kenneth the flivver before Lanai, wrote in exasperation, "You certainly were in luck your last night here with the machine. You know I cautioned you about the tires, and you forgot all about it and sailed all over the landscape. Well, Wednesday the left front tire blew up when I was at the University of Hawaii; and I expect the other to go at any time."

By now, the whole family was helping with the Lanai report. They hired a stenographer to do the typing. Walter and Winifred

Emory helped read proof. But the manuscript was still unfinished when Kenneth sailed off to school in Boston on board the SS *Maui* on Wednesday, July 22, 1922. He scribbled a chapter about Hawaiian fortifications on his lap on the train enroute from San Francisco to Chicago. Along the way he struck up an acquaintance with a fellow passenger who turned out to be a nurse at Queen's Hospital in Honolulu. Kenneth's interest in Polynesia created an immediate bond between them because her artist brother, Armstrong Sperry, had just come back from a marvelous sketching excursion to Tahiti. By the time they arrived in New England, Kenneth had accepted an invitation to visit the family in Moosehead, Maine. He spent a busy summer and early fall before reporting his activities to Gregory in a letter:

> I saw Kroeber and Boas in California, Linton in Chicago and reached New Hampshire in eleven days out from Honolulu. The time then passed too quickly but very happily with friends. In the heart of the Maine woods I canoed with Armstrong Sperry, a coming South Sea artist, a Yale graduate and two years my elder. He met Aitken and Stokes at Papeete and his chum, Oscar Schmidt, was with Linton at Hivaoa. As Sperry knew the Tahitian language fairly well and was anxious to pick up Hawaiian, we exchanged lessons and in other ways increased our enthusiasm for the time when we shall return among the islands.
>
> At Harvard, the prospect for the coming year is most promising. The museum, laboratory, and library facilities are adequate and encouraging. The courses I am taking cover the parts of the field I did not get into at the University of California; the classes are all small and informal, and I have every man [as teacher] in the department: Dixon, Tozzer, Hooton and Spinden. In the graduate school there is one field worker from Africa, one from the Philippines, one from Mexico and one from India.

At Harvard, Kenneth found himself in the mainstream of his profession. It stimulated him. Yet he discovered that Dixon, the authority on Polynesia, had never done fieldwork there. He was a textbook scholar who lectured from file cards. One day he told the class there were no fortifications in Polynesia. Kenneth corrected the professor, explaining that there were fortifications on Lanai in the Hawaiian Islands.

"What is your source?" asked Dixon.

When Kenneth admitted that he was the source, the professor appeared annoyed. "I was a little surprised by his attitude," Kenneth said later. "If it wasn't printed, it couldn't be very good. He was an indoor anthropologist. But he had the reputation because up to then there were very few people who had studied Polynesia." Kenneth

enjoyed Dr. Earnest A. Hooton, a professor who livened his lectures by bending over, his arms dangling, and lumbering around the classroom like an ape to demonstrate the physical characteristics of primates.

At Harvard there was little of the class cutting and few of the weekend excursions that marked Kenneth's career at Dartmouth. When he wasn't studying, he worked on the Lanai report. In a stiff, celluloid collar, he lectured in Boston to the American Anthropological Association about fieldwork in Hawaii. That was on December 28, 1922, and the lecture clearly indicates that Kenneth was not a textbook anthropologist. He enthusiastically described the value of Hawaiians as sources of information, recommending them above published writings, using as his source the trip to Kaupo:

> The native I had with me could in a moment induce the old men to talk intimately and spontaneously on any matter, and he could take down chants and lists of names as well as notes with a rapidity which made me realize that a native is the man to collect material from natives. He needs simply to be told what kind of data is wanted. . . . There is not the slightest doubt of the existence of material in the minds of living Hawaiians which will enable us to write an infinitely more satisfactory ethnography of Hawaii than if we rely on what so far has been gathered.
>
> We did not learn as much about ruins as it was intended simply because we did not get to it. I did not feel justified in coercing an old tottering native out into the thick lantana bushes in search of a circular stone enclosure to find if it was a garden patch or a pig pen when he could sit contentedly all day on his verandah giving myths, chants, data on houses, canoes, petroglyphs, bird-catching, the operation of fish shrines, and sorcery; facts which had never been recorded in the culture of Hawaii.

Kenneth took Margaret Manning to the Winter Carnival at Dartmouth the following February. But his diary is concerned more with work on skulls, letters about burial customs, and exams on Oceania. In March 1923, he wrote wistfully to Gregory in Honolulu, "We have had three continuous weeks of cold snap and I have been picturing you in Japanese slippers and wishing I was upstairs [at the museum] where I could run down and talk to you about this report on Lanai." The exchange of letters reflects a warm, fatherly attitude on the director's part and a growing confidence on Kenneth's. When Gregory wrote about an upcoming expedition to the small, uninhabited islets northwest of Honolulu, he received some advice from his assistant ethnologist:

I believe it mighty important to explore them archaeologically. At the same time, unless a man is going to make an exhaustive search and knows the trick of looking for things and clues, it would be wasted effort. . . . Do the ruins on these islands illustrate the enterprise of native fishermen from Kauai or Niihau [the nearest inhabited islands], or are they the result of a resident population, or of bands of migrants? Whatever the traces are, they are sure to be faint and easily overlooked.

The letter also recommended a fellow student, H. L. Shapiro, for one of the Yale fellowships at the Bishop Museum. Then Kenneth turned back to his books. On June 11, 1923, he took his last examination and passed, clearing the way for his master's degree in anthropology. He had completed all but the conclusion of his Lanai report. He was also ready to play a little.

By coincidence, Dr. Hooton was looking for somebody to photograph Indian skulls at the Peabody Museum. Kenneth got the job, then wrote for permission to stay the summer. His father penned an irate letter telling him to come home and tend to business. But Gregory made no objection. So Kenneth spent the summer camping, canoeing, and building a log cabin on his uncle's land at Pike while gainfully employed photographing skulls of American Indians in Boston. He didn't start home until October.

If he had any doubts that his return to Hawaii would be dull after the intellectual stimulation of Harvard, they were dispelled by a breezy letter from Gregory that caught up with him in Berkeley, California. Gregory wrote:

Dig into that Lanai report and complete it. I understand that field work on Maui is within your scheme. . . . That plan is approved and any extension of it that you think desirable. But it is inadvisable to make plans for Maui work on the assumption that you will have two or three years to complete it. Very likely you will be assigned to a job in Micronesia which will involve your saying goodby to Waikiki for some time.

Chapter Thirteen

God Throws a Switch

Micronesia gave Kenneth a new subject of study, but he soon found himself swept into a maelstrom of activity closer to home. Gregory put him in charge of a visiting celebrity, Miss Helen Roberts. Sullivan, now studying skulls of Southwest Indians in Tucson, Arizona, had warned Kenneth that she was the "American heavyweight champion of primitive music and a darned good cook." Miss Roberts proved to be rather nondescript, a bit fussy, and a genius at taking down unrecorded chants, love songs, and folk music. She had made her reputation among the American Indians. Now a group of music lovers in the islands had commissioned her to meet and record Hawaiians.

However, Miss Roberts did not speak Hawaiian. Nor did she know the old natives who could help her. Kenneth's task was to find Hawaiians who remembered the old chants and *mele*s (songs) and could translate them into English. The museum's receptionist and guide, Lahilahi Webb, lined up chanters on Oahu. Miss Roberts also wanted to record on other islands. Kenneth thought of his friend, Tom Maunupau, a native of the Kona Coast on Hawaii. Maunupau agreed to help. Thus were born the associations that produced a classic work, *Ancient Hawaiian Music*.

A trip to Kona with Maunupau also produced a budget of chatty letters from Miss Roberts to Kenneth in Honolulu. She described the complexities of musical research on the lazy Kona Coast:

> We have found a great jewel in the most remarkable old lady, over one hundred, who used to chant for royalty. . . . Her mind is perfectly clear, her eyes and ears as good as ever. . . . She is pitifully poor and lives all alone . . .
>
> We have found a fine hula performer at Kealia Beach. . . . He is better than Antone Kaoo in Honolulu, that is, he knows the ritual of the hula, but is at present very hoarse from political speeches. . . . Many of the old folks I consult are affected by throat and lung trouble . . .
>
> We had a very good old man in Kona but, valuable as he was, we could not afford to wait there a week until he and his companion got over a big *luau* which occurred Saturday in honor of Julian Yates' election. It was

said there was enough food for all who came to last a week and swipe evidently flowed like water. I was very disappointed for he knew how to use the nose flute as no one else here.

Kenneth received other letters that added to his workload. Sullivan asked for help after discovering that the physical identification of Hawaiians by racial types was proving more difficult than expected. Dixon at Harvard had already decided that there might be three or four racial types among Hawaiian skulls. There was also a question whether skeletons of tall, robust chiefs and those of small, skinny commoners represented separate racial types. Also, how did one distinguish the skulls of chiefs from commoners? Were chiefs buried in caves and commoners in dirt or sand? Sullivan added that he needed at least one thousand skulls from all parts of the island plus long bones to check his results.

Then there was Linton who wrote from Chicago for help. "I am working up my Marquesan burial caves and find, when it comes to comparisons, that the information from Hawaii is unsatisfactory and conflicting. You have a first hand knowledge of conditions and I wonder if you would be willing to clean up a few points for me?" Linton also wanted to know if chiefs were buried differently from commoners. Were bones ever placed in trees? Had coffins been used?

Kenneth answered in a nine-page letter. "There is probably a physical difference between chiefs and commoners due to environment [diet] if nothing else," he wrote. "But to say a skull is that of a chief because it comes from a burial cave, and setting up that skull as an example of the physical type of chiefs, will not do." The letter gave examples of cave and coast burials that Kenneth had seen himself or had been seen by others whom he carefully named, then went on to answer the other questions in detail.

It is a mystery how Kenneth kept up with such correspondence, duties at the museum, and his social life all at the same time. He worked on his Lanai report, helped Stokes measure tapa beaters, made up photographic plates of petroglyphs, and translated chants about the volcano goddess, Pele, as well as letters in Hawaiian from an old man in Kona, named Kelokuokamaile, about stars. On weekends he roamed the island checking out reports of burial caves. Evenings he saw Muriel Mattocks, Margaret Andrade, and Bernice Judd. In his spare time he read the logs of Portlock and Dixon, as well as *Beasts, Men and Gods* and *Glory of the Pharaohs*. He also saw a movie with Rin Tin Tin and attended the Hawaii-Oregon football game.

The pace picked up in February 1924, when he took a trip to the island of Hawaii as the guest of Helen Roberts' father. In March, Gregory conferred with Kenneth about Micronesia. "Verbally, I chose this field," he wrote in his diary on March 11. "Expect to go in a year." Also, by this time he had been selected as the archaeologist for a short expedition in July to two small islands, Nihoa and Necker, northwest of Honolulu. That meant additional study and preparation. In April he finished his Lanai report.

Then the direction of this headlong activity changed as abruptly as if God had thrown a switch and set Kenneth on a new track. It began on Wednesday, May 28, 1924, when Gregory called Kenneth in to explain that a Florida capitalist, Medford R. Kellum, had purchased an old, four-masted lumber schooner in San Francisco. He was having the vessel refitted with new diesel engines and luxury accommodations for a cruise to the South Seas.

Gregory said he had persuaded Mr. Kellum to take a party of Bishop Museum scientists along on the expedition. Dr. Stanley C. Ball, zoologist, would be in charge of this group to include Gerrit P. Wilder, botanist, who was taking his wife as a volunteer assistant and French interpreter. Kenneth would go as the museum's ethnologist and would also be allowed a volunteer assistant since the generosity of Mr. Kellum appeared to be boundless. The vessel measured one hundred seventy feet, was being fitted out like an ocean liner, and would be equipped with a complete scientific laboratory.

Kenneth felt like Cinderella after a visit from her fairy godmother. His feet hardly touched the ground as he walked out of Gregory's office. Micronesia faded into insignificance, replaced by the magical names on his new itinerary that included, among others, Tongareva (Penrhyn), Manihiki, Rakahanga, and Pukapuka. The first order of business would be to choose his assistant. He had plenty of friends who would go for the adventure. But Kenneth wanted someone who would be of real help, who was knowledgeable about Polynesia and spoke the language, and who could afford to spend six months away from home without pay. He knew only one person who fit these criteria and that was Armstrong Sperry, the artist who spoke Tahitian. Kenneth sent a cable to Maine, and a stunned Sperry immediately accepted.

News of the trip leaked out on Sunday, June 29, in The *Advertiser.* The brief story hinted in the closing paragraph at Kellum's financial capability: "Mr. and Mrs. Kellum came here several months ago, and not finding a suitable apartment at Waikiki to rent, bought the Bottomley place at Kahala beyond Diamond Head . . . Mrs. Kellum is a niece of the late Andrew Carnegie."

The story moved to the front page on July 3 as Kellum's expedition caught the public imagination like the plot of a romantic silent movie. The *Advertiser*'s Lorin Tarr Gill revealed that this was to be only the first of several scientific voyages to extend over a period of three years. No South Sea island would be immune from exploration. Anthropological knowledge of the Pacific would be extended by leaps and bounds:

> It is a dream of the Bishop Museum come to realization—the proposed cruise of M. R. Kellum's schooner yacht to the South Seas—for, according to Dr. Herbert Gregory, director, it makes possible a survey of the little known islands in the Central Pacific, the sponsorship of which would be utterly beyond the financial possibilities of any one scientific institution . . .
>
> The islands to be visited on this first cruise appear to offer much of botanical, ethnological and zoological value.
>
> Malden Island . . . is five miles long and four broad and rises to a maximum height of thirty feet above the sea. . . . Four Europeans and fifty natives make up the population. . . . Ancient ruins, believed by some to have been built by the South American Incas, and by others to have been left by the early Chinese navigators, will be investigated for the first time.
>
> Tongareva [Penrhyn] . . . consists of numerous low islets connected to a reef around a lagoon twelve miles long and seven miles wide. . . . In 1913 the population of 400 included only one white man besides the agent. . . . There is communication with Rarotonga five times a year . . .
>
> Manihiki . . . is an atoll of five by six miles with no opening into its small lagoon. Its population in 1899 was 580. . . . Robert Louis Stevenson was much impressed by the inhabitants of this island . . .
>
> Pukapuka . . . is the northernmost of the Danger Island group. . . . The population is 500 natives under Rev. Kare of the Seventh Day Adventist Mission and the missionary report for 1909 says of them: ". . . They are little removed from heathen yet after forty years of teaching, and most of them pierce their ears with big holes and wear earrings. The people are generally poor and have not enough clothes to cover them. They certainly do not need many in this hot climate, but many still use skirts made of the coconut leaf."

This story appeared on Thursday while Kenneth was getting his gear together for the expedition northwest to Nihoa and Necker, a project that demonstrated Gregory's genius for exploring the Pacific at practically no cost to the trustees. Members of the scientific party would be guests of the U.S. Navy on board the USS *Tanager*, a minesweeper. The *Tanager* had taken a museum party to the northwest islands in 1923. But that expedition had not carried a person experienced in archaeology.

Kenneth's job as usual would be to survey, photograph and describe ruins, and to collect artifacts. Stone images and implements brought back by an earlier expedition testified to past occupation of these remote islands. Had these people been far-ranging fishermen from the nearest inhabited Hawaiian Islands, Niihau and Kauai? Were they migrants passing through, another race? Had the colony settled permanently? Why did they leave? There would be plenty to keep Kenneth busy during his stay.

The *Tanager* sailed out of Honolulu Harbor at 5 P.M. on Monday, July 7, 1924. Dr. Gregory, L. A. Thurston, Walter Emory, and a crowd of bystanders waved goodby. Nihoa, the tip of a volcano hardly bigger than a small farm in the Midwest, lies about 250 miles northwest of Honolulu. In the late afternoon on Tuesday, the island rose on the horizon like a great, lonely boulder. The *Tanager* wallowed to windward and came to anchor for the night. At first light in the morning the crew lowered boats. Kenneth helped load his equipment, eager to begin this new adventure.

Oars propelled them into the lee of Nihoa where waves surged against the island's precipitous sides. A sea shelf provided the only landing and the boat, rising and sinking with the surge, made an unstable platform from which to jump to shore. Higher up were caves where the scientific party established headquarters as the boats ferried food and camp gear from the ship.

Kenneth scouted the rugged, rocky island. Its bleakness gave him new respect for the prehistoric people who had discovered this remote outpost and had inhabited it, at least for a while. The ruins left no doubt of that. Kenneth recognized garden terraces in the gulches where there was a few inches of soil. Yams and sweet potatoes and sugar cane would grow there when it rained. "Surprised at the extent of ruins and amount of soil," he scrawled into his field notebook. "Swarms of sooty [terns], noddy terns, grayback terns, frigates, boobies; noise deafening."

A little later he stopped again to scribble, "At 8:05 [A.M.] in bluff shelters . . . found a perfect stone bowl in plain sight, also a large cowry shell bored with a hole at one end on top of *paepae* [house platform]. Also plenty of grindstones. Looks good."

The evidence indicated that the people who had built the house were Polynesians. He found a fishhook made of human bone similar to Hawaiian fishhooks of the same type. There was a typical Hawaiian stone lamp as well as more cowries, each punctured with holes for use as bait on a line attached to a squid hook. The same artifact was found throughout Polynesia.

For four-and-one-half days Kenneth collected and photographed and took notes, too busy almost to eat. To make the most of their time, the party divided into two: one group scouting for ruins, the other coming behind to excavate cave shelters and to measure. One day Commander Samuel Wilder King brought a boatload of his sailors ashore and cleared away the underbrush from a village site. When the last boat pulled away from the island, Kenneth was convinced he had recorded all the sites and collected every artifact of value to the museum to be found on Nihoa. All they left behind were thousands upon thousands of birds.

The *Tanager* sailed for Necker, nearly 125 miles away, at 3 P.M. on Sunday, July 13, and landed its party the next day. Necker appeared even more inhospitable than Nihoa. From the thwart of a bobbing whaleboat Kenneth looked up at the island's sawtooth profile etched sharply against the sky. There were no comfortable caves in which to sleep, only niches in the rock where members of the shore party nestled like cliff dwellers at night. Since there was no anchorage, the *Tanager* circled the island during their stay.

Kenneth soon learned that Necker's dramatic skyline was in reality a row three-quarters of a mile long of thirty-four shrines, their upright slabs outlined in profile from the sea. He had seen a few similar platforms with uprights on Nihoa but never on the inhabited islands of the Hawaiian chain. The shrines puzzled him. They were quite distinctive yet rudimentary; stone platforms with a raised terrace in back where the upright slabs stood. And the slabs, whether five or seven or nine, were always in odd numbers. Had he stumbled upon a new race of Pacific islanders who worshiped in a manner different from Polynesians?

The idea of a new race did not seem likely, although he found scant evidence at Necker on which to base a conclusion. Only one cave on the hot, barren island showed habitation for any length of time. He did find a few stone bowls of the same type scattered all over Nihoa. His best guess was that Necker had been used as a fishing resort by the people of Nihoa. They might also have come here to collect bird feathers or to capture turtles. But the shrines baffled him.

When Kenneth returned to Honolulu he spoke carefully to *The Advertiser*'s museum reporter, Lorin Tarr Gill. "The ruins are a mystery," he admitted. "In some respects the temple remains bear a resemblance to the . . . Hawaiian *heiau* sites, especially in their dry masonry work and in the fact that their surface is sometimes paved with pebbles. . . . It is believed that the natives of Nihoa occasionally went to Necker to fish though it is not at all certain that they had anything to do with the temple ruins on Necker."

The mystery of Necker Island fascinated him but there was precious little time to solve it. He had photographs to develop and notes to work up and sketches to draw. July sped into August. By that time his September departure for the South Seas was only a month away. He was too busy to celebrate the appearance of his first major publication, *The Island of Lanai*, on August 14, 1924. Kenneth did breathe a little easier when word came down that the refitting of Kellum's schooner had fallen behind schedule. She would not arrive in Honolulu until November. Maybe he could get his report on Nihoa and Necker in by then.

It was not to be. Kenneth received an invitation from the Kellums for an evening of introductions and socializing on August 29. By this time they were living in a new home on the other side of the island in Kailua. Mrs. Kellum did not act like an heiress to the Carnegie fortune. She was a hunchback with a pleasant, unassuming manner. Her wiry, white-haired husband, it turned out, had gotten his start as a charter boat captain in the sport fishing business. He was a practical sort of fellow. If a bit vague about the scientific goals of his expedition, he knew exactly how he wanted it documented—on movie film. Kenneth discovered that he had been elected official cameraman, director, developer, and projectionist. To date he had never operated a motion-picture camera, much less developed the film. He would have to learn fast while getting everything else done before the boat sailed. The mystery of Necker Island must remain a mystery for the time being.

Thank goodness his friend, Armstrong Sperry, arrived on Tuesday, September 9, to help. Kenneth put him to work running errands, learning darkroom procedure, and reading up on the central Pacific. Their goal was to compile a dictionary of Polynesian words used on the islands they were to visit.

Kenneth consulted Hawaii's pioneer movie photographer, Ray Jerome Baker, at his Waikiki studio about filming motion pictures. Baker let him practice with a camera he had built himself. It really wasn't all that hard. The apparatus looked like a black box of soda crackers on a tripod. A crank on one side turned the reel that exposed the film inside the camera. The trick was to crank out the proper number of frames per second because whatever speed you cranked, that was the speed of the action. Focusing and judging the exposure settings was pretty much like operating any other camera. Kenneth quickly got the hang of it. Baker sold him the camera and taught him to develop movie film.

On Sunday, October 4, he wrote in his diary, "Developed first roll of movie film. Called on Muriel Mattocks." A week later, "Devel-

oped another roll of movie film. Arm [Armstrong Sperry] doing it."
His social life proceeded at the same frantic pace he set at the
museum; picnics, beach parties, hula recitals, and dinner dates with
Arm and various young ladies, but mostly Muriel Mattocks.

On October 6 he penned a breathless letter to Gregory:

> I doubt if I was ever happier over anything as I am over this truly great
> and ideal opportunity to work in Central Polynesia, or more grateful to
> anyone [than] I am to you for making it possible."

PART THREE

A ROMANCE OF
THE SOUTH SEAS

Chapter Fourteen

Cruise of
the *Kaimiloa*

Kenneth Emory's magic carpet to the South Seas arrived in Honolulu Harbor at 1:30 P.M. on Friday, October 31, 1924. She had been rechristened *Kaimiloa* (the long search) at Sausalito, California, where workmen had transformed the twenty-four-year-old workaday schooner into a palatial yacht. Her 180-foot-long hull gleamed with white paint. Her four masts towered 130 feet into the blue Hawaiian skies. Staterooms had been built over her main deck with a new promenade deck covering the staterooms. Their portholes extended three-quarters of the length of the ship.

Her new equipment reflected owner Kellum's respect for technology as well as creature comforts. The vessel carried a 7-horsepower engine to hoist the anchor, a 5-horsepower motor for raising sails and lowering boats, a 2-horsepower motor for pumping salt water to the air pressure tanks in the toilets, a 1-horsepower motor for fresh water circulation, and a 5-horsepower motor to run the cold storage plant. This facility stored enough meat for thirty persons for ninety days and produced two hundred pounds of ice every twenty-four hours, insuring a sufficient supply for cocktails.

Kenneth was ready. He had produced pages of equipment inventory purchased, borrowed, or requisitioned from the museum: five still cameras, two movie cameras, film, an Edison Fireside Phonograph with three horns, a spare belt and arm, one speaking tube, two recorders, two reproducers, a brush, screw driver, oil can. He had shopped for hundreds of unlikely items including thumb tacks, lamp wicks, a three-gallon bucket, fifteen feet of rubber tubing, and a book of litmus paper. His stock of trade goods for dealing with the natives included two dozen rings, two dozen bracelets, bead necklaces, a dozen toys, colorful ribbons, and cigarette holders.

He went on board first thing Saturday morning to inspect the laboratory-darkroom that Kellum had promised to provide Bishop Museum scientists. It was located in the hold in an area fifty feet long, running fore and aft between bow and amidships, and it was as bare as Mother Hubbard's cupboard. The darkroom would have to be installed during the week before the *Kaimiloa* sailed.

Kenneth's diary entry for Saturday reads, "Down on the boat most of the day . . . Meeting at Kellums." On Sunday he wrote, "On the *Kaimiloa* early. Carpenters on darkroom." He spent most of Monday seeing to the installation of his pans and printer and drying racks. "Busy superintending job on *Kaimiloa*," he wrote on Wednesday. There would not be time to try out the equipment before the boat sailed. On Saturday he and Arm packed up their gear at the museum and loaded it on the yacht.

The round of going-away parties kept him occupied outside the darkroom. On Tuesday he finished in time to attend a dinner hosted by the Wilders for the expedition party. His parents had Armstrong Sperry and other friends to dinner. The Kellums held a reception on board the *Kaimiloa* on Saturday afternoon. Federal Judge William T. Rawlins lent gravity to the occasion with a speech about the importance of the voyage to mankind, and the Royal Hawaiian Band provided spirited music.

The *Kaimiloa* sailed at 4 P.M. Sunday, November 9, from Pier 10. But Kenneth was not on board. He had been assigned the task of recording the historic departure on movie film. While the resplendent white yacht sailed past Diamond Head, he was bouncing up and down in a motor launch with spray flying, trying to keep the movie camera dry as he wound the crank to keep tension up on the spring that turned the reel. He and other members of the scientific party would join the *Kaimiloa* in Hilo on the island of Hawaii.

At least it gave him time to breathe. The next day he took the movie film to Ray Jerome Baker for developing. He could pause and restudy his memorandum of instruction from the museum director. It still seemed too good to be true. The expedition was to investigate Malden, Starbuck, Tongareva, Manihiki, and Manua (Manu'a) islands during the first three months. By the end of the first year's cruise, approximately August 1925, the scientists could expect to visit outlying islands of the Societies and the Tuamotus. The chief of the party had full authority, in consultation with Mr. Kellum, to select the islands to be visited and the time to be spent on each. The entire cruise was expected to last three years with the first major destination being Samoa.

"Sailed on *Haleakala* for Hilo at 5 P.M. . . . Moonlight and smooth," Kenneth wrote in his diary on Friday, November 14. He checked in at the Pacific Hotel, then went to the yacht for more work in the darkroom. The next day, "Worked on yacht—first lunch on board."

The splendidly appointed dining room measured twenty-eight by twenty feet with four tables seating six each. Two courteous Japanese served the food prepared by a black cook whose wife acted as maid for the smallest Kellum children. The waiters had a busy time because the passenger list included Mr. and Mrs. Kellum, four children, four guests, six in the scientific party, two tutors for Kellum's oldest son, and a ship's doctor. The ship's officers also ate in the dining room.

For some reason, two of Kellum's guests decided in Hilo not to continue the voyage. Kenneth mentioned the change in plan to a newspaper reporter. When he returned to the ship, he found his host conducting an investigation. "Mr. Kellum told us whoever gave that report is not going on the trip," Kenneth recalled later. "Well, I'd given it. Boy! Whew! That's the limit. All that preparation and not to go. So I decided to take the bull by the horns. I went right to him and just told him I didn't know I was causing anybody any trouble so I didn't see that was a reason I shouldn't be going." Kellum relented. Kenneth moved his things on board and that night showed movies on deck he had taken of the *Kaimiloa*'s arrival and departure in Honolulu.

Kellum's unexpected anger did not dampen the excitement of their departure from Kuhio Wharf in Hilo at 2:30 P.M. on Wednesday, November 19. "The native music boys played *Aloha Oe* on our deck as we waved farewell," Kenneth wrote in his log of the voyage. "The [interisland steamer] *Haleakala* and the [ocean liner] *City of Los Angeles* signalled us with their horns and we replied with our shrill, more highly pitched whistle. We had all been decorated with leis. The scene on deck was a merry one. Kauka [botanist Gerrit Wilder] and the native boys did the hula. At 3:30 such as were going ashore embarked on the pilot boat . . . They circled us a couple of times, the native boys singing *Aloha Means I Love You* and other appropriate songs with lusty voices. Then we were left to ourselves."

A shipboard routine developed the next day in spite of seasickness. Kellum's oldest son, Medford, a student at the Georgia Institute of Technology, practiced taking sun sights in the morning while his father chatted on the stern with Kenneth and botanist Wilder. A young lady named Gladys Laughlin, whom Med Kellum had invited along, promenaded on deck with a female friend while little Jimmy Kellum and his baby sister played. In the afternoon Med Kellum studied with his tutors while Kenneth and Armstrong Sperry boned up on their Samoan.

The next morning they developed the movie film Kenneth had taken at Hilo. The film looked like it had been shot in a fog because Kenneth had never used the new printer before. Wilder and zoologist Ball, chief of the scientific party, installed shelves in the laboratory and a drainboard for the sink. Ball's assistant, D. G. Rogers, was still too seasick to work. That night, Kenneth showed footage he had taken and one of the Hollywood movies the Kellums had brought on board.

As usual, he was much too busy to be bored. All six members of the crew were Marshall Islanders from Micronesia. Naturally, they ate in their own mess hall and did not mingle socially with the passengers. But Kenneth couldn't wait to strike up a conversation with them. He cornered Charlie Johmur, the boatswain, while he was at the wheel and could not escape. They soon found a common bond. Johmur said he and his friends were all from the atoll of Jaluit and had sailed to Hawaii in a German schooner at the outbreak of World War I. They were shelled and burned by a Japanese man-of-war just outside Honolulu Harbor and had shipped out of Hawaii ever since. Kenneth said he remembered watching from the Thurston cottage on Tantalus as the German schooner went up in flames. From there the conversation led to tattooing, mat weaving, dance, and how to construct a Marshallese drum.

"Wilder, Ball and I submitted two alternative routes for our course from Christmas to Samoa," Kenneth wrote in his diary on Tuesday, November 25. "Kellum is very keen to make short runs so that we will probably go to Malden, Starbuck, Penrhyn and then run for Samoa, stopping for a day at Manihiki and Suvarov [Suwarrow]."

On the face of it, the entry gives no indication that a dispute had arisen between the scientists on board the luxurious *Kaimiloa* and their genial host, but it can be read between the lines. Kenneth had laid in a supply of film sufficient for three weeks at Manihiki and three weeks at Suvarov, indicating the scientists had anticipated much longer stops at these atolls where the potential for scientific discovery was greatest. It was not until the end of the voyage in a letter to Gregory that Kenneth described what happened when the scientists presented their schedules to Kellum:

> Without dreaming that Mr. Kellum had settled in his heart to stay at Fanning and Christmas the greater part of the time spent at anchor between Hawaii and Samoa, we allotted a day at Fanning and about four or five days at Christmas Island. When he saw the short time we had down for those islands he assumed that . . . we were unwilling to stay longer.
>
> Instead of talking over his wishes with any of us first, he told everybody else that we had no regard for his or Mrs. Kellum's pleasure and that we were trying to act as if this were the museum's boat and not his. He worked himself into a perfect fury about it and then gave vent to it, bowling us over with the utmost surprise. He said he was going to go where he

pleased, stay just as long as it suited his fancy, and a great deal more better left unsaid.

There was no convincing Mr. Kellum that we fully realized the *Kaimiloa* was his boat, that he had put a tremendous amount of worry and thought into the cruise, and therefore deserved to have such recreation and enjoyment with it as he could and, furthermore, we could use our time to advantage wherever we were.

Kenneth gave Gregory one possible explanation for the blowup. His letter said he believed that even before the *Kaimiloa* had departed Honolulu, Kellum regretted inviting the scientists on board. Another explanation might be that Kellum's unpredictableness came out of the bottom of a bottle. His son said years later that his father had a drinking problem, which is why he himself learned to drink sparingly. Med Kellum said he does not remember a dispute between his father and the scientists. This may be because it did not involve him directly.

The elder Kellum took a particular dislike toward Dr. Ball, leader of the scientific party, who did not drink, smoke, or swear. "Ball was an ingrown New Englander," Kenneth explained. "He was very sober, very quiet and not very social. He spoke slowly. He was rather fussy and meticulous. Mr. Kellum told me once, 'Ball is an old prude.' Kellum tried to avoid eating when Ball was in the dining room." Members of the scientific party, as Kellum's guests, did their best to paper over the disagreement. In spite of the strain, Kenneth's diary reveals his delight the next morning when he saw his first atoll, Fanning (Tabuaeran) Island:

Wednesday, Nov. 26, 1924—I awoke at 6 A.M. and started to close the port hole which is flooded every morning when the decks [above] are scrubbed down. As I looked out I was taken by complete surprise on seeing a long, black line against the rosy glow of dawn. . . . The familiar shape of coconut trees was thrust up . . . and silhouetted sharply against the colored light.

Kenneth was so excited he shouted for his roommates. Steck, one of the tutors, threw on a kimono and rushed up on deck. Arm jumped out of bed and followed Kenneth in his bare feet. Soon the Kellums were roused and, half dressed, gazed from the port rail like children on Christmas morning. Kenneth described the scene in his journal:

The water was smooth and the sky clear except for gray banks off the horizon. The lights from the rising sun were exquisite. We watched the foliage turn to gray-green, then a bright green. A white line of surf showed clearly and, beyond, the blue-green shallow water between reef and shore.

Kenneth recognized a gap in the surf line as the pass in the reef. But he was not prepared for his first adventure in braving such a narrow opening in the roaring combers that pounded the reef. He wrote:

> We dropped anchor and blew our whistle for the pilot. A gray launch came from somewhere in the lagoon. On it was a part native, whom we learned was Hugh Gregg, and two Gilbertese boys who wore only kilts or *riri*. Gregg shouted through a megaphone, "Follow me," and away we steamed into the swift current flowing out of the lagoon through the pass.
>
> It surely was exciting for we headed toward the south [side] of the pass where the water was deepest. There was a question if we could turn in time to avoid [hitting the reef]. The *Kaimiloa* turned slowly at first and it looked as if we were going [aground] for certain. We spied natives running through the coconut trees to the beach. [They were] clad in scarlet kilts and looked very dark and savage.
>
> Our schooner finally bore her nose into the current and made steady speed against it. I could easily see the ocean bottom all the way into the lagoon. Once inside, the waters were deep and quiet and of a most vivid sky blue. [The lagoon is encircled by a] thin band of land set with tall, dense groves of coconuts. It was as wonderful a sight as any of us had imagined an atoll might be.

The *Kaimiloa* anchored one hundred yards from the copra settlement of Fanning Island Company, Ltd. Kenneth had to wait until 4 P.M. before a boat took him ashore with the Kellum family. Brown-skinned children in scarlet kilts stood silently on the beach eyeing the visitors with intense curiosity. They spoke a language Kenneth did not understand. He wrote later in his journal:

> We learned that nearly all the natives at this camp had been recruited only the month before. They were far more primitive then we expected they would be. They had never seen white children and did not know what to make of [eight-year-old] Jimmy [Kellum] who soon had them all in tow. Arm and I wandered through the native camp.

Kellum's lack of interest in the scientific arm of his expedition became evident the next day when the ship's boats were put to use for sport fishing. The scientists had to hike to an archaeological site and beg a ride back in the launch of Major Burn-Callendar, manager of the copra plantation. Kenneth remained ship-bound again on Friday. He passed the time developing film.

On Saturday morning a note arrived on board from Burn-Callendar saying he would show Kenneth a ruin provided they go immediately, return by noon, and he could find a boat to take them. Kellum consented to the use of the ship's large launch. Kenneth frantically collected Armstrong Sperry and young Rogers, Ball's snail and insect collector, and set out at top speed across the lagoon. Sperry and Rogers hurriedly cleared palm fronds and coconut husks from a large temple ruin sixty feet square built of cut and joined stones. While Burn-Callendar and Kenneth took measurements, Kenneth discovered a cornerstone cut in the shape of an L. The ruin tantalized him. "I was not half through photographing and note taking when the time was noted to be noon," he wrote in despair when they returned to the ship.

His frustration vanished after lunch when the entire ship's company went ashore to watch the Gilbertese workers perform dances native to their islands in Micronesia. Mrs. Kellum and Kenneth brought movie cameras. He was so enthused over the chance to film native dances that he couldn't make his new camera work. The journal describes what happened:

> They began dancing in earnest before I had warning. My film jammed. I opened the camera to fix it and in my excitement opened the magazine also and ruined a 200-foot-roll [of film]. Luckily I had another 200 feet and Mrs. Kellum was winding away on this part of the dance. She soon had her troubles, too, and lost as much film as I did. [But] When her troubles came my camera worked beautifully. Between us we ground away on all parts of the dance.
>
> I was immensely interested and excited for I had never expected to run into natives dancing in unaffected style and in purely native garb. They had on their *riri* or grass skirts, neck bands of colored beads, wreaths of *ilima* flowers, and pieces of coconut leaf lying on the breast and tied behind the neck. . . . The songs which were genuinely Gilbertese were strikingly Japanese-like in sound . . . and they gave them with the utmost vigor. All the young men who could gather around a wooden grocery box did so, and beat the time with their right hands while they chanted or sang. In the Gilbertese dances they clapped their hands together only, or [slapped] their hands against their bodies.

While the dance costumes were authentic, the girls wore theirs over dresses that modestly covered their breasts. Major Burn-Callendar and Hugh Gregg cajoled the women into removing the dresses for their final performance. Kenneth saw that they did so reluctantly and then were so cold to the dance that the Gilbertese head man had to jump in and get them going. Obviously the costumes had been censored for public consumption. Kenneth learned from a Gilbertese that they were to dance for themselves at eight o'clock that night. He and Arm and Rogers sneaked off after supper to watch.

This time there was no formality. A dance began to the beating of the box. A thin-faced, intelligent-looking man took up the chant. After a few verses, men and women rose and began a pantomime, arms extended, making quick movements, faces turned upward in rapture. Others jumped in, arranging themselves in ranks of four or five. By the time the dance ended, the tempo had become so rapid that the chanting was reduced to heavy grunts on the off beat. Children of both sexes mingled underfoot trying to imitate their elders. Kenneth wrote later in his journal:

> Now there was nothing shy about them. They sang magnificently. One young fellow, as handsome as Apollo and over six feet tall, had a deep and powerful voice which rolled out so vividly that I was delighted to listen to him. When he danced he did so without any apparent exertion. With his arms raised he looked like a giant. Remember all the natives were naked except for a short kilt or a mat or a grass skirt. In the dim light of the dance house they made an impressive picture.

The next day brought Kenneth back to his role on board the *Kaimiloa*. He worked in the darkroom with Arm and Steck from early morning until 11 P.M. developing 600 feet of movie film and stills taken of the dancing. They might never have finished if Kenneth had not installed an electric heater under the film drying rack. "With two electric fans and this heater going we were able to dry the film in two hours," he explained in his journal. "Once before when we tried drying film under these conditions . . . it became a mass of soft gelatin."

On the morning of Monday, December 1, Kenneth escaped once more with Major Burn-Callendar to look at another ruin. On the way across the six-mile-wide lagoon, Kenneth and Arm persuaded the Gilbertese boatman to teach them two dance songs, "Ua O Nei Rawa" and "Taratara." On the site they found two large blocks of cut stone before the noon bewitching hour arrived. During the return trip Kenneth told Burn-Callendar that Fanning Island ruins were Polynesian and had been built by temporary settlers probably from Tonga or perhaps from the Marquesas or Samoa.

Zoologist Ball and botanist Wilder, meanwhile, spent most of their time on the yacht. Kenneth reported that they asked Kellum for a boat to collect marine zoological specimens and were told,

"What do you think this is, a ferry service?" Kellum wasn't speaking to Ball at all so Ball tried to be useful by fixing up the laboratory. Then Wilder made the mistake of asking their host when they might be moving on to Christmas Island. After that, Kellum didn't speak to the Wilders either. Kenneth said he provided communication between the scientific party and the owner of the yacht.

Tuesday found Kenneth back in the darkroom preparing for a showing of the dance film to the performers themselves. By the time he had spliced the movie together and came on deck it was 8 P.M. The *Kaimiloa* had been decorated like a Christmas tree with red, white, and blue lights strung from the stern over the mastheads to the end of the bowsprit. The Gilbertese squatted on deck watching their first motion picture, a five-reeler about New York entitled *City of Illusion*. Kenneth squatted down among the workers. "The native by whom I sat kept asking me when the scenes shifted if this was still *No Yoruk*," he wrote later. "They clicked their tongues at everything strange and were much amused by all the love scenes."

The Gilbertese grew bored before the film about New York came to an end. But they stopped yawning and lolling on deck when the picture of their own dance came on. "They sat perfectly rigid taking it all in," Kenneth wrote in his journal. "They were delighted with the movie and simply roared whenever they saw one of their number make a false step. They will not forget that picture in a hurry."

Kellum invited Mr. and Mrs. Burn-Callendar to Thanksgiving dinner on board the yacht. This gave Kenneth a chance to ask the major for permission to record native singing that night, a Wednesday. Burn-Callendar granted permission, although ordinarily the natives were allowed to sing only on Saturday night because the singing often lasted until morning. Arm and Kenneth hustled off to shore with the phonograph, horns, and wax recording cylinders.

They found only a few lights burning in the Gilbertese village. It was after 9 P.M. Taps had already been blown on the conch-shell trumpet. Through one open door Kenneth saw a woman squatting on the floor weaving or sewing by lamplight. He stopped at a door where he heard a man's voice and knocked. He pushed the door half open. A whole family was in bed under one mat. The man of the house sprang up, put on his *riri* and came to the door. Kenneth asked where he could find Berika, a Gilbertese who understood Hawaiian. After that it was easy.

Kenneth and Arm set up their equipment in the dance house while Berika rounded up the villagers. They appeared out of the darkness, curious and at ease, two or three of the women dressed only in the *riri*. Kenneth described the scene in his journal:

From a rafter I slung the large horn and we induced three natives to sing *Ua O Nie Rawa* into it. But the reproduction [from a wax cylinder] was scarcely audible. We then tried the little horn. Our natives shouted into it with all their lung power, determined to be heard this time. Their song came out just one shriek. We tried another record. This time the machine refused to move the needle. [These repeated failures made the Gilbertese impatient.] After getting the natives out of bed, we [felt fortunate] that we were leaving the next day . . . [At last] I found an adjustment which fixed things. [That made everybody happy.]

We got Poia, a man who had chanted for Arm the day before, and he made a fine record. From then on it was clear sailing. First we had an old Gilbertese chant [and recorded] an ancient Gilbertese song. Then we had a man and a woman sing together. The woman was a terrible singer and they all laughed at her so she quit in the middle of the song. Last of all, we had a young native sing a Gilbertese dance song while a man on each side kept time in the usual manner of clapping. This came out excellently and we figured that now was a good time to quit so we offered cigarets. Arm passed around a full hundred.

The *Kaimiloa*'s departure added more strain to relations on board. Dr. Ball and Gerrit Wilder were eager to end the stay at Fanning, which for them had been unproductive. But the captain was delayed on his way back from the cable station, where he had gone for clearance papers, by going aground on a coral head. By the time he came on board, the tide had turned and it was too late to sail. The next day was Friday. Kellum announced that he always had bad luck when he sailed on Friday so they lay at anchor. "It was a bright day over the lagoon and I itched to get ashore but no chance came up," Kenneth wrote in his journal. Ball became more frustrated. Med Kellum said many years later that he was not aware of this dissatisfaction, which indicates that the scientists kept it to themselves.

Finally on December 6 the *Kaimiloa* steamed away from her first landfall. The coconut trees of Christmas Island to the south rose low on the horizon after breakfast on Monday, December 8. There are breaks in Kenneth's journal as well as his diary at this point, but he remembers Christmas Atoll as a barren place and the kingdom of a remarkable French priest, Father Rougier, who had left the clergy to go into business. He held the lease to Christmas, one of the largest and most productive atolls in the Pacific.

The *Kaimiloa* entered the lagoon through one of the passes in the reef and came to anchor off Paris, the name Rougier had given his copra headquarters on one side of the immense lagoon. London lay on the other side. In this remote but well-organized corner of the South Seas the scientists at last were able to collect as many bugs and shells and plants and fish as they could find. Father Rougier instructed his nephew and his plantation managers, Monsieurs Coulon and Pugeault, to extend his guests full cooperation. Ford trucks took them wherever they wanted to go.

They spent three busy days camped near Paris where Kenneth measured graves and did some excavating while Ball and Wilder happily explored the underbrush. Then they boarded the *Kaimiloa* and moved to a new anchorage off London on the other side of the lagoon. A truck drove them twenty-two kilometers to an abandoned village site. There Kenneth and Arm spent four days measuring and excavating house sites as well as graves. Ball and Wilder added all sorts of flora and fauna to the museum's collections.

Kenneth again found traces of the ubiquitous Polynesians. He had not made up his mind about the ruins until their last day in the camp when Monsieur Coulon gave Dr. Ball a shell adz he had found on the sea side of the ruins. The adz was indisputably Polynesian. "This find is not only significant but our falling into possession of it is great good fortune," Kenneth wrote in a journal entry. "The adz is indisputable evidence that the Polynesians were here. That may account for the presence of the Polynesian rat, the little bird, Akiko-kiko, the groves of coconut trees seen by Captain Cook in 1777 and some of the graves, cairns and house sites."

Father Rougier and Kellum got along famously. Kenneth said he was under the impression that Kellum wanted to buy the island from the priest. Med Kellum said it was not like that. In any event, Christmas kept the yacht owner entertained for nine days. During this time the two-masted schooner *Malaya* dropped in on her way west from the Galapagos Islands to mend some sails. Then Father Rougier's own schooner, the *Roy Summers*, arrived after a month-long voyage from San Francisco. Wireless messages kept the atoll in contact with the outside world and, at night, a radio on the deck of *Kaimiloa* broadcast dance music from a hotel in San Francisco over the star-spangled lagoon.

When the *Kaimiloa* sailed from Christmas Island at 2 P.M. on December 17, she carried three new passengers: Father Rougier, his nephew, and a Mademoiselle Pugeault. Kenneth said she was Father Rougier's girlfriend. Med Kellum doesn't remember her being on board. Whatever the case, the new passengers added fuel for speculation among the scientists. All they could do was speculate because Kellum hardly confided in them and Father Rougier, an imposing figure in his full, white beard, kept to himself.

It was not long after their departure that Kellum dropped his bombshell. He announced that the *Kaimiloa* would not be going to

Samoa after all, but would head for Tahiti where Rougier had his home. The voyage of a year would be cut to less than two months. There was absolutely nothing his shanghaied scientists could do about it. They didn't even try. By that time, one of the tutors and several of the crew members had also incurred Kellum's displeasure. It was best to tiptoe around him. Kenneth, Armstrong Sperry, and young Rogers remained in his good graces and maintained a friendly relationship with the Kellum family.

A sailor aloft sighted Malden Island at 2 P.M. on December 20. But it was not until 3:30 that the passengers on deck saw the low, barren platform of coral jutting from the ocean. Kenneth went down to work in the darkroom. When he came up on deck again at 5 P.M. a skiff with five excited Polynesians aboard was coming alongside. The head man yelled out in fine English, "Do you wish to anchor tonight?" "Yes," the captain shouted back. The head man offered to lead the way. He said his name was Pita Bob, foreman in charge of six guano diggers, the only inhabitants of Malden. They were all from Rarotonga in the Cook Islands and they had not seen a boat since last May.

The sun had set and darkness was closing in as the *Kaimiloa* approached the island. There was no lagoon at Malden, not even an anchorage, because the island sloped so steeply into the water. The owners of Malden Island Property, Limited, engaged in digging and selling guano as fertilizer, had therefore installed a mooring buoy to which their ships could fasten while loading. Pita Bob and the captain were just able to see the buoy in the dim light. A sailor heaved a line to the Polynesians in their boat so they could make it fast to the buoy. Kenneth's journal describes the exciting climax to this hair-breadth arrival:

> Before the Rarotongans could fasten the line to the buoy, we drifted off too far and the line pulled away. We had to bear off and come up again, this time in the dark. We were all anxious. Med played the searchlight on the water. We had about given up hope of finding the buoy and the natives when someone made them out. When they came along side, we put two kerosene lanterns in the boat and Med got in with them.
>
> We bore off, made a wide turn and came up again against the wind and current which is here very powerful. After another hard struggle, the natives succeeded in putting the rope onto the buoy. Med was on the buoy himself to help tie the rope. He said he could hear sharks all around him. Even so, when one native lost his oar, he jumped overboard in the dark and swam to it.

Considering the hazards to navigation at Malden, it seems understandable that Kellum had not wished to risk his yacht here.

Besides, the guano island, covered by bird dung, was the most god-forsaken place they had seen so far. Yet to the scientists it represented a fascinating challenge. In 1825 the British frigate *Blonde* had sighted such imposing ruins on the island that the ship's artist, Dampier, had sketched them. Who had built these great stone structures? An opportunity to find out would make the entire voyage worthwhile. Kenneth's journal describes what he saw the next morning:

> At the first touch of pink light on the trade wind clouds, which I could look out to as I lay on my bunk, I jumped to the floor, put on my clothes and went on deck to observe by daylight Malden Island. There she lay 400 yards away. She presented a steep, white beach half a mile long, the westerly coastline. Midway between the northwest and southwest points stood the settlement, a long line of neat buildings joining one another like a New England farm establishment. It was off this group of buildings we lay fastened to a great buoy. Back of the settlement a few coconut trees lifted their fronts high enough to be seen above the roofs. On the northwest point a dozen *pukatea* [*Pisonia*] tree clumps were all the trees we could see. The land spread away in the shape of a fan, flat and brown, covered only with bunch grass, *ilima* bushes and a few weeds. From up in the rigging I could see a depression, filled with water, which occupied a large part of the interior of the island.

They would have to land through the surf. The scientists had no idea how long they would stay until Kellum told Kenneth to pack enough grub for two days. With the Rarotongans at the oars, the launch headed for shore. Surfing in on a boiling comber was like arriving on a roller coaster. Kenneth got out his movie camera to film the next boatload. It got crosswise to the wave and almost swamped. The other passengers soon returned to the ship but the scientists remained on shore where Pita Bob offered them accommodations in workers' huts.

But the scientists didn't spend much time there. For two days, from dawn to sundown, they worked furiously in an orgy of measuring and collecting. Here was virgin, unrecorded territory. The meticulous Ball counted thirty-two semi-wild hogs, about fifty cats and three goats on the island, and reported that the rat was extinct. He pounced on dragonflies, spiders, two kinds of silverfish, an earwig, several specimens of black beetle, two types of moths, two species of ants, and pill bugs. He listed every species of bird on the island: noddy terns, red-footed boobies, sooty terns, frigate birds, white terns, blue-faced boobies, common boobies, tattlers, plovers, and Tahitian curlews, and counted them all.

Kenneth was just as busy. He found the temples Dampier had

sketched one hundred years before. One of them measured one hundred feet by fifty feet. Its low walls, eighteen inches high, were curbstone blocks of limestone cut from the reef and set edgewise into the ground. Coral rubble inside the walls formed a platform on which a second, smaller platform had been built. On top of this was a stone box eight feet long, four feet wide, and three feet high. The box had partly collapsed.

A second temple, identical to the first but half as large, stood two hundred yards away. Kenneth found smaller ones built on the same plan on the opposite side of the island. Hundreds of house sites, marked by coral curbstones, clustered around the rim of the island. All of these Kenneth recognized as monuments to a former Polynesian people who had discovered this forbidding island and populated it for a while. Was there no island in this great ocean the early Polynesians had not tested for habitation?

The Rarotongans not only understood Kenneth's and Kauka Wilder's Hawaiian but spoke English with a New Zealand accent, their home islands being under the protection of that nation. Pita Bob killed one of his precious pigs to provide a feast for his guests on Monday, December 22. Then the scientific party embarked through the surf. The *Kaimiloa* sailed at 5 P.M.

By the time they reached Tongareva (Penrhyn) two days later, the novelty of arriving at a South Sea atoll had worn off for most of the passengers. For Kenneth, after working in the darkroom all morning, the magic was still there. He wrote in his journal:

> We sighted land and coconuts dead ahead at 3 o'clock. The islets of Penrhyn [Tongareva], each carrying a very tall forest of palms, stood in a line stretching far to the left and right. Pearly light filtered upon the islands through a thin overcast. It was quiet and hot. A flock of plover twittered by our bow flying low on the water. A few solitary frigate birds soared overhead. As I stood on the bowsprit, watching the land come into view upon which I had set my heart to visit, I could hear the hissing sounds made by flying fish as they skimmed in fright over the smooth water.

Kenneth was not so thrilled by the Tongarevans, Polynesians all, who sailed out in a boat. They swarmed on board and then stood without a smile or displaying any of the curiosity other natives had shown on first sight of the luxurious *Kaimiloa*. Kenneth explained why in his journal:

> One young native, catching my eye, beckoned me aside and said, "Want pearl?" He showed me a small bottle full of softly shining pearls.

Not knowing a thing about pearls and suspecting these natives to be pretty shrewd, I stayed clear of buying except to trade a shirt for a dozen small ones. The Wilders and Kellums were gathering in pearls by the hundreds. The natives became terribly excited and seemed ready to part with anything for a pair of trousers or a shirt. When Mr. Wilson, the pilot and chief commissioner of the island, came on board hardly anybody noticed him except Mr. Kellum and the captain.

Tongareva proved to be a picture postcard of the South Seas: tall palms reflected in the lagoon, blue wreaths of smoke rising in the still evening air, thatched huts nestled among the coconut groves. The islands encircling the lagoon were lush and tropical and Kenneth found out why during the two days he scouted for ruins. It poured rain the whole time. He and Armstrong Sperry, soggy as sponges after a thirty-mile circuit of the lagoon, returned with only a few place names and the location of some fish ponds.

When the *Kaimiloa* sailed on Sunday morning, December 28, Kenneth was back in the darkroom developing movie film. He kept at it on December 29. His diary entry for December 30 reads like an old refrain, "At sea. Developed pictures all day. Cloudy, rough." The captain expected to arrive at Tahiti before midnight the next day. Kenneth's dream voyage appeared to be over almost before it had begun, his hopes for three years of South Sea exploration a pipe dream. Neither he nor anybody else in the scientific party knew what would happen next.

Yet he was not discouraged. In fact, he could not in his heart feel sorry that they had substituted Tahiti for Samoa as their destination. Fabled Tahiti, capital of the South Seas! All of his life he had wanted to see this enchanted island. He would cope with his future the Polynesian way: enjoy today and let tomorrow take care of itself.

Society Islands

Maupiti
1925 Survey
1962-63 Dig

Motu Motu
Pass
o o

Bora–Bora
1925 Survey
1963 Restorations

Vaitape

Tiva

Tahaa

Uturoa

Fare

Raiatea

Marae
Tuputapuatea
1925 Survey
1962 Dig

Maeva (Maraes) 1925 Survey

Huahine

Tetiaroa

Pt. Venus

Papeete

Papenoo

Opunohu Bay

Cook Bay

Moorea
1925 Survey

Afareaitu
1960 Dig

Marae Arahurahu
Marae Mahaiatea
1925 Survey

Tautira

Tahiti 1925 Survey

**Tahiti
Nui**

Tahiti Iti

Te Pari

Maiao

Windward Islands

Leeward Islands

Legend

Voyages Made in 1925 and
Retraced in the 1960s

Chapter Fifteen

Thank God
I'm Still Here

The new year, 1925, dawned on the *Kaimiloa* lying at anchor in the placid bay of Papeete, on the island of Tahiti. She had slipped through the pass in the dark without a pilot only three hours after the new year began. Now she made a festive picture in her white paint, wearing her colored lights and dressed in gay, bright signal flags from stem to stern.

Kenneth Emory stood on her deck gazing toward land with the other passengers as the sunrise etched Tahiti's fairy-tale mountains against pink and purple clouds. The black, jagged skyline gradually turned a rich, tropical green. Papeete sprawled along the curving shore, a miniature, one-story city of four thousand inhabitants. Kenneth watched a white horse hitched to a carriage plod along the waterfront street past a wooden church by the shore, and observed wooden stores painted lively colors, a tall white church set back from the bay on a wide street, and a great flowering tree.

Uncertain about Kellum's plans, the scientists asked to go ashore. He made no objection and seemed relieved to be rid of them. Armstrong Sperry, who spoke French, took Kenneth in tow. They hiked along the waterfront to the Hotel du Port, which was not a hotel at all but a rooming house with a cafe downstairs. Guests went down the hall to the toilet and cold shower bath.

To Kenneth it didn't matter. He was in a dream. His window looked out over the bay with a view of the South Seas. The streets he strolled with Arm seemed familiar yet delightfully different. He recognized the tropical trees. But he could not understand the clerks in the stores. French baffled him and Tahitian, spoken rapidly, eluded his grasp. The people seemed to him characters out of South Sea novels: traders in white suits, Tahitian women in folds of calico and huge hats billowing streamers, Chinese storekeepers, native schooner skippers, French bureaucrats.

Mechanization had not yet taken over Papeete. It was like stepping back to a time of elegant carriages and shays and surreys. Bicycles wheeled silently along. The most common mode of transportation was "Train Number Two" nicknamed after the number of legs required for walking. Schooners outnumbered steamers in the harbor. Most of all Kenneth sensed a style, an attitude, an atmosphere that distinguished Papeete from Honolulu. It was compounded of French élan, Tahitian charm, and the smell of tropical flowers.

The scientific party celebrated the new year that night on the veranda of Hotel Tiare, also known as Lovaina's Hotel after its very large and well-known lady proprietor, now deceased. She had fed Paul Gauguin when he was down on his luck and starving. Somerset Maugham had dined on her veranda. It was still the same: flowers on the tables, excellent French cuisine, Tahitian waitresses with dark eyes and sensuous smiles. Residents of Papeete still strolled by to glance at the veranda and see who was new in town.

Arm brought his accordion and Kenneth his guitar. They sang the Tahitian songs Arm had taught Kenneth in Maine, creating a buzz of interest on the veranda. Some of the diners recognized Arm from his previous visit. But who was this other young chap? In remote Papeete such information passed rapidly on the coconut wireless. That night, for the first time, Kenneth consented to drink liquor. He couldn't recognize the taste, of course, but he thinks it was champagne.

The Wilders and Ball with Rogers took rooms at Hotel Tiare. Arm began the next day introducing Kenneth to old friends. An English-speaking member of the large Drollet clan invited them to a dance the following evening in honor of visiting French university students. The elite of Papeete was there as well as important visitors. Kenneth met a slender, middle-aged Englishman with a red mustache and a hyphenated name, George Pitt-Rivers, which he recognized from the Pitt-Rivers Museum in Oxford. It turned out that George's father, an anthropologist, owned it.

Pitt-Rivers and Kenneth had breakfast together the next morning. In the afternoon Kenneth visited Papeete's little hole-in-the-wall museum and its amateur director, Mr. Ahnne, a school principal and president of the Société des Etudes Océanienne, whose membership comprised Tahiti's intellectual set.

Uncertainty hung like a cloud over the scientific party. Nobody knew what Kellum's plans were, nor did Ball feel inclined to ask. They sat around trying to decide what to do. Kenneth said he believed Kellum would like nothing better than to be rid of them if there were a graceful way out of his dilemma. Then he could sail wherever he pleased. Arm and Rogers agreed. Kenneth added, like a young man newly in love, that he'd much rather work in Tahiti than go back on board the *Kaimiloa*. There was plenty for them to do here.

A plan about how to take advantage of this unexpected landfall had already formed in his mind. Handy, who had headed the Marquesas expedition in 1920, had returned with his wife to Tahiti in 1922 to study, among other things, Polynesian religion. In the course of his research he had measured and described a number of temple ruins. But Handy was neither trained in archaeology nor much interested in the subject. If French Polynesia was anything like the Hawaiian Islands there must be plenty of ruins that nobody had bothered to document. Here was a job waiting to be done and Kenneth didn't see why he should not be the one to do it.

Ball and Wilder were in favor of heroically sticking it out on the yacht according to the museum plan. After all, Kellum had a responsibility to fulfill his promise of assisting the scientists in their work. Kenneth argued that Kellum could still do this if they abandoned the *Kaimiloa*. Money was not his problem. Why not ask him for return fares to Honolulu and to finance whatever research they conducted here or on the way back? Wilder warmed to this idea. They began to figure out how much each of them would need for expenses in addition to transportation. Kenneth came up with a sum of $375. Wilder advised him to double it to $750. They agreed that Kenneth should sound Kellum out about their plan.

On Monday, January 4, Kenneth went back to the *Kaimiloa* to clean up the darkroom. Kellum, friendly and affable, talked vaguely of cruising through the Tuamotus to the northeast, then back to Honolulu. Kenneth explained to him that the scientists felt Tahiti offered as fertile a field for research as Samoa, especially for himself. If Kellum were to sponsor this work they could all fulfill their obligations to the museum without continuing the cruise. The owner of the *Kaimiloa* appeared not only relieved but grateful.

Ball met him to work out the details the next day. Kellum's generosity blossomed once more now that he wasn't required to sit around and twiddle his thumbs while scientists collected rubbish. Kenneth went with him to the Banque de L'Indo-Chine to have a deposit made in his name.

"You think you'll need $750?" asked Kellum.

"Yes, sir."

"We'd better double that," said Kellum, and wrote a check for $1,500.

The next day the owner of the *Kaimiloa* fired his captain, the first mate, and a tutor. They invited the jubilant scientists to an "indignation party" that night. But Kellum hired them back the next morning. Kenneth and Arm collected their gear from the ship and settled in at Hotel du Port. On Saturday, January 10, the once-a-month mail boat arrived. He spent the next two days scribbling letters of explanation. He wrote Gregory the following:

> I do not see that there could have been a more favorable outcome, under the circumstances, than the present plan. Mr. Kellum will subsidize our work over the period of time which would have been taken by the cruise. We can accomplish more this way than by having a small company of scientists travel on a yacht bent solely on pleasure and guided by a very genial man who has no interest in or understanding of the actual field work which needs to be done . . .
>
> I am going to stay here for at least three months before returning to Honolulu. Then I hope to return by such a way that I may at least see the principal groups of Polynesia, excepting the Marquesas. . . . Sperry will keep me company but he will be on his own and pay his own expenses except when I need his help on a trip. Papeete will be my base and I expect to go out even to some of the Tuamotu Islands. I shall watch the trading schooners and adjust movements accordingly.

Now Kenneth had all of French Polynesia to explore, islands that only a lucky few scientists had studied: Moorea, Huahine, Bora-Bora, Raiatea. Every morning when he awoke he said aloud, "thank God I'm still here."

Chapter Sixteen

Ashore in Paradise

A steamer bound for San Francisco sailed from Papeete on Tuesday, January 13, 1925, with Kenneth's letters, Dr. Ball, Rogers, and Med Kellum's two tutors on board. Kenneth watched them go without a qualm, impatient to begin his great adventure. He was twenty-seven years old, single, and exactly where he had always wanted to be. His experience in Haleakala, Lanai, and Nihoa and Necker qualified him in a unique way to work in Tahiti. He would be the first archaeologist to survey the ruins of French Polynesia. That was the goal he set for himself.

Kenneth and Arm decided to keep their rooms at the Hotel du Port and take their meals at Hotel Diadem, the finest in town. With $1,500 in the bank, Kenneth could afford it. The daily cost totaled 32.47 francs ($1.50) for both food and lodging.

Arm immediately began sketching. Kenneth wrote a letter to Edward Handy, asking his help and advice, to go out on the next mail boat. He developed photos on board the *Kaimiloa* one day, hiked into Fautaua Valley behind Papeete to search for ruins the next, and, a few days later, lunched with Frank Stimson, an American fluent in both French and Tahitian. Stimson worked as an accountant at Maxwell's Store, had a degree in architecture, and knew Handy and other Bayard Dominick scientists from their trips to the South Seas. He was compiling a Tahitian grammar. As an old Tahiti hand, he collected artifacts and possessed a rich fund of knowledge about island history, legends, schooners, and native women. Kenneth was surprised to find such a first-rate mind in Papeete.

Rain made quagmires of Tahiti's dirt roads and kept Kenneth on a leash within a few miles of town all during January. On sunny days he got out his camera to photograph petroglyphs in a nearby valley and the stone god in Stimson's collection. Kenneth had to find another darkroom when the *Kaimiloa* began sailing back and forth between Tahiti and Moorea. Kellum bought a valley on Moorea for Med, who was now engaged to Gladys Laughlin. The landlord at Hotel du Port made no objection to Kenneth's photographic activity, so he installed some pans and the printer in his room. On Tuesday, January 27, he wrote in his diary, "Fixed motion picture drying rack and camera. Finished reading *The Dude Wrangler*. Drank too much white wine at Diadem."

When rain kept him indoors, Kenneth studied French. A young lady named Natalie Drollet gave him lessons. She was pretty and charming but he had no illusions. Natalie's cap was set for Armstrong Sperry. Nevertheless, until the rain stopped and he could comb the island for ruins, Natalie's lessons occupied Kenneth's time more productively and at less cost than white wine at the Diadem.

Kenneth's pace picked up on February 6 when he bought a purple bicycle just unloaded from a French steamer in from Bordeaux. Then he learned that the steamer *Hauraki*, on her way to San Francisco, was due in five hours. Kenneth had letters to get on her before she sailed. He jumped on the new purple bicycle and pedaled for the hotel. Mrs. Selover, wife of an American copra trader in Papeete, flagged him down. She said she was hurrying to get clothes together for her husband in case he decided to run up to the Tuamotus.

"Whether he goes or not depends if he can find a companion," she explained. "Could you go?"

"I'd like nothing better," said Kenneth.

"They sail at eleven o'clock."

"But it's nine o'clock now."

"That's why I'm in such a hurry."

"I can't possibly make it by eleven," Kenneth told her. I have a museum report and letters to write."

Kenneth pedaled on to the hotel with less enthusiasm than before. The atolls of the Tuamotu group were poor relations of French Polynesia, sparsely populated and economically unrewarding because of their remoteness. They were so inaccessible that libraries in museums contained little more on the Tuamotus than a few accounts by missionaries and explorers. None of the Bayard Dominick scientists had been there. Why did such a rare opportunity have to come on mail day?

He settled himself to finish his report to Gregory. At 10 A.M. a note arrived from Selover urging Kenneth to see him in his office. It would only take a few minutes. The copra trader had met archaeologist Robert Aitken on his way to the Australs and knew how to tempt a young scientist.

"We're only to be gone a week," he said smoothly. "We are sailing on the fastest schooner out of Papeete. You'll have a chance to size up the Tuamotus which will help you in any plans you make later to visit those islands. It won't cost you anything. I'd like to have some company."

This time Kenneth didn't refuse. With Arm's help he packed a few clothes, a camera and notebooks, and ran for the quay. An hour later he was sitting with Selover on the cabin roof of a small, two-masted schooner, *Tiare Faniu*, sailing out of the lagoon and feeling quite satisfied with himself.

Only the first page of the journal he kept on this voyage has survived. A brief entry in his diary on February 7, 1925, reads, "Off Kaukura [atoll]. Fine weather. Made six knots. Sighted the island at 11 P.M. by moonlight." The next day, "Came up to the island at daybreak. Landed at Kai Tahiti." Photos Kenneth took at Kaukura show an untidy village of native houses with tin roofs. The *Tiare Faniu* sailed at noon for nearby Arutua (atoll), where Selover had another store, and arrived at 3 P.M. Selover finished his business the following afternoon. They sailed back to Kaukura that night and spent the next day fishing with a villager named Mahinui before sailing back to Tahiti on February 11.

Kenneth made no discoveries on this sightseeing trip. He didn't have time to look for ruins. But the voyage introduced him to and gave him confidence in the mode of travel he would have to use in this remote part of the world—schooners commanded and crewed by Tahitians. He also learned how to survive by himself on an atoll, by living with the people of the island. "The natives fed and housed us while we were there," he said later. "They invited me to stay."

Heavy rains kept him in Papeete during February. His social life suffered from a different constraint—his lack of French. Evenings with the Drollet family, calls on the Wilders, and luncheons with visiting Americans hardly matched his social calendar in Honolulu. We can assume that he accepted gratefully an invitation to the fancy costume ball, sponsored by an athletic club, on February 21 in the Palais Theatre.

The Palais Theatre did not live up to its elegant name. This social gathering place was a large wooden barn-like building that would have been called a dance hall in a less-imaginative community. However, Kenneth knew from the ball there in January that adornments of leafy boughs and branches, and decorative bows and colorful streamers could make a lot of difference. More important, it was a place to meet beautiful young ladies of wit and intelligence. Daughters from the best families in Papeete would attend the ball.

Kenneth had discovered that Tahiti's reputation for friendly females was deceptive. Oh, it was easy enough to acquire a live-in companion; Quinn's saloon, famous throughout the Pacific, provided Tahitian women in all shapes and sizes. But the desirable daughters of respectable families did not associate with the patrons of Quinn's—sailors and beachcombers and other riffraff. The thirty-five-year-old woman who tended the desk at Hotel du Port took a personal interest in Kenneth, teasing him in French with a phrase that taught him something about culture values when he finally learned what it meant, "Do you have an erection?" He was not ready for such a direct approach. And getting to know a proper young lady required an introduction.

His diary entry for Saturday, February 21, reads, "Called on Wilders A.M. Had [developing] tray made and worked on costume P.M. Developed pictures. Evening; fancy dress ball. Went as pirate." The best reason for choosing a costume so out of tune with his personality seems to be that it was easy to assemble: a pair of ragged pants, shirt open at the neck, bandana tied rakishly over the brow, and his hunting knife thrust inside a sash at his waist.

The Palais Theatre teemed with the cream of Papeete society in homemade costumes inspired by exotic civilizations near and far. On the bandstand a violin, piano, guitar, and oboe provided toe-tapping music. But an obstacle barred Kenneth's introduction to the young ladies of Papeete: local residents all sat on one side of the Palais Theatre while foreigners all sat on the other.

A dark, regal beauty costumed as Nefertiti immediately captured Kenneth's interest from an archaeological point of view, Egyptian excavations being much in the news. She danced gracefully with Carl Curtis, a visitor from New York of Kenneth's age and acquaintance. Her golden slippers tripped lightly in time to the music. She was vivacious and slim and quite beautiful. Kenneth had admired her from afar as he ate his lunch on the veranda of Hotel Diadem, while she dined alone or with a distinguished older man in a private room. Kenneth had assumed that this entrancing creature was married to a French official. Now he was not so sure.

The music stopped and Curtis escorted Nefertiti to the foreigner's side of the Palais Theatre to introduce his mother. As they chatted, Curtis walked away leaving Nefertiti stranded among the foreigners. Here was Kenneth's chance. He grabbed his friend's arm to find out if she was married. She was not. Kenneth demanded an introduction. Nefertiti smiled thoughtfully at the pirate, her dark eyes appraising, as they met. She accepted his invitation to dance. The straps on one of her slippers broke. She kicked them both off in a carefree gesture. About that time, Kenneth's hunting knife slipped from his sash to the floor and nearly cut off her toe.

Their attempts to communicate presented a more serious problem. Kenneth tried English. That didn't work very well. She tried French. That didn't work any better. Her rapid Tahitian made his Hawaiian sound awkward and slow. Nevertheless, he now knew her name, Marguerite, and was determined to learn a great deal more about her. He was unaware that she, and every young lady in Papeete, already knew quite a lot about him.

It was common knowledge to Marguerite that her dancing partner had arrived on the luxury yacht *Kaimiloa*, whose owner was married to Elizabeth Carnegie. Such information routinely passed by word of mouth with electronic speed. She also knew that two young Americans from the yacht, a tall one and a short one, ate at the Hotel Diadem. The short one, she had heard, played the accordion, the tall one a guitar. This one was tall. Therefore, he must be the guitar player.

"Do you like Hawaiian music?" he asked.

"Oh, no," she confessed. "It is too mournful."

The guitar player explained that he lived in Hawaii. Marguerite was much too polite to ask his profession. She was not trying to catch a man, although the shy manner of this American appealed to her. Besides, her best friend, Chiffon, wanted to meet the tall guitar player. Marguerite remembered exactly how she had learned of Chiffon's interest in the American. It was when the doctor had hurried by the dressmaking shop of Chiffon's mother with word of a suicide down the street. A Chinese storekeeper there kept two wives, a Chinese and a Tahitian. The Chinese wife, despondent over her husband's preference for the Tahitian wife, had killed herself. Marguerite and Chiffon were hurrying to the scene when they saw the two Americans walking in the opposite direction and Chiffon had confessed that she would like to meet the tall one.

Kenneth was not aware of these complications. The woman in his arms danced like a dream. She was charming, poised, and very feminine. The music ended much too soon. As a leading belle of Papeete, Marguerite was in constant demand as a dancing partner. She introduced him to her friend, Chiffon, who was agreeable and attractive. But it was not Chiffon with whom Kenneth wanted to dance. He waited his turn until Marguerite was free again, then pounced. He danced with her as often as possible until 3 A.M. when a photographer took a group picture of the guests in costume—at least those still on their feet. The next day Kenneth wrote in his diary, "Home at daylight. Slept all day."

He revived in time to motor halfway around the island to Taravau on Monday. It was his first glimpse of the Tahitian countryside and it enchanted him. Every few miles they came upon a Chinese store and a church set amid a cluster of Tahitian houses, some thatched, some with tin roofs. Pigs and dogs and chickens wandered about. He passed through grove after grove of coconut palms planted in orderly rows for the production of copra. Kenneth saw bananas and bread-fruit and mangos and taro growing in luxurious profusion. Oxen driven by Chinese worked rice paddies.

At Mahaiatea they turned off the road to a point overlooking the sea where, shrouded in underbrush, Kenneth found a temple ruin described by Captain Cook during a journey around the island in 1769. The Tahitian name for such a temple was *marae*. This one rose in stair-step platforms of beautifully rounded stones set one upon the other in a great pyramid. Valleys cut into the interior made him itch to explore on foot. If the stories he had heard were true, these valleys were thick with ruins.

Then it began to rain again, scuttling a plan to visit Raiatea, one of the Leeward Islands to the northwest. Kenneth's diary entry for Thursday, February 26, reads, "Cloudy and rainy. Worked on motion picture film and studied French in A.M. Promenade with Mlle. Ture." Since Marguerite's last name is spelled Thuret, we know from his phonetic spelling that Kenneth at least pronounced it right with the last syllable accented.

We also know that the couple did not promenade alone. Marguerite would not dream of walking with a strange man unaccompanied by a chaperone. Such things weren't done by a young lady of her social position. Her father, after all, was a French official of considerable standing and seniority in the judicial system. Kenneth, therefore, was stuck with Chiffon and several other young ladies whether he liked it or not. They chatted briskly in rapid French, as unintelligible to him as Esperanto.

He explained as best he could his interest in ruins and artifacts and Polynesian culture. This was not a subject that Marguerite had been taught was important. Her father had sent her to be educated in Paris where she had spent ten years, leaving her Tahitian mother behind. In France, with cousins and a seamstress aunt, Marguerite had acquired the female accomplishments: sewing, dancing, competence in classical piano, an infallible taste in clothing, correct speech, and decorum. During her absence her mother had died. Now Marguerite considered Paris her home although she was living with Papa in Papeete at the moment. Kenneth's enthusiasm for things Polynesian seemed to her no more strange than the hobbies of other foreigners in Tahiti. When he mentioned that he planned to photograph thatched houses on Sunday, she invited his American friend and him to the thatched beach house she and her friends rented for weekend parties.

It is not clear whether Kenneth's incentive that day was to get pictures of native thatching or to be with Marguerite. She came by in a carriage with her girlfriends. Arm apparently went with them but Kenneth rode his new purple bicycle in case he might have to pedal on to a village at Faaa in search of thatched roofing. The cottage on the beach satisfied him. Soon he discarded the camera for his guitar. He and Arm, on the accordion, serenaded the lively Tahitian ladies who were chaperoned by Chiffon's mother and Marguerite's father. The ribald Tahitians songs the Americans sang made Marguerite glance nervously at her father. Papa Thuret took it all in stride.

With sunshine drying the roads, Kenneth extended his range for recording the survival of Tahitian culture. The next day he rode his bicycle "to native village A.M. Canoe makers P.M." The day after, "Sunny. Read Macmillan Brown's book, *Mystery of the Pacific,* half thru. Read *Raiatea La Sacree.* Out on bike to canoes. Developed in evening."

By this time Chiffon had accepted her permanent demotion to chaperone for Marguerite and Kenneth when he came courting at the downtown dressmaking shop of Chiffon's mother, Mrs. Assaud, in the afternoon. The shop served also as a convenient headquarters for Marguerite's friends when not under the watchful eyes of their fathers at home. For Kenneth it was like coming to call on a sorority meeting. He was never alone with Marguerite. When he bought her an ice cream he had to treat all of her chaperones. Yet he kept coming back to do it again.

She became almost a daily item in his diary. On Wednesday, March 4, "Printed pictures, a rainy day. At 5:30 [the] girls called. Went to dinner with them at [the] Tiare [Hotel]." On Thursday, March 5, "Had lunch with Marguerite. Out to graveyard valley A.M. and to canoe builders P.M." On Sunday, March 8, "Wrote letters all day except for some time in P.M. at Assauds with Marguerite." On Monday, March 9, "Mail in from Samoa. Wrote letters. Strolled in the evening with Marguerite."

The mail boat brought letters from Honolulu. There was one from Dr. Cooke, the shell expert acting as director of the Bishop Museum while Gregory taught at Yale. Cooke wrote that Ball had returned. "I believe that your stay in the south will be beneficial to the museum as there is a lot there you can accomplish," the letter read. ". . . I find that very little work has been done on [the Leeward] Islands and for the good of the museum I think that a series of shells should be collected on all the islands that you visit. . . . Some species of shells were carried by the Polynesians in their migrations so such material as you find may be another link in the chain."

The mail boat also carried letters back to Honolulu. Kenneth typed three pages to Gregory:

Young Med is now the owner of the great and most beautiful valley of Opunohu on Moorea and plans to be back with his bride in May to work the land for copra and vanilla. The *Kaimiloa* was nearly wrecked there. . . . A storm came up at three in the morning and she dragged anchor till she grounded. It was more than twenty-four hours before they succeeded in getting her off. She must be in the Marquesas by now and she should be in Honolulu about the first of April.

I am shipping a large Tahitian canoe on her, and in the chest which I am sending my father are the negatives of the photographs taken on the way down, selected and arranged for the museum album and with the labels containing full and valuable data, typed and ready to paste in the album. He will deliver them to you.

I would like to be home in August to see you before you return East.

For two months Kenneth and Arm waited for storms to subside so they might visit the Leeward Islands of French Polynesia. Finally, at 6 P.M. on March 10, 1925, they sailed on a small steamer. This time Kenneth left the bulky Edison recorder behind. He brought with him his bicycle, cameras, notebooks, a tape measure, and the book he was reading, *Raiatea La Sacrée*. The steamer landed them at 4 P.M. the next day at a place called Uturoa inside the reef on the island of Raiatea, the administrative capital of the leeward group about one hundred miles west by north of Tahiti. For the old Polynesians the island had been a religious center. Here autos were still a novelty. The only visitors who had reason to stop here were French government officials and businessmen. Accommodations for them at Pepe Feroni's Hotel des Allies in Uturoa made the Hotel du Port in Papeete seem like Buckingham Palace. Kenneth loved every minute of it. He was making his way to the heart of the South Seas.

The steamer turned back at Raiatea, but at 11 A.M. the next day Kenneth and Arm continued their adventure on a schooner bound for an island still more remote, Bora-Bora, on the northwest horizon. Wind and rain had eroded the island's volcanic skyline into wild and magnificent shapes. They disembarked at 3 P.M. and set out on their bicycles. "Sped out many miles," Kenneth wrote in his diary.

Bora-Bora was the South Seas he had hoped to find. The dirt road wound along the shore through groves of coconut palms. Seaward the lagoon lay in placid shades of pastel, water lapping the immaculate beaches with little liquid whispers. The sound of surf, lashing the reef in mighty fury on the far side of the lagoon, reached this shore as a soft, musical drumming.

Yet Kenneth had to be careful not to be distracted because the winding road was pitted with potholes that would bend the front wheel of his bicycle if he ran over one. Holes also pitted the sandy soil like a mine field on both sides of the road. He soon saw why. Huge, red land crabs scuttled into the holes when the travelers came close.

They passed brown-skinned girls washing clothes in streams and women who tended cooking fires in the yard. Men dressed in the *pareu* walked along the road with carrying poles slung across sturdy shoulders, bananas or coconuts or taro dangling from either end of their poles. When Kenneth stopped to chat in Tahitian, the elders directed boys to shinny up coconut trees and send down drinking nuts, husked on the spot and opened with a few expert whacks of a machete.

Since there was no hotel on Bora-Bora, Arm led them to the home of an acquaintance from his first visit, a white man who had married into a Tahitian family. The family received them with warm hospitality as if they were being honored by having guests. The next day Kenneth and Arm moved into an empty one-room cottage to stay as long as they wished.

But Tahitian hospitality had its pitfalls. Family members and neighbors entered the house to examine the visitors and their belongings as casually as they extended food and shelter. They seemed to have no concept of privacy or ownership. Kenneth's illustrated book, *Raiatea La Sacrée*, attracted droves of guests who passed it from hand to hand discussing the pictures. After the first day, Friday, March 13, Kenneth wrote in his diary, "We were swamped with natives until 5:30 A.M." On Saturday he wrote, "Another day when natives in the house made it impossible to stay there. Saw heiaus and petroglyph rocks." Kenneth began photographing and measuring.

On Monday he learned that a cutter, the *Teawaroa*, would sail the next day for Maupiti, a tiny island on the outer edge of French Polynesia that was so remote only one white man lived there. Arm warned Kenneth that if he missed the *Teawaroa* on her return trip he might wait six months before another vessel put in at Maupiti. That only made the trip more exciting. This time he kept a journal in a ruled, primary school composition book. The journal began on the morning of departure:

Tuesday, March 17, 1925—At five o'clock I was called to go to the boat for Maupiti. Arm went with me. The little one-masted boat . . . was to take Terii [a fellow passenger] to see his wife. [The vessel also] carried a woman passenger with two children, two men, a girl, the captain and his son, and myself. The dawn was pink and glorious.

We moved very slowly out of the lagoon. As we entered the pass for the great ocean, all heads were bared while Terii gave a long prayer. The wind held light until we were way out [and] rain squalls gave us frequent spurts. . . . The girl played an accordion and the time went most pleasantly . . .

At three o'clock [in the afternoon] we were off two coral islets to the south of Maupiti. They stand on each side of its narrow [harbor] entrance, flat coral islets covered with coconuts. This pass is often very dangerous, the waves breaking on both sides leaving only a few yards of deep water. This evening it was quite peaceful and we glided without difficulty into the channel. In the protection of the isles we had scarcely a breath of air. Terii gave a prayer of thanksgiving as soon as we made the entrance. Gradually we moved up to the mountain at the base of which are the villages of Maupiti.

It was after sunset when we came up to the dock which we could see was crowded with natives—hundreds of them. They say there are four hundred here. After we landed at the missionary house, there were more prayers. I had dinner with them and then was led to the house of the captain where I was to stay. It was the last word in unsanitation but they gave me their best, a great bed with one dirty sheet. The mosquitoes were in swarms. There was no water with which to wash. But I got through the night.

Kenneth spent the next day hiking around the island with two teenagers named Tane and Manuela, five-year-old Tewaki, and "the kids." He found a species of ground shell. "We ate coconuts, mangoes, bananas all the way," he wrote. On Tuesday, March 19, Kenneth confessed in his journal that he still suffered from lack of privacy:

For the first time since I left Vaitape, Bora Bora. . . . Tuesday morning, I have managed to escape the natives for a few moments to myself. I am up on the slopes of the mountain on the edge of a vanilla plantation clearing. It is a fair day. The weather has been so since we departed from Papeete two weeks ago. The surf booms and froths on the great encircling reef. Within are the emerald green and deep blue colors of the sheltered water.

This morning we were to walk around the islands, starting at six o'clock. But at six, there was no sign of breakfast and the two boys in the house who were to go with me were still asleep. At seven we were ready to go but friends of my host came in to see "the book," *Raiatea La Sacree* by Paul Hugenin, in which there are many illustrations from photographs, paintings and sketches. The scenes and people are quite familiar to these people. There is a sketch of this island.

The hiking party got started at eight o'clock but the people they were supposed to meet had gotten tired of waiting so were no longer at the appointed place. Yet Kenneth's enthusiasm never flagged for the remains he found of old Polynesia still in use by living people.

It was a delight to see so many purely native houses. Some are resting directly on *paepaes* [stone platforms], others are on stilts. There are two or three meeting houses that have earth floors strewn with grass and then mats [over the cushion of grass]. Two *paepaes*, at least, are of cut coral blocks. There are two great canoe sheds where a large wooden boat is being built.

The party stopped to pick *tiare* flowers, to pause for views of the lagoon, to eat mangos and bananas and sugar cane, and to hustle by places known to be inhabited by *tupopau* (ghosts). The children also gave a wide berth to the ruins of two *marae* along the way. Halfway around the island they caught up with the guide they were supposed to be walking with. The man knew a story about every prominent rock and cave and promontory on the island, each the embodiment of a supernatural lizard or dog or canoe or pig. Kenneth scribbled it all down in his journal.

At noon we were back in the village and I had to take pictures of natives as usual. Demands to have their pictures taken were insistent. As some were friends of my host, I did not want to refuse them. The Handys have been so well remembered because of the things they did for the people that I wish to keep up the good name of our people—the Popaa [Caucasians] from Vaihi [Hawaii].

A new problem confronted Kenneth when, on Sunday, March 22, he found himself without his pants; they had become so dirty his hostess demanded to wash them.

I would like to go out but I have no trousers. I let the madame of the house have them [to wash] just before supper last night and since I have had to keep to the *pareu*. At night I don't mind wearing it. But as it keeps unloosening, I am afraid of it daytimes. Still it is most comfortable.

As usual the natives came over this morning to pore over my book, *Raiatea La Sacree*. It will be in tatters soon. They come and take it out of my travelling case without any concern.

Kenneth had discovered how insecure a *pareu* can be when he had gone out with the length of cloth wound around his hips a couple of turns and tucked in at the waist. He had hurried down the road with a group of young people to see what was reported to be a fight. All they had found was an *are'are'a*, dandies of the village prancing about in a circle in time to an accordion and harmonicas. Later he wrote about it in his journal:

> Tetane tried to stir them up. A few girls finally joined in the dance, *pae ere*, in which the natives shuffle in a circle about the players and at every other measure stop to *ori* or wiggle . . . but there was not much life to it compared to what Sperry and I had seen on Bora Bora.
>
> I had on Chinese slippers and my *pareu*. . . . They all wanted me to join the dance. As I had already been initiated at Bora Bora I did, greatly to their amusement [because his *pareu* kept coming loose].
>
> I am the first white visitor since the Handys were here three years ago. To be sure there is a white man here, Walinoski, but he is not liked, and keeps entirely to himself. I have not gone to see him because I would rather be with the natives entirely.

It is clear from Kenneth's journal that he became daily more fascinated by the people he had come to study. He described a guessing game by moonlight on the porch of the house where he stayed. The players made up conundrums to be solved by their opponents, a Tahitian version of Twenty Questions. "Here these natives showed nimble wits," Kenneth wrote in his journal. "The guesses at answers flow [rapidly], and one guessing contest was over in a minute. They showed the greatest animation in this and got keen amusement out of it. . . . I tried to follow their talk but in vain. The answers I could make out in most cases but the riddle made no sense. . . . There is always a pun on words."

Sometimes the Tahitians exasperated him by their thoughtlessness. "I had collected a lot of tiny shells," he wrote. "But a fresh young native, when I showed her what I had collected, said they were no good and slapped the box to the ground. I lost every one of these shells. Needless to say, I was mad. As it was impossible to explain why I should care for such invisible, dirty shells, I had to hold my peace."

He ate the foods of the island: taro, *pia* (tapioca), and always *iaota* or raw fish dipped in *mitihaari*, a coconut sauce. Watching how skillfully the Tahitians used the materials of their environment gave him keen pleasure. "Tane collected two ripe *fara* fruits [in the mountains] and transported them in an ingenious way," Kenneth wrote. "He took the stem and leaves of a *ti* plant and used each leaf for the warp element of a basket. For the woof he used *more*, the bark of the hibiscus. Inserting the individual fruits of the *fara*, he tied the *ti* leaves together and had a fine carrying basket."

His Tahitian improved to the point where he felt confident about asking for information. Every hour his knowledge grew because he recorded everything he saw and heard. For example, he discovered that the style of natives houses was not static but still was evolving. "They speak of a time when the houses were on the ground [not on stilts] as many of them still are. Half the dwelling houses of native style rest on the ground; twenty-nine on piles, twenty-nine on the ground. . . . The five meeting houses are on the ground."

As he became more familiar with the relationships around him, Kenneth began to understand their subtleties. On Tuesday, March 24, he described the method of calling on a young lady:

> This evening I called on Maehaa, a young native girl who helped the Handy's much. The method of calling is this: you say you are going for a stroll. You walk aimlessly along. Everyone asks you where you are going and you stop to talk many times, ending by saying you are going to the store.
>
> The kids pick this up and, lured by the prospect of cigaret butts, begin to assemble. In the region in which you have seen the one you wish to see —you never know which house as they live in different houses at different times—you stop and talk to some of the old natives.
>
> Presently on the porch of one of the nearest houses a kerosene lamp is placed and the kids call out, "Come, come, here is Maehaa." She is there, sure enough, and you have never said a word about coming or that you wanted to see her. The kids know because they have seen you give her an extra cigaret, perhaps. Nothing escapes their omnipresent eyes.
>
> There is no privacy whatever. You sit on the opposite side of the blinding lamp and everyone comes to talk and see. This evening I was treated to a display of the *fai* [cat's cradles] which were given [shown] to the Handys. Maehaa played the accordion. As the evening wore on, the others were satisfied that they had talked enough and you were left alone with the person on whom you have called. The others drop[ped] off to sleep on the verandah."

The next day the *Teawaroa* set sail on her return voyage to Bora-Bora. This time the tiny sailboat with an uncertain engine would be tacking back and forth into the southeast trade wind instead of sailing with it. Kenneth's journal describes the preparations for their departure:

> The praying took an hour. First hymns were sung. I [was about] to enter the house where the prayers were being held with a *lei* around my neck but was warned in time that it was a great sacrilege to keep flowers on when at prayer. We shook hands silently with all the old people.
>
> Another cutter sailed at the same time as ourselves. We followed it out of the narrow passage through the reef which yesterday was a rip with the tide, and waves breaking. Today great swells were breaking on both sides. The cutter ahead tossed up and down in the channel. We prayed our way through. On the other boat we could hear them singing hymns. Our captain betrayed his nervousness, in spite of our prayers, by clearing his throat often and looking anxiously about. The wind held strong and we sailed clear of all the rough water to the ocean.

Then the tedious part of the journey began, tacking back and forth against the wind to Bora-Bora which lay tantalizingly close the whole time. The rough sea made Kenneth vomit. It was sunrise the next day before the *Teawaroa* began to maneuver for the pass in the reef, and three hours more before the boat moored at the dock. "Arm was there to meet me," Kenneth wrote. "And Patiatia had my bicycle ready. He had guessed when I would come back because he had watched the sea and knew the conditions on Maupiti. . . . On the way over, Bau and others would not drink beer because 'God was on the boat.' There was no liquor of any kind on Maupiti, quite the reverse of Borabora."

Now began a strenuous ten days of uninterrupted work. It was as if his taste of living with the Polynesians on Maupiti had taught him to ignore their distractions. The day after he returned he photographed two petroglyph boulders a quarter of a mile inland at Vaiati. One of the boulders was called *ofai honu*, the turtle stone, and was believed by the old people to be the mythical parent of the island and its chiefs. The next day he concentrated on Anau Bay, a scenic cove ringed with stone ruins overgrown by jungle.

Here he found seven *marae*, including two that were the best-preserved on Bora-Bora. For the next four days Kenneth measured these ruins. He had already noticed that the architecture of *marae* he had seen so far on Tahiti was different from those on both Maupiti and Bora-Bora. An outstanding feature of *marae* on Tahiti was the stepped pyramid construction of fitted volcanic stone laid up to an imposing height. Yet in the Leeward Islands the great *marae* were built of enormous limestone slabs cut from the reef.

What did these differences mean? There was limestone to windward and volcanic stone to leeward. Yet each group of islands chose a different building material and a different method of building construction. Sir Joseph Banks, the English naturalist who sailed with Captain Cook, attributed these differences in architecture to their comparative antiquity. He believed the cruder-looking *marae* of the Leeward Islands to be older than those on Tahiti to windward. There could be other explanations. Perhaps the Tahitians on the Leeward Islands had migrated from a different place or by a different route than those of the Windward Islands and had brought along a different concept of the *marae*.

But from where? There were local variations in temple construction all over Polynesia that defied attempts to connect them by migration routes. Hawaiian temples were different from Tahitian ones, even different from those on nearby Nihoa and Necker. Most different of all were the huge stone statues at Easter Island, which seemed unconnected with anywhere else in Polynesia. What did it all mean?

Kenneth's motivation may have been a growing realization that he had come to grips with a major anthropological mystery. By the time he and Arm caught a schooner to Raiatea at dawn on Monday, April 6, he had measured fifteen ruins and recorded more than one hundred place names on Bora-Bora. There were many more ruins than he had anticipated, so many, in fact, that he knew he had not seen them all.

At Raiatea they found that the steamer *Pasteur* would not be in for a week. Kenneth and Arm took passage on a schooner that went on the reef at Huahine for a nervous hour before the rising tide floated them free. "All day moving at painful pace," Kenneth wrote in his diary on Friday, April 10. They docked at Papeete at 9 A.M. the next day as a mail steamer arrived.

That meant letters to write. His return to Papeete also meant evening strolls with Marguerite. He was able to express himself in Tahitian now. And to understand her. He learned that she would soon return to France. She listened to his plans to sail home via New Zealand. They were both strangers in paradise. The improbability of their meeting at all added poignancy to each promenade together. The moments with her, despite the intrusion of chattering chaperones, were the most stimulating of his day.

He spent almost a week developing and printing the photos he had taken on the Leeward Islands. At dinner with Stimson, the accountant, on Sunday, April 19, Kenneth described his discoveries on the Leeward Islands. They talked about *marae* architecture. Stimson was not much interested in stones but he knew quite a bit about the genealogies of the chiefs who had built *marae*. He was a mine of information and Kenneth went away full of ideas.

Kenneth awoke the next morning to watch a steamer bound for France anchor in the lagoon at Papeete. This was the vessel on which Marguerite had booked passage. It seemed incredible that time had passed so quickly. He had already been three and a half months in Tahiti, a time so rich and rewarding that he felt he had come home. Now he realized how much Marguerite had added to this experience. The prospect of her departure, before they had hardly become acquainted, appalled him. Maybe he could talk her out of it.

That evening he explained as clearly as he could with his limited vocabulary that he wanted very much to know her better. Would she consider turning in her ticket so they would have a chance to become better acquainted? Marguerite said she would. Kenneth walked back to his rooming house on the waterfront feeling very pleased with himself.

Chapter Seventeen

Marguerite

When Marguerite told her father that she wanted to turn in her ticket, he protested in French, "But it's already paid for." She answered firmly, "Cash it." Having thus committed herself at home she had now to deal with her friends: Chiffon, Muriel, Lulu, and Mimi. We can assume that they received the news with the interest it deserved because nowhere in the world are love affairs followed with such devoted attention to detail as in Papeete. In Marguerite's case, especially, the American newcomer represented a fascinating counterpoint to heartbreak.

Her friends knew, although Kenneth did not at the time, that the great love of Marguerite's life was a South Sea prince whose marriage had already been arranged. She had lost her heart to him during his stay in Tahiti. On his departure she had gone into decline, eating so little that her weight loss worried everyone. Perhaps this American was the antidote she needed.

Certainly Ahnt-Ahnt, another suitor, was not the answer, although he was well educated and handsome enough in his white linen jackets that set off his black skin. Ahnt-Ahnt was a judge, rather self-important, one of the French colonial officials called *tia tia* by Marguerite and her friends. Like all *tia tia*, Ahnt-Ahnt came from the island of Martinique. Ahnt-Ahnt ate at the Hotel Diadem, took a proprietary interest in Marguerite, and did not approve of Kenneth. One day he said to her, "You know these Americans, they come and they go." She retorted briskly, "And they return."

The truth is, Marguerite had never met anyone like Kenneth. He used an approach with which she was entirely unfamiliar—artlessness. His shy, ingenious manner appealed to her. She found herself wanting to help him. Other things about him annoyed her, such as the manicure set he brought as a gift. She never colored her nails. Besides, men in Tahiti gave women presents like that in return for favors received. She could only excuse Kenneth on the grounds that he was an American and didn't know better.

Kenneth, when he wasn't trying to get acquainted with Marguerite, developed and printed photos taken on Bora-Bora, and studied French. Time was slipping away at an incredible rate. The steamer schedules made it worse. He dispatched a cable to Gregory about it. When the mail boat arrived on May 2, he dropped everything to write letters.

The letter to Gregory, describing his dilemma in detail, is dated May 3, 1925. Kenneth explained that he wanted to return in August in time to see the director before he departed for Yale. He also hoped to squeeze in a trip to New Zealand on the way home. The *Tofua* sailed there and on to Fiji and Samoa where he could catch an Oceanic liner to Honolulu. But he didn't want to leave before the June 27 sailing of the *Tofua*, and old Tahiti hands had warned him that he might miss his connection if he cut it that close. If he didn't, it would mean sacrificing his plans for fieldwork. Kenneth added that he and Sperry were ready to sail for Raiatea, Huahine, and Tahaa on a twenty-day trip. Then he'd come back, develop his photographs, and see Sperry off for home.

The letter rambled. Additions between lines and spelling errors show that it was written hurriedly. It is no wonder. Like everyone else in Papeete, Kenneth had gotten into the habit of cleaning up all of his correspondence in one great burst of energy after the mail boat arrived and before it sailed, usually two days later. The Tahitians liked the system because arriving mail could be answered immediately, then the whole dreary affair forgotten for another month. Everybody was so busy writing letters that business came to a standstill when the mail boat arrived. People flocked to town from the country, even from across the channel on Moorea, to pick up mail and scribble answers before returning home. This grand literary holiday centered around Papeete's charming two-story, New-England-style post office where everyone gathered to gossip. Kenneth wrote thirty-three letters before the boat sailed.

He spent Monday evening, May 4, with Marguerite and set out the next day for Huahine and Raiatea, this time without Armstrong Sperry. The Christian family, descendants of *Bounty* mutineers, took him in at Uturoa on Raiatea. The clan included brothers of Kenneth's age and a sister, Elsie, who showed him ruins. He plunged happily into a bout of measuring and photographing the great *marae* of Taputapuatea.

Legends designated this immense, eerie place as the principal temple of Oro, the great Tahitian war god. Sir Joseph Banks, who sailed with Captain Cook, saw a roasted hog and a fish on the altar in 1768, as well as eight human lower jawbones hanging with a large canoe model in a house nearby. Smaller houses protected woven sennit images of the gods themselves.

Natives of the district of Opoa told Kenneth that human skulls and bones at one time were scattered through the whole length of the immense *ahu* (platform). He had never seen so large an *ahu* of its type, a long rectangle faced with giant slabs of limestone that stood up to ten feet above the ground in a wall that measured 141 feet long. A low altar, twelve feet long, nestled under the great platform. Both overlooked a rough, open-air court paved with coral pebbles and basalt blocks that extended 150 feet from the *ahu*. Most interesting of all to Kenneth was a limestone facing he found beneath the visible facing on the *ahu*. Apparently the huge platform had been built directly over a smaller one. The great *marae* stood with the ruins of half a dozen other temples on a flat, sandy point on the lagoon facing toward Huahine. Ancient Polynesians called this place Te Po (meaning the night) and the rest of Raiatea Te Ao (the day).

Kenneth spent the better part of a week getting measurements and descriptions down in his field notebook. On May 13 it rained. He jotted in his diary: "Took down chants, etc. In house all day. Evening with Christians." The weekly steamer from Papeete brought a cable, forwarded by Sperry, from Gregory telling Kenneth to stay in Tahiti as long as he wanted. Kenneth got a letter out on the same steamer to Marguerite. She was quite impressed. "It was a very simple letter," she said years later with a giggle and a blush. "It belonged to a fellow who was expert in writing letters."

Meanwhile, the attractive Elsie was also proving to be extremely helpful. She went with Kenneth on May 19 to explore for ruins on the neighboring island of Tahaa. They also attended a feast and looked for shells. At one point, while they were measuring a ruin, she stamped her foot and said, "Don't you ever think of anything but *maraes*?" It dawned on Kenneth that Elsie's cooperation might be due to something beside an interest in archaeology. Before he sailed for Tahiti on May 23 he asked if she was coming to Papeete for the big Bastille Day celebration on July 14. He would be there. Maybe they could make up a party. Elsie accepted the invitation.

Marguerite and her friends joined Kenneth for dinner on his return. A few days later he took them to the cinema to see *Blood and Sand*. Armstrong Sperry sailed for home in the *Tahiti* on Tuesday, June 2. The Hotel du Port seemed cold and lonely without him. Fortunately, Kenneth no longer spent much time at the hotel. He was too busy seeing Marguerite. That evening they walked in the moonlight. Then on June 4, "At Muriel's at 5 p.m. and with Marguerite in the evening." On June 9, "Saw Marguerite at noon." On June 10, "On bicycles went out to Haapape and Papenoo, saw ruins."

This excursion with a chaperone took them along the shore of the scenic north coast to Haapape Village at the base of a spit of land that forms Point Venus. Captain Cook had taken his observations here in 1769. Ten large basalt uprights an eighth of a mile from Point Venus marked the location of Marae Fare Roi where, according to legend, a small child unacquainted with the taboos had innocently followed a priest onto the temple. The child's father, to avert the anger of the gods, seized the boy and killed him. The road continued along the palm-shaded shore through a couple of villages to Papenoo at the mouth of a river flowing out of the interior. Here Marguerite helped Kenneth measure the *paepae*, or house platform, of Ori on a plateau above the village, a pavement 50 by 150 feet.

Marguerite had never in her life done anything like this before. In the Tahiti of her day, respectable young women were not encouraged to dabble in pagan religion. Her father had, in fact, protected her from the influence of Tahitians. She knew none of the native dances and her childhood memories of Tahitian neighbors were mostly of the noise they made during parties on weekends.

But this was different. Kenneth opened a door to the Tahitian part of her that piqued both her pride and her intelligence. She did not understand what prompted his interest in ancient ruins. A well-bred young lady of her day did not ask a man his profession. She assumed he was pursuing a hobby and would tell her in good time what he did for a living. Meanwhile, these dashing adventures added to his attractiveness.

The following Saturday her friends came along to the Marae Fare Roi, yet were horrified when she went with Kenneth among the uprights. Muriel insisted she would surely get elephantiasis from walking on the *marae*. "I will go wherever Kenneth goes," Marguerite answered. "He wants me to help him. I am sure I won't be hurt because the *akuas* know it is for a good purpose."

Yet Kenneth's strange ways often embarrassed her. She could not understand why he came to lunch in shirt sleeves when everyone knew that such informality was in poor taste. Men wore coats in public. Marguerite defended Kenneth to her friends on the grounds that Americans observed different customs. If that was so, they asked, why did he not hold her chair at the table? All American men held the chair like valets for their women. Young ladies in Papeete snickered about it. Marguerite could not answer. Was he, after all, not a gentleman? How difficult it was for a woman to make up her mind.

At the same time, Marguerite was for Kenneth a completely new experience: beautiful, vivacious, intelligent, and Polynesian. He was in love, of course. But that was nothing new. He fell in love easily. This time, however, was different because Tahiti was different from all other places he had known. He felt about Marguerite as he did not in spite of her being Tahitian but partly because of it. All his adult life he had been fascinated by Polynesians in a professional way. Now his fascination focused on Marguerite in an intensely personal way. That is why he had asked for time to get better acquainted.

Time was something he didn't have much of. For months he had waited for the rains to abate so the river in Papenoo Valley would subside to a safe level. The valley penetrated deep into the mountainous interior of the island where it widened into a great jungle-covered basin that occupied the entire central portion of greater Tahiti. The Tahitians in ancient times must have lived there because traditions spoke of chiefs and villages in the mountains. Pig hunters, both white and native, brought back tales of stone ruins in the most obscure valleys. No archaeologist had ever penetrated this wilderness. Kenneth had been chafing since January to make the trip.

At 9 A.M. on Monday, June 15, 1925, he set out with Talbot Patrick, a young American journalist visiting Tahiti; two Tahitian mountaineers, Vini and Taeaea; and seven flea-bitten hunting dogs. The path meandered along the shore of a shallow, boulder-studded stream for about a mile where it crossed the river only to veer back farther on. Cliffs soared up a thousand feet on either side. The expedition passed through vanilla plantations. Two thatched huts three miles up the river marked the last human habitation. A vast serenity closed upon them as they picked their way up the stream, slipping on the wet stones.

Kenneth wore a pith helmet, as an explorer should, and a hiking outfit with a long-sleeved shirt to keep off the mosquitoes. He carried a knapsack slung over one shoulder. Patrick sported a natty Tahitian hat of woven pandanus. Their guides made no pretense at fashion. Once the jungle closed around them they stripped to ragged shorts. Each carried a pole over his shoulder with camp gear and archaeological equipment hanging from each end. "They looked as wild and primitive as their first ancestors," Kenneth wrote in his journal. "The manner in which they handled the heavy carrying sticks and kept their balance on the glossy rocks in the swift current was an art. The bundles never dipped in the water or banged against a tree trunk."

Neither of the Tahitians seemed concerned that the bundles contained no food. Kenneth soon discovered why. Taeaea stopped at the first quiet pool. He stood quietly with a homemade spear in his hand, a light stick armed at one end with half a dozen nails. A quick jab and a flick of his wrist brought up a shrimp five inches long from whisker tip to tail end. While Taeaea speared shrimp, Vini cut a large joint of bamboo in a grove nearby. The Tahitians stuffed the shrimp into the hollow tube of bamboo, filled it with water to keep the shrimp alive, plugged up the tube with a *ti* leaf and went on their way. Oranges and bananas also grew along the trail.

That night they stopped to camp at a place called Apapauai Grotto, which was smothered in jungle and swarming with mosquitoes under the overhang of a cliff. The Tahitians expertly constructed a lean-to by tying poles together into a frame with strips of bark from *hau* saplings, a variety of hibiscus. *Ti* leaves tied to the frame in rows like shingles kept the rain out. For dinner the Tahitians started a fire on which they piled the joints of bamboo and cooked the shrimp inside. Vini and Taeaea assured Kenneth that there was no need to carry food into the valley. It was all around them.

The next day Kenneth pestered his guides for the names of the tributary streams that flowed into the river, about thirty in all, and checked each against his map. They penetrated deeper into the shadowy interior with wild, jagged skyline all around them. That day they advanced by noon to Te Pari (the cliff) where three valleys branched off to form the great basin. In ancient times Te Pari had been used as a watchtower. Vini told Kenneth a church stood at the base of the bluff in the last days of habitation. "We saw a simple, low terrace faced with stone upon which the church was supposed to have stood," Kenneth wrote in his journal.

Just beyond Te Pari they stopped to rest at Pufau Grotto, a moss-draped cavern under an east bluff, cool and damp and mysterious. Kenneth unlimbered his camera for a photo. They followed the main stream, veering now to the right, deeper into a tangle of jungle to a place called Popotaiaroa where the Tahitians built a lean-to and cooked the food gathered that day while Kenneth worked over his notes. The guides said many ruins were nearby.

They stumbled on the ruins the next morning, stone paving smothered in dead leaves and broken branches and overgrown with fern fronds. All of it had to be cleared away. What emerged was something archaeologists had heard about but never seen; a Tahitian archery platform used by sport-loving chiefs. Vini took a position on the platform, posing to show how the archers stood while shooting for distance. There were more walls and platforms farther on, all buried in vegetation that had to be hacked away before Kenneth could measure and photograph. He returned to camp blissfully exhausted by his discoveries.

Taeaea and Vini said they knew of more ruins at the end of a side stream. The next day they followed the stream into the shadow of the encircling cliffs. Here they found a complex of ruins near Ieiefaatautau Stream: a large *marae*, a terrace, an archery platform, and a house site plus smaller *marae*s. One of these caught Kenneth's eye as the remains, under rotting jungle rubbish, of a family shrine. They cleared and chopped until a little stone enclosure came into view. Three stone uprights stood on a low stone platform at one end as they must have stood untouched since the last inhabitants moved from this remote spot.

Kenneth gazed down at the primitive place of worship with a puzzled sense of recognition. He had seen shrines like this one on Necker Island, the same simple arrangement of platforms and uprights. How could that be? What could two such isolated places like lonely Necker Island and the uninhabited interior of Tahiti have in common? The answer startled him in its simplicity. They were both untouched by progress. These shrines, then, must represent an early form of *marae* that survived only in out-of-the-way places. Such unpretentious structures had been obliterated or built over in populated places as more elaborate forms of *marae* evolved. If this theory was correct, he had stumbled upon a link that at last connected early Tahiti and early Hawaii. He was so excited he had to force himself to carefully measure and photograph.

The expedition headed back downriver the next day, Friday, June 19, and emerged from the valley on June 20. Eager to put his theory on paper, he wrote all morning on Sunday, June 21. Details of all the *marae*s he had measured crowded his mind. The basic plan of each was the same, some sort of *ahu* or platform overlooking a courtyard or enclosure. It was clear to Kenneth that the *ahu* was the place of the gods and that the uprights represented either the gods themselves or the backrests where they sat.

Each family, Kenneth knew by this time, had worshipped its own ancestors. So the early settlers in Papenoo Valley and the fishermen of Necker Island had brought with them their own family gods to be placed on modest *ahu* of primitive *marae* for worship. As the population increased in coastal areas, chiefs of successful families must have built larger and more elaborate *marae* to command wider respect for their gods. The difference in building materials and types of construction would account for the wide variety in appearance of *marae* on different islands. Yet the Polynesian temple, like the Polynesian language, had maintained its basic structure down through the centuries because everywhere it exhibited all or some of three ingredients: courtyard, platform, and upright slabs. Kenneth knew he had discovered a new tool for tracing Polynesian wanderings, the places where they had worshipped.

The concept provided a staggering number of possibilities for study. First, he had to make drawings. His diary entry for Monday, June 22, read, "Wrote up notes, unpacked and drew plan of *paepae* at Papenoo. Saw Marguerite and developed pictures in the evening." By this time he was, without question, in love. He wanted to be with Marguerite all the time. The possibility that he might someday soon sail away from Tahiti without her seemed unbearable. The only alternative was to get married.

"Worked on plans [of] Papenoo ruins all day, with Marguerite in the evening," he wrote in his diary on Friday, June 26. His mother had warned him that before he proposed marriage to any girl he should look carefully at her and imagine that she was forty years old. On Saturday evening he studied Marguerite as she sat on the counter in the dress shop of Chiffon's mother. She looked better and better all the time.

When it came time to walk her home, a distance of one city block, he explained firmly to Chiffon that they would not need a chaperone. Marguerite accepted this breach of etiquette with lady-like aplomb. Kenneth walked her to the gate of the Thuret cottage, a graceful frame building with a broad veranda that looked out over a tropical garden. He could hear Papa Thuret smoking his pipe on the veranda behind a screen of vegetation. At the gate, in the tropical darkness, Kenneth asked Marguerite to marry him. She looked at him for a long time as if trying to find the answer in his face.

"You'd better talk to my father," she said at last.

Apparently this meant "yes," if Papa Thuret approved. Kenneth discovered that diplomatic negotiations of this sort must be handled delicately. Marguerite would first prepare her father for the summit conference. Meanwhile Chiffon, Muriel, and the rest said it was about time Kenneth proposed because they were tired of chaperoning the two lovebirds. Papa Thuret asked Marguerite, "What do you know about him?" His daughter answered with complete honesty, "Only what he's told me." Marguerite and Kenneth spent an idyllic Sunday at the little thatched cottage by the sea and on Monday evening she took him to see her father.

"Are you from California?" asked Papa Thuret suspiciously.

"No, sir," said Kenneth.

This seemed to ease Papa Thuret's concern, Californians apparently having incurred his displeasure in the past. Kenneth assured Papa Thuret that he loved Marguerite, and that he was gainfully employed and would provide for her. He hardly knew what to say when Papa Thuret brought up the matter of the dowry he would give her. This was something Kenneth had not even contemplated. Papa Thuret gave his consent and Kenneth found himself betrothed to Marguerite.

On Wednesday, July 1, he wrote in his diary, "To lunch with Stimson and [Dr. Robert H.] Lowie [a visiting anthropologist]. Recovering from strain." The mail boat sailed with a flood of letters by Kenneth announcing his engagement and setting back his date of departure until December. To Gregory he wrote:

> This last month I have been in Papenoo Valley, the great central region of Tahiti, and such have been my discoveries that I know I should put in considerable time in Tahiti. For example, among the *maraes* in the valley there is one clear type which is almost identical with the structures with uprights on Nihoa. The resemblance is so great as to establish a connection between Nihoa and Tahiti as regards the ceremonies at one time present in the one and the other place.
>
> I want very much to take a little time and to work up some of my material part way to see what omissions I may be making and what sort of things are becoming significant to look for, and to send in something for the museum.
>
> I have to announce my engagement to Marguerite Thuret here, a girl who can go with me and be a great help to me wherever I may be in the South Seas. She is of the region herself, being half Tuamotuan in blood, but brought up and educated in France. I realize [what] all this may imply for the future. My family have the particulars.

Events quickly showed that Kenneth was still learning what all this implied for his future. The news that he was about to marry a woman from Tahiti created a stir at Bishop Museum. Gregory consulted Handy to ask what he knew about this Thuret girl. Handy assured him that Marguerite, whom he had met during his stay in Tahiti, was a highly respectable young lady of education and refinement. The *Kaimiloa* had arrived back in Honolulu by this time. Kellum, who took a protective, fatherly attitude toward Kenneth, offered Walter Emory a ride to Tahiti in his yacht so he could look over this female his son wanted to marry. Walter told Kellum he trusted Kenneth's judgement. Armstrong Sperry, meanwhile, was reassuring Winifred Emory about Marguerite's ladylike qualities.

Back in Papeete, Kenneth discovered that being engaged had its limitations. Marguerite's eyebrows went up when she discovered that he had invited Elsie Christian to the July 14 Bastille Day celebration. Elsie would expect to be escorted. If Kenneth expected to escort two women to the fete, one of them would not be Marguerite. Either they were engaged or they weren't. Chastened, Kenneth explained his status to Elsie when she arrived. She cried.

The rest of July passed in happy activity, drawing plans of Papenoo ruins by day and squiring Marguerite in the evening. He hiked back into Papenoo Valley on July 18 and camped at Pufau Grotto for five nights. The expedition excavated the dirt floor of the cave. All they found were cooking stones and three pig bones. But Kenneth measured more *marae*.

On July 28 Marguerite helped him find a cottage. His diary entry for Saturday, August 1, reads, "Moved from Hotel du Port to the cottage at [the] mission. Marguerite helped me clean up in the afternoon." He paid no more in rent at the cottage than he did for his room at the Hotel du Port. A third of the Kellum fund remained. He felt like a millionaire.

He worked hard on the Papenoo material but there were interruptions. On August 4 he met one of the colorful characters of the South Seas, Robert Dean Frisbie: beachcomber, writer, storekeeper, alcoholic, and protégé of authors Nordhoff and Hall. "Here comes Frisbie from Pukapuka [an atoll in the Cook Islands] with a native wife and a native man, an old timer from that island, and a collection of fishhooks, bowls and pounders," Kenneth wrote. "He also has an extremely beautiful Pukapuka canoe which I shall try to persuade Kellum to buy for the museum. It follows the ancient workmanship faithfully. Here is first hand information to be had from a very important point and one from which nothing whatever has been brought to light."

A cable from Kenneth's parents on August 17 set his mind to rest about their attitude toward Marguerite. "Our love and blessing to you both," the cable read. The mail boat five days later brought the engagement ring, his grandmother's, which he had sent for. But the arrival of the *Kaimiloa* on August 24 created a complication. The ship's doctor took Kenneth aside and told him he had heard that Marguerite suffered from tuberculosis.

This bombshell, apparently based on a rumor caused by Marguerite's weight loss, worried her more than it did Kenneth. What if his parents heard that their future daughter-in-law had tuberculosis? She hurried to a specialist in the colonial service for a medical examination that would lay the rumor to rest. But the mail boat was still in and his office was closed while he took care of his correspondence. She begged him to examine her. He did so and found nothing wrong.

Kenneth and Marguerite received an invitation to dinner and a movie on board the *Kaimiloa* on August 26. Marguerite felt that Kellum had decided to dislike her but her charm won him over. About this time Marguerite told Kenneth about her lost love. She handed him a packet of letters so there would be no secrets between them. Kenneth kept them overnight and gave them back the next day.

"Did you read them?" she asked.

"No," he said. "They are your own."

By now her friends were asking when she and Kenneth were going to get married. They hadn't yet set the date when author James Norman Hall, age thirty-seven, announced his engagement to Sarah Winchester, age seventeen. James and Sarah decided to be married on September 17. Such a secret could not be kept in Papeete. As usual, it became garbled in transmission. Marguerite's friends smiled knowingly when she told them she had not set a wedding date. They already knew it was September 17.

"Everybody says we're going to be married on September 17," Marguerite complained one day.

"Well, why don't we?" answered Kenneth.

"All right."

Marguerite wanted to be married at Paofa'i Church, to which her mother had belonged, so she went to the minister and reserved September 17. When Sarah Winchester discovered she was sharing her wedding date with Marguerite, she moved her own date up to have a clear field. On September 10 Kenneth hiked into Punaruu Valley to measure *marae*s. He returned in time to be measured for a white suit while Chiffon's mother sewed Marguerite's wedding gown, white with a veil.

They attended a ball on board the battleship USS *Seattle* on September 12. The next day they paddled out to the *Kaimiloa* in the graceful little twenty-three-foot Pukapuka canoe Kenneth had purchased out of Kellum's funds. What with wedding announcements to send home and the old man from Pukapuka to question about the canoe, Kenneth hardly had time to breathe. On the day of the wedding, he wrote in his diary, "Married Marguerite at Paofa'i Church. Beautiful day. Learned canoe lashings."

Marguerite did not want a large affair. Against her father's wishes she invited none of his friends in government nor her own circle, only her "adopted uncle" and his wife and a couple who stood up for Kenneth. The service was in French. Kenneth needed prompting from the minister about when to say, "Oui." After the ceremony the minister presented him with a huge family Bible. Kenneth gave him all the money he had in his pocket. When he told Marguerite, she convulsed with laughter. Married couples were always presented with Bibles. One didn't pay for them. "But I thought you're supposed to give the minister something," Kenneth protested. "He took the money."

They drove in an open touring car festooned with ribbons to the Hotel Diadem where the black female chef from Martinique outdid herself with an intimate dinner of roast duck served in the private dining room. There were toasts in French that Kenneth could hardly follow. Then the wedding couple went home to his cottage by the mission.

Chapter Eighteen

The Honeymoon

Marriage agreed with Kenneth. Years later he admitted that this was his first relationship with a woman that was not platonic. "Oh my, I was in heaven," he said. Both he and Marguerite were innocents in paradise. She had never learned to cook. Every morning, Kenneth hopped on his purple bicycle and pedaled downtown to pick up pastry and fruit. "He was very brave," Marguerite recalled. She put up curtains and adopted a stray kitten who stored melon rinds under the cottage. The newlyweds took noon and evening meals at the Hotel Tiare. After a week of visiting and auto rides, they invested in a bicycle for Marguerite. She pedaled with Kenneth to Paea Valley on Friday, September 25. The next day carpenters started work on a darkroom in the cottage.

Kenneth's theories about the importance of the *marae* in the ancient culture of the Society Islands kept expanding. He explained in a letter to Gregory that the ruins he had found represented three major cults. One, apparently, had once been universal but eventually was followed only by people of the interior. Another cult had predominated on Raiatea and the other Leeward islands from early to historic times. A third cult had been in full flower on Tahiti and Moorea when the first Westerners made contact there. Kenneth added:

> The most significant thing about these ruins is that each type is duplicated somewhere else in Polynesia and when we come to trace the larger distribution I am sure we shall make some most solid discoveries.

A honeymoon to Moorea became a busman's holiday for Kenneth and, for Marguerite, a totally new experience. They sailed on Tuesday, October 6, in a small yacht owned by a New Zealand couple named Gray who lived across Opunohu Bay from Med and Gladys Kellum. The honeymooners had brought their bicycles and, on October 8, set out on a trip around the island. Marguerite, exhilarated by the unbounded energy of her new husband, tried to keep up with him. She was coasting down a hill when the front wheel of her bicycle hit a crab hole. The bicycle went flying one way, Marguerite another. Kenneth came back to find her laughing with excitement.

"We stopped at the first house we saw," she remembered later. "There was a tragedy that [had] just occurred. We saw a woman there who said that her husband had been poked by a *nohu* [poison fish] and he was in great pain. Ohhh. He heard somebody was there and he came around. He was a childhood friend of mine. Xavier Teroo was his name. It was quite a surprise to him. His pain stopped and we stayed there."

Kenneth, of course, took a photo. It shows a charming frame house with a tin roof and a veranda enclosed on two sides by ginger-bread railing, all shaded by a spreading breadfruit tree and tall coconut palms. It soon became clear to Kenneth that, with Marguerite along, he would have no difficulty making contact with the Tahitians. She had entrée everywhere and took precedence over him on the social scale. Tahitians referred to the two of them as "Marguerite *ma*" (Marguerite and company).

On this first expedition with her husband, Marguerite followed him from *marae* to *marae* trying to be useful. "He put me to work," she explained later. "I helped him measure and draw. It was one of my good points." A photo shows her posed at Marae Nuurua, a slender young woman with brown skin and short, dark hair. She wears a dress with a long-waisted belt, white shoes, and a wooden bracelet above her left elbow. Her head is tilted and she smiles pensively. She wears a different dress in every photo. "Kenneth was going to outfit me in one of those *palaka* [cotton drill] pants," she said. "It was horrible."

One day they were alone on a *marae* in the jungle when a boar with great, curving tusks came out of the underbrush. "Then we saw the sow and all her little pigs," said Marguerite later. "I looked around for a place where I could climb. But they were more afraid of us." To her the honeymoon seemed a magnificent adventure. "It was all just the complete unknown," she said. They worked their way from ruin to ruin around the island staying with Tahitian families along the way. Kenneth collected several skulls. On Saturday, October 17, they returned to Papeete and unpacked.

Kenneth had no time to rest. There was his annual report to write, unusually important this year because he had a great deal of work to document as well as a request to make of the museum trustees. Marguerite still wanted to see her relatives in France. Kenneth had a different reason for wishing to visit Europe. The oldest and most rare artifacts from Polynesia had been collected by the first Western explorers in the Pacific. Most of these artifacts were in

European museums. Brigham had long ago made the grand tour, but his survey was hardly complete. As the leading museum of Polynesian culture, the Bishop should possess an inventory of Polynesian material all over the world. Why not combine such a treasure hunt with a visit to Paris for Marguerite? He wrote to the trustees:

> By April first I should have everything packed and be ready to leave. At this point I can see the possibility of an opportunity of an exceptional nature which may not come again with such favor for years, if ever.
> I see that I might with perfect ease board one of the [French] liners going directly from here to [Europe] and spend four months among the Polynesian collections [in museums] of France, Germany and England . . .

Kenneth pointed out that the opportunity to meet European anthropologists, to speak French and German, and to study the collections of major museums would be the best preparation possible for a doctor's degree. He added:

> It costs much less to reach Europe from Tahiti than it does from Hawaii. . . . Mrs. Emory is quite familiar with Europe and her relatives and friends are mostly there so that I would require her company if only as a guide.
> I understand also that it is sometimes the custom to grant the members of the staff a sabbatical year at the end of five years. If that is true in my case, the time is near and nothing could be more appropriate or helpful than to have it now. In July I will have been with the museum five years.

He mailed the report, than started work on two articles he had promised Mr. Ahnne, president of the Société des Etudes Océanienne of Tahiti. The first article described a petroglyph near Papeete, the second recounted his study of stone ruins. For the first time, Kenneth made public his *marae* discoveries. This article is remarkable less for its boldness than for its conservatism. Kenneth did not claim to have found a new tool for studying Polynesian migrations, merely that *marae*s in French Polynesia appeared to represent different cultures from island to island and from interior to coast. He conceded only, "It is possible that these differences were originally linked with separate migratory groups to the islands . . ." In his determination to be scientific he had wrung his excitement and enthusiasm of discovery from the text, leaving only colorless fact.

He was so busy at the typewriter that Marguerite could not find out from him what clothes to take to Huahine for a month's stay.

She had never been there. "I must say, we did not speak the same language. Not yet, anyway," she said later. "I only knew enough of the English for tea parties and things like that. He said, those were the clothes to take. But he didn't give me a suitcase where to put those things in. That was my business. When he got out his suitcase, it was his working equipment, not his clothes in it."

So began an adventure both Marguerite and Kenneth remember with nostalgia. When the schooner *Vahine* sailed from Papeete Harbor on a calm sea at 6 P.M. Wednesday, November 18, 1925, Kenneth had to rush from last-minute picture printing. Kenneth had loaded his bicycle. The deck was crowded with Tahitians. Marguerite had never sailed on a craft where everyone slept on deck because it was more comfortable than the stuffy cabin. She and Kenneth brought their mats topside and staked out their space. Naturally, they created considerable curiosity among the other passengers.

"On the schooner people said, where are you going?" Marguerite recalled later. "They told us there are no hotels on Huahine. We are just going, I said. Oh, I must say that on board during the night that fellow there said, you come to my place. My family lives in Maeva."

To wile away the time, some of the Tahitians amused themselves by making string figures, or cat's cradles. The figures were quite elaborate, some requiring the use of toes as well as fingers, and each one told a story from Tahitian mythology that the performer chanted as he or she dexterously formed the string figure. Kenneth asked to learn so the Tahitians taught him several of the intricate evolutions.

The *Vahine* arrived at the town of Fare on Huahine at 8 A.M. This port capital of the island, asleep under tropical trees, made Papeete look like a metropolis. There were no automobiles nor accommodations for travelers. "But, you see, you call on the chief and it is his duty to take care of you," Marguerite explained later. "I had to learn all of these things. So the chief got us in. And he said, what was bringing us there. Kenneth explained we were going to Maeva. He went on his bicycle to investigate that place. And he returned to get me. We went there."

Exactly how, neither can remember. Maeva is on the other side of the island from Fare, a long way by bicycle and even longer on foot. But it was worth the effort because at Maeva they found a graceful cluster of thatched cottages on stilts along the shore of a serene lagoon. They moved in with the family of their friend from the boat, a husband and wife and their little girl, to share a single large room with no beds nor tables nor chairs.

"You just can't imagine how very different it was," Marguerite recalled. "Because, remember, I am French. I played hoop under the Eiffel Tower. They were very nice. They fed us. We sat on the deck and they presented the food to us on leaves. Oh yes, complete care; food of the sea, shells. There were mountains of shells. Oh my, they were the soul of the Polynesian race. Those people sleep on a mat. However, they had cushions. You lay down and put the cushion against the wall."

Again, the family referred to their guests as "Marguerite *ma*." "It was always 'Marguerite *ma*,' come and eat," she said. "Oh yes, it was always me and my husband. He was the stranger. You see, I was Tahitian blood. I was the person."

The family awoke very early in the morning. After breakfast Kenneth and Marguerite went along the lagoon shore to the imposing array of *marae*s, which formed a somber counterpoint to the pleasant village; at Maeva were concentrated all the major *marae*s of the island. Like the great Marae Taputapuatea on Raiatea, the *ahu*s of these temples were constructed of huge coral slabs set on edge to form tall platforms. Walls of rocks ran farther out into the lagoon to form fish traps. Kenneth wrote later:

> It is obvious to anyone who reads the accounts of [missionaries] Ellis or Tyerman, and has visited Maeva Village, that it has changed little since their time [1818]. The fish traps and ruins of *marae*s have remained practically unaltered, and about the same number of natives houses line the shore.

"Those *marae*s were white coral slabs, elegant," Marguerite recalled. She brought sewing to wile away the time while Kenneth measured and photographed. The villagers could tell him little about the history of the temples. He knew from accounts of missionaries and Tahitian scholars that one *marae* was dedicated to the sacrifice of turtles. Marguerite accidentally discovered the function of another temple.

"Kenneth had finished his work [that day]," she explained. "I went behind a slab to relieve myself. I saw something [carved on the slab]. I called to him, come and see what I see. He was really finished and wanted to go. I insisted. He came and this was a canoe petroglyph." They were on the *marae* where canoe makers worshipped.

For Kenneth the grouping of temples at Maeva added another detail to his growing store of information about the evolution of the *marae*. Obviously, the size and importance of the *marae* in Tahiti was determined by the social organization it represented. The great

Marae Taputapuatea on Raiatea was in the nature of a national temple, fulfilling a religious function for more than one island. The large *marae*s at Maeva fulfilled religious functions for the population of the island of Huahine alone. On Tahiti there were *marae*s that functioned for the various districts of the island on which they were located. The small shrines that survived inland functioned only for single families.

Such hard-earned knowledge also taught Kenneth how much more there was still to learn about the people of old. Working with the ruins was like trying to reconstruct a whole society from scraps of rubbish. There were continual surprises. One evening as they sat in the house after dark both he and Marguerite heard a strange noise that sounded like a cross between a whir and a hum, "Whooooor, whoooor." Neither had heard anything like it before. Kenneth noticed in the moonlight that his host was moving his arm and that a string led from his hand out the door. The man was flying a kite. It proved the next day to be a superb example of craftsmanship: half as tall as a man and equipped with a bamboo hummer.

Having Marguerite along made their month-long stay on Huahine an extended honeymoon. She went with him every day. An old man with rheumatism took them across the lagoon in a dainty sailing canoe for splendid adventures. "Shhhhhhhh, we went like this," said Marguerite, imitating the sound of the canoe surging through the water. "On the other side there was a family, very neat family. And do you know those people were making [French] bread every other day. Marvelous."

It was all new and exciting to Marguerite. "You see, we were not on the ocean but a lake [lagoon], a tongue of land went over there. And here they closed the water coming in in such a way the tide would bring fish and they couldn't get out. So they didn't have to go fishing. A ripple came on the water and, oh, the fish came, you see. They go and get it. There was a school teacher, a young fellow, and his little brother. When we had to go places across the water, Kenneth would carry me. And he would kiss me. The little boy would say, 'Now comes the kissing time.' "

They boarded a schooner at noon on Sunday, December 12, for the overnight sail back to Papeete on a rough sea. Kenneth became very sick. The day after they landed he developed eight packs and twelve rolls of film. By the time he had finished cleaning up after the Huahine trip it was time to celebrate Christmas. A driving rain brought in the new year, 1926. On January 9 a letter arrived with exciting news from Gregory at Yale where he was in the teaching half of his year:

I am suggesting to the acting director that the following be presented to the trustees: Recommend that Kenneth P. Emory be authorized to continue his field work in the Society Islands until April 1st, 1926 and to spend such part of the remainder of the year 1926 as he thinks profitable in studying collections and literature in Europe and America; that in addition to the full salary $1,000 be allotted to Mr. Emory as travelling expenses.

Twenty days later another letter arrived from acting director Cooke, saddled with the task of finding the $1,000. He didn't seem as enthusiastic as the absent director. Cooke wrote:

Dr. Gregory wrote me suggesting sending you $1,000 to apply on your expenses to France, but as he did not say where I was to get the money, and as the 1926 budget is fully accounted for, I am not sending the money. However, I am not conversant with Gregory's sources of supply, and will leave the matter up to him. I presented your request for leave of absence to the trustees at the last meeting, with Gregory's recommendation, and it was approved.

Kenneth refused to be discouraged. He worked through January and February trying to accomplish what he had set out to do before sailing for Europe. On March 8 he wrote to Gregory:

I am not worried because I think there must be somewhere in the budget a recognition that I am still in the field doing active work, and that I must be brought back to the museum without . . . being forced to swim. The fare for one from here to Honolulu is between $300 and $350. If I am allowed that, that is something. If, however, there could be $1,000 as is your wish, I could not ask for more. With salary and $300 or $350 it is possible for me to engineer though I will be painfully cramped. . . "

In the same letter Kenneth wrote that he was sending 583 negatives, the Pukapuka canoe, and his photographic equipment to San Francisco by sailing vessel for reshipment by steamer to Honolulu. He also told Gregory of a decision that would affect the rest of his life:

The Tuamotus are the last great area [of the Pacific still] untouched, and probably the hardest to tackle because of its tremendous extent and the difficulties of inter-island communication. If the Bishop Museum is considering pushing into that area, and if volunteers are scarce, I would not be averse to the idea of going there . . .

Kenneth wrote out the address of Marguerite's aunt in Paris, stuffed it into the envelope, and hoped for the best. Marguerite went to get a passport for their trip to France. At the passport office, she was shocked to learn that by marrying Kenneth she had lost her French citizenship. Furthermore, she was barred from American citizenship as an Asiatic because U.S. law classified Polynesians as Asiatics. To make matters worse the passport official was the uncle of a young man who had once hoped to marry her. Was he punishing her because she had not married his nephew?

Papa Thuret was furious when he heard that the official had not given her a passport. "You go back," he ordered. "He *must* give you a passport." So Marguerite went back to convey Papa's sentiments to the official, who then issued her an illegal passport. In the midst of the suspense, the passenger freighter that was to take them to France arrived several days sooner than they expected. Marguerite and Kenneth were still packing when they learned that the ship, *El Kantaru*, would leave in three days instead of the usual five or eight. They almost missed the sailing.

"You see, we were packing, packing," she explained. "Every day I was struggling to get packed. I was exhausted and we went there just in time to catch the boat. Papa was there at the foot of the gangplank. I started crying. And he said, 'Courage.' I kissed him goodbye. So I went on board. He didn't stay. He stood there awhile and then walked alone and I was watching. He never turned back."

Chapter Nineteen

The Cardboard
Suitcase

"Sailed at 8:30 [A.M.] on *El Kantaru* for France," Kenneth wrote in his diary on Thursday, March 25, 1926. "Rain ceased from 6 to 9. Rainy and cold all day. Four thousand five hundred twenty miles to Balboa [Panama Canal Zone]." After their hectic departure, both he and Marguerite welcomed the lazy, pampered life of sea travel: good food, reading, deck sports, playing guitar.

The *El Kantaru* made its unhurried way east falling farther and farther behind schedule. Off Panama on April 14 they sighted battleships, submarines, pelicans, and islands, and anchored by moonlight off the tropical shore. Their trip through the canal locks kept the passengers entertained past noon. On Friday, April 21, the *El Kantaru* docked at Martinique where Kenneth and Marguerite made the most of a two-day stay that in actuality turned into four.

Kenneth spent three weeks studying French as they steamed slowly across the Atlantic. By this time they were so far behind schedule the steamer's larder began to run out of food. Passengers complained, especially about the lack of butter and sugar. Kenneth and Marguerite lost weight. They passed the sturdy profile of Gibraltar on May 12, and made their approach to Marseille the morning of Saturday, May 15. A sudden, furious windstorm called the *mistral* delayed the docking until 10 P.M.

The first thing Kenneth did the next day, after they landed in the rain and cold, was head for the local museum. Probably to Marguerite's relief it was closed on Sunday. They went sightseeing and on a two-day visit to Cannes, yet Kenneth chafed at the delay. It was to be a preview of their stay in Europe; Marguerite eager to share with her new husband fashionable places on the continent, Kenneth determined to ferret out every Polynesian artifact between London and Rome.

They arrived in Paris by overnight train at 9:45 A.M. on Saturday, May 22, and were met by Marguerite's aunts and assorted cousins. Aunt Lucy was horrified by her niece's loss of weight. Marguerite weighed 101 pounds, Kenneth 129. Aunt Lucy took the couple to lunch, steered them through customs, and brought them home for dinner at 78 rue d'Assas. Marguerite's family reminded Kenneth of his own in New England, but he had to struggle to keep up with their rapid conversation in French. The next day they strolled along the Champs-Elysees. Only a severe cold kept Kenneth out of the museums.

A letter from Gregory bearing cheerful news was waiting when they arrived. As good as his word, the museum director had found $1,000 for traveling expenses, a draft for $500 of which was in the envelope. The other $500 would be forthcoming when Kenneth needed it. A letter also arrived from George Pitt-Rivers, the English-man Kenneth and Marguerite had met in Papeete, inviting them to visit the Pitt-Rivers' little house in Dorset. Kenneth's answer on May 30, after a week amid the sophisticated delights of Paris, reveals clearly why he had come here:

> My object in this European trip is to obtain full descriptions of Polyne-sian specimens not available for study at our Bishop Museum, and espe-cially specimens from the Society Islands and the Tuamotus. . . . It is especially important, therefore, that I have access to these collections in the British Museum . . .

By coincidence, Pitt-Rivers had followed his letter to Paris. He took Marguerite and Kenneth to an elegant supper show, repeated the invitation to his little house in Dorset, and promised to get Ken-neth an invitation to attend an annual meeting of the British Associ-ation for the Advancement of Science, Anthropology Section, in August. The show was entertaining, the food superb, and Pitt-Rivers spoke fluent French. Marguerite thoroughly enjoyed the evening.

She had looked forward to exploring with Kenneth the ambiance of Paris, which she considered her home. In many ways it could have been his city, too. The graceful, soaring Eiffel Tower had been built in the year of his birth. A colony of expatriate Americans lived there, including Ernest Hemingway. Hemingway was just Kenneth's age, and his first best-selling novel, *The Sun Also Rises*, came out while Kenneth and Marguerite were in Europe. Paris sparkled with creativity. Pablo Picasso was in his surrealistic phase. The first exposition of Art Deco took place the year before Marguerite and Kenneth visited. The Charleston and American jazz had taken over Paris.

Kenneth found all of this diverting but he had come to work and there was no keeping him out of the museums. His search for Poly-nesian artifacts began on June 1. He found the Polynesian collections at both the Trocadero and the Mission Museum closed to the public. That meant writing letters to get special permission. Then the directors had to meet to give approval. Kenneth fretted at each delay and, with his poor command of French, he had to recruit Marguerite as his translator. Instead of exploring romantic Paris she found herself working as his secretary.

His diary details their activities in the City of Light. On June 6 they visited Musée de l'Armée, and on June 7 the Musée de la Société de Mission. On June 9 they finally got in to see the Polynesian collection at the Trocadero. They found themselves alone before the Tahiti exhibit. The only other person in the large hall was a small, pretty young woman at the Samoa exhibit. The woman came over to ask Kenneth in French if he had a key to the capes. He hesitated and she said, "Do you speak English?"

She was obviously American and an anthropologist since she had permission to see the closed exhibit. Kenneth knew that a University of Columbia graduate, who had joined the American Museum of Natural History in New York, had been in Samoa while he was in Tahiti. He had heard about her because she had stopped to study at the Bishop Museum on her way to Samoa.

"You must be Margaret Mead," he said.

"You must be Kenneth Emory," she answered.

They began an animated conversation that Marguerite felt was in poor taste because the woman called Kenneth by his first name although they had not even been introduced. "It's just not done," she explained years later.

Kenneth continued to drag Marguerite on his Parisian-Polynesian sight-seeing tour with a working visit to Musée d'Ethnologie on June 14. Then it was back to the Trocadero. Marguerite enjoyed much more meeting Margaret Manning, Kenneth's former girlfriend from New England, who was visiting Paris with her mother. They had lunch together and Marguerite pronounced Margaret "a lady" which, to her, was high praise. When asked later what Margaret was doing in Paris, Marguerite answered, "Spending money." By June 18, Kenneth was able to report to Gregory:

Mr. Real, assistant to Dr. Verneau of the Trocadero, was delighted and quite overwhelmed by our [Bishop Museum] Marquesan publications I showed him today. He was not aware of them! And yet this is the largest and by far the most important ethnological museum in France—and they have a fairly good library, mostly of old and rare books. But our works are not there. Our formidable list of publications and a few samples makes a hit every time. Of course, it is of more help to us than a hour's speech.

On June 19 Kenneth and Marguerite set off on a whirlwind, month-long tour of museums in Italy and Switzerland. They ransacked three museums in Turin in three days, Marguerite acting as interpreter. She did get in a bit of sight-seeing in Rome because Père Dubois of the Mariste Mission took them to the Catacombs, the Basilica of St. Paul, the Colosseum, as well as the exposition at the Vatican on Wednesday, June 23. "I had been to Italy before but never with anyone like Kenneth," she said. "All he did was go to museums." Kenneth wrote ecstatically to Gregory from Berne, Switzerland, on July 9:

> This is the end of three very active weeks since we left Paris. . . . At Turin I recorded a very small collection of Polynesian arms, but most important there, we learned exactly where to go and whom to see in Rome.
>
> The big Missionary Exhibit was closed but luckily the things from Oceania had not been removed. From the head of the Catholic Mission in Western Polynesia, Pere Dubois, I gained access to the collections and had the help of an assistant as well as of Mrs. Emory for five days of recording. . .
>
> Only a few objects were rare, but they were very rare—a carved head which was originally on the bow of a Marquesan canoe; an ark containing religious relics from the Tuamotus; a superb Marquesan bow; are among the pieces most interesting to us.
>
> I was greatly surprised to find in the Royal Museum of Ethnography at Rome a truly remarkable East Polynesian collection. Fifty-three hafted, ancient ceremonial adzes from the Cook Islands, and ten hafted adzes from Tahiti were the first things to take my attention. . . . The history of each specimen is carefully given by a tag. It took me another five days to note down these things, and I left Rome very tired but contented with the results.
>
> We arrived in Berne four days ago. Prof. Zeller gave us the most cordial and delightful welcome we have yet received and the Berne Municipal Museum is the handsomest we have yet visited. The thirty-five precious objects Weber, who was Cook's artist, collected from Tahiti we were allowed to handle and minutely record. I finished our work here this morning. We leave . . . tomorrow morning for Sion in the mountains where we are going to have a little rest before attacking England and Germany.

On the way back to Paris Kenneth stopped at the Neuchatel Ethnological Museum and found "a splendid Marquesan collection, a rare collection of seventeenth century Tahitian tapas, a Tahitian wood idol and a remarkable Marquesan urn." He talked the conservator, Monsieur Delachaux, into photographing fifteen of the artifacts in return for Bishop Museum publications.

By the time they arrived in Paris on July 22, Aunt Lucy had arranged a medical appointment for Marguerite. She was examined and x-rayed on July 26 and pronounced fit. Kenneth continued his unrelenting study of Polynesian artifacts at the Trocadero, measuring and taking notes. The end of summer was creeping up on him. Reluctantly he wrote Gregory on August 2 that there would not be time for Germany:

> I have about four more days at the Trocadero but I must leave for London tomorrow to attend the meeting of the British Association [for the Advancement of Science]. . . . Then I shall come back to Paris to get Mrs. Emory. . . . Then I shall be at the British Museum until we sail [for the United States] . . .
>
> Nothing would have pleased me more than to have passed four whole months right in Germany where I could have gotten a good grip on the language. [But] Our boat was a month late leaving Tahiti, and retarded ten days enroute, so an already too short summer was cut still shorter for us. Yet, I cannot complain.

Marguerite insisted that Kenneth be properly dressed in England. She took him to a "very chic" shop, where a friend of her aunt worked, for a suit and a tuxedo. She also made him replace his battered suitcase. He wanted something nice and heavy in leather. She explained that leather was old-fashioned and talked him into a lightweight grip similar to modern airline luggage. Kenneth called it his cardboard suitcase.

Marguerite stayed behind in Paris when he boarded the train for England. Pitt-Rivers took him in tow at Oxford. Kenneth spent five days talking shop with British scientists at the annual conclave of the British Association, met an Egyptologist, and examined a collection of Pitcairn adzes. Then he accepted an invitation to Cambridge where he spent two days recording Polynesian things at the museum. In Paris, Marguerite had bought tickets for the opera to celebrate his return from Oxford. When Kenneth didn't return she had to go with her cousin.

After two hectic days together in Paris, they caught the train for London with four minutes to spare. This time Kenneth took his bride to the British Museum where he went to work recording the best Polynesian collection in Europe. The tracing she did of a petroglyph motif they discovered on a bamboo quiver delighted her husband and gave her a sense of accomplishment. They worked together for five days through the week of August 25 until 6 P.M. Saturday, when they set out for Pitt-Rivers' little house, Hinton St. Mary, in Dorset.

On arrival they were met by a butler at the entrance of a sprawling country mansion surrounded by acres of manicured estate. When they went up to dress for dinner, Kenneth found that the valet had laid out his tuxedo. He managed to get into the thing but he had forgotten how to tie a bow tie. His host came to his rescue saving Kenneth the embarrassment of calling for help from the valet. Marguerite had a marvelous time and made a big hit with Pitt-Rivers' two small sons. During a four-day stay they lunched with Pitt-Rivers' aristocratic mother, motored to Stonehenge, and viewed the family museum.

Kenneth had booked their passage to New England through Canada because of Marguerite's false passport. "We thought it would be safer to come in the back way," Marguerite explained later. So they boarded the SS *Montrose* at Liverpool on September 4, after a flying visit to the Liverpool Public Museum, and sailed for Quebec at 5 P.M. In spite of their apprehension they breezed through customs and immigration, and on Saturday, September 11, arrived in Pike.

This time it was Marguerite who struggled with the language barrier. But Kenneth's New England relatives delighted her. "I was thrilled," she said later. "I was received with open arms. Kenneth's uncle, Bertram Pike, [had] married a belle from a southern state. She teased me, 'You and I, we are from the South.' Grandmother Pike, a Canadian, was a teacher of Latin and French when she married Kenneth's grandfather. She and I could speak."

Kenneth borrowed a car. His wife, for the first time, observed his technique behind the wheel. "He drove like mad," she said. "I was puzzled by this little boy I [had] married." Kenneth introduced her to the lakes and forest trails he loved. They picked blueberries and spent a week in the log cabin he and his hiking pals had built. A Dartmouth classmate named Don slept in the second bedroom and did the cooking because Marguerite still couldn't do that very well. When she complained of feeling nauseated in the morning, Marguerite learned from another of Kenneth's classmates, who had become a doctor, that she was pregnant. The news came as a pleasant surprise. Her only real problem was the cold. She hadn't dressed for it.

At New Haven they stayed with Armstrong Sperry. But Helen Roberts, the spinster folk music specialist who had been in Hawaii, complained to Kenneth that he was neglecting her. So he and Marguerite moved in with Miss Roberts. She lived in a small apartment. The next day, while they were dressing for a dinner engagement with several of Kenneth's old professors, Marguerite felt a stabbing pain in her chest. She was so ill that Kenneth called a doctor instead of going to dinner.

The doctor told Marguerite she was suffering from pleurisy and ordered bed rest. Her temperature read 99-plus on the thermometer. Every breath pained her. To make matters worse, Miss Roberts obviously did not want a bedridden guest. "She was mad as can be," said Marguerite later. "She wanted to get rid of me the worst way. And she was so disagreeable to Kenneth. I thought the end of my life had come. It was so painful, painful, very painful. There was nothing I could take for it. I just had to wait."

Kenneth hovered over Marguerite for five days while Miss Roberts made things unpleasant. By that time the fever had gone down and Marguerite felt better. Kenneth asked if he could leave her for a couple days to study the Polynesian collection at the American Museum of Natural History in New York. "I don't think Kenneth could stand Miss Roberts any longer," Marguerite said later.

He caught the 7:30 A.M. train on November 9. Former college chum Harry Shapiro met him at the museum. Shapiro had joined the staff as a physical anthropologist. Margaret Mead threw her arms around Kenneth's neck in greeting. She was married to a man named Fortune. Kenneth learned that the museum staff had nicknamed her "Miss Fortune." For two days he spent every waking moment poring over Polynesian artifacts. He slept in Armstrong Sperry's New York studio and returned to New Haven in the evening of November 10.

"Marguerite much better," he wrote in his diary. But it was more than two weeks before she could get out of bed. By that time December had arrived. They packed for the last time and on December 3 boarded a train heading west. Closson joined them in Chicago, rode the train to San Francisco, and sailed with them for Hawaii. Now that he was actually going home, it seemed to Kenneth more dream than reality. He couldn't believe two years had passed since he had sailed from Hawaii on the deck of the *Kaimiloa*.

PART FOUR

IN TOUCH
WITH THE GODS

Chapter Twenty

The House is on Fire

Kenneth Emory stepped off the SS *Maui* at Honolulu on December 14, 1926, quite a different person from the overworked bachelor handyman of the *Kaimiloa* expedition. Married, soon to be a father, he felt the gravity of his twenty-nine years. He would never shed the diffidence that permitted others to step ahead of him, but the warm reception he and Marguerite received on the dock and at the museum increased his sense of worth.

"Marguerite and I went out to the museum in our flivver," he wrote in his diary on Wednesday, December 17. Gregory was there, surrounded by his aura of scholarly authority. Kenneth carried off his introduction of Marguerite by making a pun from her Tahitian family name, Marae, on her mother's side. He boasted that he had not only made a thorough study of stone ruins in Tahiti but had brought back his own Marae.

Kenneth enthusiastically described his tour of museums in Europe. "The biggest collection of Polynesian artifacts in the world is at the British Museum," he told Gregory. The museum director quietly but firmly instructed Kenneth he must never say that. Bishop Museum claimed the world's greatest collection of Polynesian artifacts. The reputation of Bishop would suffer if one of its ethnologists went around extolling the superiority of another museum. But a stubborn streak in Kenneth, born of his New England background and scientific training, would not permit him to compromise the truth. Years later, he still got annoyed every time he thought about it.

There were a lot of changes to catch up on. Kenneth found Handy at the museum. The tall, aristocratic Virginian was now an ethnologist on the staff. His latest project was a study of Polynesian religion. Stokes still had not finished his reports on Honaunau and the Australs because he was so meticulous he could not commit himself to a final draft.

A part-Maori medical doctor from New Zealand named Peter Buck, and also known as Te Rangi Hiroa, had joined the staff as ethnologist and was working in the Cook Islands. Kenneth knew

him only by his amazing reputation as a Polynesian who was proving that his race could excel. Buck had graduated from medical
school with honors, had served in Parliament, had earned three
medals for bravery during World War I, and was now writing excellent ethnographic reports.

The changes at the Emory household affected Kenneth more
directly. Closson had married since leaving Hawaii and was the
father of two small boys. His wife, Rachel, after the birth of their
second son, had come down with a nervous disorder the family
referred to as sleeping sickness. She was now an invalid in Hawaii,
unable to control her limbs, and spent six months of every year in
the care of the Emorys and the other six months with her parents
who rented a house in Honolulu for that purpose. Closson came to
visit Rachel and the children every Christmas.

So Marguerite and Kenneth moved into a busy household. There
was plenty to do. Rachel needed care and her youngsters, Buddy,
four, and Dick, six, had to be tended. Marguerite helped although
Haru San, the maid, insisted on feeding the boys. Winifred Emory
invited guests over to meet her new daughter-in-law. A few of them
spoke French. "I had no problem filling the time on Bates Street,"
said Marguerite.

Two weeks after Kenneth and Marguerite moved in with his parents he took her on their first house-hunting tour. Marguerite
recalled that it was Kenneth's idea they build a home rather than
rent, using her dowry as a down payment. Walter Emory promised to
draw the plans. They looked at lots in tropical Manoa Valley, at
Alewa Heights on a ridge overlooking the city, and in Kalihi's low-
rent district near the museum.

On Monday, January 10, 1927, the real estate agent took them to a
new development called Dowsett Highlands in prestigious Nuuanu
Valley. It was on a hillside covered with tough, tangled guava thick-
ets pierced by a paved road. Neither electricity nor mail service had
reached that far up the valley and only one or two lots had been sold.
Marguerite immediately decided this was the place. They picked
out the smallest lot, drove up the following Saturday night to
admire the view by moonlight and, on Tuesday, January 18, bought
the lot for forty-five cents a square foot, for a total of $5,707.

At the museum, Kenneth talked with Gregory about plans for the
next few years and learned that he would probably be going to the
Tuamotus on his next round of fieldwork. Then he settled down to
write his report on Nihoa and Necker. On the morning of Tuesday,
February 1, he watched an outdoor pageant on Waikiki Beach to
mark the opening of the Royal Hawaiian Hotel, a sprawling pink

palace set amid coconut palms. The Hawaiian warriors, he noted with dismay, wore long johns under their *malos* so as not to offend the missionary element.

As the months passed, Marguerite became heavy with their child. Thelma Boyum of Maui called to pay her respects on Thursday, June 9. She was the young lady who had sparked Kenneth's first interest in girls and Marguerite found her quite attractive. Thelma wanted to show them her new place in Honolulu. "She *drove* you know, so fast!" Marguerite recalled later. "We didn't want to lose her in our car. Kenneth raced around the corners. That's when the pains started but I didn't say anything." By midnight the pains were coming continuously. Kenneth drove his wife to Children's Hospital where she gave birth at 7:30 A.M. to a six-and-one-half-pound baby girl they named Tiare.

In August the Bishop Museum trustees rewarded Kenneth for five years of service by promoting him from assistant ethnologist to ethnologist and raising his salary to $3,500 per year. He found himself in the hospital about that time with an inflamed appendix. After it came out, the ether made him nauseated for three days but Gregory didn't let him rest. An important manuscript entitled *Ancient Tahiti* by a Teuira Henry, a native scholar in French Polynesia, had arrived at the museum and the director was impatient as usual to get into publication. "Gregory almost invariably underestimates the time necessary to do a good job and in his effort to economize often cuts down where it hurts the most," Kenneth wrote later.

The manuscript had already been worked on by Handy. Then it was assigned for editing to Marie Neal, a botanist with little background in Polynesian ethnology. Gregory told Kenneth he wanted an index in two weeks. Kenneth refused to tackle such an impossible task so Gregory turned it over to Miss Jones, the museum's editor, who produced a skimpy, inadequate index after fourteen days of gargantuan labor. Now Kenneth was trying to correct the errors of others in a last-minute read through the text.

By the time Kenneth emerged from the hospital and finished the *Ancient Tahiti* manuscript, the house in Dowsett Highlands was almost completed. On Saturday, September 17, he wrote in his diary, "Served orange sherbet at our home, the first initiation of our table and tea set. Tiare, Marguerite and I slept in our new house for the first time." He neglected to mention that the beds had not arrived so they slept on the floor. "Very uncomfortable," Marguerite said later without enthusiasm. "One of those crazy ideas."

Kenneth sailed the following Monday on invitation from the Kauai Historical Society to clean up and study Lohiau's ruins at

Haena. Lohiau's ruins are a *heiau* dedicated to the hula. Kenneth spent a week with six Hawaiians cutting away underbrush to display the temple for public viewing, as well as documenting the site, a poetic place by the sea with a view of Kauai's breathtaking Napali coastline of black, brooding cliffs.

Electricians finished wiring the house in Dowsett Highlands for lights on Friday, October 7. The painters rolled up their splash cloths the next day. Marguerite moved into her new home on Sunday, October 9. The following Friday, disaster struck. She was home alone when the water heater started to hiss. Marguerite had yet to master the fine points of cooking. She had not even started on domestic technology. There she was alone in a new subdivision with no near neighbors and a water heater about to explode.

Fortunately, the house was equipped with a telephone. Marguerite frantically dialed the museum. When Kenneth came on the line, she was so excited she forgot to speak English. She gasped, *"La maison est en feu,"* which means "the house is on fire." Her startled husband got her calmed down sufficiently to tell him about the hissing water heater. A repairman came out and fixed it.

In all honesty, cooking did not appeal to Marguerite's sense of creativity. Give her a length of fabric and she could design a stunning gown. Sit her at a piano and she would play the classics. But there was something menial about cooking. Besides, the grocery store was a mystery to her. She couldn't tell pork from beef or lamb on a meat counter. "When I thought of meat, I thought of the animal; pig, cow, sheep," she explained later. "Chicken was easy."

Now, for the first time in her life, she had to cope with a kitchen and grocery shopping. First, she called Chun Hoon's Market, operated by a Chinese family in lower Nuuanu, to order by phone. The clerk at the other end of the line could not understand her French. Marguerite went to the store where her bewilderment increased among the myriad assortment of foodstuffs. One of the Chun Hoon clan took pity on her and filled out her shopping list.

"You know, the Chun Hoon family, they adopted me," she said later. "The whole family was working there and the oldest woman said, come have tea with me in the back. Then, you see, one of the younger ones went to school in Switzerland. She had become a trustee of the Honolulu Academy of Arts and she spoke French. She was in accounts in the office upstairs. When I went shopping with my basket, you know, they put things inside there, presents."

Maids to help with the housework and the care of Tiare proved a much thornier problem. First Florence quit. Kenneth's diary recorded Florence's return at 6 A.M. on Sunday, October 23. But she quit again the next day. On Tuesday, October 25, the diary read, "A maid came A.M., left for good P.M." Georgina came to work the following evening. Marguerite said later the trouble with maids resulted from inexperience on both sides.

"You know, I had no experience about housekeeping," she explained. "Everything had always been done for me. Ach, those maids. We got them through the YWCA. They were young girls, very inexperienced. They worked after school. One of them let Tiare put an open safety pin in her mouth." Every time a maid left, Marguerite had to go back to the agency and plead with the man for another. Once he laughed at her because she was in tears. Georgina, however, proved competent and willing. She doted on Tiare and taught her to speak English by singing nursery rhymes.

The Tuamotus now occupied Kenneth's mind as a dream of the future while he closed in on his Nihoa-Necker report. He knew the Tuamotu job would be considerably more complicated than the work in Tahiti. Few places in the world were so isolated as the broad, one thousand-mile-long crescent of lonely atolls lying north and east of Papeete. There was no scheduled transportation at all, no accommodation for travelers, no means of communication with the outside world, no doctor to treat illness or accident. The work would be uncomfortable, strenuous, and risky, but it would also be exciting. This was virgin territory for scientists and a last opportunity to make contact with ancient Polynesian culture. An expedition would be expensive. It must be planned with extreme care to make it worthwhile.

Language would be the first obstacle. Kenneth was reading everything he could find in the museum library about the Tuamotus, which wasn't much. He had already learned, however, that the natives spoke several different Polynesian dialects. A study of those dialects and how they came about could hold a key to the larger question of Polynesian dispersal around the Pacific. No anthropologist anywhere spoke the dialects.

There was not time for Kenneth to learn the dialects and work up the dictionary that should be part of the study. Besides, language wasn't his field. He'd have more than enough to do handling the archaeology and ethnology. The expedition needed a linguist, and the only qualified person Kenneth could think of was an amateur in Papeete, Frank Stimson, the bookkeeper at Maxwell's store. Stimson had a genius for language, was writing a Tahitian grammar, and possessed an amazing capacity for hard work. Better still, he was already in Papeete where Tuamotuan islanders frequently came to visit or live. He could begin studying the dialects immediately.

First Gregory had to be convinced of Stimson's capabilities. Kenneth became Stimson's bargaining agent at the museum, not a comfortable assignment. Gregory wanted to spend as little as possible on a salary for Stimson who held a high regard for his own worth. Kenneth could tolerate a bit of ego as the price for a successful expedition. And Stimson's letters offered tantalizing hints of the discoveries to be made in language study. He wrote that he had collected complete lists of "Nights of the Moon" from sixteen different island groups and was studying their divergence. Nights of the Moon are the Polynesian names for days of the month universal throughout the Pacific but pronounced and spelled differently in different island groups. These differences could be measured to determine migration patterns. What made it so exciting was that nobody knew the lists could still be reconstructed. Stimson wrote to Kenneth:

> I needed the Easter Island list in order to support certain conclusions I had drawn . . . but never dreamed at this late date that the remotest possibility existed of recovering it. Not one Easter Islander whom I questioned could remember a single night. And then, as I had given the matter up as quite hopeless, I dropped in on ex-Queen Marau in order to discuss the probable meaning of some old Tahitian names. She brought out an old dogeared and faded notebook of her brother Paea in order to show me an old Tahitian list that she remembered it contained, and there, on another page, I found a complete list of the Easter Island nights of the moon! It had been recorded by Paea as a young man . . . nearly sixty years ago.

On Friday, January 6, 1928, Kenneth wrote in his diary, "Handed in Nihoa-Necker report. Talked P.M. on Stimson." Gregory was being cautious about Stimson. Kenneth wrote to his protégé on January 17, "He seems definitely to have made up his mind that you are the one to tackle the language problem, if anyone should be set to do it, but much to my surprise, he holds a low estimate of the value of such studies . . . "

A diary entry on February 8 reads, "Began work on Tahiti manuscript . . . " and on Tuesday, February 21, "Stimson is appointed to work with me in the Tuamotus." But the proposal was considerably less ambitious than Stimson had hoped. Gregory offered Stimson a two-year contract at $2,500 a year with $500 annually for field expenses as a member of the expedition in the charge of Emory.

Kenneth knew that Stimson wanted five years and had compromised on three, and that he dreamed of doing a grand study of Polynesian dialects showing comparisons with other cultures. All without a degree in philology. "This two-year appointment is certainly the best thing that can now be gotten out of the Bishop Museum or Dr. Gregory," Kenneth wrote. ". . . It has a been a struggle on my part to secure two years and a large enough sum of money to enable you to investigate the Tuamotu dialects in a fairly favorable manner."

As usual for Kenneth, this correspondence and his work on the Tahiti manuscript was squeezed in with other projects. He had found another method of dating the occupation of Polynesian islands by linking the genealogies of chiefs with the temples they built, a merger of archaeology and ethnology. Bill McKern, who had gone to Tonga in 1920, was using the same technique for Tongan tombs and the dates fit neatly with Kenneth's for Tahiti. On February 27, 1928, he wrote to Tozzer, his former professor at Harvard:

> The Society Island *marae* is of the same construction as the Tongan *langi*, though not nearly so well put together. They are restricted to the Leeward Islands and date not earlier than the 13th century. The stepped-truncated pyramids of Tahiti and Moorea are about a century later in appearance. The genealogy on which the above deductions are based is checked by Maori and Rarotongan genealogies, so we can't be far wrong. All Hawaiian *heiau* of any size certainly are subsequent to the 13th century. The earlier temple form is to be seen in the ruins of Necker Island.

Stimson accepted his appointment with gratitude. "It is difficult for me to tell you how much I appreciate all you have done, and all the trouble you have been taking in order to get me a 'start' in research work . . . " he wrote on April 30. "I have talked the matter over with Nordy [Charles Nordhoff], Knapp, [James Norman] Hall, and others of the old crowd of friends here, and we are all in agreement that I *ought* to take the chance . . . " To prepare himself, Stimson enrolled in short courses at the Linguistic Institute at Yale at his own expense.

The correspondence between Stimson and Kenneth provides a unique insight into the Tuamotu expedition, which was to become legendary in the Pacific. On May 8, Kenneth described some of his ideas and how Stimson fit in. "Stokes has set on foot the theory that the Maori of New Zealand came from the western Tuamotus," he wrote. "Dr. Buck believes the theory highly plausible and I find a surprising amount of data in support of it against Tahiti as being the heart of the Maori land of exodus. The evidence which seems to be the most striking . . . comes from the language. This is wholly a matter for the philologist [Stimson] to decide."

Kenneth wrote that as an ethnologist he would approach the same problem with a study of navigation, canoes, and warfare. While the Marquesan islanders, living north of the Tuamotus, compared with the New Zealand Maoris in tattooing, cannibalism, and warfare, they were poor navigators. "The Tuamotuans have the same wealth of tattooing, were just as rapacious, but have always been excellent navigators and are nearer to New Zealand," Kenneth wrote. He added that the purpose of the expedition was to investigate these ideas, not champion one or the other. "We are not out to prove any theories, but to collect all the data for and against each hypothesis which has plausibility."

He wrote that his studies showed the vast Tuamotu Archipelago not to be a uniform area culturally but divided into at least four groups. "I consider it advisable to concentrate on the central and east part of the Tuamotus at the start because these are the most difficult of access and their isolation has kept the native culture in a greater state of purity," Kenneth wrote. "I wish you would tell me how these divisions strike you and also what preliminary divisions you would make on the basis of language alone."

Stimson wrote back from Yale that he was working on the Nights of the Moon, giving them mathematical value and putting this on a map to show interisland or inter-swarm affiliations. With habitual lack of modesty Stimson reported that Dixon, on hearing about this technique, had said, "your work is positively thrilling." Others were also impressed by Stimson. The head of the Linguistic Institute permitted him to enroll in four courses instead of the usual two permitted each student.

While Kenneth prepared for the Tuamotus, Marguerite applied for U.S. citizenship. She had filled out the application on May 12 with their neighbor, William Twigg-Smith, who was publisher Thurston's son-in-law, and Gregory as witnesses. The shock came on June 30 when Federal Judge Rawlins declared Marguerite ineligible for citizenship. As a Polynesian she came under the restrictions of the Asiatic exclusion act. "Oh boy, it hit us like a ton of bricks," Kenneth said later. "It was very serious. If she was not permitted to live here, she would have to go back to Tahiti."

The problem was with U.S. immigration laws, which classified Polynesians as Asiatics who were excluded from gaining citizenship in the United States. Marguerite could remain in the U.S. only if she could show that she was more than 50 percent Caucasian. Her mother had always told her that she was pure Polynesian on that side of the family. Yet she remembered that her brothers had blue eyes. Harry Shapiro at the American Museum of Natural History in New York, an authority on the subject, advised them that the first mixture of pure Caucasian [her father] and pure Polynesian [her mother] does not produce blue eyes. Therefore, a Caucasian or two must have slipped into the family tree on her mother's side.

In July Kenneth composed a letter to the judge marshaling his anthropological evidence for Marguerite's Caucasian blood. There was a hearing on July 3. Fortunately, Shapiro came to town. He turned the judge's chambers into a lecture hall for physical anthropology, demonstrating by the color of Marguerite's skin, the shape of her nose, and the configuration of her head that she was more Caucasian than anything else. Kenneth also testified as an expert witness. The judge overturned his first decision and ruled that she could take the examination for citizenship.

On September 20 Margaret Mead came to dinner. The next day Marguerite took her exam. She passed and on Tuesday, September 25, 1928, received her naturalization papers as a U.S. citizen. "Oh, I cried when I swore," she said later. "I cried because it was such a trial, the whole business."

Chapter Twenty-one

Murphy's Law

Gregory approved the final plans for the Tuamotu Ethnographic Survey on August 28, 1928, authorizing Kenneth Emory to lead an expedition through the most remote atolls in the world where hotels and transportation schedules did not exist. No sane travel agent would have accepted such an assignment. Fortunately, Kenneth had always been an optimist. And he didn't yet appreciate the pitfalls of chartering copra schooners. Information from Captain Brisson in Papeete had been encouraging. Kenneth dashed off a letter on August 27 to Stimson, addressed to catch him in San Francisco on his way back from Yale, with the good news:

> Gregory has informally consented to allowing me until the end of 1930 to work on the survey of the Tuamotus, and thinks the museum can back us on boat hire to the extent of $5,000 . . .
> Mr. H. Grant has offered the *Stella* for $750 a month including a captain, mate, cook and four sailors. We pay for fuel, oil, grub. That seems a reasonable offer. But we cannot take the boat now and hold it, nor when we do take a boat, can we hang on to her until we are through . . .

On September 24 Kenneth sent more news to Stimson. Gregory had increased the budget for boat charter to $8,000 over two years with a total budget of $10,000. The expedition leader wrote to his assistant, "So far as I know, this is by far and away the most liberal endowment promised any of our expeditions . . . To change the subject again, what are the chances of installing a radio set on our boat? Have the semi-diesel engines a strong enough dynamo to run electric lights, radio and movies? Is there an amateur radio man in Tahiti who could be taken along?"

Stimson was not an optimist, especially about Tahiti schooners. Years of experience in the business had taught him to believe in Murphy's Law: if anything can go wrong, it will. Besides, he was a little miffed because Kenneth had gone to someone else for advice. His letter from Papeete, dated October 14, brought Kenneth back to reality with a thump:

When I arrived here Mons. Henry Grand asked me to inspect his boat, the *Stella*, upon which he claims to have spent some 40,000 francs in the naive expectation that the Museum would charter her. He told me that he got his information from [Captain] Brisson who had said that the matter was as good as settled . . .

The *Stella* was the *Tiare Apetahi*; she is about 40 years old, and in spite of anything that Grand may say, I consider her not far removed from a death trap . . .

Stimson went on to list five other schooners. The deck of the first was so rotten it had come away from the sides on her last trip. An iron bar and a turnbuckle now held her together. The engine of another schooner commonly gave trouble, which rendered her help-less because she was a bad sailor. On the other hand, two small but fairly new and extremely well-built fishing boats might be fixed up and hired for the same price as the charter of a larger schooner.

Chastened, Kenneth hastened to assure his touchy assistant that "All our dealings concerning boats and the business of the Tuamotu expedition go through you until I arrive." This did not help much. The boat charter business kept getting more complicated. In his next letter, Stimson admitted that he may have been hasty in his judgement of the schooner that was falling apart. She had been pur-chased by a new owner. "I now believe the boat will be in fair shape when repairs are completed," Stimson wrote. "A new, full-diesel engine of 55 horsepower has been installed. . . . These are far and away the most economical engines to have. Consumption of fuel is really extraordinarily low."

All this information about diesel engines and turnbuckles gave Kenneth the sensation that he was trapped in quicksand. There was little he could do about it two thousand miles away in Hawaii. On October 22 he wrote:

I have not yet had time to devote my whole attention to the Tuamotu trip, so that my propositions to date should be a little incoherent and not thoroughly thought out. I am trying to bring my Tahiti work to some sort of termination by the end of December, and then have a few weeks entirely free for making final arrangements for shoving off. I am going to try to make the *Makura* arriving February 2 [1929], but I am really doubt-ful about being able to come until the month following.

If Kenneth's letters were somewhat scatterbrained, Stimson's were the opposite. He wrote rapidly with no mistakes on a specially constructed typewriter that printed italics when he wished. His computer brain strove mightily to find order in the chaos around him. In addition to itemizing the ideas in each letter, he numbered his mailings in an effort to keep track of Kenneth's questions that were sixty days in the answering. By that time several older letters had passed between them. It was like running a business from information in newspapers arriving once a week two months late.

Kenneth's ingrained optimism and his Polynesian attitude kept him sane. Stimson's frustration began to show by December and there were several very good reasons why. He wrote stiffly:

> The last month has been quite a severe strain on all of us. There has been an epidemic of influenza . . . and after practically all of the family had recovered from the former we had four of our household down with the measles! They are just now getting over it. There have been over two hundred deaths in Papeete during the last six weeks . . .

But that was not the worst. Stimson's quarterly check from the museum, which should have been sent in October, did not arrive in November. It also missed the December steamer. Now it would be January before he could hope to be paid. Since Stimson was now working full time for the museum, his only other income was the interest on several small mortgages. Keeping a stiff upper lip he wrote hopefully, "I cannot imagine the money will fail to arrive in January." He enclosed a carefully compiled list of steamer sailings to Tahiti in 1929 for the benefit of the museum's muddle-headed treasurer.

By means of an incredible ability to botch things up, the treasurer failed to get the October check on the January steamer. By this time Stimson bowed to the inevitable. "It is doubtful if I shall get away for any short trips to the [Tuamotu] islands [as you requested] until you arrive. I am sorry but it is certainly not my fault," he wrote on January 9, 1929.

In Honolulu Kenneth was still trying to finish his Tahiti manuscript. His sailing date had been pushed back to February 14 with arrival scheduled in Papeete on March 2. He wrote to Stimson on January 15:

> We moved out of our house yesterday to turn it over to those who have rented it. Now we have to pack, have ourselves and Tiare vaccinated and inoculated . . .
>
> I will bring enough cameras and film to supply all of us, four still cameras and three moving picture cameras. I will have motion picture film developed at the coast if Petit [in Papeete] cannot handle it, although I can give him formulas, supply chemicals, and a developing outfit.

The last half of January and the first two weeks of February passed in a blur of preparation. Kenneth received a letter at the last minute from an English anthropologist, Sir Humphrey Barclay at Chislehurst, Kent, which was not encouraging. "I envy you your trip to the Islands, although I suspect that the Puamotus [sic] are hardly the place one would choose for a holiday. Nor do I suppose there is much left [to discover] on the Islands."

Another last-minute letter, this one from Stimson, contained better news. He had found just the boat for them, an American yacht, the *Chance*, owned by several Yale graduates willing to sell her because they were tired of their voyage in paradise. This superb vessel could be bought at a sacrifice for only $12,000. Later she could be sold to recoup most of the investment. Stimson talked Wilder into writing a letter of recommendation on the matter to one of the trustees.

Since the price came to more than the entire budget of the expedition, it doesn't seem likely that Kenneth took the offer seriously. But the idea of buying a boat and selling it later, rather than chartering one, intrigued him. He and Marguerite bundled Tiare on the steamer and sailed to San Francisco where he wrote to Gregory again about the yacht and hoped for the best.

Then a more immediate worry drove boats from Kenneth's mind. On the voyage to Papeete, Tiare went into convulsions from milk poisoning. The ship's doctor proved to be incompetent. For two days Marguerite and Kenneth tended their baby. "We thought we had lost her," Kenneth said later.

The Emorys stepped ashore from a ship's boat on the sunbathed quay of Papeete to a warm and cosmopolitan welcome. Stimson was there with his Chinese-Tahitian wife, as well as a Bishop Museum party waiting for a boat to Rarotonga where they would complete a study of the Cook Islands. In the party were kindly Dr. Cooke and his wife from Honolulu, and the Bishop Museum's new part-Maori ethnologist from New Zealand, Peter Buck, and his stout Caucasian wife.

Buck, about fifty years old, made Kenneth think of a Polynesian chief. The man wasn't large in physical stature but he carried himself that way. He was gracious, articulate, and dignified. Marguerite was very impressed. She felt that Buck's wife didn't measure up to him at all.

Stimson's wife, Mere, insisted the Emorys move in with them until they found a place of their own. She was plump, jolly, and capable. The two Stimson toddlers and little Tiare, plus Mere's

Tahitian relatives and friends who floated in and out, made the Stimson home a busy place. There were so many distractions that her husband rented a beach cottage for $16 a month where he could pour over his word lists in solitude among his neatly ordered bookcases. "So peaceful and inspirational a place it is to work that I have begged him to let me share a corner," Kenneth wrote to Gregory.

The more Kenneth saw of J. Frank Stimson, the more grateful he was that they would be exploring the Tuamotus together. Stimson was almost too good to be true. The man was so dedicated to research that he worked ten to twelve hours a day. "We have an immense amount of typing to do," Kenneth wrote. "Most of it has to be done by ourselves as it consists largely of reducing to readable form native manuscripts [collected by Stimson] in which words are run together, proper names uncapitalized, verbs and adjectives capitalized, periods scattered throughout without any rule. Then the beautiful linguistic work Stimson does he alone can type on his complex machine."

Stimson wrote with a facility and command of language that Kenneth envied. His mind worked with a machinelike precision. While Kenneth arrived at conclusions by carefully adding one fact upon another, Stimson made breathtaking, intuitive leaps toward understanding. It was amazing to find all this in a man who had isolated himself for fifteen years in Tahiti after abandoning a career in architecture.

Stimson's mental prowess did not, however, solve their transportation problem. Gregory vetoed purchase of the American yacht *Chance*. They would have to make do in the Tuamotus with less luxurious accommodations. Kenneth went to the waterfront to watch as two Tahitian copra schooners were hauled ashore for repairs. Their scarred, rotting bottoms shocked him. "I must confess . . . my first reaction was that I would never trust myself at sea in them. . . . Yet they would cost us at least $10 a day, bare boat charter, and $40 a day extra for running expenses, or $1,500 a month altogether," he wrote to Gregory.

Author Charles Nordhoff, who designed sailing boats as a hobby, instructed Kenneth in the advantages of building one in Papeete to his own specifications. The museum did not need a sixty-foot schooner for exploring the Tuamotus, Nordhoff explained. A single-masted cutter in the thirty-foot range would be more practical and cheaper. Properly designed, such a small craft could be hauled ashore like a canoe on atolls where there was no pass in the reef. One of the Catholic missionaries traveled among the most remote Tuamotuan islands in such a craft.

Nordhoff said he had already built four boats of this size at a cost of about $1,750 each, some $1,000 for the hull, and $700 for rigging. He hired captains at $100 a month, sailors at $24, and spent no more than $25 per month on the boat's operation. Such a vessel could be sold at the end of two years for, probably, 80 percent of its building cost, or about $1,400. Nordhoff had sold all four of his boats within a week after he put them up for sale. He recommended Ellacott, his own boat builder, and offered to supervise construction at no charge.

Marguerite's brother, Edward, who had sailed his own boat in the Tuamotus, gave Kenneth advice about marine engines. He recommended a 16-horsepower Universal model with reduction gear that would give the boat a top speed of ten knots. Edward explained that it was best to have plenty of power for breasting an outgoing current of a pass in the reef.

Unfortunately, the museum had a policy against owning boats. Kenneth filled pages with numbers about boat charters, building costs, gasoline, wages for the captain and crew, and resale price. As nearly as he could figure, building their own boat would give them transportation totally at their own disposal with captain and crew, fuel, food, and extra help at a total cost of $8 a day during the entire expedition. It would all be done within the budget. On March 29, 1929, he wrote a letter to Gregory that he hoped would not get him fired:

> It is a bit disconcerting that the museum has made a decision not to purchase boats or accept them as gifts. But your grant of authority to us to make any arrangements we like for transportation, so long as it does not involve the museum beyond the funds officially involved, will allow us to go ahead with the plan [of building our own boat]. . . . We feel our responsibility to the museum . . . requires our shouldering whatever risks and responsibilities may be incurred . . .
>
> We will now need more money by the steamer arriving the end of May. Will you please, therefore, instruct . . . [the museum bookkeeper] to send me $3,000 and to be sure it catches the May steamer. We will probably have to pay for the boat itself in May, for the engine in June, and we will be off in July for a long, hard cruise of three or four months.

By this time, Marguerite and Kenneth had found a cottage of their own, but Kenneth didn't spend much time there. Harry Shapiro arrived from New York to follow up on a pioneering study in genetics he had done in 1926 among the survivors of the *Bounty* mutineers on Pitcairn Island. He was interested in the whole problem of physical characteristics of Polynesians. When he heard that Kenneth was about to launch an expedition into the unexplored Tuamotus, he asked to go along. The opportunity of adding a physical anthropologist to his team delighted Kenneth. But it meant helping Shapiro take measurements while they packed for their first voyage, by chartered schooner, to the northwestern Tuamotus. On April 15 Kenneth wrote to Gregory about the vicissitudes of this trial run:

> This is the last letter I will be writing from Papeete for some time because it looks certain that we sail tomorrow for Takaroa. . . . We had thought to be on the sea two weeks ago. The delay is characteristic of the local boats. At the last moment, realizing we were impatient to get off and that not another boat is going for another fortnight, the owners of this boat raised our fare to treble the normal amount. When we protested they hinted that we might not be allowed passage under any consideration; that they took those they pleased to . . .
>
> During the last two weeks, we have turned to helping Shapiro with his anthropometry. I rounded up a bunch of Tuamotu natives so that Shapiro could judge for himself if they were a nondescript lot or if they had types of their own. . . . The outlook for physical anthropology and linguistics is very bright . . .

As leader of the expedition, Kenneth was striving mightily to stay within his budget. From a man named Brooks of the yacht *Chance* he had picked up $750 worth of movie film for $200. Another $200 had gone into building a darkroom in his cottage. There he would develop for Shapiro six hundred five-by-seven-inch negatives and the same number for himself, as well as 8,400 feet of motion picture film. Pacific Coconut Products Company was supplying a marine engine for the boat without charging an agent's commission in return for a free copy of Henry's *Ancient Tahiti*. Since no money from the museum had arrived yet, Kenneth earnestly requested that it be sent to the Banque of Chin Foo so that Marguerite could pay the boat builder $800 while he was gone.

Takapoto and Takaroa, their first objectives, lay some three hundred miles northeast of Tahiti. Takaroa, the seat of a once-powerful tribe, the Vahitu, had at one time dominated the whole area. Its accessibility made it an ideal point at which to break into the Tuamotuan chain while their own boat was under construction. Kenneth's journal for the voyage states that the expedition set sail on Monday, April 15, 1929, in the schooner *Pro-Patria* with two Mormon missionaries and forty Takaroa natives on board.

The members of the expedition provided a study in contrast. Stimson was short and stout, in his forties, and so sure of himself he might have been mistaken for the leader. Something of a dandy in dress, he always wore a coat and a natty straw hat. His nickname was Ua. Shapiro, tall and gangling, stood over six feet and moved with scholarly serenity as if he were browsing in a library at Cambridge rather than sailing a schooner in the atolls. During this period Kenneth sometimes appeared in steel-rimmed glasses and odd-shaped hats, which made him look something like a missionary.

During the launch they all waved farewell to Marguerite and Tiare and Mere Stimson on the beach. On the open sea the swell made Kenneth queasy. Stimson and Shapiro felt no qualms and Kenneth controlled his by taking out his guitar and strumming along with the Takaroans who had brought two guitars and a ukulele of their own. Kenneth stayed on deck with the Mormon missionaries during dinner. That night he slept in the fresh air on a Tahitian mat on top of the cabin. The stuffy cabin made him seasick.

On the third day they arrived at Takaroa, where they unloaded their gear on a blinding, sunbaked beach. They spent the afternoon negotiating for sleeping quarters in the neat village that was almost like New England in its cleanliness and strict religious spirit. Kenneth wrote in his journal that Stimson and Shapiro lodged in the house of Faukura while he took the house of Tara. He added, "To cook for us, Faukura gave us the daughter of his wife by her first husband and his wife's sister, Vahine Rii. Both have white blood and are slightly under sixteen years of age."

Kenneth had come to measure ruins, Shapiro to measure natives, and Stimson to compile word lists as well as legends and genealogies. The natives could hardly have recognized the trio as scientists based on appearance. Only Shapiro carried anything that remotely resembled laboratory equipment. A case one and one-half feet wide and one and one-half feet long by three inches thick contained the calipers he used to measure heads. A cloth tube about two and one-half feet long contained a telescoping gadget to measure height and breadth of bodies. Since Shapiro had studied medicine, he also carried a first aid kit.

In practice all three spent much of their time with Shapiro's anthropometry because he had only six months to spend in the Pacific. Kenneth explained how they did it in a letter to Gregory:

> This business of measurements certainly consumes time and energy. Rounding people up, explaining why we want to measure them in a way that satisfies them, and keeping them humored while the slow work goes on takes as much time as the 25 minutes to each person for the measurement, observation and photograph. While Stimson asks questions and records, I photograph and Shapiro measures and observes. In this way, we sometimes handle three to four natives an hour for several consecutive hours.

Then something is bound to happen as when a little boy came rushing up to tell us his playmate had a fishhook in his finger. Shapiro was an hour getting to him, cutting to the bone to extract the hook, and dressing the wound. We have callers with ailments all day [now that] Shapiro's reputation [has] spread around.

After two weeks we [have] broken down [their] suspicion and distrust . . . [but we cannot] clear them entirely of the idea that we are fine meat for money. We are soaked to the limit at every turn even though we keep to French prices and not those they get from American yachts touching at Takaroa.

On Friday, May 3, they hired a cutter to take them to nearby Takapoto. The rigging was so rotten that a puff of wind snapped a rope supporting the upper boom. Kenneth's letter to Gregory describes their difficulties on arrival:

There was only one canoe on the beach. The owner said we might have the use of it to get ourselves and baggage ashore for $6. We beat him down to three and so sullen were all the other natives in the village over our unwillingness to give six times the regular price that not a hand was lifted to help us for several hours . . . in spite of our strong letters of recommendation to the chiefs.

By evening, however, we had half the population on our side. My Hawaiian music, Shapiro's string figures, and Stimson's banter brought us in harmony with nearly all of this tough lot within another day. Out of fifty adults, we were able to get measurements of forty-one.

I wasted a day on the lagoon in a sailing canoe [to scout for ruins] having hired the canoe and man for the day for $3.50. We started out for the other end of the lagoon, a distance of ten miles. A mile from the end, the top boom of the mainsail broke in half. The next day we hired a cutter for $8 and went over the same ground [again] plus enough to reach our destination.

The cutter was two days late to pick them up. When it arrived, the sea was too high to risk cameras in the surf. "The providential and totally unexpected arrival of the *Stella*, bound for Takaroa, delivered us from our plight," Kenneth wrote. "They had a good whale boat and a crew to take anything through the surf."

By this time Shapiro and Kenneth had taken a sufficient number of measurements. Kenneth wanted to check on the progress of their boat in Papeete and Shapiro hoped to squeeze in a quick trip to the Marquesas. They decided to return to Tahiti in the *Stella*. Stimson was determined to stay. It had taken him three weeks to cajole and bulldoze the suspicious Takaroans into letting him see their manuscript books of genealogies and chants. He would remain until he

had copied them. So Kenneth set out with Shapiro on a three-day voyage in the *Stella*, which he said later was as uncomfortable as any he ever made. Here is how he described it:

> Harry Shapiro and I [sailed] on the miserable copra tub *Stella*, which they have been trying to charter to us at the bargain price of $1,000 a month. . . . The distance from Takaroa is 300 miles as the crow flies when he follows his nose and doesn't turn his head; but counting the waves we climbed and skidded down and the circles we made when the man at the wheel dozed, we probably covered 500 miles.
>
> The *Stella* makes five or six miles an hour when hitting on all cylinders which is not very often. . . . There was no going below as the cabin was half filled with copra which gives off a hot, oily-sweet smell that is nauseating. So we sat in two chairs which we had brought with us, bracing our feet against boxes and hanging onto loose ropes of the rigging for forty-nine unending hours without being able to sleep or take a morsel of food . . .

Kenneth had never been discouraged by small misfortunes. Hardship for him added zest to adventure. The expedition had survived its first encounter with the difficulties they could expect throughout the Tuamotus. While his search for ruins so far had not been very productive, the team had made its first physical measurements —143 out of an adult population of 280 on Takaroa and Takapoto. Stimson had made a beginning on the language spoken by old people at Takaroa, and had already copied more than one hundred pages from the notebooks in which native families had written down their genealogies. It was a good start. Kenneth looked forward to their next voyage with unflagging enthusiasm.

Chapter Twenty-two

The *Mahina-i-te-Pua*

The *Stella* limped into port at 8 A.M. after a hectic night of engine breakdowns. Kenneth hurried home to find Marguerite overcome with grief. She had just received the news that her father, who was visiting in France, had died there in an auto accident and fire. Her last memory of him was their hasty departure for Europe in 1926, when she had hardly taken time to say goodbye. Now she was wracked with guilt and emptiness. But life went on in Papeete as everywhere else. Tiare came down with chicken pox. Two nieces were staying as houseguests and now Marguerite had Shapiro and Kenneth on her hands with no maid to help.

Kenneth relaxed after his strenuous voyage by taking Shapiro to a secret burial cave he and Marguerite had found in 1925 in a valley in back of Papeete. The trail led through mountain streams and under huge, majestic mape (Tahitian chestnut) trees with great, buttress-like roots to the cave in a cliff. Shapiro and Kenneth took out eleven skulls for study, as well as part of a drum. "The cliff climbing, stream wading, [and] march through the gloomy groves of mape trees appealed enormously to Harry's sense of adventure," Kenneth wrote to Gregory.

The good news in Papeete was that the boat would soon be completed. The bad news was that no money had arrived from the museum to pay for it. While Kenneth was away, Ellacott had gone to Marguerite for his May 1 payment. She explained that she didn't have the money, so Nordhoff advanced Ellacott enough to pay his men. Now another boat had arrived with no money, and the groceries for the Takaroa voyage were still unpaid.

"I am ashamed to look Ellacott and Nordhoff in the face, as well as many others [to whom] we owe money in Papeete . . . " Kenneth wrote Gregory. "Stimson's money has not once arrived as promised, and each time he has had to borrow and beg until his state of affairs is a regular joke around town."

Kenneth was doing his best to cut expenses. They had learned in Takaroa that they would need twice as many photographs as estimated because every native they measured wanted a copy of his photo. No photo, no measurement. The number of five-by-seven negatives to be developed and printed for Shapiro had grown to 1,500. It was an awesome task that would cost $332 at a local photography shop. Kenneth decided do it himself for only $65. "The man we are getting for an engineer [on the boat] knows how to develop and print pictures, so when we have him all will be well," he wrote with as much enthusiasm as he could muster. The man was Marguerite's youngest brother, Marii.

The expedition leader also worried about his assistant, now marooned on Takaroa eating fish and coconuts. Kenneth had packed $60 worth of provisions that were to feed Stimson for two months, and had rushed them on board the *Zelee* bound for Kaukura and Takaroa. The *Zelee* returned in record time, it turned out, because she got a good cargo in Kaukura so didn't bother about going on to Takaroa. Kenneth transferred Stimson's provisions to the *Tiare Faniu*, which set sail a week later and never returned at all because she burned to the waterline with every can of Stimson's provisions inside her. Kenneth wished that he had sent the provisions in the *Stella*, which sailed one day after *Tiare Faniu*, until the *Stella* returned after three days with engine trouble. "I don't know if another boat will ever get to Takaroa," he wrote to Gregory.

By June 24 the nonappearance of museum funds was driving Kenneth frantic. "We will not have enough money to do anything but sit in Papeete for the next month unless some comes," he wrote. "Shapiro is returning the first of July from the Marquesas expressly to be in time to leave the first of July in our boat. Stimson plans to return expressly for the same purpose. It will be maddening if we all have to wait here another month for a check that may not come even then."

The museum treasurer's uncanny talent for doing things wrong might have been hilarious had the consequences been less frustrating. "[He] has a genius for sending checks to the San Francisco steamer two days late," Kenneth complained. Stimson's long-delayed check was finally found by his wife in an unsealed envelope that she had tossed aside on the assumption it contained an advertisement. This was after the treasurer had received careful instructions to always send checks in sealed, registered envelopes to prevent pilfering by light-fingered postal clerks at Papeete. The $3,000 Kenneth needed so desperately had been sent to the wrong bank. Since the two competing banks in Papeete avoided communication as much as possible, it was several weeks before anybody bothered to pass along the information that the money had arrived.

Stimson returned, understandably annoyed, on Sunday, June 23, with 429 typewritten pages of copied genealogies and chants. He retreated to his cottage on the beach where he buried himself in the new material and interviewed Tuamotuan informants, leaving Kenneth to fight the battle of the boat. Kenneth enjoyed watching the sturdy little vessel take shape. Her dimensions were twenty-seven and one-half feet from bow to stern with a nine-foot beam. She was designed to carry a maximum of five people, including a captain-engineer and a sailor-cook. There would be four bunks in the tiny cabin, which meant everyone could sleep at sea except the person at the helm. The galley was a Primus stove on the deck aft.

What with photos to develop, the boat to look after, and informants to interview, Kenneth hardly had time see his wife and child. Tiare said years later that she remembers little of her father in Tahiti. On Saturday, June 29, he received a radiogram from Honolulu with the message that his father had died of a heart attack. In addition to the grief he felt, his concern was for his mother alone in the house on Bates Street.

"Our boat looks very nice shining in her new white paint as she rests on the blocks," he wrote to Gregory. "The keel is of course red, a two-inch band of green meets the red at the water line, and a one-inch band of gold runs from bow to stern at the deck level. . . . Stimson and I have chosen the name of an ancient Tuamotuan canoe for our boat. The name is *Mahina-i-te-Pua* which means 'Moonlight on the Bow Wave.' "

The launching took place on Saturday, July 6, 1929. Tiare wielded the champagne bottle and the *Mahina* slid into the water as twenty-three overdressed spectators cheered. Then they all went for a spin to Papeete Harbor. A photo taken on the occasion shows women in large hats and men in coats or ties or both, all lounging on the deck of the tiny cutter as if they were attending an afternoon tea.

Word came from Buck that he was returning for a quick holiday from the Cooks in a British gunboat, the *Veronica*, which would drop him at Raiatea in leeward French Polynesia. Kenneth was anxious to consult with his knowledgeable Maori colleague about the Tuamotus. He wrote to Gregory, "As it was of importance that Buck meet Shapiro on the question of physical measurements, and that all of us would go over the work together. . . . I put the boat in readiness to go to Raiatea to bring back Buck as soon as he arrived." The voyage would also serve as a shakedown cruise.

With Marii as captain and James Norman Hall's brother-in-law, Bebe Winchester, as crew, Kenneth cast off in the *Mahina* the evening of July 13. He was delighted by Buck's surprise two days later when the little cutter sailed under the lee of the gunboat at sea.

Buck transferred to the *Mahina* and they put into Raiatea where native singing and dancing for the July 14 Bastille Day fete was still in progress. On July 17, they coasted inside the reef to the great *marae* of Taputapuatea. There Buck honored the ancient home of his tribe. Then they headed through the sacred pass into the open sea for the return voyage to Tahiti.

A mutual respect and friendship between Kenneth and Buck, which lasted as long as Buck lived, probably began in the cramped confines of the *Mahina* enroute to Papeete. Kenneth doesn't recall what they talked about. But the letters that passed between them during this period indicate that Buck was concerned by Gregory's haste to publish after an expedition. "It has always seemed to me as if he [Gregory] wanted to do the whole of Polynesia during his term of office . . . " Buck wrote to Kenneth that year. "Gregory . . . wants the museum to churn out material in print as an advertisement to the outside world."

Whatever the conversation, it was interrupted at 8 P.M. when the engine stopped. Marii discovered that an air hole in the gas tank had let in water. It was a miserable five hours of wallowing in the heavy swell before the *Mahina* got underway again. Under the lee of Moorea the engine stopped again. This time it took Marii only an hour to make repairs. They entered Papeete Harbor at 5 P.M. on Thursday. "Our Universal marine engine makes a noise like an aeroplane so all our friends knew we were arriving," Kenneth wrote later. "They were all on the beach to greet us." That left Friday and Saturday for round-the-clock consultations about how to attack the Tuamotus. Buck started back for the Cook Islands on Sunday.

Stimson's charisma continued to arouse Kenneth's admiration. Shapiro said years later that Stimson had much more self-confidence than Kenneth did. "You see, it was new territory to Kenneth," said Shapiro. "No one had ever done archaeology in the Tuamotus before Kenneth. There was nothing to go by. There were no clues, no insights, nothing. It was really virgin territory." While they prepared for their first voyage in the *Mahina*, Kenneth wrote to Gregory. His letter clearly reveals Stimson's influence:

> We have found more than enough to keep us busy in our own work. Shapiro has been getting his Tahitian measurements. Stimson has been working night and day with three Tuamotuan scholars who were taught by learned men of their islands. One is from Anaa, one from Raroia and the other from Fakahina. . . . The three natives . . . have a far better acquaintance with the old lore than any we met in Takaroa or Takapoto.
>
> We are beginning to grasp their cosmogony and pantheon of deities, which [according to Stimson] has been woefully distorted in all the

accounts so far published due to missionary influence. Their conception of creation is almost as grandiose as the Maori and proves the antiquity of the latter in as much as most of the gods and their functions are exactly the same.

The Maori Cult of Io, the self-created, the maker-of-all-things, which has been looked upon by outsiders as of post-European introduction, and to which there is but one slight reference in the Society Islands literature . . . seems to exist in the Tuamotus with Io bearing the name of Kiho . . .

Stimson stumbled upon this quite by accident. Kiho and everything connected with him has evidently been suppressed and kept in the dark because the missionaries have identified Po with Hades . . . and Kiho dwelt in Po. Not wishing to have their great Kiho . . . called a devil, the natives seem not to have said anything about him to white men. . . . We are sure that we have opened up something of profound interest concerning which it is not too late to learn the truth.

From the Tuamotuan informants Kenneth also learned that a knowledge of the stars and the ability to navigate by them survived in Fakahina and Takume atolls. One Tuamotuan sage gave the names of fifty-five stars, another gave more than eighty names. Both said they could identify all of them and could navigate by them from their island to surrounding islands.

Marii's relations with Stimson were not as cordial as Kenneth's. Stimson assumed a haughty colonial-administrator attitude toward the Tahitians to get from them what he wanted. Apparently it didn't always work, especially with Marii. Stimson ordered the captain-engineer to have the boat ready at 3 P.M. on a Saturday to take some guests for a sail. Marii had the boat ready, although nobody works Saturday afternoon in Papeete. He waited an hour, then two hours more. When Stimson failed to appear by 6 P.M., Marii went home. Stimson arrived half an hour later. He gave Marii a tongue-lashing for failing to obey orders. Marii quit on the spot.

That meant Kenneth had to scramble around and find a new captain. He hired a skinny little Tahitian named Mora, which means "duck." On August 11 Kenneth wrote to Gregory, "Barring storms or epidemics, we should be well up in the northeast Tuamotus when this letter comes to Honolulu. Our itinerary was worked out . . . three weeks ago. . . . The sails have been tested and altered, the exhaust has been changed so that it is impossible for the engine to suck in sea water as it did the last time . . . our chronometer has been checked, a landing boat made, and a waterproof landing box made for our cameras, films, notes and other precious things."

When the mail steamer arrived on Saturday with their spare propeller and an extra magneto, they would be off.

The Emory's touring car, 1910. Kenneth is on the running board, his parents are in the front, and his grandparents are in the back seat. Their home on Bates Street is in the background. (Emory family album)

Kenneth (left) and playmate Lorrin P. Thurston perform for their admiring mothers in 1912. (Emory family album)

Kenneth and his surfboard on Waikiki Beach, about 1915. (Emory family album)

The Emory brothers, Closson and Kenneth, in 1918. (Emory family album)

Members of the Dartmouth Outing Club at the end of a hike in the White Mountains, December 9, 1917. (Emory family album)

Kenneth as swimming instructor, teaching his students lifesaving at the Aloha Camp for Girls in 1918. (Emory family album)

Kenneth's first archaeological expedition, a survey of Haleakala Crater on Maui in 1920. He poses in the excavation of a terraced platform. (Bishop Museum photo)

Arrival on the island of Lanai in July 1921 for a six-month archaeological survey. (Bishop Museum photo)

Kenneth chalks petroglyphs to photograph at Luahiwa, Lanai, in 1921. (Bishop Museum photo)

At Kahekili's Leap overlooking the cliff coastline of Lanai in 1921. (Bishop Museum photo)

Photo taken by Kenneth of Hawaiian students at Keomuku School on Lanai in 1921. The children wore their best clothes to class for their first photograph. (Bishop Museum photo)

Rare photo of visitors to Lanai in 1921 showing (left to right) Armine Von Tempsky, Armine's sister, Lorrin A. Thurston, George Munro, Kenneth, and Walter Emory. (Emory family album)

Photo taken by Kenneth in 1924 of Kalokuokamaile, an expert canoe builder at Napoopoo, Hawaii. (Emory family album)

Mysterious shrines discovered by Kenneth on Necker Island in 1924. (Bishop Museum photo by Emory)

The luxury yacht *Kaimiloa* anchored in the harbor of Papeete, Tahiti, in 1925. Moorea looms in the background. (Bishop Museum photo by Emory)

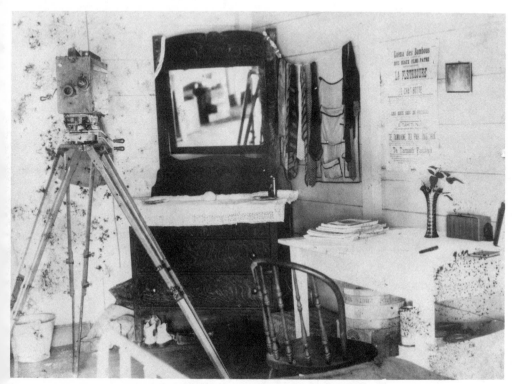

Kenneth's room at the Hotel du Port in Papeete in 1925. His hand-cranked movie camera is at left. (Bishop Museum photo by Emory)

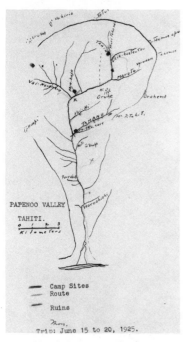

Map drawn by Kenneth after exploring Papenoo Valley in Tahiti for ancient archaeological sites in 1925. (Emory family album)

Armstrong Sperry (right) and Kenneth pose with their host on Bora-Bora in 1925. (Bishop Museum photo)

Members of Papenoo Expedition under their leaf shelter at Popo-taia-roa on June 18, 1925, on the island of Tahiti. (Emory family album)

The Necker Island type of shrine in Papenoo Valley that provided an archaeological link between Tahiti and Hawaii. (1925 photo by K. Emory in Emory
family album)

The great Marae Taputapuatea on Raiatea as Kenneth saw it in 1925. It was
restored in the 1960s. (Photo by K. Emory in Emory family album)

Marguerite Thuret at age 17. (Emory family album)

The belles of Papeete in their beach cottage in 1925: (left to right) Marguerite, Chiffon, and Taunoa. (Emory family album)

Marguerite spending her honeymoon on Moorea exploring the jungle for *marae*s. (Emory family album)

The Necker Island type of shrine in Papenoo Valley that provided an archae-ological link between Tahiti and Hawaii. (1925 photo by K. Emory in Emory family album)

The great Marae Taputapuatea on Raiatea as Kenneth saw it in 1925. It was restored in the 1960s. (Photo by K. Emory in Emory family album)

Marguerite Thuret at age 17.
(Emory family album)

The belles of Papeete in their beach cottage in 1925: (left to right) Marguerite, Chiffon, and Taunoa. (Emory family album)

Marguerite spending her honeymoon on Moorea exploring the jungle for *marae*s. (Emory family album)

Marguerite in her exploring outfit on Huahine in 1925 posing with a village friend, Henri Derien. (Emory family album)

Kenneth and Marguerite in Tahitian costumes he insisted they purchase and which she never liked. (Emory family album)

Mahina-i-te-Pua, the twenty-seven-foot cutter that transported Kenneth four thousand miles through the remote Tuamotu atolls. (Emory family album)

Members of the pioneer Tuamotu expedition photographed on Hao Atoll in 1929: (left to right) Kenneth, Harry Shapiro, and Frank Stimson. (Bishop Museum photo)

Houses on the lagoon shore at Takoto in the Tuamotus in 1929. (Bishop Museum photo by Emory)

Photo by Emory taken at Vahitahi in 1930 of the magic circle exorcising the malignant
spirit at the end of the *tipara*
ceremony. (Emory family
album)

Canoes and houses atop shell
heaps on the lagoon shore at
Reao in the Tuamotus in 1930.
(Bishop Museum photo by
Emory)

A family posing before their
house on a shell heap at Reau
in the Tuamotus in 1930.
(Bishop Museum photo by
Emory)

Winifred, Kenneth, and Tiare relaxing on the beach at Papeete during the Tuamotu expedition. (Emory family album)

The Emorys in Honolulu in the 1930s: Winifred, Marguerite, Tiare, and Kenneth. (Emory family album)

Kenneth in 1943 as a survival instructor teaching basketweaving to GIs. (Emory family album)

Soldiers learn how to husk a coconut during a class in survival taught by Kenneth during World War II. (Emory family album)

A display created by Kenneth in 1943 to teach GIs how to cook food, make a fire, build a shelter, weave baskets, and manufacture sandals without tools on an uninhabited atoll. (Emory family album)

Houses on the lagoon at Nukuoro Atoll, Micronesia, in 1947. (Emory family album)

Emory photo of Kapoi working in her taro patch at Kapingamarangi Atoll, 1947. (Emory family album)

A girl builds a fire for a ground oven at Kapingamarangi Atoll, 1947.
(Photo by K. Emory in Emory family album)

Women of Kapingamarangi, 1947. (Photo by K. Emory in Emory family
album)

At work in the anthropology office and laboratory at Bishop Museum in the 1950s. (Bishop Museum photo)

Kenneth inspects bones stored in the bowels of Bishop Museum, 1950s. (Bishop Museum photo)

Kuliouou, Oahu, shelter cave from which the first carbon date in Polynesia was taken. The photo was snapped on the day in 1955 that author Bob Krauss (right) met Kenneth (left) and Marguerite (center). (Ed Sheehan photo)

Yosi Sinoto (left) and Kenneth (right) at the South Point, Hawaii, dig in 1954. (Bishop Museum photo, Department of Anthropology)

Kenneth (center) and William Bonk (right) at the Nualolo Kai, Kauai, dig in 1959. (Bishop Museum photo)

Kenneth lands by canoe on the shore of Kealakekua Bay, Hawaii, at the foot of a cliff to explore burial caves in 1958 (first in photo series by Bob Krauss).

Climbing the cliff (second in series).

The cave entrance (third in series).

Preparing to enter the cave (fourth in series).

Wooden frame that marked the entrance to the burial chamber (fifth in series).

A looted Hawaiian cave burial (sixth in series).

Inspecting artifacts from the cave: (left to right) Kenneth, expedition guide from the Leslie family at Napoopoo, Yosi Sinoto, and Amy Greenwell (seventh in series).

Kenneth with a baby coffin that has been exposed to erosion (eighth in series).

A typical Kenneth Emory pose; exploring a shelter cave in the 1960s. (Bob Krauss photo)

Kenneth (center) with Aurora Natua talking to a land owner in the Papara District of Tahiti in 1960 to get permission to dig. (Bishop Museum photo, Department of Anthropology)

Kenneth (left) and Yosi Sinoto in 1962 examine an eroded fireplace at Maupiti in the Society Islands where the first archaic artifacts linking Tahiti to New Zealand were found. (Bishop Museum photo, Department of Anthropology)

The last portrait made of Kenneth, 1968. (*Honolulu Advertiser* photo by Carl Viti)

Chapter Twenty-three

Long Sweep Eastward

On September 9, 1929, stars burned over the village of Tautira, sprawled at the end of the road on Tahiti's eastern shore. A half-moon had risen above the jagged mountain peaks to illuminate the broad bay where the *Mahina* rode like a toy in the mellow light waiting to begin her voyage of discovery. She was loaded and ready. At supper the chief of Tautira, Ka'iarii, had announced that the weather was perfect for departure. A cold mountain breeze, the *hupe toetoe*, rustled coconut leaves as members of the expedition left the beach in a canoe bound for the *Mahina*. They stepped easily onto her low deck and helped sheet home the jib, then the mainsail. Bebe Winchester, their one-man crew, lifted a conch shell to his lips at 9:30 P.M. The lonely moan of his long blast drifted over the bay as the *Mahina* made for the open sea.

"I took the helm until midnight," Kenneth wrote in a journal he kept during the two-thousand-mile-long voyage. "Harry and Ua [Stimson] slept below. Later I tried to sleep on the roof of the cabin but had too many thoughts to drop off into a sound sleep."

At dawn they could still see the peaks of Tahiti almost sixty miles away. Mora pointed out a dark smudge on the southern horizon, an atoll twenty miles distant. There was nothing else but heaving ocean. They had already discovered that the *Mahina* was not a good sailer. With sails set and the engine at half speed, she cruised at about 6.5 knots.

Toward evening a stiff breeze chilled the five men huddled on deck. The rain that night drove them into the cramped cabin, which was furnished with two bunks on each side and, covering the engine, a wooden box in the middle that served as a table. The place smelled of gasoline. After midnight, Bebe thought he saw land to starboard. Nobody slept easily after that. Mora slowed the engine to one-fourth speed. Among the uncharted reefs of the Tuamotus safety lay in vigilance.

A glorious dawn revealed only empty ocean. At 8:15 A.M. Captain Mora sighted the faint top of a coconut grove to the northwest. An

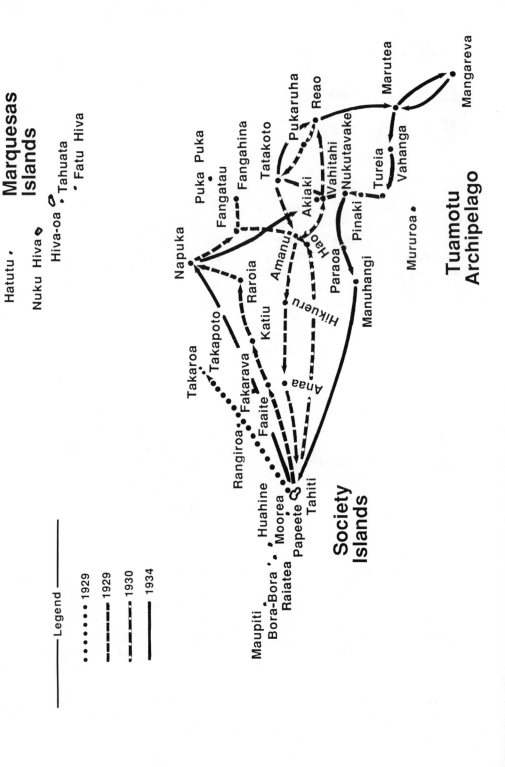

Marquesas
Islands

Hatutu •
Nuku Hiva •
Hiva-oa • Tahuata
• Fatu Hiva

Napuka

Puka Puka
•
Fangatau •
Fangahina
Tatakoto
Pukaruha
Reao
Marutea
Mangarea
•

Mangareva
•

Akiaki
Vahitahi
Nukutavake
Tureia
Vahanga

Amanu
Hao
Paraoa
Pinaki
Mururoa •

Raroia
Katiu
Hikueru
Manuhangi

Takaroa
Takapoto
Fakarava
Faaite
Anaa

Rangiroa
Huahine
Moorea

Maupiti
Bora-Bora • •
Raiatea
Papeete
Tahiti

Society
Islands

Tuamotu
Archipelago

Legend ——

•••••••• 1929
––·––·–– 1929
–––––––– 1930
———— 1934

argument began about what island it might be. Mora said it should be Faaite, their first destination. Bebe held out for Fakareva (Fakarava). Ua, who didn't trust Tahitian navigators, had brought along a sextant. By his calculations, the island was Tahanea. Forty minutes later, land rose above the horizon. It was Faaite.

They motored through the pass on the west side at 2 P.M. and dropped anchor off a neat pier of coral. About a dozen men squatted among the miserable huts of the village, watching with little interest. The expedition landed, each man shook hands formally with the disinterested Tuamotuans, then presented their letter from the governor to the chief. He read it to the villagers in their meeting house. Then things became more lively.

Shapiro measured with Stimson recording, while Kenneth explored a destroyed *marae* and a burial ground. In the evening all forty villagers sang *himene*, native songs converted to hymns, in the soft darkness. One was a song about their atoll, another was in praise of the gods Atea and Tane, the next asked their guests to stay longer, and the last was about teaching Tahitians how to count in Tuamotuan. Kenneth repaid their courtesy by singing Hawaiian songs to the accompaniment of his guitar.

The *Mahina* sailed away in the morning like a camel traveling from oasis to oasis in the desert. The weather remained perfect. Kenneth was able to eat the meal Bebe cooked on the afterdeck. That night by moonlight the captain sighted Katiu. He had never been through the pass there. The chart said it was "fit only for boats." But the canoe men at Faaite had given Mora instructions how to avoid the coral heads, so he headed right into the strong current. With Bebe at the helm and the engine at full speed, Mora stood on the bow frantically waving instructions to steer port or starboard.

The village lay about five miles beyond the pass on the lagoon shore. It appeared somber and deserted under tall coconut trees in the moonlight. But an old woman, who turned out to be Bebe's grandmother, was there. She gave them accommodations in the chief's house. Her pretty granddaughter, Mere, fetched water and put the house in order. The villagers were away making copra on the nearby *motus* (small islands) that circled the lagoon.

In the morning the expedition motored down the lagoon. Natives appeared from the coconut groves as Bebe blew his conch. One of them proved to be the chief. He read the governor's letter of introduction and called his people together. Once more the measuring began. Shapiro doctored a few natives. That night instead of singing there was a dance, described by Kenneth in his journal as a native highland fling. He and Shapiro tried to participate, raising howls of

laughter. It was 10:30 P.M. before they let Kenneth put down his
steel guitar.

At 6 A.M. the villagers gathered to say farewell. The chief returned
a basket—in which they had given him canned fruit—filled with
shells. Bebe's relatives gave him five chickens, and a patient of Shapiro's gave him a fowl and a beautiful cowrie. The sea grew rougher
as the *Mahina* continued her long sweep eastward. This time their
destination was Raroia. By the time they came up to Taenga the sea
was very rough. Mora tried to put in at Taenga but great waves were
breaking into the pass and the current boiled in a menacing crescent
half a mile out to sea. Kenneth wrote in classic understatement, "It
looked bad for us. The captain said he knew the pass well and was
not afraid to try it, but he admitted we might not make it."

They ran north under the shelter of the atoll where they found
quieter water to anchor during their supper. Mora told his passengers to go to sleep. He would wait a few hours. If the wind did not
get any worse he might make a run for Raroia. During the night Kenneth was awakened by the starting of the engine. The weather had
cleared and the wind was more moderate.

At dawn, Raroia, the largest atoll in the Tuamotu Archipelago,
rose on the eastern horizon amid a spectacular sunrise. They pushed
through a mild current in the pass and anchored off the deserted village. The chief came on board. His villagers were on the *motus* making copra, so they headed toward them until a rope caught in the
propeller. The chief stripped to his *pareu*, dived in, and freed the propeller. It still wouldn't turn. Mora discovered the housing had torn
loose. He was fifteen minutes fixing it.

Underway again they came upon canoeloads of villagers under
sail. Kenneth filmed them with a movie camera from the bow. He
was much impressed by an intelligent, vivacious old man who came
on board. He turned out to be Teiho o Tepagi, the greatest-living sage
of the Western Tuamotus.

On the way back to the village the *Mahina* ran out of gas in the
after tank. Moreover, they discovered to their consternation that
only ten gallons remained in the forward tank. "Happily a tank of
gas has drifted ashore on this island and we will be able to buy it,"
Kenneth wrote in his journal. Then the measuring began. He spent
the rest of the day snapping photos.

The next morning a weather-beaten schooner, the *Roberta*, arrived and landed ten cases of gasoline for the *Mahina* while the measuring continued. In the evening, Teiho staged a *himene* and spear
dance for the visitors. He sat on a box to one side, springing up at the
start of each song to explain it: an ancient *fangu*, or chant, about

Raroia; a *fangu* converted into *himene* and beautifully harmonized; a lament; a striking piece about shooting and breaking the heavens with bow and arrow; then a ghost chant and love songs. Old Teiho eloquently interpreted each piece with oratory and humor.

At Raroia, as on the other atolls, Kenneth was dismayed by the tawdry look of rusty tin roofs. They radiated heat and turned the houses into ovens. Grass thatch gave an elegant appearance and kept the houses cool, but it was old-fashioned in the eyes of the young people and more work than putting up a tin roof. Some of the houses contained beds and a stick or two of furniture. The beds were status symbols, never used except for visitors, and the furniture in actuality made the houses appear barren. The artistic weave of an old-style pandanus mat in addition to a few hand-carved wooden implements was warmer and more appealing.

Again and again Kenneth told himself they were just in time. The old ways were passing, even on these remote outposts of Polynesian culture. Native women were much impressed by shoes, perfume, and store-bought dresses. Men no longer made their fishhooks or carved canoes out of logs if they could find lumber. Steel tools had replaced shell and bone. Yet the ways of welcoming visitors with song and dance had not changed since the days of Captain Cook. And although Christian religion had crowded out the old gods, there still were old people who had practiced the old religion as children before the missionaries came. And younger sages such as Teiho who remembered the teaching of grandparents. But there wasn't time on this trip to interview Teiho intensively. They would send for him later when they returned to Tahiti.

At 10:45 A.M. on September 20 they sailed for Napuka. "The night was long and wretched," Kenneth wrote in his journal. "Spray broke over us from the bow. Water leaked everywhere through the deck and roof of the cabin. It was cold. To add to the discomfort of the motion, we had rain . . . So it was with joy we sighted Napuka close by in the northeast at 9 A.M."

Children ran along the shore in excitement. There was no pass at Napuka. An old canoe paddled out, and Kenneth sent back a message to the chief. Finally a large, modern canoe put off and took the visitors ashore. There Kenneth saw old-style houses. He wrote in his journal, "It was a strange sensation walking through this truly native village with more than a hundred pairs of awestruck eyes upon us. . . . Harry started measuring and Ua recording while I went through the village on a first look around. The lagoon beach presented a superb sight with fifteen canoes, mostly of the ancient form, drawn up."

The isolation of the atoll had preserved, or perhaps developed, curious peculiarities in language, physical types and culture. There was so much of interest on Napuka that they stayed five days. Then the weather turned foul and they were shorebound six days more. Kenneth kept busy photographing and measuring canoes. He visited the ruins of four temples and took notes on houses. Shapiro measured sixty-five natives, and Stimson compiled a list of 1,500 new words. They spent the morning of Friday, October 4, packing and getting out through the surf to the *Mahina*. She sailed for Fangatau at 2 P.M. in fine weather.

An overnight sail, with one stop to repair a sputtering magneto, brought them at 11 A.M. the next day off the village at Fangatau, another atoll without a pass into the lagoon. The *Mahina* stood off and on for four hours before a boat came out. The atoll proved to be the wealthiest of all, having extensive coconut groves for producing copra. There was even a road and a truck on the island, and a resident Caucasian. Yet the place had a strangely deserted look and there were few young people.

The expedition had settled in at Fangatau for five days when word reached the village that the wreckage of a schooner had washed ashore on the northeast coast. That afternoon Kenneth rode in the truck with Fangatau's resident white man to the scene of the wreckage. They found a piece of gunwale with a nameplate that read *Roberta*, the vessel that had delivered their gasoline at Raroia.

Fangatau proved to be a storehouse of ancient learning. Stimson recorded a chant commemorating a canoe landing there twelve generations before 1900, or about A.D. 1600. The atoll was the home of two great sages, Temiro a Paoa, who was born in 1841, and Kamake a Ituragi, born in 1858. A younger sage from Hikueru, Fariua a Makitua, had married a daughter of Temiro and was on the island. Fariua showed the Temiro's family *marae* to Kenneth, and pointed out stars and gave their names. On Thursday, October 10, Fariua brought his father-in-law, who was eighty-nine years old, to visit. The scrawny, moody, alert-eyed old man had been twenty-eight years old when the last ceremony was held on the family temple in 1869.

He had grown defensive about his worship of the pagan gods after years of missionary teaching and the ridicule of younger members of the family who considered him senile. Yet he insisted on taking his guests to the family *marae*, even though it threatened rain. They, he understood, wished to learn what would soon be forgotten.

The *marae*, like many others Kenneth had seen in the Tuamotus, reminded him of the primitive structures on Necker Island and in the interior of Tahiti. He saw the same upright slabs of uneven number—the backrests of departed, unknown gods. But they were not unknown to old Temiro. Kenneth listened in astonishment as he recited their names with the familiarity of long acquaintance: Haao in the north, Tare in the south, and Paoa in the main slab in the center. Temiro explained that the slabs must always be in uneven number so that the main god might sit in the middle. There were names not only for the places of the family gods but also for the stone backrests themselves. Those few moments in the sun on the ruins of a pagan temple made all the hardships Kenneth had suffered worthwhile. Now he knew not only that this form of early worship had existed in the Tuamotus as well as Hawaii and Tahiti, but some of the gods themselves had come alive.

Temiro came to the house the next morning to record chants. The island was so rich in ancient lore that Stimson stayed behind to record while Kenneth and Shapiro sailed on to Fakahiva for three days of measuring. There they learned the fate of the *Roberta*. She had gone ashore at 11 P.M. on September 21. The captain and sailors on watch, exhausted after a hard trip, were asleep on a calm sea when a current quietly drifted her onto the reef. Her rotten hull broke up completely in thirty minutes.

On the *Mahina*'s return to Fangatau, water began spurting through the driveshaft—weakened when it had been wrenched loose at Raroia. Mora stopped the engine to caulk the leak. Faithful Fariua brought them ashore in his canoe through heavy surf. Stimson was waiting with the truck to take them to the village. Busy days followed as Kenneth measured *marae*s, hunted for artifacts, and interviewed the old man. In the evenings there was dancing and singing.

Tanned and lean, the trio of scientists sailed for Amanu for more measuring. By this time they had been among the atolls for three weeks, entirely out of touch with the outside world. Their crisscross route had taken them more than one thousand miles in a sailboat twenty-seven and a half feet long. Yet they had covered only half of the vast sweep of atolls and were behind schedule. Shapiro was eager to go on to Reao at the far end because the physical type there was so distinctive from all the others. Were they survivors of a race before the Polynesians?

The barometer dropped to 136 as they packed for the voyage to Hao, their next destination. They arrived safely through the pass on November 5, in spite of a worrisome vibration in the propeller housing. By this time they were into the season of rain and storms. The endless measuring began again. Kenneth recorded place names from the chief and, kept indoors by the rain, typed them. On November 9, a Saturday, the expedition members met to decide where to go next. Mora, who was not prone to exaggeration, told them it would be risky to try to reach Reao with the propeller shaft vibrating the way it was. They voted to send Kenneth back to Tahiti with the *Mahina*. Shapiro and Stimson would wait for the first schooner going east. They would charter it to Tahiti via Reao and have it lay over there long enough for Shapiro to take his measurements.

On November 11 Kenneth divided the provisions and at 1 P.M., set sail from Hao with nineteen passengers on board including men, women, and children bound for Amanu, Hikueru, and Tahiti. They carried with them chickens, pigs, and bundles of food and clothing. Kenneth, down with a raging cold, huddled miserably in his bunk as the *Mahina* met the ocean swells. "I finally got good and sick," he wrote in his journal.

Fortunately, the voyage to Amanu lasted only a few hours. There the *Mahina* tied up in the lagoon and Kenneth got a full night's sound sleep. They sailed in the morning with four passengers, two for Hikueru and two for Tahiti, and fifty drinking coconuts piled on deck, gifts of the villagers at Amanu.

"Tahiti is ahead!" Kenneth wrote in his journal. "At 2:30 [P.M.] engine trouble. Dirt in the gasoline and a leaking stuffing box. . . . The engine stopped on an average of once every four hours all afternoon and all night. But never for more than 20 minutes." They landed their Hikueru passengers the next day. "At 10 P.M. we departed for Anaa. An hour out, engine trouble again . . . A rough night with the engine stopping plenty of times and the rumble of the shaft increasing alarmingly."

The journal continued: "Thursday, November 13—At 6:30 [A.M.] we were having all kinds of trouble with the engine . . . the sea was big with plenty of wind. It looked bad to me. I thought we would be lucky if we reached Anaa by machine and it seemed too windy to sail. At 10 A.M. we saw Anaa plainly. Mora had noticed the reflection of the lagoon in the clouds sometime before. I could not make out this phenomenon clearly until we were very near. A greenish vivid blue light appeared on the underside of the clouds."

Captain Mora tried to anchor the *Mahina* in the bay but the wind was too strong. So he put to sea again and headed for Tahiti. "It took courage to face that long traverse in heavy seas with our engine likely to go bad on us at any moment," Kenneth wrote. "But we are anxious to get home before the weather becomes worse which Mora feels it surely will at the full of the moon. After all, the machine will probably pull us through. Here we go! It is 7:30 P.M."

That night they ran out of gas in one tank. The engine stopped and Mora didn't get it going again until 8 A.M. They hoisted the sails but even with a strong breeze the *Mahina* would move no faster than three knots. They pushed on, the propeller shaft pounding with each revolution. The engine broke down for the last time at 1:30 P.M. "At sunset we could see Tautira," Kenneth wrote. "It was full moonlight. We drifted along at 7 knots. At 3 A.M. Saturday, November 16, [1929] we came through the pass [at Papeete]. What a relief and what a joy. I jumped ashore and walked impatiently home."

Chapter Twenty-four

Return from the Atolls

Marguerite got out of bed and welcomed her husband with some dismay. He looked like a tramp—unshaven, dirty, and in need of delousing. The first thing she did was scrub him. There was something else on her mind. She said later that she and Mere Stimson had conferred about the possibility that their husbands were going wild in the Tuamotus. Mere had heard on the coconut wireless that Stimson had taken a Tuamotuan virgin of twenty as his *vahine*, or mistress. Marguerite said there are things a wife cannot scrub off her husband—a question mark.

Kenneth's journal does not mention this problem. But he explained later that a visiting, single male without a *vahine* in the atolls was fair game for the young, unattached women of the village. One Bishop Museum anthropologist, he said, had fathered a child in the islands. He said it was a difficult situation for him since he had a wife and daughter in Tahiti. Also, he did not want to bring home a venereal disease. To protect himself, he said, he sometimes formed a platonic relationship with a woman, preferably older and a good informant, who did his cooking and washing and chased away the younger, aggressive women. "It worked perfect in some places and not so perfect in others," he said.

Shapiro, later recalling the voyage, agreed that there were no social nor cultural prohibitions against sex in the Tuamotus. "They took it as if that was to be expected and normal between a man and a woman," he explained. Asked if Tuamotuans would think something was wrong with a man if he did not take a *vahine*, Shapiro said, "I don't know. But that would be my guess. They'd wonder what the matter was." He said the expedition did not stay long enough on most of the atolls to form romantic relationships. As for Hao, where Kenneth left Stimson and Shapiro, "Kenneth didn't stay there very long so I don't recollect what his life was like at Hao . . . But Frank had a woman he was living with. I had a house of my own." Shapiro said he saw no venereal disease in the Tuamotus.

Long-time Moorea resident Medford Kellum, who arrived in Tahiti with Kenneth on the *Kaimiloa* and who knew Stimson for thirty years, said, "He was very interested in sex. I don't think Kenneth was—not to that extent. He was a normal human being. But Stimson was more than that. He was almost obsessed with sex." Asked if this might have offended Kenneth, Kellum answered, "I don't think that it offended him. He probably learned something. It probably gave him ideas." Asked if it was in character for Stimson to laugh at Kenneth's naivete about sex, Kellum said, "I think it is."

In any event, Kenneth was glad to be back. And he was proud of what the expedition had accomplished. He wrote to Gregory:

> We have so many genealogies [we don't bother with them unless they are ten generations at least] that we . . . laboriously copy . . . down identical ones without knowing it. When you learn that one genealogy has 3,000 names, and another 1,700, and another 1,000, and that we have over 200 genealogies, you will forgive us for not remembering all of the names. We have 80 names of stars from Anaa, and about the same number from Fangatau. We have the names of about 70 historical canoes, and the names of their masters. It took me four days to make a rough index of Stimson's three typewritten, loose-leave volumes of chants, genealogies and traditions . . .
>
> At Napuka we were held . . . by stormy weather . . . a week longer than we had planned. This enabled me to see most of the *maraes* . . . and to record about all [the information] to be had on ancient houses and canoes. Stimson completed his basic word list and recorded about 1,500 words of this curious dialect for his comparative Tuamotuan dictionary. Shapiro measured nearly all the adult males and half of the females . . . Fangatau could have kept Stimson and myself busy another month . . .

Even before his arrival in Papeete Kenneth had begun to worry about Stimson and Shapiro on Hao. On his way back he had learned that the two schooners they expected would stop at Hao had been rerouted to other destinations. Nine days after Kenneth's return, the schooner *Pro-Patria* sailed from Papeete to load copra in the eastern Tuamotus—Reao and other atolls. Kenneth instructed the captain to pick up Shapiro and Stimson on the way.

Later he learned that the engine of the *Pro-Patria* had broken down just before she reached Hao. Under sail she had bypassed the atoll, so that a rival schooner would not sneak ahead and get the copra. The *Pro-Patria* was at Vahitahi, beyond Hao, before Kenneth could make radio contact. This time he asked the captain to return to Hao after he picked up his cargo. Meanwhile another schooner was reported to be at Hao but she did not have a radio. Kenneth could only wait to find out if Shapiro and Stimson were on her. By this time it was December 6.

What he didn't know was that Stimson and Shapiro expected him to return for them in the *Mahina-i-te-Pua.* Shapiro said many years later that he understood Kenneth had gone to Papeete for more gasoline and that Stimson became more and more angry at Kenneth for not rescuing them. It is not clear how Kenneth was supposed to accomplish this. Nevertheless, the scientific castaways were understandably impatient to escape from the atoll. "I know that Frank very definitely expected Kenneth back well within the time we were there," said Shapiro. "He got very upset and rather angry with Kenneth. He thought Kenneth was neglecting us. . . . Frank talked about it quite a lot."

Meanwhile Kenneth was doing his best to have Stimson's two-year contract with Bishop Museum extended. "If Stimson and I are to complete the survey of the Tuamotus this coming year, there is going to be no time to work up reports or to translate more than a fraction of the great wealth of . . . material we have . . . " Kenneth wrote Gregory. "It would not be fair of me to demand all his time helping me in the field up till his last day, and then leave him to struggle with his reports and with translations during nights and Sundays while he worked at Maxwells or held down some similar job to support himself."

Shapiro and Stimson finally turned up in Papeete two days after Christmas, after spending the better part of two months on Hao and without ever getting to Reao. Kenneth said he remembers no unpleasant feelings on their return. Shapiro said Stimson complained to Kenneth. Marguerite remembers that Mere Stimson said she broke a chair over her unfaithful husband's back, and asked Marguerite what she had done to Kenneth. Mere, however, seems to have had a sense of humor. Marguerite said she and Kenneth were invited to Stimson's for dinner. Mere served a whole suckling pig. As a joke, she placed apples between the pig's hind legs and sprigs of parsley in the crotch. Marguerite said several American guests were somewhat shocked by this *pièce de résistance.* "It was very gay," she giggled.

While the *Mahina* was being repaired, both Stimson and Kenneth struggled to digest their staggering volume of research materials. They were also interviewing Tuamotuan informants. In addition, Kenneth had Shapiro's photos to print and develop. Marii, short and chunky and competent, became his darkroom assistant. Stimson found a splendid Tuamotuan informant from Taiaro, Paea, who had a photographic memory. "He tell all the story of the family, of the land, of the lagoon, of the fish," said Marii. "Extraordinaire memory. . . . That's why Emory tell me maybe three, four like Paea. Maybe last in the world. After he go, finish."

In each letter to Gregory, Kenneth stressed the need to keep Stimson on beyond his two-year contract. "We do not need so much more time in the field . . . than originally planned . . . " he wrote on February 3, 1930. "But we have had to work too fast and too blindly. Stimson and I have both got to take some time to study and to learn, and not spend all our time collecting. It is not enough to take down a chant . . . we must know enough or learn enough to be able to ask the questions and understand the questions essential to comprehension not only of the meaning of the chant, but [of] its place in the folklore, music, history and social organization. The vocabulary of the chants must be in the four or five thousand."

The *Mahina* was being equipped with a waterproof ventilator to keep the cabin habitable when the portholes had to be shut down in rough weather. There was nothing they could do to increase the headroom, three feet from deck to ceiling, except not to sit up too fast. It was twelve inches between top bunk and ceiling. The expense was more than Kenneth had anticipated. They had already expended $3,500 on the boat.

Letters from Honolulu informed him that his old mentor, Stokes, had been fired. Handy wrote, "Poor old Stokes is out of the museum for good—the only solution for a hopeless psychological short circuit, I guess. . . . [He] is trying to complete [his reports on] Rapa and Honaunau at home, I believe, and hoping for some sort of job at the Normal School in connection with Hawaiian crafts."

Kenneth could not be quite so unemotional about Stokes. He wrote to Gregory, "I am sorry Stokes does not seem to give you any satisfaction. I am afraid we who have come [after him] to the museum, and are under everlasting debt to Stokes for all he did so willingly for us, have not given him the encouragement, sympathy and help he needed. When the museum was making its adaptation from the old to the new, Stokes was my anchor . . . I shall miss him greatly when I go back . . . and deplore not having his large, exact, and mostly unpublished knowledge to draw upon."

Shapiro sailed home to New York with his photographs. Then a report arrived that guano diggers on the island of Makatea in the Tuamotus one hundred miles northeast of Tahiti had unearthed ancient artifacts. Marguerite's friend, Mimi Pearson, was married to the director of the phosphate company. He invited the Emorys for a visit to see the artifacts. Marguerite's uncle lived there. She had never seen her mother's brother and was eager to go along. So she and Kenneth and little Tiare all set out together.

One unusual feature of Makatea is its geological structure as a raised atoll, a small, high island thrust out of the sea on a bed of coral. "There was no landing," Marguerite recalled later. "You had to wait for the boat to come up to the edge, then somebody grabs you." The workers had dug up twenty-six stone adzes and nine pounders as well as many bones. The overseer had built a small collection of excellent specimens. Kenneth explored three burial caves and learned of three others. For Marguerite, the highlight of their ten-day trip was Mimi's big house and the visit with her uncle whose Tahitian name meant, "the chiefs enter the heaven of the universe." He told her that her mother's name meant, "where Maui stood to noose the sun." He was a brown-skinned man in a *pareu*, small boned and of medium height, who greeted her with dignity and flawless courtesy. The suggestion that there must be white blood in the family amused him. Marguerite was very impressed.

The Emorys returned to Tahiti and another adventure. Repairs and improvements to the *Mahina-i-te-Pua*, including an iron shoe on her keel, were nearly completed. She was launched on Friday, March 21, 1930, and sailed immediately for a trial run to Taravao, in the isthmus of Tahiti, with the Emorys and a party of French men and women on board. They explored a grotto inland on Saturday and, on Sunday, Kenneth set out on foot with a male guest, Andre Ropiteax, a wealthy wine distiller, up the coast beyond the end of the road.

The Tahitians named the backside of the island *Te Pare* (the cliff) because great coastal walls of basalt plunge into the sea. Deep, tropical valleys guarded by *Te Pari* were inhabited in days of old by people who came out by canoe or by precarious cliff trails. Kenneth and Ropiteaux were crossing the face of a cliff where a waterfall made the path slippery when Ropiteax lost his footing and slid over the edge.

"God, I was horrified," Kenneth said later. "He fell into the water and disappeared. I saw him come up and a big wave went over him. No more Andre. I looked and looked until he waved from a long way out. He was swimming to a place where he could climb out of the water." Kenneth scrambled down the cliff to help his cut and bleeding friend back to the end of the road. "I gave him my shoes," Kenneth said. "On the way, I cut my feet on the coral."

A week later the coral cut began to fester. A week after that, the doctor lanced the infection to let it drain. But the infection grew worse. By Monday, April 14, Kenneth was in bed with a swollen foot. Marguerite dressed it three times a day. Nothing helped. On Thursday, April 24, the doctor cut painfully deep to expose the core of the infection. At last, the sore began to heal. By the middle of May Kenneth was interviewing Tuamotuan informants. But it was another week before he could walk.

Meanwhile, his mother had agreed to visit Tahiti. He was bogged down in expense accounts with only $1,196 left of his $10,000 budget. The captain of the port, a self-important bureaucrat, ordered Ellacott to stop repairs and put the *Mahina* in a regular, and much more expensive, drydock. Kenneth had to go to the governor, who told the port captain to mind his own business. Then a local French history buff accused Stimson of stealing a manuscript that he had purchased in a box of old books from an Englishman on Raiatea. Yet Kenneth kept his temper. "All these bothers are part of the game and I do not mind them now," he wrote to Gregory. "Dealing directly and frankly with the people responsible seems to smooth out the difficulty in a short time."

With Stimson holed up in his beach cottage deep in word lists, Kenneth struggled to prepare the expedition for its longest voyage, three months in the remote atolls. News from Honolulu was both good and bad. Bishop Museum trustees voted to give him another $4,000 to see the Tuamotuan survey through. But Gregory ordered him back by the end of the year. Kenneth pleaded for another five months to work up his material in Tahiti rather than Honolulu. His mother arrived, but there was little time for visiting with the approach of June and their departure.

On this voyage Kenneth was determined to have a radio. Since it was too expensive to hire a radio man, he would operate the set himself. First he had to buy one. Once more Marii showed his versatility. He had worked as a radio technician for the government and had helped install the station in the Marquesas and also on Raiatea. Now he put together a little battery-operated transmitter and receiver, simple enough for Kenneth to operate, from directions in an amateur radio journal.

"I build [it] in two, three days; finish," he said. "I build very small; two tubes, detector and amplifier with dry cell. . . . Put in box so you can carry. Weighs five, six, seven kilo with batteries and antenna, special wire on a spool. You arrive somewhere, string antenna out, put on radio and tap with key." Marii said he taught Kenneth Morse code in Tahitian because there are only twelve letters in the alphabet.

Kenneth got his radio operator's license on Friday, June 13, amid frantic preparations to be off. Mora had quit, twice, so they would sail with a new Tahitian captain and crew, Vanoa Gooding and Tane. "Rushed things onto boat," Kenneth scribbled into his diary on Monday, June 16. "At 6 P.M. decided not to go until 6 A.M. Tuesday. Packed late into night. Mother, Marguerite and I sad over parting."

The next morning Kenneth and Stimson were on the dock at 6

A.M. The captain didn't make an appearance until 7:30 A.M. They got away at 8 P.M. on June 17, 1930, and promptly ran upon a coral head. The captain strung a line from the top of the mast to a nearby rock and heaved, tilting the stranded *Mahina* until she slid off her perch. With the iron band on her keel she was no worse for wear. But the weather was so rough they put into Tautira and laid over one more day. Marguerite said later the Tahitians were making jokes about the expedition's slow start.

It was not only slow but rough. They sailed for the Tuamotus at 6 A.M. Heavy swells rolled in from the southeast. In the evening they hove to in the lee of Mehetia for shelter during supper. "Rough night at sea," Kenneth wrote. "Slept in dingy on deck." The next day, a storm hit at noon and drove him into the stuffy cabin in spite of his seasickness. "Between 11 A.M. and 9 P.M. terribly rough, wind strong first from one direction, then another," he wrote. He was horribly sick and felt miserable.

"This blow drove the schooner *Zelee* onto the reef at Arutua, 140 miles to the north of us, and broke her into a total loss," he wrote later. "The *Mahina-i-te-Pua* rode through twelve hours of mountainous seas, like a submarine, losing her foresail and giving us a good scare. I never believed a twenty-eight-foot boat could survive such torture. Our captain had been on a schooner during the hurricane of 1906 and comforted us by saying that we were in a mill pond by comparison."

It was hardly a propitious beginning for what Kenneth hoped would be the crowning achievement of his career.

Chapter Twenty-five

Vahitahi

The four men on board *Mahina-i-te-Pua* squinted into the sunrise for a glimpse of Akiaki, the last stepping stone to their primary destination, Vahitahi. They saw nothing but birds and restless ocean. It had been such a fine night at sea that Tane had fallen asleep at the tiller. Now they were not sure of their position. A rough southeast wind came up. They passed an anxious morning on the empty ocean. A noon sight, the accuracy of which was questionable, placed them fifteen miles south of their course.

Tahiti lay six hundred miles due west. For the past ten days the *Mahina* had plodded steady eastward. They had paused at Amanu to dry out things and try the radio. It was like a new toy for Kenneth, although Stimson was not so enthusiastic about remaining in contact with civilization. Every day at Amanu, Kenneth had hunched over the tiny set patiently tapping on the key. Once Marii had answered.

For three more hours their eyes scanned the horizon. At 3 P.M. they sighted a sail. It proved to be the schooner *Pro-Patria* on her haphazard circuit of the atolls to pick up copra. They were grateful that she had survived the storm because she carried their provisions for the coming month on Vahitahi, the place they had selected for an extended stay. The atoll lay in the eastern Tuamotus beyond Hao. Its people spoke their own dialect, one that Stimson had not yet studied, and were culturally distinctive. One reason for this was the isolation of Vahitahi. There was no pass into the lagoon. Schooners loaded precariously off the reef and stayed no longer than necessary.

The atoll, a smear of grayish green on the horizon, appeared at 3:30 P.M., putting them twenty-seven miles off course. By 5 P.M., the *Mahina* was anchored off the village. Kenneth and Stimson, still in his coat and Panama hat, went ashore over the reef where great grooves were worn into the coral by canoes launched there over the centuries. The village did not overlook the lagoon but lay on the ocean side of the island, a sprawl of awkward, boxlike, wooden houses, a stone Catholic Church, and the inevitable Chinese store. A few villagers greeted them and offered their best accommodations, the second floor of an ornate, two-story house.

The next day, June 30, 1930, Kenneth wrote in his diary, "Landed our stuff. Took all A.M. Set up radio." Stimson went looking for a more congenial place to live. "He could never rest until he had found a *vahine*," Kenneth said later. The *Pro-Patria* showed up at noon and Uria, the radio man, helped Kenneth check out his set. But they could not raise Marii. That night Kenneth played his guitar for the villagers, and there was singing and dancing.

Vahitahi is a low island four miles long and a mile wide which, with the reef, enclosed a lovely lagoon in shades of pastel to deep blue. A thick stand of trees on the lagoon side of the island provided a pleasant contrast to bare reef on the other side. Two large, handsome voyaging canoes under thatched shelters made Kenneth eager to ask questions. They were made of hand-hewn planks of *kou* wood sewn together in the shape of whale boats, a modern adaptation. He also found parts of an ancient sailing outrigger: the bow, stern, and two pieces of keel. But there was no one to ask about them. Most of the population of not quite one hundred was away on Akiaki, twenty-five miles to the northwest, making copra.

On Thursday, July 3, Kenneth set sail in the *Mahina* to find Tangi, the last of the sages of Vahitahi. "Akiaki is a perfectly round, flat island without a lagoon, one mile in diameter," he wrote. The *Mahina* rounded the south side of the island and came up to the village. A lone Tuamotuan, the chief, paddled alongside in a canoe. Kenneth stepped precariously in and they shot over the reef. A solemn, suspicious crowd waited on the beach, afraid that Kenneth was a French official come to seize their land in payment of debts. They broke into friendly chatter when they learned why he had come.

They said they remembered only one visit to Akiaki before his by a vessel other than copra schooners. That had been twelve years ago when an English or American boat hove to off the village. The villagers had a clear memory of the occasion. Someone on shore who had been to Papeete, recognized the word "coconut" shouted from the yacht. The villagers loaded their canoes with coconuts and paddled out. They returned with a bag of flour and many tins of food, an incredible windfall.

Tangi fit perfectly a missionary's description written in 1870 of Vahitahi people: "They are distinguished by slender bodies, flaming, harsh and savage looks, very mobile features, and extravagant pretensions." On this observation Kenneth wrote, "Among many of the real, old Tuamotuans, I have marked a certain fierceness and pride entirely lacking in the present generation. An air of ferociousness was certainly cultivated by the ancients."

The *Mahina* ran to the lee of the island for the night because there was no place to anchor or dock. As dusk fell the people gathered in front of Kenneth's house. He asked Tangi if they would give him a sample of their *ere*, a form of singing Kenneth had not heard before. Tangi immediately ordered silence and told them of the request. From somewhere in the darkness a woman's voice chanted, "*te maro o Tupuho-e a i.*" Another woman repeated the line and the response came in a full-throated, strange, yet simple harmony. Tangi pranced before the singers through the verses, grimacing and making defiant gestures as he acted out the putting on of the sacred *maro* of their great ancestor Tupuhoe, which was the theme of the song.

Kenneth's appreciation brought one *ere* after another. When he asked for a demonstration of their *haka*, the dance for which they were renown throughout the Tuamotus, the young people sprang up and heaped piles of dry coconut leaves in the open spaces among the thatched houses. They set the piles on fire. Tangi ordered his daughter, Kohemingo, to lead the *haka*. Her command scattered the villagers. They returned in a few minutes bedecked with garlands of sea vines from the beach, and formed two lines—the women in front.

Kohemingo gave a long, quivering shout, "E-eeeeee-hi," which was answered by the dancers. Silence fell, broken only by the crackling of the fires and a steady throb of the dancers' feet stamping in slow rhythm. Kohemingo broke the silence with the shrill line of a chant, the first line of the song and the signal for the dance to begin. Arms and hands waved in rhythm to a rapid counterpoint of hips and feet. Kenneth wrote later, "Towards the end of the song the tempo soared to a frenzied climax. The dance and song ended in a deafening shout which, dying away, left a stillness poignant with warm emotion and beauty."

It was as if the spirit of ancient Polynesia had broken through the restraints of modern culture. Tangi grabbed a stout carrying stick and leaped into the firelight to lead savagely the next dance. "For the *haka* is not worthy of its name if it does not brutally arouse the sexual instinct out of all sleep . . ." Kenneth wrote. "In the generation of Tangi's father, the *haka* was often a piece of magic to drive the hot winds of desire into fury and turn them loose that all nature might become fecund—that there might be an abundance of coconuts, pandanus nuts, turtles, fish, and children . . ."

The next day, after visiting two *marae*s, Kenneth watched the villagers cook the first turtle catch of the season. He sat under a coconut tree, fascinated by a naked child of four years heating a coconut shell half full of turtle blood and scrambled turtle eggs over a burning coconut husk. Suddenly a heavy thud startled Kenneth out of his daydream. A large green coconut, weighing about ten pounds, had fallen between his hip and his camera twelve inches away. He learned later that a child had been killed several years before by a falling coconut, the only such fatality the villagers could remember. But Kenneth never sat under a cluster of coconuts after that.

The *Mahina* returned to Akiaki for Kenneth because he had told the captain he wanted to take the chief and Tangi to Vahitahi. But the surf was too high. Even so, a man whose son was dying on Vahitahi asked to go. Kenneth gave him permission with instructions to the captain to come back when the weather moderated. "The villagers seemed deeply moved by my giving this man a chance to see his son for the last time," Kenneth wrote. "The surf kept up its heavy pounding for three days but I was content to be stranded with these people. I had the chance to explore the tiny island and . . . saw taro, banana and sugar cane growing in ancient excavations, and a big artificial pond in which turtle were kept for time of need."

Monday, July 7, proved to be a busy day. First the *Mahina* hove into view, then the *Tiare Tahiti* arrived to load copra. Kenneth invited Tangi, Kohemingo, and the chief, Takaoa, to sail with him to Vahitahi in the *Mahina*, so they might escape the incredible confusion of returning by canoe with dogs, cats, pigs, and chickens. The canoes arrived at Vahitahi the next day as the weather threatened again. "Last night the wind boxed the compass," Kenneth wrote. "Our boat had to keep running from one side of the island to the other." That night the wind turned to a strong *maraamu* (west wind). The *Tiare Tahiti* arrived from Akiaki at 8 P.M., but made no attempt to land passengers.

Since the Tuamotuans could not pronounce Kenneth, they called him Keneti. It was Takaoa who suggested the next day that they haul the *Mahina* out of the water to safety. Otherwise she must sail up and down the island day after day, night after night. Her tired crew had only to fall asleep and she could drift to destruction on the reef. Kenneth gratefully accepted the chief's offer. He knew that there was an ancient ceremony attached to the process of hauling ashore a large voyaging canoe. The opportunity to record such a ceremony might never come again.

First the *Mahina* had to be unloaded. That took a day. On Wednesday, July 9, Kenneth wrote, "Tangi assembled the people and drilled them in the ancient chants used in bringing a *pahi* [canoe] over the reef and to land." They placed coconut fronds on the coral as skids for the keel. The next day the ocean was dead calm off the village. Kenneth unlimbered his movie camera. Later he described the scene:

All over four years of age were out in the ankle deep water on the reef, ready to haul on the two long ropes. Tangi took up his strand near the end of the reef where the yacht would first touch.

He chanted while the *Mahina-i-te-Pua* moved slowly toward the reef. As he finished [the chant], his daughter led a rousing *haka*, then all took up the ropes. The *Mahina* rose on a slight swell. Tangi yelled, "Take up the slack." Then he shouted the first line of the hauling chanty. All joined in the song and pulled . . . marching towards the beach. The yacht rode gently onto the reef and, when the waters receded, was high and dry.

But, according to the program, she was supposed to slide straight to the sands. By herculean effort, stirred on by chants and cheers, the people dragged her some forty feet inland. The chief had underestimated our weight and overestimated the strength of his people. The captain hit upon a scheme of lying the boat on its side and skidding it on a greased plank. That gained thirty yards and the boat was safe for the night. The natives were exhausted and numb from exposure to the cold wind and rain.

Another attempt the next day to haul the *Mahina* to land produced the same results. Only half of the population turned out now that the excitement was over. The mail sack carried in the *Mahina* from Amanu had contained a letter from the government office at Papeete deposing the present chief. "He associated his fail with us," Kenneth wrote. "To add to the discouragement, most of the natives were in bed with severe colds. Tangi was in bed." A promise of a barrel of flour and a pig for a feast restored the workers' spirits sufficiently to drag the *Mahina* within one hundred yards of the beach. She would be all right unless a big north sea blew up.

Tangi announced the next day that after Keneti's feast his people would perform for their guests the *tipara* ceremony, a signal honor. The *tipara* ceremony had died out on all the atolls except Vahitahi and the last performance there had taken place seven years ago. Preparations went forward in secrecy. Tangi refused to tell Stimson and Kenneth anything about it until they saw it themselves. Kenneth suspected this was partly because the songs and dances were half forgotten. The old people assembled to revive their memories and straighten out the order of events. Kenneth wrote later:

> The *tipara* anciently was held only in times of famine. *Tipara* means "to beg" and the essential feature of the ceremony was the formal begging by those who did not have from those who did. We believe that behind it all was originally the idea to amass enough food so that dances and magic rites might be performed which would stir up nature to produce the food for which they were sorely in need.

Hence the highly erotic character of so many of the songs and dances, and a probable explanation of why we know so little of such ceremonies, depending as we do on the writings of missionaries for all that involves a real knowledge of the language.

The feast of Keneti was scheduled for Bastille Day, June 14. Ceremonies opened at 8 A.M. with a flag raising and speeches. Songs and dances lasted until 11 A.M., when the feast began. The expedition had supplied an eighty-pound pig. Villagers took most of the food home. At 1:30 P.M., the old dances began and lasted until 5 P.M. when a shout went up, *"boti, boti!"* The *Mahina* was awash in huge surf tumbling over the reef. Everybody ran to the beach and hauled the boat one hundred feet nearer to the shore. All this kept Kenneth hustling as he shot movie film and took notes.

Preparations then began for the *tipara* ceremony. Tangi was sick in bed but Stimson got from him an outline of the ceremony and feast. Kohemingo directed the dancers. The ceremony began at 9:30 P.M. on July 16. Kenneth described it as follows:

> A group seated at one end of the village began a low, drawling chant. They chanted for an hour. We were then requested to extinguish our lamp and the glow of our cigarets. Any sort of fire would prevent the *kaha*, a certain malignant spirit, from joining and aiding the begging expedition.
>
> By the light of the bright stars alone, that part of the ceremony called the *hangahanga ki te maunga*, the building of the canoe, was silently performed. A procession of two files, one of women, the other of men, symbolized a raiding canoe. The *kaha* were represented by men armed with spears. They announced their arrival by rushing about scratching the sands with the points of their weapons while someone chanted.
>
> When all was in readiness, the canoe moved underway to a dignified, beautiful chant. One line was, "Which star shall I steer by? I will steer by the star, Gana." The procession swung off and disappeared in the deep gloom of the coconuts. Their song filled the night with lovely harmony.

Kenneth and Stimson did not follow the canoe as it voyaged through the village. Instead they walked around to wait on the other side at the place of "the anchoring of the canoe." Both files finally arrived and sat down to chant and wait until moonrise. Kenneth and Stimson sat through five hours of monotonous chanting. At moonrise a cloud cover made it a matter of debate. Those who believed the moon had risen won. Once more the canoe set sail.

The sailors chanted, "The shadows pass. Your path is flecked with moonlight." They drew near the first house and the singing changed in tone: "Come infants, come young people, come mature people, come. Babies at the breast, come. Old men bent up on their mats, come." As the song ended, two men approached the door with spears raised, snarling with anger. The chanting rose once more, "Give some food. Give some food." The *kaha* slapped the house violently with their spears so no one could pretend to sleep while the chanters taunted, "It is a holding back of food, holding back of food." The taunt of stinginess produced a bag of flour through the door. The canoe visited each house in the village.

Exhausted, Kenneth stumbled onto his sleeping mat. But the villagers were sent out to gather food the next day. Women went into the brush for pandanus nuts. Children collected coconuts. Men launched their canoes into the lagoon or over the reef into the ocean in search of fish and turtles. The food gathering went on for two days and on each day a fisherman caught a turtle. Later, Kenneth described the food preparations:

> The morning of the third day, the village was gay with smoking ovens. Five great earthen ovens had been prepared for the cooking of the feast; one for pig, two for smaller food, and two for turtle. One of the turtle ovens was for roasting the body whole, the other for semifinal cooking of the various cuts and the internal organs. All meat for the feast is only partially cooked. The people do not eat together where the feast is spread . . . but each family or group of friends take their share off to the house.

Two great coconut leaf mats were spread in the center of the village, one for the food and the other for guests—those who had stayed at home and given the food to the begging party. The beggars stood on the other side, singing, each decorated with a neatly braided headband of coconut leaf. Two older girls escorted each guest to the feast. Kenneth was cranking his movie camera when a couple of girls pulled him firmly to the mat, indicating by their determination that this was not a show, it was a *tipara*.

Kenneth and Stimson sat in the places of honor and were required to taste each dish and pronounce it good before it was divided among the other guests. "We could conscientiously swear to the deliciousness of most of the food," Kenneth wrote, "especially for the pandanus kernels which one might easily mistake for California pine nuts. But there were certain queer looking internal organs of the turtle which we sampled very gingerly."

There was more dancing and, during an interval, a spear drill—two files of men rushing across the field, alternately fighting and fleeing. Each time they met they swung their sticks in ritual battle that produced resounding whacks. They thrust and parried vigorously. Their performance ended the dancing. Everybody went home to gorge. Kenneth wrote, "We were informed the next number on the program, its conclusion, was for each one to seek out and spend the night with his favorite. Such an event being so commonplace in these islands, they nearly forgot to mention it as a necessary part of the ceremony."

Yet the *tipara* was not over, for the evil spirits, *haka*, were still about. They must be gotten rid of or bad things would happen. The exorcising ceremony took place two nights later. "The prelude was a curious affair," Kenneth wrote. "It seems that to make sure the people had not changed the songs or invented new dance movements, they must go through all the dances once more in front of two old people representing ancient chiefs who, dancing and singing with them, would be their critics. Nowadays, instead of the two old men, two young men dress up in outlandish odds and ends and simulate aged, decrepit persons. They are the objects of ridicule and the source of hilarious amusement. The appearance of the old crones emerging out of the darkness on the road was a masterpiece of acting."

A masked boy helped each of the ancient creatures crawl forward, croaking a chant. They hobbled through the steps of the dances, creaking arms making the proper motions while the audience convulsed with laughter. The "old-men dance" continued for two hours without boring the villagers. At last it was time to conduct the serious finale of the *tipara*.

The canoe formed again and, chanting, exactly retraced its path, stopping at each house and beating it. Close to the starting point the dancers halted and crouched down. The *tukau* (leader of the chants and dances) cried, *"Ti ho vik vik! Ti ho vik vik!"* In answer the dancers rose and crossed the right foot over the left, then the left foot over the right while they uttered, *"Huuuuuuuuuu,"* three times. They formed a circle around the *haka* who made vain attempts to escape the magic spell while the dancers chanted. Finally, the two men in the center fell to the ground, clutched the imaginary evil spirits, and strangled them. The *tipara* ended formally with the burning of all the paraphernalia used during the ceremony: decorations, leaf stalks, baskets, garlands, and headbands.

One of the pagan chants had brought Stimson alive with excitement. It ended with the words *ko-kio*. He translated that to mean "all is Kio's," Kenneth explained later. At last Stimson had found hard evidence of the existence of the supreme Polynesian god in the Tuamotus. This was the same deity that Handy had speculated upon in his book on Polynesian religion, and the god that was called Io by the Maoris in New Zealand—a god whose existence was kept secret on pain of death by a select cadre of priests. Kio must be the Tuamotuan equivalent of the Maori god Io.

In spite of Stimson's excitement, Kenneth did not read so much into the prayer ending. The *tipara* prayers seemed to end in various ways that gave them no special significance. What is more, the Polynesian gods Kenneth had encountered in the Tuamotus were familiar: Tane, Atea and Rono, Wakea and Papa, as well as Tetu—the beginning. Of course, that did not mean a supreme god did not exist. The whole purpose of scientific inquiry was to explore such possibilities.

So Kenneth and Stimson went to Ruea, an old woman who had given them chants, and asked about the meaning of *kio* in the prayer ending. Kenneth said later Ruea told them the only Kio she knew of was Kio Tu Papako, a legendary ghost who had popped up before in Kenneth's researches. Kio Tu Papako, common in the Tuamotus, was certainly not a supreme god. Stimson was insistent. "He told her about the Io cult in New Zealand," Kenneth recalled later. "That it was so sacred no one could reveal it on pain of death [and] that he believed she had been taught that Io was Kio. Her only reply was that she knew of Kio Tu Papako, Kio the ghost." Stimson continued to believe that the natives were afraid to tell him the truth.

Kenneth's little radio set proved a great comfort to him as well as a source of exasperation. The day after the *tipara* ceremony, he tried for two and a half hours without raising Marii, although Kenneth heard him clearly. He didn't know that his antenna had to be strung toward Papeete or the signal would not go in that direction. Also, Kenneth's call signals proved too difficult so he used his initials, KPE, instead. An operator in New Zealand complained about his unauthorized call sign. In addition, Marii had agreed to set 6:30 A.M. as their transmission time. But on Vahitahi Kenneth discovered that this was exactly the moment his bowels moved, so they had to broadcast one-half hour later.

On Monday, July 21, he reported in his diary, "Heard Marii and he heard me. Learned that Marguerite and Tiare are well and that our goods are on the *Moruroa*." Yet, he couldn't make the set work consistently. On Tuesday, July 22, "Waited patiently all day for Marii. He called me a few minutes in the A.M. and P.M. but did not hear me." The next day, "Marii called me this A.M. but didn't hear me." Kenneth had better luck on Thursday when he got through on the first try and learned that the *Pro-Patria* was bound to Vahitahi with money for the expedition, and that the *Moruroa* would soon arrive with their supplies.

Each brief contact meant a triumph for Kenneth. He did not talk only to Marii in Papeete. He listened to transmissions in Morse code by radio operators on the schooners wending their unpredictable ways through the atolls. And he could call them in any one of four different languages after his technique improved. The little radio changed his status from castaway to subscriber on a one-thousand-mile-long rural party line.

The radio made all the difference. After the high surf had battered the *Mahina* on the reef, Captain Gooding inspected her for damage. The exhaust pipe came off in his hand. Stranded without contact it would have been difficult to decide how to cope with this disaster. Stimson and Shapiro had cooled their heels on Hao for two months because they expected schooners that never came. Now Kenneth could call them. This time they decided to send Captain Gooding back to Papeete in the *Moruroa* to repair the exhaust pipe. She arrived on July 27, 1930. "Was very happy to have news and food," Kenneth wrote in his diary.

On Vahitahi, Stimson and Kenneth differed considerably in their handling of the natives. Both methods must have been effective. Stimson projected himself as an authority figure: decisive, masculine, of superior knowledge. He was good at banter and he had a flamboyant appeal. Kenneth treated the Polynesians as his equals, people from whom he could learn. His approach was soft and unspectacular, his appeal was artless. Bengt Danielsson of the *Kon Tiki* expedition, who later knew and liked both men, compared Stimson to a warrior and Kenneth to a sage.

"He hounds the natives till they produce their books, or come through with any other of his wishes," Kenneth wrote later to Handy. "Then he indulges them with all the soft soap the French love. . . . It cost him such an effort and such an amount of thought to win them over that he thinks it is a much more difficult feat than it is, and that for winning them over he deserves a lot of credit— which he certainly does."

Stimson was so convinced of the superiority of his methods that he lectured Kenneth, especially on the importance of becoming intimate with the natives in order to win their confidence. Kenneth wrote to Handy, tongue in cheek, that if Bishop Museum anthropologists adopted Stimson's field methods, all their wives would divorce them. Kenneth added, "Stimson . . . lays his success to these new methods rather than to what I consider the true cause, namely, his absolute facility with the language and his unflagging energy."

In spite of their differences, the two men worked well together.

Stimson, who was proud of his strong grip, carried a hand instrument with a spring that measured hand strength. Since the Tuamotuan men prided themselves on strength, Stimson took great pleasure in squeezing his machine harder than they. Kenneth said his own grip was the weakest. But he could swim, and the Tuamotuans also prided themselves on their skill in the water. Stimson dared the Tuamotuans to swim against Kenneth.

"We set the date for July 21 with three of their best swimmers," said Kenneth later. "Stimson was the referee and got us started. They made a tremendous splash, not very efficient. I . . . kept up with them splashing around. On the way back I just simply lit out. They were looking behind all the time to see where I was. I was sitting on the beach when they finished." Kenneth's victory over the fifty-yard course appealed mightily to Stimson, and the Tuamotuans immediately learned Kenneth's stroke.

The weeks passed in steady activity. Kenneth typed an article about the *tipara* ceremony for *The Honolulu Advertiser.* He took movies of the natives landing a turtle. His contacts with Marii became more frequent and professional. "Tahuka gave me his manuscript [genealogy] book," he wrote in his dairy on Saturday, August 2. The next day, "Had Tahuka and Nicola to dinner." He learned more string figures and the legends they told.

With Stimson settled domestically in another house and expanding his word lists, Kenneth decided to make a run to Tahiti and back. He worried about Marguerite and Tiare. The dictaphones that Kenneth had ordered to record chants should have arrived by now and would require special handling. Most important, Kenneth could never endure to remain stationary for long. When the *Pro-Patria* appeared on the horizon at dawn on Tuesday, August 12, he "rushed to be off on her."

Years later, he described the voyage. "The *Pro-Patria* was a big schooner. Couple of masts and a pretty good sized crew," he said. "The captain just wore a pair of shorts and a shirt. Very unassuming. The crew were Tahitians and Tuamotuans. Tuamotuans were very good [sailors]. I slept in the little cabin, a table in the middle with bunks on both sides. Or you can sleep on deck. On a mat. We always carried mats. Sleep with one side over you. Use some clothing for a pillow. Those Tahitian mats are very good. Standard luggage. And a *pareu*. You tie it up [around your belongings], throw it over your shoulder, and there you are . . . I did have a suitcase but I was the exception that way."

They put in at Tatakoto to load copra while Kenneth learned string figures and photographed canoes as well as the chief. The *Pro-*

Patria wended her leisurely way to Amanu where the current was so strong in the pass she couldn't get into the lagoon, then to Hao where they did get in to find only six people in the village. The others were away making copra. A brisk breeze brought them to Hikueru, then on to Anaa where the *Pro-Patria* took on fourteen tons of copra—all transported in sacks from a pile on the beach in the ship's boats. The crew worked until 11:30 P.M.

Kenneth arrived in Papeete at 7 A.M. Monday, August 25, 1930, looking like a beachcomber. Little Tiare cried in fright when the strange, unshaven man appeared at their door. Marguerite scrubbed him. "It was not a wife's dream to have a husband return from the Tuamotus," she confessed later. Kenneth wrote in his diary, "Marguerite and Tiare looking splendidly."

The next day he put Marii to work printing his film while Kenneth caught up on his accounts and got the dictaphones out of customs. "The wax cylinders were very fragile," he explained later. "Each machine had a speaking tube which led from the horn to the cylinder. The dictaphone was hand wound. It had a case. You could carry it."

Kenneth had booked passage in the *Tiare Tahiti* heading back to the Tuamotus on the following Monday, but the departure was delayed so he and Marguerite had a chance to visit until late afternoon on Wednesday. He sailed at 5:15 P.M. with Captain Gooding, the repaired exhaust pipe, and a dictaphone with several boxes of wax cylinders. They arrived at Vahitahi on Thursday, September 11, after a voyage of seven days and eight nights, to find Stimson engrossed in translations.

The captain set to work repairing the *Mahina* and getting her ready to be launched. Kenneth and Stimson urged Tangi to let them photograph and record the chants and dances of the *tipara* ceremony. The villagers had skidded the *Mahina* to the water's edge when the captain came down with the grippe and a stiff neck. He was on his back and Kenneth was swimming in the lagoon on September 22 when a girl came running to the village. Waves were battering the *Mahina* and had washed out the underpinnings that kept her from rolling over. "Great excitement," Kenneth wrote in his diary. "Passed an anxious night. Three men slept on the boat. Luckily [the] wind shifted to the southwest."

The next day Kenneth reported, "Natives at boat eight hours without rest." That night she slid into the water unharmed. And the next day, "Started people trying to record . . . music." Kenneth wrote later, "That was September 25, a Thursday. Friday morning early I sailed south for a reconnaissance survey of Nukutavake, Pinaki and Vairaatea, leaving Stimson with his *tipara* and his god, Kio. Coming back after a few days we were ready for the recording of the songs and chants of the *tipara* on the dictaphone and for the cinema of the dances."

Then a labor dispute arose. One faction at Vahitahi insisted they be paid for their performance. Neither faction wanted the scientists to record and film the other faction. "Things looked bad for a few days," Kenneth wrote later. "Stimson called a council of war, and he with his firm hand and I with my gentle hand, finally got them going again, each of us secretly claiming the victory."

With pagan songs and dances on the rampage again, Stimson and Kenneth extended their stay into October. It was a final frenzy of activity. On October 4, Kenneth wrote in his diary, "Ua recorded chants A.M. Prepared to record P.M. but people all in the lagoon after great school of fish. In evening fell asleep with fatigue." On October 7, "Took down some songs A.M. on dictaphone. Ua had it all P.M. Began cinema of dances. Recorded eight." On Thursday, October 9, "In afternoon took movies of eight men in spear dances and in part of the *tipara* ceremony. Very busy with dictaphone and dances." On October 11, Kenneth took movies of the end of the *tipara* ceremony.

Their three-month stay on Vahitahi ended on October 15. "People helped us load," Kenneth wrote in his diary. "Made us a present of food and chickens. Very gloomy." They arrived at Reao at noon the next day. "Between the measuring of men, I took cinema and photographs and ran the dictaphone," Kenneth wrote later to Gregory. "I made a complete circuit of the island recording their fine *maraes*, so different from all others in the Tuamotus except those of Pukarua."

It took Kenneth a week on Reao to make contact with Marii in Papeete because he had changed his radio frequency. They remained two and one-half weeks, and it was not until the last week that the natives gave them a welcoming ceremony: "two pigs, ten chickens, five sennit skeins, two mats, a great many coconuts and a very pretty presentation with ancient songs and dances. Took down records in the evening."

They had reached almost the eastern end of the great sweep of atolls that comprise the Tuamotus. There was no time to go farther. "*Mahina-i-te-Pua* sailed for Takoto and home at 8 P.M.," Kenneth wrote in his diary on Monday, November 3, 1930. But he and Stimson did not sail in her. By radio, Kenneth had arranged passage in *Pro-Patria*, ready for a homeward voyage with a full load of copra. She would take a little longer than the *Mahina*, but twenty-five dollars extra for the 725-mile trip would assure them a dry passage for themselves and their film and dictaphone records. It being the stormy season, in the *Mahina* they might be soaked the whole way.

"As it turned out," Kenneth wrote later, "an exceptional . . . ten days of beautiful weather followed, and we regretted not having come by *Mahina*, Stimson in particular. He hates Chinese schooners."

Chapter Twenty-six

Worry about Stimson

Each of Kenneth's expeditions seemed to begin by fits and starts, slowly gather momentum, and end in a burst of activity. Now, after his return to Papeete, he entered the frantic final stage of his Tuamotu survey. There were endless loose ends to tie up: the writing of his annual report, chants still to be recorded by Tuamotuan informants in Tahiti, translations to be agreed upon, the boat to be sold, and film to be developed and printed. Gregory had grumpily agreed to give him until the end of May 1931 to finish up in Tahiti, but only if it didn't cost extra. Kenneth tried not to waste a minute of it.

A first priority was to sort out the material and agree on how to handle it. "Collaboration seems the only solution for an important half," Kenneth wrote to Handy on January 3, 1931. "But how are we to collaborate [after my return to Honolulu] with two months between every exchange of thought? . . . An easy solution would be to have him [Stimson] come to Honolulu were it not that both he and I need the help of local Tuamotu scholars in working up our material—Stimson in particular . . .

"He has a great fund of energy and he is keen and quick. He needs, however, to go through a period of steadying so as not to be swept off his feet by his enthusiasms. Also, the fact that certain of his abilities seem to have no limit rather blinds him to his limitations. . . . It will be well for him to learn to cooperate with us . . ."

To Gregory, who had written Kenneth impatiently that the translation of chants, songs, and folks tales was not his job, he wrote back:

The ethnology is inextricably tied in with the chants and prayers, and largely dependent on them for its authenticity. Therefore it is imperative that I go over this material with Stimson before we separate. The place to go over it is here where, when the material is incomprehensible or too incomplete to serve, we can fall back upon the inestimably valuable help of Tuamotuan scholars in Papeete.

Should Stimson work up these chants entirely independent of me, it would mean a big delay for ethnology [Kenneth's responsibility]. And I will have lost the chance to bring the ethnology of the Tuamotus up to a par with what will surely be the quality of the linguistics and physical anthropology.

Kenneth's letter indicates that Stimson had become openly critical of his handling of the expedition. "In Stimson's opinion he could have handled it better," Kenneth wrote. "He will undoubtedly have the chance to prove what he can do, and to profit by our mistakes as well as our successes. . . . If, as Stimson would claim, we had extraordinary good luck in getting through happily with my planning, fortunately we did not have the extraordinary bad luck he prophesied. Some reasonable chances have to be taken or we would have lost invaluable time and far exceeded our budget. I found that Stimson's stern hand and condescension, the traditional colonial method which some ethnologists keep and some discard, was for me incompatible with my character and rarely necessary . . ." What has survived of this letter appears to be a first draft. It is not clear whether Kenneth mailed it or what parts of it he mailed.

The inexhaustible Paea was still in Papeete. Stimson worked with him as a paid informant to capture the subtle shades of meaning of the chants. Marii remembers meeting schooners in from the atolls. When he found Tuamotuans on board, he hustled them to Kenneth's house where he took their oral histories and genealogies on the dictaphone. "Put roller [wax cylinder] on," he explained. "Turn the horn to you and you tell all the story." Then he snapped their photographs.

Kenneth sold his radio for $155. But the boat was not so easy. The colonial governor expressed his readiness to buy it for 35,000 francs ($1,400). Then bureaucratic delays set in. Kenneth came down with a cold. The leading anthropologist from New Zealand, H. D. Skinner, and his wife arrived and had to be shown the island.

On January 21 Kenneth wrote in his diary, "Had breakfast with Ua. Read over his Kio paper all morning." The paper disturbed Kenneth. He said later he did not feel that either he or Stimson was ready to publish their Tuamotuan material. There were too many unanswered questions. Now Stimson was prepared to announce his discovery of a supreme god in the Tuamotus, and gave Ruea on Vahitahi as one informant—the woman who had told Kenneth and Stimson she had never heard of such a god. Apparently she had later told Stimson that she agreed with him.

"I just couldn't believe my eyes," Kenneth said later. "But . . . he [Stimson] swore, you know, that he had checked this . . . So until I had a real good chance to check, I didn't dare say anything at the time. It's all beautifully written up. . . . I didn't know to what extent he had worked with Ruea and developed material." In spite of what Kenneth remembered, his subsequent correspondence with Stimson indicates that they had heated arguments at this time about the translations.

Kenneth's headlong rush to wind up the expedition continued. A diary entry on February 20 reads, "Packed canoe from Pukarua." On February 23, "Worked on plans of Mehetia *marae*s. Out to inspect . . . overhauling of *Mahina-i-te-Pua.*" On February 27, "Busy packing specimens for Honolulu." Fariua and his striking wife, Reva, arrived from Fangatau on March 27 and agreed to work with Kenneth as a paid informant. Then Paea came to work with Kenneth. By this time he was keeping the dictaphone, Marii, and a stenographer busy to get it all down. Stimson was working at the same pace at his own beach cottage with the informants.

Kenneth's concern about Stimson's preoccupation with a supreme god increased a few weeks before departure when Fariua told him that Stimson kept asking if he knew anything about a Kio cult at Fangatau. Fariua said he had told Stimson, "I know nothing of such a cult. But as soon as I return to Fangatau I will ask the old people and, whatever I can learn from them, I will write to you." Fariua said Paea was giving Stimson false information about the cult of Kio. About the same time Marii told Marguerite to warn Kenneth that the informants were playing tricks.

One of the basic rules of anthropology in Kenneth's day, as well as at present, was not to lead an informant. Anyone who worked in the South Seas knew that islanders were eager to please. If they sensed an anthropologist believed a certain way, they felt it discourteous to correct him especially if they were being paid. Stimson made no effort to conceal his interest in a supreme god. In fact he seemed determined to wrest its secret from his informants. Was Paea, the Tuamotuan sage, telling Stimson what he knew he wanted to hear about the god Kio?

The best evidence for Kenneth's concern about the Kio cult at this time comes from a letter to Handy dated April 26. He wrote:

> Stimson's paper on the cult of Kio in the Tuamotus goes by this mail, the result of five months of hard toil on a few precious fragments of chants and scattered bits of information, by an energetic and swift moving mind never fatigued by routine . . . in handling details.
>
> I would rest easier about this erection were its keystone not too much our Anaa informant Paea who, unfortunately, was fairly familiar with the

Io cult in New Zealand before giving most of his information and who seems to have been held back from revealing the Tuamotu cult more by lack of information than by unwillingness. In my own work with him, I have found him more than ready to oblige by composing words or ideas originating with himself when no other source was available.

Paea has an enormous stock of chants, genealogies, legends, but no more than many others, and you know by taking liberties with such knowledge it is possible to turn out stuff bearing all the earmarks of the real thing. I will heave a sigh of relief, and am sure Stimson will also, if Paea is not the sole living repository of this lore for the western Tuamotus, and if another can give material checking him. . . . Skinner said no native could lie so beautifully . . .

We have a great body of religious chants about which hangs no shadow of intervention and these need to be translated and worked up. I wish now Stimson had chosen this solid field in which to give his exhibition of mental gymnastics and left the shaky part of the Kio cult, though more sensational, until some further confirmation could be had.

On Friday, May 22, Kenneth went to bed with a sore throat and cold brought on by overwork. He took an aspirin and drank hot wine. The next day he and Marguerite packed. That afternoon they boarded the SS *Makura* bound for a visit to New Zealand. He had hardly accomplished everything he wanted to do in the Tuamotus. But he was bringing back 1,500 photos, recordings of 250 native songs, 2,500 feet of movie film, and 400 artifacts. The expedition had measured more than 500 Tuamotuans and had collected 2 sets of 5 loose-leaf notebooks of 400 typewritten sheets each, 10 museum notebooks, a file of 2,000 place names and a dictionary file of words and meanings numbering in the tens of thousands. All of this was material about to be lost. They had done it by traveling 4,000 miles in a 27½ foot boat. Theirs was a unique achievement performed against formidable obstacles. But he was still worried about Stimson.

PART FIVE

THE GODS
IN CONFLICT

Chapter Twenty-seven
Stimson's Cult of Kiho-tumu

Marguerite took first prize at a fancy dress ball on the voyage home. It was poor preparation for the grim reality of economic depression they found in Honolulu the summer of 1931. Harry Shapiro reported from New York that unemployed workers were living in hovels made of packing crates and were selling apples on street corners. He had been shocked by the nation's plunge into poverty. The Great Depression did not hit Hawaii that hard, but even Handy, who liked to assume a pose of amused detachment, was concerned about cutting back programs at the museum.

He put it this way, "Unless somebody finds the pot of gold at the end of the rainbow or gets out grandma's stocking, it is going to be necessary to call off Dr. Buck's trip to the Horne Islands. . . . Now when Gregory says the museum can't pay Buck's expenses for a six months' field trip, you know we are *actually*, not just psychologically, hard up."

Kenneth and Marguerite moved in with his mother until the tenants in their own house found a new place. Little Tiare, age four, spoke only French. She could not understand her grandmother. Kenneth made the rounds of used car lots where his training in anthropology didn't help much. He tried Fords, Chevrolets, and finally settled on a Nash. At the museum, in his third floor office located above the director, he began unpacking the archaeological cargo he had brought back from the Tuamotus.

A decade in the director's chair had made Gregory impatient and dictatorial. He was inaccessible to the press. Raymond Fosberg, a young botanist who later went to the Smithsonian Institution, remembers Gregory from this period as "a hard nosed, contrary, arbitrary bastard. His usual inclination, if you suggested something, was that he'd do it just the opposite. Yet he could be most charming." Laura Thompson, beginning a long career in anthropology, remembers a place down the hall from the director's office known as the "Weeping Room." It was where staff members went to unburden their despair after a frustrating interview with Gregory.

Much more disturbing to Kenneth was the way his trouble with Stimpson followed him to Honolulu. He would soon discover that their disagreements were to become the major frustration of his career. Among aficionados of the South Seas, the controversy has provided a continuing subject of speculation. Anthropologists who got involved tended to be embarrassed by it. Since they seldom talked about it in public, most of the information that has circulated is based on gossip and hearsay.

Kenneth found that Stimson had written to Ed Bryan as well as Handy about his great discovery of the supreme god Kio, and had mailed them translations of chants. Then Kenneth received a letter from Stimson announcing that Fariua, who had accused Paea of lying about the existence of Kio, had also come around and was giving Stimson Kio lore. Stimson's letter of July 20, 1931, described the conversion of Fariua to the Kio school in his typical enthusiastic fashion:

> All the time that you and I were working with Fariua I felt that there must be some reason why he would tell *you* one thing and *me* another. . . . So I planned a deliberate campaign . . . five weeks ago . . . to break down his reserve; it was a long shot but it was worth taking.
>
> I told him that a great *tagata tahutahu* [sorcerer] had told me that in a former existence I had been a high-priest of Kio. . . . I showed him Conan Doyle's book of spirit photographs, and I worked on his superstition in every way that my knowledge of Polynesian character suggested. For several days his reply was the same: to wait until he could see Kamake [the great sage of Fangatau]; he said that he felt sure that *if* Kamake knew about the Kio lore he would be willing to tell me . . .
>
> But a day or two afterwards he turned up in the morning and told me that his grandfather [Temiro of Fangatau] had appeared to him in his sleep the night before, and asked why he concealed the knowledge in his heart from me. When he replied that Temiro himself had laid the *tapu* on him never to divulge the sacred *paurau mahauhau* . . . Temiro—the dream apparition—replied that he released him from the *tapu* . . .

Stimson wrote that old Paea was now jealous of Fariua for his superior knowledge of the supreme god. "To my surprise, instead of the supreme god being Kio, as I had anticipated, it is Kiho-tumu," he added. The expense money left by Kenneth to pay Fariua had run out, Stimson explained, forcing him to pay Fariua out of his own pocket. But Stimson obviously felt the money was well spent because of the Kiho material Fariua had given him. Stimson was plunging ahead in the pursuit of more Kiho lore about which, he wrote, Bryan and Wilder were enthusiastic.

This letter and those to other museum staffers from Stimson alarmed Kenneth. He put down his thoughts for Handy:

> Thanks for letting me see the new Kiho chants of Stimson and his letter. They enable me to understand what is back of this apparent sudden releasing of Kiho lore on the part of . . . Fariua. A perusal of the chants convinces me that these are nothing more or less than the Tetumu chants and lore which Fariua was trying to bring to the attention of Stimson just before I left. Stimson's insistence that Tetumu was Kio caused Fariua to draw somewhat within himself. . . . I am afraid that the expiration of the little fund I left in Papeete to feed and house Fariua and his wife for four weeks, in order to enable them to help Stimson on Fangatau translations, has been the deciding factor in Fariua giving in to Stimson [so that he would continue to be paid] . . .

Kenneth wrote a stiff letter to Stimson on July 26. He repeated what he had said to Handy about influencing Fariua and added that he was disturbed to find in Stimson's translation the omission of a phrase, *po kino*, as it was sung in the original text by the informant. *Po* means "underworld home of dead spirits" and *kino* translates as "undesirable" or "evil." Apparently they had discussed this in Tahiti. Stimson contended that the association of evil with his supreme god was due to missionary influence and, therefore, he omitted it from his text. To Kenneth, changing the text of a chant for any reason was a serious breach of ethics.

He also objected to Stimson's introduction in which he belittled Fariua's wife, Reva, because she refused to concede the existence of Kio. Kenneth wrote, "I am not just disturbed, I am alarmed over the apparently uncritical frame of mind with which you seem now to be pursuing your investigation of the cult of Kio or Kiho."

Three days later, Kenneth's sense of fair play made him send Stimson another letter. "Your beliefs about Kiho may be right," he wrote. "There is no insistence that I am probably right." But he reminded Stimson that omitting words to suit the translator can forever remove the possibility that other meanings might exist. Kenneth wrote, "The tendency you have to assume you know more than your informants is a dangerous one. . . . We are not out to teach the Polynesians grammar or our conception of their beliefs. We are out to record what they know, as they know it. To do that . . . we have to keep our minds as sensitive as we can to every little breeze of thought that flows. Your increasing knowledge of the language opens you to this opportunity. But that opportunity is spoiled if your own ideas are so noisy that those of the natives cannot be heard."

Stimson answered on August 15 in the tone of a older brother lecturing a younger one:

> Really, Kenneth, I *quite* appreciate your point of view because I *understand* it. But what made me hot under the collar at the time (sorry I lost my temper once) was that I felt (and still feel) that you should defer to my judgement in matters of *translation* which belonged particularly to my field, and wherein I felt that my judgement must, necessarily, be more likely to be right since *I was constantly perceiving* little intangible evidences—straws that showed how the wind blew—in my daily intercourse with my informants, which I literally could not make you see as I (in my more intimate association with them) saw them . . .
>
> I have no desire to receive credit for your work, and I'm sure you don't want to receive credit for mine; why not forget our differences of opinion which—after all—are not fundamental, in the sincere desire to garner the utmost we can out of our splendid material, you in your field, and I in mine?

Yet to Kenneth their differences could not have been more fundamental, and Stimson's assumption that they were based on professional jealousy hurt. How could he convince Stimson that the chants they had been privileged to record must not be used to satisfy one theory or another but rather as a priceless resource to be made available to scholars for all time? There would not be an opportunity like this again. The importance of their material, the possibility that it provided a last true glimpse of ancient Polynesia, made Kenneth hesitant about publishing at all until the entire body of chants had been translated, checked, and evaluated. But Stimson would not wait. He charged ahead with sublime confidence in his superior knowledge.

The Nash refused to start in August so Kenneth had the carburetor fixed. Then the door wouldn't shut. The Rockefeller Foundation scheduled a visit to look over the museum before deciding whether to fund more research. Kenneth asked for money to prepare one thousand feet of his Tuamotu movie film for showing to the visiting committee. The museum turned him down so he talked a donation out of an affluent friend, Atherton Richards.

By September, Buck and Handy had read some of Stimson's translations and had found that they generally rang true. Kenneth's relief shows in his letters to Stimson. Yet he continued to offer criticism as the translations progressed. "If you think I am hopeless, it is probably because I am purposely taking the opposition—finding all the faults and weaknesses I can while your work is still plastic . . . [and] . . . before your work appears in immovable, hard print . . ." Then he picked the translations apart, pointing out inconsistencies, contradictions, and alternative translations that filled eighteen typewritten pages.

In November he wrote to Stimson, "Gregory has walked off with your manuscripts and is probably circulating them among the trustees. He enjoys good writing and clear presentations. Albert Judd [president of the trustees] is an admirer of your writing. . . . In three or four weeks letters from you will probably be here to shoot along to publication. Don't expect me to gum up proceedings. I have said what I have to say. . . . So long as it is not to be assumed that I subscribe to everything said, I have no objections to the publication of your manuscripts exactly as they stand at this moment, although I believe you will eventually regret having said some of the things you say and having committed yourself to certain theories so wholeheartedly."

With the blessing of the director and president of the museum, work on the manuscripts moved forward quickly. "Gregory is all set to put your manuscripts right into the editorial and printing mill," Kenneth wrote on December 11. A letter from Fariua helped ease Kenneth's concern about Gregory's eagerness to publish. The Tuamotuan assured Kenneth that he had told Stimson the truth about Kiho-tumu, and that there was in his home at Fangatau a book in which the chants were written.

With the new year, 1932, Kenneth went back to work on his manuscript about archaeological ruins in Tahiti. He finished writing about stone construction on February 13 and began a study of genealogies the following month. Marguerite was pregnant again and not feeling very well. Maids came and went.

The letters between Kenneth and Stimson continued to be pointed but friendly, with Kenneth offering criticism intended to improve Stimson's translations. Sometimes they came to agreement. Stimson defended his freedom to translate esoteric meanings that only he with his deep understanding of the Tuamotuan language could grasp. At one point he advised Kenneth that "Buck should leave linguistics severely alone." Kenneth conceded Stimson's superior knowledge of the language but questioned the literary licenses he took. Both Buck and Kenneth believed in more literal, and less literary, translations.

"Buck's and my criticism that you have a tendency to over-refinement, is not to be dismissed quite so categorically," Kenneth wrote. "We mean [that] the delicacy and extreme refinement of European thought, expressed in high flung phrases of Shakespeare or the Bible, gives a flavor which is foreign to the Polynesian mind and does not adequately bring out its own strength and beauty."

Kenneth gave as an example Stimson's description of Tuamotuan dance movements: "they pirouetted through the figures of the dance . . ." The phrase, Kenneth wrote, calls to mind dainty figures whirling on tiptoe, flitting in and out through graceful arrangements. Yet films of the slow *haka* show a lazy, graceful swaying of hips, swinging of arms, and opening and shutting of hands. In the fast *haka* there is vigorous stamping, sudden and abrupt movement, and around this the strong scent of coconut oil and tropical blossoms.

As for Buck's linguistic ability, Kenneth added, "When I read an abstract of the Tahaki legend at the Anthropology Club, Buck got up, ran through the Maori versions and the Cook Island versions, and chanted chants occurring in all of them. I had just [also] read the two Maori versions and a Cook Island version similar to the one he gave and was therefore able to observe the faithfulness of his memory. You would have thought he had the legends in his hands, and had read them through a moment ago."

Stimson wrote back about his tendency to overrefinement, "I believe you are absolutely right. I sent one of my carbon copies of the *Great Legend* to my sister and brother-in-law (the author, VanWyck Brooks—his life of Emerson will be out in April) . . . and they both feel just as you and Buck do about all words derived from the Latin. My sister has sent me a long list of suggested changes, substituting anglo-saxon words for words of Latin derivation, and I must admit they are improvements."

The two men clashed again after Stimson wrote to Buck and misquoted Kenneth to his own advantage. Kenneth wrote in open anger, "What was your motive in twisting my remarks and then implying that I was twisting Buck's?" Then he quoted exactly what he had said. Kenneth added, "What makes for the greatest difficulty is, to be perfectly frank, you do not seem to be playing a square game, and [are] more interested in demonstrating your superiority than in discovering the truth . . ." He continued, "I am mindful of the remark in your letter to Buck, 'while criticising each other frankly, we should not go so far as to suspect each other's integrity of purpose or character.' Then, I ask, why undermine my faith in your integrity or purpose or character by making statements you know perfectly well I know not to be true . . . ?"

The correspondence does not show an answer to this until months later when Stimson wrote, "I'm glad that you have written me frankly about your criticism. I am never offended at frank criticism, but I'll admit I *was* offended at some of the things you said, such as that I had bribed Fariua. The thing that hurt was that you could think I would do such a thing; but I believe now that you said some things thoughtlessly without stopping to figure out how they must seem to me, and I think it was mainly due to *plain worry* . . . I am only too glad to assume that you have gotten over such ill-feeling . . . and hope that we shall work together in complete harmony for our best interests and the best interests of the museum."

The Rockefeller Foundation, impressed by Kenneth's movies of the Tuamotus, came through with funding for 1932 and 1933 to insure continuation of work in progress. Ed Bryan, now curator of collections, said he didn't know how the museum would have raised enough to carry on otherwise. In a letter to Stimson, Kenneth warned, "Unless things pick up by the end of 1933, we are in for a siege, all of us." The museum's revenues might be cut in half. He wrote that he had considered putting Marguerite and the children in her house in Tahiti, and camping on some Polynesian island with Buck where they could live and work.

Gregory himself took over the editing chores for Stimson's manuscripts. The *Mahina* remained an unsold white elephant. In Tahiti, Kenneth had loaned the museum $100 to be paid out of the sale price of the boat. The loan was still unpaid. Now the Emorys had no money for a baby carriage and baby clothes. They scraped along with a dollar or two left in the bank at the end of every month.

This time Marguerite's labor pains began on July 22 after a shopping excursion to Piggly Wiggly, a new grocery chain store in Honolulu. Kenneth took her to St. Francis Hospital that night. A baby girl, Winifred, was born at 8:02 A.M. on July 23, 1932. Kenneth wrote in his diary, "All well. Brought mother and Tiare in from Lanikai. They stayed over." The next day, "Cooked dinner myself and stayed home. Very tired."

In May, Stimson began to look for hidden Kiho meanings in the *tipara* ceremony. By June, he had found evidence of the supreme god in Tahiti as well as the Tuamotus. Then, in August, came "stunning confirmation" of an Io cult in Hawaii. His capacity for work fed on itself. He wrote to Kenneth, "Please don't quote me . . . but I believe my new book of legends will not be equalled anywhere in Polynesia, except perhaps by the Fornander collection of Bishop Memoirs; Paea really has a wonderful memory; he does not remember as *accurately* as Fariua, but he actually knows ten times more of the ancient legends. His new material runs over 250,000 words. And it is nearly all legends."

Kenneth, who was in his final write up of Society Island *maraes*, read about Stimson's recording of new material with pleasure. But he was not much impressed with the new Kiho discoveries. They had another disagreement about Stimson's tendency to see the supreme god wherever he looked, under names including Io, Kio, Ia, and Kiho.

The controversy refused to go away. In January 1933, British anthropologist Raymond Firth of New Zealand stopped at the museum for a day on his way to England where he would work up his notes after a stay on the Polynesian island of Tikopia. Firth's research and writing about Tikopia would make the small, slim, articulate man a towering figure in Pacific anthropology.

Kenneth wrote to Stimson, "One of the first things he [Firth] asked me was concerning your discovery of Io in the Tuamotus." Firth told Kenneth he suspected the New Zealand Io cult was not ancient but a post-contact development. In that case, Io would simply be the Polynesian rendering of Jehova.

"But . . . if we had undisputed evidence of this Io in the Tuamotus, he would have to revise his opinion," Kenneth added. "I said that, unfortunately, our evidence is not yet beyond dispute, that if the cult of Io should be proven to be post-European in New Zealand, the same might prove to be the case in the Tuamotus. There was not one of our informants who was not saturated with the Bible."

Kenneth added, "What a pity that I cannot smother grave doubts, and that I am morally bound not to conceal them when called upon for an opinion. . . . You may think I am opening an old sore in bringing up this subject. But let's not be silly about it. We have got to face the facts sooner or later, and considering our chosen calling, we ought to be able to face them together." Stimson answered on January 30: "There is nothing to be gained by discussing the authenticity of the Tuamotuan accounts of creation and a supreme god until my evidence has been placed before competent Polynesian scholars . . ."

A month later Kenneth wrote, "The plates for your first book have just been made up and look very nice. Your second book is now being put into galley." The cold, hard type was set. Kenneth felt he had done all he could to insure that Stimson's enthusiasm for Kihotumu would not embarrass the museum. Stimson was, after all, his protégé.

Chapter Twenty-eight
Pick a Buick

It was like having a toothache go away. With Stimson's manuscripts committed to type, Kenneth turned his energy to activities he enjoyed a lot more. One of them was the Anthropology Club, organized during his stay in the Tuamotus. The club had survived a battle between its founders, Stokes and high school science teacher T. T. Waterman, about whether members should read research papers at meetings or do folk dances and have fun. Lectures won. Kenneth didn't mind a bit. He attended every lecture and gave a few himself.

Kenneth, Handy, and Buck also lectured to the Hawaiian students at Kamehameha Schools. Lecturing for Kenneth was no longer a painful purgatory. He discovered that preparing lectures tended to stimulate new ideas. One of the topics on which he was asked to talk to the students was Hawaiian navigation, a subject that fascinated him but for which there was no hard information. By the time Captain James Cook arrived in 1778, the Hawaiians had stopped their transpacific voyages and were merely sailing between islands in the Hawaiian chain.

Kenneth was preparing for his lecture when he remembered something Fariua had told him about guiding on stars, how a Tuamotuan would choose the star that would lead him to the island he wished to find. When that star rose too high to follow, the navigator would drop it for a star that rose from the same *rua*, or pit, and that followed approximately the same path across the sky.

Kenneth began to fit this into what he had learned about sailing from island to island in the *Mahina*. Given the fact that the old Tuamotuan navigators could name 150 stars, what would prevent them from guiding on more than one part of the sky? If the sky was overcast forward, the navigator could take his sight astern from a star that followed the proper *rua*.

Then there was the direction of the wind and the set of the waves, all as familiar to the Tuamotuan as the path in front of his door. Why couldn't the ancients use such navigation aids just as well as copra schooner captains? The flight of seabirds provided another hint of the direction in which land lay. Finally, it seemed likely that the navigation system of the Hawaiians would be similar to that of their Polynesian cousins, the Tuamotuans. Kenneth's lecture on Hawaiian navigation produced a long story in the *Honolulu Star-Bulletin*. But he was careful to explain that his explanation was only a theory because nobody knew how the Hawaiians navigated.

He and Marguerite took lessons in ancient hula once a week as a respite from penny-pinching. Their teacher was Keahi, a Hawaiian woman whose niece, Iolani Luahine, later became Hawaii's premier dancer of *kahiko*, or ancient hula. Keahi lived in a little cottage in Kakaako near the waterfront in an area that at one time had been noted for prostitutes.

"She was from a long line of hula teachers," said Marguerite. "Keahi was poor. She was making quilts. That was how she made a living." Kenneth said Keahi taught him drumming and chanting so he could accompany the dancers. Margaret Titcomb, librarian at the museum, and a man named Sam Albers were also in the class.

The Anthropology Club and the hula classes flourished in the same period that a commercial attraction in Waikiki called the Lalani Hawaiian Village offered tourists a sampling of Hawaiian culture. Thatched buildings under coconut palms off Kalakaua Avenue provided a setting for evening hula shows, dancing, and scheduled *luaus*. Hawaiian entertainers, both amateur and professional, gathered there.

Of more interest to Kenneth was Kuluwaimaka, age 79 in 1933, who had been a court chanter for King Kalakaua half a century before. Kenneth clearly recalled later a visit he and Marguerite made to Lalani Village with Gregory's secretary and her husband. He said, "They put Kuluwaimaka on show there because he was an old time Hawaiian who could chant. I remember listening to him chanting at the village; chanting away, chanting away. One time he stopped. He looked at the audience. They were all *haoles*. He was wasting his breath chanting to them. And he said, 'Shit.' "

"He cried," added Marguerite. "He cried, you know, because it was beautiful and it meant so much to him and nobody was appreciating it. It was so dramatic. He belonged to another age, you know. An old man. It was really sad."

Kuluwaimaka became a cause célèbre among aficionados of Hawaiian culture. The museum had no money to spend on recording the chants, so the staff chipped in $35 to make dictaphone records. Then Kenneth found a visiting yacht, the *Zaka*, equipped with the latest recording equipment. Kenneth's diary for Thursday, March 23, 1933, reads, "Got Kuluwaimaka ready for recording with *Zaka*."

The next day, "On yacht at 9:30 for test of sound outfit, did not work." On Sunday, March 25, "All A.M. testing out sound outfit of Crocker's *Zaka*. Kuluwaimaka recording."

Still Kenneth wasn't satisfied and Theodore Kelsey, a young *haole* with a gift for language, provided another opportunity to preserve Kuluwaimaka's rich repertoire. "When I met him, Kelsey was studying Hawaiian," said Kenneth. "The thing is, all right, what would be interesting would be to record all the chants that Kuluwaimaka knew. To get what would be the stock of a chanter, an official chanter. All right, we would not only take it down in song but in writing, in dictation. Kelsey was a son-of-a-gun for studying Hawaiian; hard worker, son of a man in Hilo who worked on a newspaper."

Gerrit Wilder made a plea before the Anthropology Club on May 10 for the preservation of Kuluwaimaka's chants. On June 3 Kenneth wrote a report on the chants with a request for $100 to pay Kelsey thirty-five cents an hour to take the dictation. Club members donated the money. A letter to Handy dated June 9 explains what happened:

> I hope Gregory does not take me too severely to task for stirring up interest to put this thing through. We are confronted with the choice of having Kelsey do it or not having it done at all. A careful perusal of the chants . . . will convince anyone that we will never again have such an opportunity to hear ancient Hawaiian *mele* [songs and chants] or *ole* [speech], or hear about them.
>
> Kuluwaimaka has now given Kelsey 104 chants of which over 90 have already been chanted to the dictaphone. Kelsey has handed over to me for temporary safe keeping at the museum 20 records and the fully annotated texts of 76 of these chants. Nine of the texts are various prayers, 17 are *hulas*, 20 are Pele and Hiiaka [goddesses of the volcano and hula, respectively] chants, 23 are *alii* [pertaining to chiefs] chants. We do not know how many more he has stored in his mind but we are pressing on as long as they continue of the same quality as those he has given.

For Marguerite, the major event of 1933 was the arrival in April of a French school ship, the *Jeanne d'Arc*, with 150 cadets on board. Honolulu boasted only a limited number of French-speaking residents. For an event like this they rallied around the tricolor to provide hospitality for the visitors and to converse in their mother tongue. Besides, the cadets were young and dashing.

Kenneth and Marguerite greeted the ship at dockside, then invited several of the young Frenchmen to dinner. One of them was a skinny fellow with a beak nose whose brilliant conversation thoroughly charmed Marguerite. Kenneth was also mightily impressed by the cadet's grasp of things scientific, especially in marine matters. "That young man will go far," said Kenneth when the ship sailed. The cadet's name was Jacques Yves Cousteau. He so enjoyed his visit with the Emorys that he later sent them an invitation to his wedding.

The hula lessons and supervision of the Kuluwaimaka recordings were all done in Kenneth's spare time. He had finished the final revision of his writing on Tahiti stone ruins and had begun to dig into his Tuamotu notes. Meanwhile, there were plans for another expedition in spite of the museum's money problems. Kenneth wrote to Buck who was teaching at Yale: "I have my hands full putting our Tuamotuan material in shape before next March when I expect and hope to have the chance to return to the eastern Tuamotus for six months intensive field work."

Kenneth had more good news about Stimson: "I am greatly relieved to find much of Fariua's and Paea's account [in Stimson's manuscripts] corroborated by material we copied from manuscript books, practically everything except the name of the supreme being. Also, Stimson seems to be taking a more reasonable attitude toward my doubts, admitting them to be natural if unjustifiable in the light of his linguistic reasonings and his intuition. The straight translation work he is now doing is excellent . . ."

Three weeks on the island of Hawaii with his former Hawaiian tutor, Tom Maunupau, gave Kenneth a chance to begin studying the archaeology of the Big Island. They landed with Marguerite at Kailua in Kona from the steamer *Waialeale*, drove to Napoopoo the next day for canoe races, and took in the luau and dance at Kailua that night. Marguerite sailed at midnight for Honolulu.

From then on it was work. Kenneth interviewed Tom's father on fishing, and also learned two canoe lashings used to tie the outrigger to the hull. From an old native singer, Kaipo, Kenneth got songs. Then he joined two other friends for an expedition to the bleak, lava-covered South Kona coast in search of burial and refuge caves in lava tubes, some of which extended for miles.

Less than a month after Kenneth returned to Honolulu, Margaret Mead came to dinner. Then he was off again at the request of the Kauai Historical Society to investigate a *heiau* on the Wailua River known as the Birthplace of Chiefs. His excavation revealed new stone structures and resulted in the first *heiau* restoration in Hawaii in modern times.

Stimson's first publications came out in September of 1933. Kenneth gave his opinion of the finished product in a letter to his friend in Tahiti: "*Tuamotu Religion* and the *Cult of Kiho* read smoothly and clear up many passages I have come across in our notes, and throw great light on the past history of the world as the Tuamotuans conceived it, and in turn on the Tahitian accounts of the same phenomenon. As I go over our material . . . I hope to stumble across items which will clear up the points which still trouble me, and which will confirm and strengthen your findings, and possibly further illuminate them."

This friendly but qualified endorsement of Stimson's Kiho cult reveals that Kenneth continued to have doubts and does not square with a note he sent a few days later to Gregory: "His [Stimson's] *Tuamotu Religion* and *Cult of Kiho* bring together and beautifully explain the fragments of creation accounts and chants with which the manuscripts we copied were rife; and these fragments, written down before Paea and Fariua were questioned [by Stimson] regarding Io, confirm their accounts in such large measure that little ground is left to attack them. In its essentials, the cult as outlined by Stimson, in so far as the Tuamotus is concerned, is, I now believe, unassailable."

It may have been that Kenneth really had come around to Stimson's view, although that seems unlikely. It would have been more in character if he were trying hard to be a team player, to forget his differences with Stimson and demonstrate his support of a museum colleague. For whatever reason, this is the only unqualified endorsement of Stimson's Kiho cult ever made by Kenneth and it came back to haunt him.

The museum's new expedition to the South Seas took shape by the end of the year. Funding came from the Rockefeller Foundation, the Hawaii Sugar Planters' Association, the Charles M. and Anna Cooke Trust, and the J. B. Atherton Estate. Gregory once more put Kenneth in charge of Stimson. Their correspondence indicates that Stimson had expected a more exalted role for himself and that Kenneth was determined to keep a tighter reign on his colleague. On November 13, Kenneth wrote:

> I would shift our emphasis now from fact gathering to fact understanding. . . . For example, we have a technical description of . . . [Tuamotuan] . . . music, but we understand very little of how their music functioned in their life. Before the white man came, on just what occasions did they sing? How much of their life was given to singing? At Napuka they sang nearly every night. But was this not in commemoration of someone who had died a few weeks before?

Kenneth went on to say that he was more interested in sensitive reporting than in theories. They would leave that to students and professors at universities. He also mentioned their differences of opinion in the past about the meaning of Tuamotuan terms, *toki-oho*, for example. Was this prayer ending a reference to a supreme god, or a euphemism? Kenneth added pointedly, "I would like to be present when you ask the Hao natives what this word means."

Stimson's answer on December 5 made it clear that he did not intend to back away from his claim to superior knowledge as a linguist or his right to question Kenneth's methods:

> I fully agree with what you have to say about 'fact understanding.' In fact, we ought to have had, long ago, a typewritten list of questions covering the sort of information that is most wanted—any trained ethnologist ought to be able to write out such a list from memory . . . Stokes sent me, years ago, a series of questions to ask the Rapa natives. This will help, but it was planned especially for Rapa, and is not quite what I need.
>
> Now, if we are going to work together again, we ought to clear up and get rid, once and for all, of several little 'points of friction' and irritation that have no place between colleagues. . . . I recognize your ability in your own field and am always ready and willing to defer to it; but in my field—which is strictly linguistics—there is nobody in the world who can tell me how those old Tuamotuan chants ought to be translated. I am stating a perfectly obvious fact when I say this . . .
>
> I want you to try to realize—and accept—my plain statement that I am not trying to 'distort' *any* of my translations, but merely trying to give, to the best of my understanding and ability, their true and authentic meaning.

The year 1934 opened with an incredible stroke of good fortune for the Emorys. They received a visit from Kenneth's "Aunt" Frances from Pike, the waif his grandfather had taken into the family. Late in life, to the astonishment of all the Pikes, she had married Harry Noyes, a wealthy Buick dealer. Now she registered at the Royal Hawaiian Hotel and did her best to display her affection for Kenneth.

He was still driving the second-hand Nash which, by this time, had become a rattletrap. Uncle Harry, therefore, instructed his calabash nephew to go down to the local Buick dealer and pick out a new car as a gift from Aunt Frances. This generosity created a dilemma of status for Marguerite and Kenneth because nobody at the museum drove a Buick, not even the trustees and least of all their underpaid ethnologists. The Emorys compromised on a green Pontiac that caught Marguerite's eye and because it came with driving lessons. It was the last good deed of Harry Noyes' life. He died before he had a chance to ride in the new car. Marguerite and Kenneth helped Aunt Frances arrange the funeral, which was held on February 16, 1934.

This time, as the new Tuamotu expedition loomed, Kenneth wasn't saddled with its planning. He could enjoy the publication on Thursday, February 23, of his *Stone Structures in the Society Islands* and a party the next night hosted by the Wilders for scientists chosen by Gregory to go adventuring in the South Seas. It was a big party and Kenneth turned out to be the only scientist there who had been in the Tuamotus. Most of the others were younger than he. It made him feel like a veteran, but that didn't dampen the keenness of his anticipation to get started.

Chapter Twenty-nine

The Mangareva Expedition

Months before it began they called it the Mangareva Expedition, because that grim, craggy archipelago, beyond even the inaccessible Tuamotus, had become a symbol for the farthermost reach of the Bishop Museum. It was in scope the single most ambitious research project the museum had ever undertaken. There was to be not one field party but three, each with a different mission and all working at the same time in a remote ocean area one thousand by two thousand miles. It would be as if Lewis and Clark had set out to find bugs and snails and exotic plants instead of a route to the Pacific.

The planning, supervised by Gregory and clearly intended to be his crowning achievement, was to become a model for Bishop Museum expeditions in the future. To solve the transportation problem the museum had chartered two vessels. The first was an eighty-seven-foot-long, seventy-five-ton converted fishing sampan out of Honolulu, the *Myojin Maru*, renamed the *Islander*, under the command of veteran Pacific hand "Wild Bill" Anderson. He had sailed with Kenneth ten years before to Nihoa and Necker.

This 200-horsepower, shallow-draft, high-prowed craft had been converted to a floating laboratory that would transport a team of five, including malacologists, botanists, and entomologists on a scientific tour of fourteen islands in the Southeast Pacific where malacologists, botanists, and entomologists were rarer than the species they were trying to find. They would penetrate beyond Pitcairn in the east and as far as Rapa in the south.

The other vessel chartered for the voyage, a trading schooner based in Papeete, was the *Tiare Tahiti*, skippered by Bob Burrell. She would be at the beck and call of the second field party, Kenneth and Stimson, as they continued their linguistic and ethnological studies in the Tuamotus. The *Tiare Tahiti* would also become a magic carpet for the third field party under Peter Buck when he returned from Yale to explore Mangareva with Kenneth as an assistant. In typical Gregory fashion, this efficient team would "clean up" the Southeast Pacific in less than twelve months.

For malacologist Montague Cooke, now nearing the age of retirement, the Mangareva expedition fulfilled a lifelong dream. The lure of South Sea adventure called also to journalists. Captain Anderson filled his crew with the morning *Advertiser*'s waterfront reporter, Alexander MacDonald, and the evening *Star-Bulletin*'s telegraph editor and arts writer, Clifford Gessler. To protect the museum against unauthorized reportage, Gregory had Gessler and Mac-Donald as well as all scientific members of the expedition sign an agreement not to publish articles about the expedition without the approval of the director.

But not only *haole* newspaper editors were eager to print stories of the expedition. Enterprising Yatsutaro Soga of the Japanese language paper *Nippu Jiji* learned that the diesel engineer on board the *Islander* was a Japanese-American. Soga sent a reporter to the dock to fetch the diesel engineer, who proved to be an extremely bright young fellow, Yoshio Kondo, who had taken work on fishing boats because there were no other jobs during the depression. Soga quickly taught him how to use a camera, gave him some pencils and paper, and promised him a modest stipend for any stories he might send back. Neither Soga nor Kondo were aware of the agreement not to publish without permission.

Meanwhile, refitting of the *Islander* had fallen behind schedule. The new deckhouse, built as a combination dormitory-laboratory, made the boat look so topheavy that self-appointed waterfront experts predicted she would tip over. More frustrating to Captain Anderson was Cooke's firm resolve not to have women on board. Anderson knew from long experience that, next to the captain, the cook on a long voyage filled the most important position. His wife was one of the best ship's cooks in the Pacific and he wanted to take her along. Cooke refused.

In disgust, Anderson set out to hire a cook. A young man of Portuguese descent was fishing from the dock. Anderson went up to him and asked, "Can you cook?" The startled fisherman blurted, "No." Anderson said, "Good. You're hired." The young man's name was Ernest.

The *Islander* was scheduled to sail from Honolulu at 2 P.M. on Sunday, April 15, 1934. However, the wavelength of their radio had been changed the day before so the crystals had to be reground. The heavily loaded sampan did not leave until 6 P.M. Practically everybody including Ernest got seasick right away.

Kenneth retired to his bunk. He said all he could see of botanist Harold St. John across the cabin were his toes at one end and a shock of hair at the other. Botanist Raymond Fosberg, then a graduate teaching assistant at the University of Hawaii, said later, "The sampan had a peculiar motion, a combination of pitching and rolling. I had been seasick before but not like that. I was seasick during most of the voyage except when we were on land."

The fact that the deckhouse leaked didn't help. "As an economy measure, the museum had hired a house carpenter instead of a shipwright to build it," explained Fosberg. "When it rained the roof leaked. Spray from the waves came in through the walls. My bunk was wet most of the time. Food got moldy." In addition, the drinking water became contaminated by diesel oil.

But by far the most severe hardship was brought on by Ernest. He hardly knew enough about cooking to heat soup. For the first meal he served hardtack and a liquid nobody could decide was tea, coffee, or cocoa. Everybody lived on oranges from crates Cooke had brought on board. Gessler observed, "Oranges have this merit. They taste the same going both ways." The course of the *Islander* could be traced by orange peels floating astern. After that, it was canned corned beef one meal and canned salmon the next. Botanist St. John said later, "In seven months, Ernest never set table successfully. Within two days, the kitchen was filthy." The meals everybody enjoyed were seafood dishes prepared by Yoshio Kondo after they caught fish.

The *Islander* made a welcome stop at Fanning Island, then continued to Papeete to pick up Stimson and entomologist Elwood Zimmerman. Kenneth did not remember in later years how Stimson and he greeted each other on his arrival in Tahiti. Fosberg recalled, "Stimson and Emory didn't get along." Yet Kenneth's diary on Wednesday, May 9, reads, "A.M. writing letters. Lunch with Ua [Stimson]." By this time Mere and Stimson had divorced, but Mere hosted a feast, just the same, for the scientific party the night before departure.

As far as Fosberg can remember, Stimson was not on board when the *Islander* sailed from Papeete on Friday, May 11, 1934. "He was off on his own, travelled by copra boat," said Fosberg. Baskets of papaya, limes, pineapples, and coconuts cluttered the sampan's deck. Oranges swung in fiber nets and bunches of bananas swayed with the rolling of the boat. Scientists as well as the crew lounged about in brightly colored *pareus*.

The next day they anchored off the grim, black lava shore of uninhabited Mehetia. The third landing party swamped and sent Gessler skidding over sharp, slippery rocks. He struggled ashore wet and bruised and bleeding. Shell, plant, and bug collectors immediately disappeared into the bush. Gessler elected to follow Kenneth to the ruins of melancholy *marae*s where they measured and turned up a few bits of bone. They found a deserted village brooding in mellow sunlight among tall banana plants. For Gessler it was a haunting experience. Kenneth jotted into his diary, "Found new *marae*. Left island 2 P.M."

The plan to put Kenneth off at Reao Atoll, where he intended to finish the work begun in 1930, ran afoul of a government quarantine to control leprosy there. Kenneth decided instead to head for Napuka, one of the most remote islands in the northern Tuamotus, where he, Stimson, and Shapiro had spent five of their most productive days in 1929. Reluctant to go ashore alone, Kenneth asked Gessler to come with him to Napuka. The journalist accepted eagerly. He took notes of their adventures and later published his first book, *Road My Body Goes*, about the trip. The only personal record Kenneth left is his line-a-day diary.

They sighted the feathery tops of palm trees, then Napuka's solid, white coral church, on Tuesday morning, May 16, 1934. The island lay in the majestic embrace of weathered, brick-red reef. There was no pass. The *Islander* anchored in the calm sea while Kenneth and the mail went ashore in a canoe with a Tuamotuan gendarme to get permission to stay. Then the sampan's cutter, a canoe, and a row boat all made three trips through the surf to bring supplies as well as Gessler to the beach.

For Kenneth, this was all familiar. But it was a novelty for Gessler and he made detailed notes of the landing: children swimming to the sampan with chickens under their arms, canoes paddled by Tuamotuans in tall hats, a lad carrying a ukulele made from a sardine tin, the police chief attired in a huge mustache and a blue cap trimmed in red braid, worn only for such state occasions.

Chief Maono himself carried two suitcases. He led the way down one of the four arrow-straight streets of the village to a house that had been emptied, at cost of Banque d'Indo-Chine notes, for Kenneth and Gessler. The stout house, with walls of woven coconut leaves and a high roof of thick pandanus thatch, stood on blocks of coral three feet from the ground—out of the reach of pigs. The single room was furnished with a chest, an empty box, and some bottles. Two doors, hanging on leather hinges, provided entry at either the ocean side or the inland end. The walls swung out to provide air and light.

The next day expedition leader Cooke reported that he agreed, at Kenneth's request, to take twelve natives to Tapoto. Instead of twelve, thirty-seven natives came on board with chickens, mats, calabashes, and food. Cooke added, "If we had not limited the number, the entire population would probably have come along."

Captain Anderson traded empty oil tins and tobacco for ducks, chickens, and coconuts. The natives wanted to sell him a pig. Anderson protested that his crew and passengers could not eat all the meat before it spoiled. The Tuamotuan businessmen urged him to solve that problem by inviting them to dinner.

Life on Napuka settled back into more routine activities with the departure of the *Islander*, but her impact was not finished. A few days later the entire village, including Maono, came down with colds. Kenneth explained to Gessler, as he doled out aspirin to be taken with hot water, that the *hota*, or respiratory infection, swept most atolls on contact with visiting boat crews who brought the germs with them. Since there were no handkerchiefs on Napuka, the villagers blew their noses into their hands and hurled the mucus out through the open doors.

On Thursday, May 17, Kenneth wrote in his diary, "Straightened out things in house. By 10 A.M. finished, cooked first meal. Rest of day trading and buying specimens. Spent $16 and purchased seventy-nine specimens. Gave phonograph concert to natives in evening." The cheap, hand-wound phonograph Kenneth had brought from Hawaii proved on Napuka to be a priceless miracle. Villagers listened to the scratchy recordings of Hawaiian music with the same intense interest they displayed in advertisements in the American magazines Kenneth had stuffed into his luggage.

Soon the days merged into a relaxed round of taking down place names, legends, chants, and taking and developing photos. Kenneth mapped the arrangement of houses and took careful notes during the distribution of a papaya harvest to study the social structure of the village: how many family groups, the number in each family, and how they distributed themselves among the houses and divided up the land. One day he gave the village a bag of flour. All the women immediately set to work baking bread in earth ovens. It turned out to be the consistency of soggy pancakes, but the villagers gorged themselves. The next day everybody was constipated.

Chief Maono received a summons to testify in Papeete about an administrative matter. Panic swept his subjects. Kenneth tried to assure them that the chief was not being arrested. The parting was no less emotional and charged with grief.

Before it seemed possible, five weeks had passed. But the *Tiare Tahiti* did not appear. Kenneth had no way of knowing that adverse winds, repairs to the schooner, and other complications in Papeete would stretch their stay on Napuka to nearly ten weeks.

Kenneth and Gessler adapted easily to the lifestyle and spontaneous time schedule of the Napukans. Gessler took notes on the after-dark activities of the *taurearea*, village teenagers, who met without chaperones out in the palm groves in the moonlight to dance and make love. Kenneth explained that *taurearea* means "time of enjoyment." Gessler reported that he asked one of the women if parents did not object to their young people making love half the night. The woman explained that parents were pleased when children developed normally.

On Friday, June 15, Kenneth wrote in his diary, "In forenoon to Teufi's house. Studied old *fangus* [chants]. Slept seaward." Sleeping seaward was a way to escape the mosquitoes. Villagers built portable shelters made of woven palm-frond panels on the windward shore, and slept there on hot, still nights. Kenneth said later he did most of his recording of old, pagan chants at night because the villagers, now devout Christians, wanted to wait until their children were asleep.

The diary records Kenneth's dogged work schedule: "July 4, Made map of Napuka, typed all A.M. Rested P.M. A steamer passed at 5 P.M. to south." "July 5, Typed all A.M. except for taking several dances from Tagia. Afternoon visited Teufi—*marae* ceremonies." "July 6, Developed two films A.M. Nap P.M. High wind today, east northeast. Will hold back boat [*Tiare Tahiti*]."

After about two months, the villagers decided that Kenneth and Gessler should be adopted into Napukan families and given new names appropriate to local history. There was much discussion about which family deserved new members and what their names should be. Kararo, in whose house Kenneth and Gessler lived, felt a certain proprietorship. The son of chief Maono, who had been furnishing Kenneth and Gessler with coconuts, argued that this already made them part of his family. Temae put forward a claim based on the resemblance of Kenneth to his own dead son. But the role of foster parents went to Tehau, the police chief, and his wife, Teroro-tu. Since Tehau and Teroro-tu were near kin to Kararo, and through him to both Maono and Temae, everybody was satisfied.

Gessler became Mokio-ariki, the name of a famous chief, and Kenneth received the name Tuhoe, after the great-grandson of the original Mokio-ariki. Out came the genealogy book from a chest in the corner and in went the names. When the Tuamotuans asked Gessler for his genealogy, he sang a portion of the *Nibelungen Lied* naming "Gunther und Gernod und Geiselher [Gessler] der Junge." He learned that henceforth he must not take a woman of the family as his sweetheart, for she was now his sister.

The renovation of the old village well provided Kenneth with another example of Napukan political as well as social and economic organization. On learning that the well was to be improved, Kararo—known as the village miser—laid claim to it because it was on his land. The men met to discuss this matter. They decided against Kararo on the ground that the well had been in use by the entire community since ancient times as was clearly described in the chants. Therefore, communal title to the well had been established.

Work on the well went forward for more than a week. The younger men carried, dressed, and placed the stones. The older men fished, harvested papayas, and cooked for the workers. Tehau named the workers for each division, but they seemed to know what to do without bossing. To Gessler it was an eloquent example of the Biblical injunction: "From each according to his ability, to each according to his need."

Gessler reported that it was impossible to be alone in the village, that he gradually ceased to demand privacy but still preferred the company of a few to the many. One night he walked alone to admire the haunting beauty of a moonrise over the lagoon. Two little girls spied him and came running, laughing and chattering. They asked why he was not singing and dancing. He said he wanted to look at the moon on the water. They considered this new thought, then turned the conversation to the goddess Hina who, after exploring the earth, sailed to the moonrise and entered the moon country. The girls knew that the shadows on the moon are from the bark of a tree from which Hina makes clothing for the gods.

Kenneth had brought with them a carefully planned ration of canned food. He and Gessler, unlike the Napukans, cooked and ate inside the house. Yet the villagers insisted on giving them food: raw tuna and cakes of nutty bread baked over hot stones in wrappings of leaves with chopped papaya and coconut. Maono's son at first, then their adopted parents, Tehau and Teroro-tu, supplied them with young coconuts from which they sipped clear, pure water. They drank little else.

Scraps of information piled up in Kenneth's notes. Fishing lore alone provided an endless well of detailed information: hand fishing, spearing, torching, netting, fishing with hooks, snares, poisons, stone weirs, fish ponds, angling, and decoy fishing. There were small hooks, large hooks, eel hooks, shark hooks, trolling hooks, bone hooks, wooden hooks, turtle shell hooks, pearl shell hooks, and hooks fashioned from bits of iron. There were barbed hooks, barbless hooks, one-piece hooks, composite hooks, and hooks made with attached lures. Every aspect of Napukan life—houses, canoes, planting, cooking, plaiting, music, amusements—demanded the same close attention to complex detail.

There was little time to worry about being castaways. The *Tiare Tahiti*, twenty-three days out of Papeete, put in a long-belated appearance on Saturday, July 14. Kenneth wasn't ready to leave. To give himself time to finish his work, he sent the schooner to neighboring Tepoto Atoll at the request of the Napukan natives. Gessler went along. The *Tiare Tahiti* sailed on July 18, and Kenneth worked desperately with old Temae to take down all of his chants. He finished by the time the schooner returned on Saturday, July 21, 1934.

But a new and far more serious delay kept them on the island. Gessler returned from Tepoto with an infected finger. Against the advice of the Napukans, Kenneth opened the infection with a pair of sterilized scissors. The next day Gessler's hand was swollen as far as his wrist. The infected finger became as big as his thumb. Kenneth refused to sail until the infection went down. But it didn't.

They consulted Paunu, a *tahunga* (sage). The old man quickly diagnosed the infection as a *uruaitu*, ghost-head, and asked Gessler who had cause to work sorcery upon him. Gessler said he had no idea, that he had done nothing intentionally wrong. Paunu then decided Gessler had walked too close to a graveyard.

Gessler asked the old man for treatment. Paunu said he would make his magic only if other medicines failed. His daughters, Roki and Tauhoa, applied a medicine of the crushed young leaf buds of the *karauri* and the *piupiu* mixed with chewed coconut leaf. The poultice did not help. The next day the pain and swelling had moved up to Gessler's arm. He shook with fever. Still Paunu, a faithful member of the Church of the Sacred Heart, hesitated to apply magic. He advised Gessler to let Toriu and Tinaia, older women, treat him by *rakau nati.* If that failed, Paunu would invoke the gods.

That night Toriu came to the house bearing a half coconut shell filled with a thick, reddish liquid threaded with gold. She explained that it was made of the root and bark of the *karauri* and the *horahora.* Both Kenneth and Gessler knew that the *horahora* tree was called *noni* in Hawaii, and that its bitter-tasting apple was much used by Hawaiians for medicinal purposes.

Tinaia washed Gessler's hand and brushed the red liquid on the swelling with a white feather. Then Toriu chopped the ends from a bud coconut and placed it under Gessler's arm to cut off circulation and block the spread of infection. She advised him to leave the coconut there all night. The natives sat waiting, leafing through the pages of American magazines. Toriu was worried. She told Kenneth that the evil spirit had gone under Gessler's left shoulder near the heart.

Gessler was out of his head most of the night, tossing and reciting poetry. The next day he improved. Tinaia brushed a smaller area of his arm with the reddish liquid. She explained that she was forcing the evil spirit back to the spot where it entered. Tinaia applied the poultice used before. This time it brought the infection at the base of Gessler's finger to a hard, high dome, like a skull. That evening Kenneth wrote in his diary, "Cliff is a little better. Under native care his infection burst today."

Now Tinaia changed the poultice to yellow laundry soap, the kind that arrived at Napuka on trading schooners in long bars that smelled of lye. Shaving off slivers with a knife, she applied them to the sore and bound it again. The old bandages she took away to be buried or burned. On Friday, July 27, Kenneth wrote, "Cliff is up and around. Finger much improved." On Saturday, "Cleared out our house, leaving typewriter and suitcases on shore." And on Sunday, "Embarked the last of our stuff and sailed from Napuka by 10 A.M."

The next day, on a rough sea, they sighted Fangatau where Kenneth intended to question Fariua about his conversion to a belief in the existence of the supreme god, Kiho-tumu. Fariua came out in his canoe to meet them, surprised to see Kenneth once more on the island. Reva, his tall, striking wife, greeted them on shore. She brought the subject up first. Alone with Kenneth while walking to the house she said there was no book, as Fariua had written Kenneth, containing written chants of Kiho.

Kenneth and Gessler stayed in Fariua's house. That night, after a long evening of chanting by Fariua and Reva, Kenneth asked if he might see the book in which the Kiho-tumu chant was written. Fariua brought out his genealogy book. The chant was there but recently written, Kenneth said later. He asked Fariua if he would chant it for him as he had for Stimson. The Tuamotuan sage began the chant, faltered, and stopped. He said to Kenneth, "Keneti, a funny thing happened. After I gave those chants to Stimson, they disappeared from my mind."

By this time Kenneth had come back to his original view; the cult of Kiho-tumu existed only in Stimson's fertile brain. The natives had given him what he wanted to hear in return for the money he payed them as informants. Kenneth became more convinced a few days later on Vahitahi where they found Stimson. Ruea, the woman who had admitted to a knowledge of a supreme god named Kio after first denying it, was also there. Now Kenneth found that Stimson's two Bishop Museum publications about the supreme god had

caused a storm of controversy on Vahitahi, and severe criticism of
Ruea.

"*Awe* [too bad]," angry natives told Kenneth. "Those are the lies
Ruea told Stimson." Ruea herself said she had given the information
to Stimson to please him. This time Kenneth learned that the
phrase, *to-kio*, which Stimson insisted meant "all is Kio's," was the
contraction of a phrase, *to-kiofa*, and had several other meanings.

From Vahitahi, Gessler sailed away on board the *Tiare Tahiti* to
Papeete where he found a letter from the managing editor of the
Honolulu Star-Bulletin telling him his services were no longer
required because he had been scooped on the Mangareva expedition
by the *Nippu Jiji*. Kenneth sailed with Stimson in the *Moana* to
Tatakoto Atoll. They went ashore for another month of research.

Kenneth said later that he and Stimson buried their differences
when working together. They lived apart to avoid irritating one
another. On Thursday, August 30, Kenneth wrote in his diary, "Evening at Ua's end of the village." On Friday, "Working on houses and
food. Along border of lagoon, a nap there. To bed early." On Saturday,
"Typed all A.M. on pandanus food. Afternoon out to *marae* Ahu-tu."

Their disagreement about the cult of Kiho-tumu did not go away,
however; neither retreated from his respective position. Stimson, in
his annual report to the museum, later proclaimed that on Tatakoto
Kenneth had not only heard a chant to Kiho but had recorded it on
the dictaphone. The name of the sage from whom the chant came
was Te Uira "who is unquestionably the most learned bard of all the
Tuamotus, not excepting Fariua . . . He was taught the lore of Kio
by his grandmother of Vahitahi who was the mother of the Vahitahi
sage, Tagi . . . "

This claim severely annoyed Kenneth when he learned of it. He
later wrote to Handy: "And what about Te Uira, the lone Vahitahi
sage up in Tatakoto who gave Stimson fifty-four Kio chants. . . ? He
is [now] admitting freely to his fellow men that he knew nothing of
a supreme god named Kio before we came. When taken to task by
the old chief of Vahitahi, for altering their chants to please Stimson,
he replied, '. . . no te moni ia' [for the money]."

Buck arrived on September 5 in the schooner *Moana* with a
packet of letters from Marguerite, the first in seven months. They
all embarked in the *Moana* for Mangareva where the French administrator, Emil Brisson, invited them to stay in his large, comfortable
house. After the barren atolls, this was incredible luxury.

The volcanic peaks of Mangareva and its sheltered bay gave the
island a fairy-tale appearance. Kenneth thoroughly enjoyed working
with Buck, whose Polynesian ancestry and fluent command of the

language won him immediate entrée with the natives. Even Stimson's claim to have found a Kiho convert in the leading sage of Mangareva didn't raise Kenneth's hackles as usual because Buck had observed Stimson's methods and was not impressed.

For nearly two months after Stimson returned to Vahitahi in the *Moana*, Kenneth prowled for ruins and caves and artifacts while Buck talked to the people about their folklore. On Friday, September 27, Kenneth wrote in his diary, "Climbed over . . . mountain looking for burial caves. Haneriko Vovovae was my guide." On Tuesday, October 9, "Up to Te-ana-tetea cave—burial cave of kings. Excavated bluff shelter back of our camp." On October 13, "Helped Buck translate traditions." On Sunday, October 14, "Morning collected two adzes. Afternoon: Mrs. Brisson's birthday. Danced in evening." On October 31, "Developed film. Prepared for leaving."

Mangareva proved to be a disappointment for Kenneth as an archaeologist because a determined Catholic priest named Laval had destroyed all the *marae*s after his arrival in 1834. However, Kenneth found that the nearby atoll of Temoe had been peopled from Mangareva. On Temoe he discovered a *marae* distinctive in pattern and different from others he had seen in the Tuamotus.

To join Stimson, Kenneth sailed in the *Tiare Tahiti* at 2:30 P.M. on Monday, November 5, with a fine breeze. They island-hopped among atolls with musical names: Marutea, Vahaga, Teuraruro, Tureia, Pinaki. On Pinaki, Kenneth found Stimson busy recording. He had not been successful in finding informants who knew about Kio but he had discovered any number of Kio chants, Kenneth reported to Buck. Stimson insisted that Kenneth accompany him to nearby Nukutavaki because a genealogy book was located there that would once and for all establish the existence of the cult of Kiho-tumu. Kenneth agreed to go.

He wrote to Buck that Stimson's young informant who claimed to know about the book changed his mind at the last moment. He "tried like a captured animal to escape," Kenneth wrote. The family hastily explained that the part in the book about Kio was probably already torn out due to its sacredness. Nevertheless, Stimson shoved the unfortunate informant into the boat and off they went to Nukutavaki. There they found the book with about a dozen of the middle pages missing.

"This is of course where the sacred and esoteric knowledge . . . reposed," Kenneth wrote to Buck. "It was clearly a very old tearing out of pages. Here and there throughout the book, pages also were torn out, as is the case with nearly all of these books—this being their source of writing paper."

Kenneth sailed for San Francisco on Wednesday, December 5. His great adventure in the Tuamotus was ending not at all the way he had anticipated when it began. He spent ten impatient days in San Francisco, then sailed for Honolulu on December 18. The ship docked at 6:30 A.M. Christmas morning. Marguerite and Tiare were there to meet him. At least, coming home for Christmas partly compensated for the trouble he knew lay ahead at the museum.

Chapter Thirty

The Painful Period

"Somebody must be lying," said Gregory with distaste.

"That's right," Kenneth answered. "I believe somebody is lying."

"It may be that either you or Stimson will have to go at the end of the year."

The two men sat in the director's second-floor office at the museum. The date, according to Kenneth's diary, was Friday, February 15, 1935. This is the only record, besides Kenneth's memory, of the meeting at which he told Gregory what he had learned about the cult of Kiho-tumu during the Mangareva expedition; that he now believed the cult existed only in Stimson's mind and that he was afraid Stimson had altered chants to make them conform with his convictions. Gregory, who earlier had instructed Kenneth to leave the translating to Stimson, may have told Kenneth he was meddling. But the meeting produced results.

"Gregory to ask Stimson to come," Kenneth wrote on February 16. So they would have it out. And it might cost Kenneth his job. If that happened, Kenneth told Buck, there would be nothing worthwhile for him to live for. The museum was his whole commitment. Kenneth remembers that Buck assured him privately that Stimson didn't have a leg to stand on.

Yet Buck did not say so for publication. It would, after all, be like washing the museum's dirty linen in public. Handy had become even less supportive. Kenneth said later he believed it was because Handy found Stimson's concept of a supreme god attractive. It agreed with his own theories. Handy also may have been reluctant to take sides in what he considered an argument without profit.

But sides had already been taken. Gregory had personally edited and pushed through the Kiho publications. It would be embarrassing to concede now that they were fabrications. Moreover, Albert Judd, chairman of the trustees, admired Stimson. He became decidedly cool toward Kenneth about this time.

"One morning when I came to work five minutes late, he was standing at the steps of the museum looking at his watch," said Kenneth. "He also took me out to the courtyard one day and quizzed me about the identification of a tree. Of course, I could identify the tree. But I mistook the one he pointed at and identified the wrong tree. He corrected me as if I were a school boy. It was humiliating."

Marguerite clearly remembers this painful period. She said she wrote to a friend in Tahiti, a woman whose husband had died, who owned an island that produced copra. "I asked if she could use Kenneth in any way," said Marguerite. "The answer came back, 'We will find a place for him.' Kenneth might also have gone into photography."

He could have spared himself this anguish had he simply done what Buck, in all probability, urged him to do—concede Stimson the privilege of making his own mistakes. But Kenneth was not constituted that way. It was like the time Gregory had ordered him to say the Bishop Museum owned the world's greatest collection of Polynesian artifacts when Kenneth knew very well it was not true at the time. There was a stubborn, New England streak in him, parallel to his shy and self-effacing personality, that would not permit him to compromise the truth.

Some of his colleagues said later they found his persistent hounding of Stimson unattractive and unprofessional. That they put it down as a personality conflict. The whole controversy was, in broad perspective, merely a tempest in a teapot. Only a very few Polynesian scholars knew there was a controversy and even fewer cared. But Kenneth did care. There was nothing, including Marguerite, that he cared more about. And it had nothing to do with personality.

The Tuamotus offered a last opportunity to make contact with the gods of old Polynesia through chants that had survived from ancient times, handed down orally from sage to sage who preserved the chants in their memories. The last of these sages were still alive and, in a few years, would be gone. There would never again be another opportunity like this. Brigham had let a similar opportunity pass in Hawaii. The last priests of Tahiti were gone. Only in the remote Tuamotus had the old chants persisted in their purity, revealing the relationships between the Polynesians and their gods. To have these fragile snapshots of the past tampered with to satisfy a personal conviction was, to Kenneth, immoral. It must be stopped.

There was another reason for Kenneth's exasperation with the way Stimson manipulated the old chants. They named the gods and expressed the prayers that had been used on the *marae*. Kenneth had begun his interpretation of the temple ruins. How could he be sure which gods were worshipped there and in what manner if he was not confident that the chants as translated by Stimson conveyed what the old priests had said?

At the same time Stimson continued to insist that his work was distinct from Kenneth's, and that Kenneth should stick to archaeology and let Stimson do the translating. Stimson did not question Kenneth's archaeology. It was presumptuous of Kenneth to question Stimson's translations because no one knew the language better than he. For Kenneth to interpret the religious concepts of the chants was to take credit that belonged to Stimson. Kenneth could see no distinction between the ruins and the chants performed there. To him they were two expressions of the same thing and each added meaning to the other. So they must dovetail.

It was doubly exasperating to know that Stimson had ability in his field bordering on genius. He knew the language. His capacity for work amazed everyone. He could grind out translations with a rapidity and an inexhaustible energy that awed Kenneth. But that awe had come full circle and now added to Kenneth's distrust. Stimson's energy was like a motor gone out of control. The longer it continued to operate, the more dangerous it became.

A Belgian naval training ship, the *Mercator*, interrupted the Stimson controversy by arriving in Honolulu on Friday, February 22, 1935, with members of an expedition from Easter Island on board. Marguerite was delighted by the opportunity to speak French again. She and Kenneth took Dr. Lavachery, director of the Musée Royale in Brussels, and linguist-ethnologist Alfred Metraux to a luau in Waikiki and lunch at the Oahu Country Club.

The visit gave Kenneth a satisfying look at Easter Island culture and a chance to talk about the mysterious, monumental stone sculptures erected there centuries ago. He said later that he had already recognized them as glorified slabs on a Necker Island *marae*, an elaboration different from that which took place in other isolated parts of Polynesia. In Tahiti the primitive *ahu*, or platform, supporting the slabs had become a huge, stepped pyramid. On Raiatea it had become a great wall of upright slabs. In Hawaii it had assumed various monumental shapes. On Easter Island the slabs themselves, seats for the gods or representations of them, had grown into enormous sculptures.

The departure of the *Mercator* on February 26 set Kenneth to work in earnest on *marae* ceremonies. On Friday, April 5, he indexed Nukutavake chants, the next day began indexing Vahitahi chants, and on the following Tuesday finished indexes of Hao and Tatakoto chants. The indexes gave him a quick and reliable picture of where the chants diverged and how closely they paralleled. He wanted the information at his fingertips when he sat down with Stimson.

On June 25 he wrote to Johannes C. Anderson, editor of the *Poly-*

nesian Journal, in Wellington, New Zealand, with a warning about Stimson's Kiho material. The *Journal* printed scholarly articles in the field of Polynesian research. Its circulation was small, yet included anthropologists all over the world. For Kenneth the letter amounted to a declaration of independence. Whatever the consequences, he would no longer paper over his disagreement with Stimson to protect the museum.

Stimson arrived on the *Lurline* on Thursday, June 6, and checked in at the Blaisdell Hotel downtown. Kenneth and he were both on their best behavior when they went out to dinner that evening. They had lunch the next day. On June 11 they saw the Kamehameha Day parade together and attended the lei sellers' luau. Marguerite explained later than the two men were, after all, friends of many years. "That trouble was a professional thing," she said.

But the trouble was what had brought Stimson to Hawaii. Kenneth said Stimson carried with him the original genealogy books of Paea and Fariua, which did not mention Kiho, and his card-file Tuamotuan dictionary. He never did produce the incontrovertible new evidence that his letters claimed existed. Three weeks passed before their confrontation. "Had it out for four hours before Handy and Buck," Kenneth wrote in his diary on Monday, July 15. There is no written record of what they said.

Kenneth said later that he brought to the meeting wax cylinders of the chants recorded before Stimson had worked with the informants. A comparison of the chants with Stimson's translations, Kenneth said, showed substitutions of Kiho for other gods. "Stimson admitted that in some cases the informants were influenced," Kenneth recalled. There are indications that Stimson agreed, in the future, to indicate with footnotes where he deviated in his translation from the original chant.

Yet Kenneth mentioned no reprimand for either himself or Stimson. Kenneth recalled later, "Stimson said, 'I'm not prepared.' Anyway, it just sort of blew over." Perhaps Handy and Buck themselves couldn't agree who was right, or they felt that both Kenneth and Stimson were entitled to their opinions. It may have been that the purpose of the meeting was to resolve the controversy by quieting both adversaries and sweeping their disagreement under the rug.

If so, it didn't work. Subsequent correspondence between Kenneth and Stimson shows that neither was satisfied. Stimson had not received the adulation he longed for. Kenneth did not feel vindicated. Stimson was still free under the aegis of the Bishop Museum to spread the gospel according to Kiho-tumu. Yet Kenneth benefited in several ways from Stimson's visit. Gregory called him in and told him to get cracking on his own version of *marae* ceremonies. Handy suggested that Kenneth use the Tuamotu material on religion in which he had confidence to write an article for the *Polynesian Journal*.

More important, Kenneth had copied Stimson's Tuamotuan card-file dictionary on photographs, for museum records, before Stimson took the cards away with him. With a magnifying glass, Kenneth discovered that he could read the dictionary from the negatives. He filed the negatives in alphabetical order in a shoe box. At last he, or any other scholar, could make use of Stimson's linguistic research without having to accept his theories on Polynesian religion.

On September 6, 1935, the Bishop Museum trustees announced in *The Honolulu Advertiser* that Gregory was retiring in 1936. Dr. Peter Buck, Te Rangi Hiroa, doctor of medicine, who held the Distinguished Service Order of the British government, would be the new director. Gregory would also retire as Silliman professor of geology at Yale University and Buck would be appointed professor of anthropology at the Yale graduate school. Thus the close relationship between Yale and the Bishop Museum would be preserved. Kenneth was delighted by the appointment of Buck, the first Polynesian to be in charge of a major scientific institution.

In Papeete, Stimson was working at full steam on a new paper for the *Polynesian Journal*. He had discovered Kiho in a chant of the Pomares, the last ruling family of Tahiti. "I think it will be a knockout, though it seems self-complacent to say so," he promised the editor. "Obscurities and apparently irreconcilable statements recorded throughout the whole of Polynesia seem to be almost magically dissolved by the unequivocal evidence of the Pomare chant."

By this time a correspondence had sprung up between Kenneth and Bishop Herbert W. Williams, a linguist and the author of a Maori dictionary, who lived in Napier, New Zealand. Williams had been assigned by the editor of the *Polynesian Journal* to critique Stimson's articles. Kenneth had always respected Williams as a scholar. Now his sympathetic interest gave Kenneth encouragement. In a letter dated April 6, 1936, Kenneth explained:

> I am left in a situation from which I would like to escape but my conviction . . . allows me no peace. I am therefore facing the situation squarely. . . . As I go along with my work on the ethnology of the Tuamotus, I am assembling all the material on religion which could not have been influenced by Stimson . . .
>
> Handy . . . has recommended that I write an article for the *Polynesian Journal* putting forth my opinions and the evidence on which they are

based. . . . As soon as I have in manuscript form all the material on religion which has my absolute confidence, then I shall feel free to deal with the problem raised by Stimson's work.

Bishop Williams answered bluntly, "I am afraid it is your duty, painful as it may be, to put the facts before the public in the interests of science."

But Kenneth, in his careful way, was not willing to do this until he had checked every chant. It was an illuminating experience. In some cases he found that Fariua and other Kiho informants had given as many as ten versions of the same chant. He soon established to his satisfaction that Stimson's "esoteric" chants were genuine enough except for one essential point: Kio or Kiho had been substituted for Tani, Tangaroa, Rogo, Atoa, Ru, Maui, or other Polynesian gods and demigods.

The Kiho informants, he discovered, were inconsistent in assigning chants to the supreme god. One informant assigned one chant to the god, another informant assigned a different chant. And they placed the god name at different points in the chant as if the chants had different sources. However, the chants in which Kiho was not involved agreed remarkably. Each informant, from whatever island, assigned the same chant to the same god. And the god name appeared in the same places in the chant as if each informant had been handed down the same chant. Meanwhile, Kenneth was learning a lot of Tuamotuan.

Unlike Gregory, Buck patiently tolerated such slow analysis of a subject about which hardly anybody was interested. Months passed. Page after page of research piled up. Now Kenneth began his own translations. Bishop Williams provided advice about word meanings. Kenneth plodded ahead, learning as he went along.

From San Francisco, Gessler wrote that he had sold a book about his adventure with Kenneth on Napuka. But he had taken far too few photographs. Could Kenneth supply some? Buck was not happy about giving Bishop Museum photographs for use in a commercial publication. Kenneth pointed out that Gessler had been a volunteer member of the expedition. The book would publicize the museum. Gessler got his photographs.

While Buck's name added romance and scholarly prestige to the museum, he had not provided any money. In fact, he didn't really care about that part of being a museum director. It was the research that interested him. The museum's precarious financial situation hit home in a memo from the director that Kenneth received on November 27, 1936, reappointing him ethnologist at a $3,600 per year. He had not had an increase in salary for ten years. The memo read:

> For your private information, I have to tell you that owing to the lessened income derived from the Museum's endowment, the Museum has had to cut down its various appropriations in order to balance the Budget . . .
>
> The Trustees regard the annual appointments as being for the 12 months specified and do not consider that they are in any way bound to reappoint members of the staff for another term of 12 months. . . . It is possible that the Trustees . . . may wish to retrench by reducing the appropriation for salaries [in 1938] . . .

Ever since he had returned from the Mangareva expedition, Kenneth and Marguerite had been in debt. There was never enough money for clothes, car repairs, upkeep of the house, or entertaining. By the end of each month they were lucky if they were not overdrawn at the bank.

A newspaper reporter who worked in Honolulu in 1937 recalled the museum's hand-to-mouth existence at that time. She said Kenneth telephoned her with an idea for a story. At the museum she found him sitting among dusty files and cardboard boxes in what looked like a storeroom. "What's the story?" she asked. "Let's go to your office and you can tell me about it." Kenneth answered, "Are you kidding? We're broke. This is it."

Yet he had never before contemplated the possibility that he might be fired. He had always taken his reappointment by the museum for granted. The uncertainty, he said later, gave him a crushing sense of failure. He had felt ever since the controversy with Stimson began that he was under a cloud in the eyes of the trustees. Would they use his attempts to correct Stimson's mistakes as an excuse to let him go? Whatever happened, he must get to the truth.

On January 18, 1937, he handed in the last of his *marae* manuscript to be typed. A month later, February 16, he finished a five-hundred-page manuscript on *Tuamotu Religious Beliefs and Practices* and routed it to the director with a letter. Buck responded without enthusiasm: "I do not wish that this subject [the Kiho controversy] should be revived at the present time. We are all too busy with our own creative work to waste time on debatable material. . . . Now that you have got the main part of the work over that has caused you so much worry, I hope you will be able to devote your best efforts to material culture."

But Buck seemed unable to apply the same discipline to Stimson in Tahiti where, as a Bishop Museum associate in ethnology, he was still writing articles promoting Kiho for whoever would publish them. It was not until a visiting anthropologist blew the whistle on Stimson that Buck appeared to take notice. The anthropologist was Alfred Metraux, who discovered that a colleague in the east was about to take Stimson's museum bulletins about Kiho at face value. Metreaux alerted Kenneth who wrote a letter explaining the problem.

In the meantime, Stimson translated a chant about Easter Island for the *Polynesian Journal.* Once more it was Metraux, recently returned from Easter Island, who sounded the alarm. He went over the article with Buck. On May 4 the director was finally moved to take some action. He wrote a discrete letter to the editor:

> What I have to say to you is strictly confidential. Stimson is a member of the Bishop Museum staff and I would not like to have him think that I went behind his back. The fault is really my own for allowing stress of other work to interfere with my writing to Stimson before this. He sent me a copy of his paper on Kiho and Io in Easter Island. I went over it carefully with Metraux.
>
> His [Stimson's] interpretation of various objects in the chant are wrong in a number of instances . . . many of the native words have a different local meaning to what they have in the dialects with which Stimson has been working. . . . There are a number of things in Stimson's translation that are not present in Easter Island: limes, grasshoppers, candlenut trees, owl, breadfruit, coconut crab, bees . . .

A short expedition up the cold, cinder-covered slopes of Mauna Kea on the island of Hawaii in August took Kenneth's mind off the Kiho controversy. With a geologist and a forester he slogged to 11,000 feet where they explored fourteen or fifteen old shelter caves in the cinder cones. Below each cave rose a huge pile of gray-blue basalt chips. Scattered over the piles were broken and half-finished adzes. Kenneth found five hundred adzes on one mound.

The caves and the adze quarry nearby were known to hunters and hikers but had never been examined by an archaeologist. It was here the old Hawaiians had come to mine the dense basalt from which they made cutting tools, taking shelter from the raw, high-altitude cold in the caves while they chipped and shaped the adzes. The caves spread along a contour two miles long. It was the largest Stone Age factory in the world.

But it was not the caves or the quarry that piqued Kenneth's interest. He had come to search for shrines and he found five, each with five to fifteen stone uprights in alignment, each upright a slab of dike basalt two to four feet high. As he expected, the primitive shrines were similar to those he had found on remote Necker Island, not like the prominent coastal *heiau*s in populated parts of Hawaii.

So the adze makers on Mauna Kea, like the fishermen of Necker, had clung to the earliest form of Polynesian temple while their more sophisticated contemporaries were building larger and more impressive places of worship. He had found one more link that bound Hawaii to Tahiti and the Tuamotus and, most likely, to Easter Island.

A month later a letter arrived from the *Polynesian Journal* editor announcing that he had rejected Stimson's provocative articles for publication and had returned them. "It was like overcoming an infatuation," wrote the editor. But Bishop Museum published Stimson's *Tuamotuan Legends* as Bulletin 148, with chants Kenneth found to be altered. And Stimson sent along a manuscript of translations of Hao chants that disturbed Kenneth even more.

At the end of November, with Buck's approval, Kenneth mailed an article of his own to the *Polynesian Journal*. The manuscript was a compilation of century-old Tahitian accounts of creation that mention Kiho only as a secondary god. He had already started on two more articles that expanded on his views of Stimson's supreme god and gave his reasons.

The articles, to anyone but a dedicated scholar of Polynesian religion, are hopelessly dull. The translations have none of Stimson's poetic imagery. They bristle with sources that Kenneth makes no attempt to glorify. The narrative is as pedestrian as instructions for repairing the kitchen sink. It is bare, factual writing without humor or romance or any speculation at all. To a colleague, Earnest Beaglehole in New Zealand, Kenneth explained what he was trying to do: "It is Stimson versus the truth and not versus K. P. Emory. That will be clear when my material comes out."

Chapter Thirty-one

Half a Doctor

The articles Kenneth wrote for the *Polynesian Journal* exorcised the spell Stimson had cast over him. It was like the beginning of a long convalescence. He still bore the scars of the battle and Stimson would always remain a sore point. But now there was energy for enthusiasm about other projects. One weekend early in 1938 he piled Tiare and Winifred into the car and drove over the Pali to a lonely, windblown beach, called Mokapu, near Kaneohe. While they were swimming, Kenneth saw that skulls were exposed in the sand dunes.

On their next picnic he brought digging tools. His excavation uncovered more skulls and bones, the remains of an extensive Hawaiian dune burial. Over the following decade, Mokapu became Hawaii's largest source of skeletal material for scientific study.

"We had a regular thing going over there, picnicking and picking bones," he said later. "Tiare and Winifred collected. I'd photograph each burial in place. So we have not only the skulls but the method of burial. We found that very few things were buried with them. Among the things were little birds. I can't understand that. It must have been part of their burial ceremony and connected with their religion."

Tiare was not so enthusiastic about skulls and bones. They haunted her, like the deserted *heiau*s she visited with her father, with dreams of death. Winifred didn't seem to have fears like that. Closson's kids, Dick and Buddy, were living with Kenneth's mother. They sometimes came along. And Captain Bill Anderson's daughter, Marion. It was like a treasure hunt.

Meanwhile, Kenneth turned his hand to building displays at the museum. "We are rearranging Polynesian Hall," he wrote in his diary on January 11, 1938. On January 17, "Painted Maori case." The next day he put the artifacts in. Through January and February he built displays for artifacts from Tahiti, the Tuamotus, Tubuai and the Cook Islands, Wallis and Futuna, Samoa, Mangareva, and Easter Island.

A request in May for a sabbatical in Europe didn't come to anything because there was no money at the museum for traveling expenses. But the Emory family finances received a boost toward the end of the year when Castle & Cooke, Ltd., one of the "Big Five" companies downtown, hired Kenneth to write articles about Hawaiiana, at $20 an article, to appear as weekly institutional newspaper advertisements. The articles, which continued through August 1939, added $500 to the family budget, one-third of Kenneth's salary at the museum over the same period.

He called the series "Flying Spray." The articles started with voyaging canoes: felling a tree, building the canoe house, carving the log, weaving the sails, and sewing on the gunwales and caulking them. The voyage came next, and included discussions on provisioning, waiting for the wind, navigating by the stars, and locating the land. Then Kenneth put down in short, popular form the legends of voyaging in the Pacific: a return voyage to Tahiti from Hawaii, the arrival of breadfruit in Hawaii, and the voyage of the priest Paao who came to build the great *heiau* of Mookini on the island of Hawaii. "It was fun," Kenneth said later.

Buck, on the advice of both Kenneth and the editor of the museum press, held up publication of a new Stimson translation because it strayed even further from the original than those he had done before. Margaret Mead came through on a cruise with her new husband, Gregory Bateson, in March. Kenneth spent all day on the boat with them.

In April, Dr. Cooke at the museum received an angry letter from Stimson about Kenneth. "Made statement to trustees concerning my position vs. Stimson," Kenneth wrote in his diary the next day. By this time, apparently, even Albert Judd had become suspicious of his man in Papeete. "Wrote letter to Buck [at Yale] and had good talk with Dr. Cooke," Kenneth wrote in his diary on Monday, April 24. At last his colleagues believed him.

"Flying Spray," and its $20 a week income, came to an end in August. Then a crisis arose at home. Kenneth's mother began pressing him to move his family in with her and save on expenses. Marguerite would have none of it. She suggested he take care of his mother while she and the girls sailed to Tahiti so they could learn French.

While this standoff continued, Kenneth confided in a university professor, Denzel Carr, who taught anthropology and sociology, and read forty languages and spoke eight. Shyness was not one of Carr's traits. He was always making a trip somewhere at somebody else's expense. In fact, he had just returned from Okinawa on a grant from the American Council of Learned Societies in Washington, D.C.

Carr offered the perfect solution to Kenneth's dilemma. Let Marguerite go to Tahiti. That would leave Kenneth free to do what he had always wanted if he were not tied down. Kenneth said what he wanted most was to get his doctorate degree at Yale. Without a doctorate, they would never give him a raise at the museum. Carr thought this was an excellent idea. Kenneth reminded him that he didn't have the money to go to Yale. Carr did not consider this a handicap at all: why not apply for some sort of scholarship? This thought had never occurred to Kenneth.

Carr became Kenneth's volunteer agent, public relations representative, and advisor on bureaucratic paperwork. On March 30, 1940, the Yale University Graduate School wrote to Kenneth informing him that he had been recommended for a scholarship covering tuition, registration, and health fees. In April the Council of Learned Societies approved a study aid grant for Kenneth of $400. The money would cover traveling expenses. Next, Kenneth reapplied for a sabbatical from the museum. He was given the sabbatical, since it would not cost the trustees anything except his regular salary.

He interpreted all this as a personal vindication. "Today the trustees and Peter [Buck] demonstrated they are behind me," he wrote when his sabbatical came through. "All the terrible worry of the past five years was not necessary. Faithful work paid. You get out of life just what you put into it."

One of the requirements for his doctorate was enough facility in French and German to understand scientific reports in these languages. Kenneth felt he could get by in French but he didn't have any knowledge of German. So, in addition to digging at Mokapu and working on the material culture of the Tuamotus, he took German lessons.

Then, in July, Stimson turned up ready to do battle over Kiho but nothing much happened. "Went over some Kiho evidence with Buck. Very tired," Kenneth wrote in his diary on Saturday, July 20. On the following Tuesday, "Stimson and I met before Dr. Buck and Cooke." The next day, "Had satisfactory p.m. with Dr. Buck." Kenneth could not recall what they said at these meetings. Apparently the director supported his position about Stimson's supreme god because the museum did not publish any more of Stimson's work and Stimson was later dropped from the museum staff.

Kenneth was now trying to put the controversy behind him in preparation for Yale. At the last minute, however, his mother had a heart attack. He felt guilty leaving her but there was no turning back. He sailed at noon on Friday, August 15, for San Francisco.

"Crossing the plains," he wrote on August 27. He explored the National Museum in Washington, D.C., and then headed for New Haven, Connecticut.

There he found himself in an assemblage of brilliant minds and sensitive egos. "Schedule made out," he wrote on Tuesday, September 24. That was with the help of anthropologist Dr. George P. Murdock, whom Kenneth described as a very "smooth customer." "German exam a week from today," he wrote in his diary. Kenneth studied German for five hours on Thursday, five hours on Friday, six hours on Saturday, and another five hours on Sunday. On Monday morning he took his first class from his old friend Alfred Metraux, an intense little man with a bald head, and studied German all afternoon. "Passed German exam," he wrote with huge relief on Tuesday. "Had conference with [Bronislaw] Malinowski."

Most of the other students were much younger than Kenneth's forty-three years. Even some of his professors were younger. Dr. Wendell Bennett and Metraux had worked under Kenneth at Bishop Museum. None of them had Kenneth's knowledge of the Pacific. A person with less ego might have been unable to adjust to such a loss of status. Nothing in Kenneth's diary indicates that it bothered him.

He tried his skis on the golf course after the first snowfall in November. But mostly it was work. Malinowski, a blond Pole who intimidated students with his brilliance, was the star of the faculty. He had published an acclaimed work that dealt with a primitive economic system among the Trobriands in New Guinea. Malinowski and Kenneth did not think on the same wavelength. "He was bent on the theoretical approach," Kenneth said later. "He was more interested in the social end, the nonmaterial side. I liked material culture. It was more solid, trustworthy." Their differences in approach to anthropology and in writing style may have been the reason Kenneth struggled under Malinowski for whom he was writing a paper on *marae*s. "Malinowski's class—bad showing," he wrote on Friday, December 20.

Three days later he was on his way to spend Christmas with relatives. "This has been a year of critical struggle," he jotted during that vacation. "I am glad it is safely past. To have continued without this break away for new orientation would have been fatal."

Kenneth spent the second week of 1941 on the *marae* paper, then concentrated on a paper about the Philippines. In February he started writing about oceanic influences in South America. By then he was lonely and homesick. He began to see a lot of a very intelligent and chic female student, Rhoda Proctor, who was being courted by Alfred Metraux. It was about this that Marguerite decided to join him instead of going to Tahiti. But that good news was followed by bad. "Mother passed away last night," he wrote on Saturday, March 8, 1941.

Marguerite and the girls arrived in the cold on a special passenger train, the Wolverine, on March 18. The next day they picked up a Buick 41, and had the children fitted with warm clothing. Tiare and Winifred ran right out and built a snowman. "Children on sleds," Kenneth wrote on March 22 in Hanover. They drove back to New Haven to hunt for an apartment. By the time they found one, spring break was over and the grind for final exams began.

"Studying with might and main," Kenneth wrote on April 28. On May 3, "Studied all day." On May 7, "All day studying for exams." His oral exam, the climax of his six months' trial, came on Saturday, May 10. Kenneth wasn't sure he would pass. A friend, Henry Silverthorn, had been flunked. To calm himself he drove with Marguerite into the country and walked in the woods. They came back to New Haven and he was ushered into a room where six of the leading anthropologists in the United States sat waiting to quiz him.

It was not nearly so difficult as he had feared. "You see, no questions were asked about Polynesia because, you know, I could answer better than any of them," he said. "Anyway, they were very nice and I managed all right." How did he feel after the exam? "Damn good. Marguerite and the children and I drove out into the country and had dinner at an inn."

Then it was play time. For two months the Emorys visited friends and relatives between New England and Washington. On July 30 they began a cross-country trek back to the West Coast. They drove across the Badlands of South Dakota; visited Yellowstone National Park in Wyoming; crossed over to Glacier National Park on the Canadian border, where Tiare and Winifred saw three bears; stopped to admire Crater Lake in Oregon; then finally drove south to view the giant redwoods.

"Oh, it was fun," Marguerite recalled later. "We cooked with all sorts of stoves. Ohhhh, and there were little animals trotting around." On the plains Marguerite saw her first hobo, a ragged fellow standing by the side of the road trying to hitch a ride. She was afraid of him. But her Polynesian breeding made her insist that Kenneth stop so they could explain to the hobo that they were too much in a hurry to pick him up.

"You know what he said," Marguerite remembered with a giggle. "He said, 'I'm in a hurry, too.' We picked him up, yes. That's when I learned what a hobo was." She was much less interested in a dance by the Chippewa Indians. "Not very artistic," she said later. "Thruuuum, thruuum, thruuum. Oh, how boring."

In Hollywood they put the Buick into a garage to prepare it for shipment to Hawaii. The Emorys sailed from Los Angeles for Honolulu in the *Lurline* on Friday, September 5, and arrived on September 10, 1941. Kenneth was still only half of a doctor. "I have worked off all the requirements for a Ph.D. in anthropology except for the dissertation, which is to be done here at the museum under Dr. Buck," he wrote to the editor of the *Polynesian Journal* on October 3. "As soon as this is finished and accepted, I will have my degree." In November he got started on his dissertation. Kenneth had not the slightest premonition that the world would fight the greatest war in its history before he finished it.

PART SIX

WAR AND SURVIVAL

Chapter Thirty-two

This is War

Kenneth always got up at dawn with the birds and fishermen. He did so on December 7, 1941, and drove alone down Nuuanu Avenue, then across on Beretania Street to St. Andrew's Episcopal Cathedral for the early service at 6 A.M. Toward Punchbowl on Queen Emma Street stood the old house Walter Emory had rented for his wife and two baby sons in 1900.

Honolulu was a considerably different place now. For one thing, the population had increased to 180,000, about four times the total in 1900. Poor people rode to work in electric trolleybuses, not mule-drawn trams. Horses and carriages had given way to automobiles. Four-engine Pan American Clippers spanned the distance from San Francisco in only fifteen hours. Twin-engine Sikorsky flying boats flew between the islands. Kenneth had never traveled that way, of course, because it was too expensive.

St. Andrew's, a handsome stone church with gothic windows and a hushed interior, provided a place of refuge in a world of change. Not that Kenneth minded change, but life in Honolulu had grown hectic. Soldiers and sailors from beefed-up military bases gave the streets a different complexion. Workers recruited from the mainland were pouring into Honolulu by the thousands to take jobs at the Pearl Harbor Shipyard. The sudden increase in population had created more traffic, a housing shortage, and lines at movie theaters.

Yet on this sunny morning only a few early risers like Kenneth disturbed the Sunday calm. You could throw a brick down Bishop Street in the heart of the business district and not hit anyone. There was no need for policemen to direct traffic at the intersections because there was no traffic. It was still cool and fresh in the dappled shade of Nuuanu Avenue as Kenneth drove home from church to the old house on Bates Street. He and Marguerite were living there to take care of their invalid sister-in-law, Rachel. They had rented their Dowsett Highlands house to a navy commander and his wife.

Kenneth parked the car and was mounting the front steps when a series of explosions intruded on his Sunday morning mood. They were powerful, menacing explosions. His first thought was that the navy must be conducting maneuvers. The explosions came from the direction of Pearl Harbor. He went out on the lawn where the view was better. Columns of ugly, black smoke rose into the serene sky. His neighbor, William Twigg-Smith, who lived in the old Thurston house, hurried out to join him on the lawn. As they stood gazing toward Pearl Harbor a formation of planes flew over. On the end of each wing was the rising sun of Japan.

"This is war," said Twigg-Smith in disbelief.

Kenneth went inside. Marguerite said he was very pale. He told her, "We are being bombed." They turned on the radio. Outside, antiaircraft fire erupted and shells rained down on the city. One of them exploded on nearby Liliha Street. "At first, we didn't know they were antiaircraft shells," he said later. "The radio kept telling us to be calm while we were quivering there."

The explosions finally stopped, but smoke continued to soil the sky. The phone kept ringing as friends called to exchange information, but nobody in the neighborhood knew what to do. Marguerite called the children inside. The little Japanese daughter of Twigg-Smith's driver was playing with Winifred. Marguerite sent her home. Kenneth went outside and walked to Nuuanu Avenue. A jeep went by with one small, scared soldier riding in back and holding a gun. To Kenneth, the frightened soldier was a symbol of his own futility.

They heard shots during the night. At dawn the next day, air raid sirens went off. It proved to be a false alarm but made the threat of a Japanese invasion more frightening. Ruth, the Japanese woman who took care of Rachel, came to work silent and tight-lipped. But Shimi, the maid and cook who had two grown sons, was voluble in her anger. Marguerite had sent clothing to her parents in Japan. Shimi told her, "I am so sorry, so sorry. My parents wrote to tell me something is going to happen. They reminded me that I am the mother of American citizens. My duty is with my children."

Kenneth went to the museum. The exhibition hall remained closed. Suddenly the research of half a century seemed vulnerable to destruction. Priceless negatives were stored in the photo laboratory on the third floor. One blast and they'd be gone. Only glass and the polished wood of exhibition cases guarded idols and feather cloaks that could not be replaced at any cost. No one at the museum had contemplated an invasion and the looting that followed. A room on the bottom floor of Konia Hall had a strong lock. The staff hastily moved the feather cloaks and idols there. Kenneth and Buck brought down the negatives, then their own files.

A concrete block building at the old Thurston place next door to the Emorys became the neighborhood bomb shelter. The publisher had died in 1931. Now his daughter Margaret, who had married Twigg-Smith, occupied her father's house. The bomb shelter had been his study, and cabinets of land shells still stood against the walls. People collected there at night, not because it was safe but because it was cool. Twigg-Smith had installed an electric fan. Blackout curtains turned the Emory house into an oven. Sometimes fifteen to twenty people gathered there to comfort each other and play the radio.

The museum became a haunted house in the nervous weeks that followed; the doors were closed to the public, and it was so quiet that Kenneth could hear the ticking of a pendulum clock on the floor below his office. Yet there was an incredible amount of work to be done. The archives contained thousands of pages of unpublished manuscripts, typewritten chants and legends, single copies of reports and journals, and field notebooks. None of these items could be replaced if a bomb turned the museum into rubble.

Kenneth knew that a technique called microfilm could reduce whole books to a single spool of film. He began at once to copy manuscripts. On April 21, 1942, he wrote to W. Wedgewood Bowen, curator of the Dartmouth College Museum:

> We are seeking a place on the mainland where we could leave on deposit for the duration of the war photographs of specimens in our museum and . . . film covering our unpublished manuscripts. . . . We feel that Dartmouth . . . would be safe from bombs and, at the same time . . . there would be no likelihood of [the material] being completely lost or thrown out. . . . We were not able to secure safety film and as a result have to do the copying on nitrate film. The film will be packed in two tins each containing a thousand feet . . .

Bowen offered the use of a fireproof vault in Bissell Hall on campus. Microfilming is a tedious job that can be done by a student, yet Kenneth did it himself because there was no one else. One by one, other staff members departed to fight or to take glamorous war jobs. At age forty-four Kenneth felt lonely and useless. But the work had to be done. The dissertation for his doctorate now seemed unimportant. He was too busy even to think about it.

At home, the war for Marguerite and Kenneth created inconvenience as well as danger. Gasoline and food were rationed. They started a garden in the backyard to raise vegetables. The children at school were issued gas masks, which they hung on trees and forgot to take home after play. The yardman at the Dowsett House stopped coming, so Kenneth had to mow the lawn himself. Then the tenant turned out to be an alcoholic. One night he went to sleep with a cigarette in his hand and nearly burned down the house. He was barely sober enough most mornings to pilot his car out of the driveway. His wife escaped to the mainland. They got rid of him only to be saddled with two young, single naval officers who kept women, which offended Marguerite.

Kenneth joined the Businessmen's Training Corps. They drilled on weekends and patrolled their neighborhoods at night to enforce the blackout. In various entries, Kenneth's diary records this patriotic period: "Drilled P.M., rapid fire." "Air raid 10 A.M., alarm. Up to house P.M., cleaned yard." "Last night a Jap plane dropped three bombs back of Punchbowl, awakened us at 2 A.M. Put films and dictaphone records under cover at the museum." "Received tin hats P.M." "On docks, Businessmen's Training Corps." "Parade—issued rifles and ammunition. To movies P.M. Greta Garbo." The latter entry was for May 31.

Playing soldier became deadly serious the next day, June 1. Kenneth wrote in his diary, "Bad news. Put on alert. Rumor. Midway has fallen." "We just held our breath," said Marguerite later. "We knew if Midway was lost, Hawaii would be next." A Japanese landing in Hawaii would mean fighting from house to house. That night Kenneth patrolled the neighborhood from 3 A.M. to 6 A.M., along with young David Twigg-Smith. In the darkness, every sound made him jump.

Still there was no news of the battle. The Japanese could land at any time. "On guard with David 8 to 12 [P.M.]," Kenneth wrote on June 3. "Rainy. Machine gun fire." That turned out to be a jittery businessman spooked by shadows. They were all jittery, ready to shoot at anything that moved, even each other. On June 4 Kenneth wrote, "On guard 12 A.M. to 3 A.M. Clear, starlit. With Ken Barnes."

An announcement of the U.S. naval victory at Midway Island, the turning point of the war with Japan, came the next day. The immediate danger of invasion was over. "Promoted to 2nd Lieut.," Kenneth wrote on June 5. "Alert off. News of Midway repulse of enemy." Honolulu settled down to the task of coping with the blackout and rationing and a lack of replacement parts for things wearing out. Kenneth sent off a box twelve inches by twenty-four inches, containing two 1,000-foot reels of microfilm, to Dartmouth. Then he doggedly began making spare copies of photographs recording the museum's most important artifacts. When he finished with that he went to work taking pictures of artifacts that had never been photographed.

It seemed the war had passed him by. Anthropology had no place in his nation's battle for survival. He might have tried to enlist but his eyes didn't pass muster. Besides, somebody had to stay and take care of the museum.

Chapter Thirty-three

Castaway's Baedeker

Clark Ingraham had gone to Dartmouth with Kenneth. Now he also had a commission in the U.S. Navy and orders to join an aircraft carrier at Pearl Harbor. Ingraham, however, arrived before the carrier so it was only natural that he call Kenneth with an invitation to dinner at the Halekulani Hotel in Waikiki, a favorite wartime rendezvous of handsome officers and their girlfriends. Admiral Chester W. Nimitz was known to be a particular friend of Mrs. Clifford Kimball, the matriarch who ruled the Halekulani with an iron hand. She once complained to him that his pilots were flying dangerously low over the hotel to salute their buddies. The buzzing stopped.

Marguerite had a marvelous time that night. She recognized quite a few daughters of old island families on the arms of dashing young officers. Romance vibrated at every table. It was not an evening to count the cost of heartache but to live each moment to the fullest. While Marguerite lost herself in the ambiance of love by the sea in wartime, Ingraham worried about what would happen to his fliers if they were shot down over the Pacific. Even if a man managed to reach a desert island, he would starve to death in a week. Nobody could stay alive on one of those miserable sand spits.

Kenneth disagreed. He explained that desert islands were mostly a Hollywood invention. Polynesians had been living on atolls for centuries and survived very well. Even uninhabited atolls provided food and water. Take the ubiquitous coconut palm. Each young nut contained nearly a pint of water so pure it could be used as plasma. The meat provided food, the shells utensils, and the husk fuel. The problem was that most young men in the service hadn't the foggiest notion how to go about husking a coconut. So they starved in the midst of plenty.

Ingraham asked if Kenneth could teach his fliers to husk a coconut. Kenneth said it would be easy. All a person needed was a pointed stick. Plant the blunt end in the ground, bring the coconut down hard on the point, and twist. Once you got a strip of husk off, just keep ripping off strip after strip until the nut emerged. Crack it open on a rock and eat the meat. Better still, first punch out the eyes in one end and drink the water. That way, it wouldn't go to waste. Kenneth explained that all of this could be done without even a pocket knife. The Polynesians didn't have iron until the white man arrived.

Kenneth described the shellfish that grew in lagoons, a mainstay of the diet on inhabited atolls. It only had to be picked. Kernels of the stickery pandanus tree contained starch and sugar. Children ate it as candy. The thick leaves of pigweed that grew along the beaches made a juicy and nourishing salad when there was nothing else. Even an island without streams or springs had a store of rainwater in a lens riding below the ground surface and above sea level. Every native village had a well that tapped this source. The water was brackish but it kept people alive.

This was a subject as familiar to Kenneth as putting on his shoes. In fact, he explained that he had quickly learned in the Tuamotus not to go barefooted. The temperature of the sand under a tropic sun could get up to three hundred degrees. Only natives, insulated by thick callouses, went without shoes. A flier beached from a life raft or floating in a life vest would probably be unshod. Burned feet could keep him immobile and helpless on the island. The first thing he should do is make sandals from coconut husk, a simple procedure that required no tools.

Ingraham listened in fascination. Would Kenneth put this information down for aircraft carrier pilots to study? It could save a lot of lives. That dinner at the Halekulani took place on Wednesday, October 14, 1942. Kenneth had just returned to work on his dissertation and had made a good start. But he put it aside to write *Castaway's Baedeker to the South Seas*. Ingraham took it to the Intelligence Center, Pacific Ocean Areas, and found an enthusiastic reception. Immediately, officers on other aircraft carriers wanted copies.

Then *The Honolulu Advertiser*, now published by Lorrin P. Thurston, Kenneth's Punahou classmate, got wind of Kenneth's do-it-yourself survival book. Reporter Dorothy Bentar splashed an interview with Kenneth over the front page. The headlines screamed, "Invaluable Advice for Unfortunate Airmen, Coconuts Sufficient to Sustain Life."

Edgar Sckenck, the innovative director at the stylish Honolulu Academy of Arts, who had already done two shows designed to attract service personnel, immediately recognized a winner. He called Kenneth to ask if they might work together on a show at the Art Academy that would include materials such as coconuts and palm fronds with demonstrations about how to use them to survive on a desert island. Kenneth agreed with Buck's consent. The museum had reopened to the public after the Battle of Midway, but the director was content to let the Academy of Arts put on skits and entertainment.

On December 15 Kenneth wrote in his diary, "Edgar Sckenck came out to prepare exhibition for *Native Lore for South Sea Castaways.*" On Christmas Eve Kenneth picked out pictures of fish and birds for the exhibit. It opened on January 6, 1943, to a turn-away crowd. Kenneth starred as survival instructor: weaving palm fronds, making sandals, and cooking in an earth oven. *The Advertiser* called him a modern Robinson Crusoe and took full credit for bringing this life-saving effort to the attention of the public.

The crowds continued to come, especially servicemen. Colonels, commanders, and captains in the U.S. Marines called to make appointments for survival demonstrations. On January 8 Kenneth lectured to a group of fliers. By January 12 he had four lectures a day. Buck reluctantly offered to help out. On January 20 Kenneth wrote in his diary, "Five lectures. Evening at Army & Navy YMCA. Dr. Buck helped with one."

Kenneth could not demonstrate survival in the South Seas without materials. When he was not lecturing he ran around hunting for coconuts and palm fronds. Mrs. Albert Judd offered the coconut trees in her yard, hoping to have them cleaned at no charge. Kenneth hardly had time to eat. By this time Buck had changed his mind about skits and entertainment. When the show closed at the Academy on January 31 it reopened at the museum.

Kenneth installed a thatched village in the courtyard, including a sleeping house, lean-to, cooking house, *imu* [earth oven], and coconut grater. The museum's school for castaways opened on February 16. On February 19 Kenneth lectured to Marine fliers, the next day to antiaircraft gunners, and the day after that to a class of dive bomber pilots. On February 25 he gave eight lectures to soldiers in the Ranger & Combat School.

By this time, fortunately, he began to get help. Loring G. Hudson, an English and history teacher at Kamehameha Schools, volunteered as assistant lecturer. The army assigned Kenneth a truck and some GIs to comb the island to fill his insatiable demand for coconuts, palm fronds, pigweed, pandanus nuts, and bamboo. Kenneth revised his *Castaway's Baedeker* and illustrated it with his own drawings. He called the booklet *South Sea Lore.* It was published by the Museum Press and became the museum's all-time bestseller.

In April Kenneth received a request for an article from the *American Museum of Natural History Magazine.* Then the *Saturday Evening Post* did a two-page spread on his school for castaways. Admiral

Nimitz praised the school in a nationwide radio broadcast. By this time Kenneth and Hudson were setting up a Jungle Training School in tropical Kahana Valley on the windward side of Oahu where servicemen bound for the South Pacific could practice survival training.

The popularity of Kenneth's survival course created several unforeseen difficulties. An ambitious army colonel in charge of the Ranger & Combat School decided that the lectures fell under his jurisdiction and that Kenneth should be given an officer's commission in his command. Kenneth had no intention of surrendering his freedom to military bureaucracy. Yet Buck was not willing to compensate Kenneth on the museum payroll for his extra work.

Wartime inflation had sent prices skyrocketing in Honolulu. Kenneth could no longer support his family on the museum salary. And the girls would soon be ready for college. He kept borrowing money to pay emergency expenses. The army finally gave him an alternative by offering to pay both he and Hudson for teaching the survival course as an official military function. Hudson, who was still getting $100 monthly from Kamehameha Schools, asked for not less than $400 a month from the army. Kenneth, as director of the school, put his value at $500 per month for an average of fifty hours work per week.

The general refused to pay $500 per month because Kenneth was getting only $300 at the museum, as he had been for almost twenty years. A Colonel H. H. Ristine, in charge of negotiations, offered to compromise on $385.75. Kenneth wrote to Buck in despair: "If the Bishop Museum is willing to make up the difference between $385.75 and $500, or $115 a month, while I should operate the school, then I can accept Ristine's offer. Ristine himself suggested that the museum do this as I would be freed of many lecture hours and would have ample assistance, and so could give more time to museum affairs, actually, than in the past months."

The trustees agreed to the terms and Kenneth, for the first time in his life, began to earn the magnificent sum of $6,000 per year. There is no doubt that he earned it. He lectured to fliers, chaplains, nurses, infantrymen, gunners, sailors, and WACs. Margaret Titcomb, the museum librarian, worried about his health. He slogged through the jungle at Kahana Valley and swam with men half his age to the reef at Waianae to demonstrate how to gather food. A letter to Rhoda (Proctor) Metraux, his classmate at Yale, explains how he felt about it:

> Since returning from Yale, I have made two good starts on my dissertation. The first was just before the 7th of December and the second just

before being drawn into the work I am now doing. I could have gone on with my writing just the same but it seemed terribly selfish. . . . It has been a satisfaction to show how anthropology can be turned to very practical purposes. . . . The men I have trained make a sleeping mat out of a whole coconut leaf in a few minutes, and in another few minutes this can be converted into a stretcher or a hammock.

The classes continued at the same frantic pace into 1944 as U.S. forces captured beachheads in the South Pacific. "Thirty-six fliers in photo recon—heavy planes," Kenneth wrote in his diary on February 28. And on May 1, "Left for Maui on Navy transport plane. Prepared for lectures all day." On May 2, "Morning lecture at Puunene Airport Theater. P.M. lecture at Kahului Fair Grounds." On June 22, "Gave lecture to G-3 C.P.A. Battle of Saipan reported. We have caused the Japs to withdraw."

Kenneth received word at 5 P.M. on Wednesday, September 13, that he would be leaving in two days for Espiritu Santo, the northernmost island in the New Hebrides (Vanuatu) chain, located below the equator on the way to Sydney, Australia. He would set up an advance base Jungle Training School and advise on how to handle the natives. It is not clear whether the military command understood that Kenneth's field of expertise lay in Polynesia while the inhabitants of the New Hebrides are Melanesians, a different race entirely. Kenneth didn't bother to instruct his hosts. He was delighted by his first opportunity to study Melanesians.

Kenneth took off at 8 P.M. on Friday, September 15, in a C-54 transport plane from Hickam Air Base, accompanied by a group of thirty men of the Jungle Training Corps. They flew through the night 1,630 nautical miles to Canton (Kanton) Atoll, a desolate flyspeck in the ocean wastes, where they landed at 5:30 A.M. They set their watches back to 4 A.M. while the plane was refuelled.

The blinding glare of the rising sun as it reflected from the coral sands of Canton reminded Kenneth of atolls in the Tuamotus. But the dusty airstrip, flat as a tabletop with each end nearly dipping into the ocean, was something new. He had associated these tiny, remote atolls with precarious canoes and shabby copra schooners. Now the mighty effort of war had swept over them, grinding them through the maws of progress and technology, changing them forever. Was it for better or worse? It was exciting, no doubt about that.

They roared into the air at 5:30 P.M., local time, and five and one-half hours later sighted the first shoals of Fiji. The reefs and shoals passed beneath them in miniature, dainty and beautiful, their terrible struggle with the surf tamed by distance. Then inhabited islands came into view, jewels of jungle. The C-54 landed at Viti Levu at noon for lunch. There it was Sunday, not Saturday, because they had crossed the international dateline.

"Impressed with tremendous speed," Kenneth scribbled into his diary. "The islands are in our back door now. Seeing them with the New Hebrides in the offing is like a dream."

Another three and one-half hours took them to Espiritu Santo, where Kenneth saw his first wild parakeets flying among the coconut palms. It was only 4 P.M. The group had dinner in a military mess hall and tumbled into bed. Kenneth awoke at 5:30 A.M. and strolled into the forest. He saw ground pigeons and swallows. They filled the air with music just before dawn.

Espiritu had become an international military outpost, the staging area for General Douglas MacArthur's reinvasion of the Philippines—already underway. At Espiritu Santo the British occupied the coast, Americans had a large base inland, and the French claimed general jurisdiction. Nobody had bothered to ask the natives for permission to camp, Kenneth said.

At the moment that didn't concern him, however. He set out after breakfast with Lieutenant David Akana from Hawaii to look around. They saw papayas, coconut palms, big breadfruit trees (but no fruit), a Polynesian chestnut in fruit, two kinds of limes, wild pumpkin and tomato and, on the beach, large Tridacna shells. Fresh water ran luxuriously out of the forest onto the beach. They had time to get acquainted with a Melanesian boy and two women before lunch.

At 1 P.M. the colonel and major escorted them along a trail hacked through the jungle three-quarters of a mile inland to the training area. Kenneth saw rattan as well as water vine for the first time, and bamboo containing water up to one-third of every joint. Mountain apple grew in profusion around the camp area. Nobody with any sense could starve on islands so richly endowed.

He supervised the construction of a thatched village and the survival training went ahead through September. The camp was in the upland, cold and misty like the volcano country on the island of Hawaii. There were plenty of army instructors now, so Kenneth spent a lot of his time adding to his store of information: Melanesian words, place names, and names for plants.

By October he had made contact with French planters and had found informants in the native villages. His notebook bristled with information. The ground ovens of the Melanesians on Espiritu Santo differed from those he had seen before. There they used small heated stones below and large stones on top of food wrapped in bird of paradise leaves, called *ravaro*, and covered the whole not with dirt but with more bird of paradise leaves. They wrapped fish in *ti* leaves.

The natives fished with bow and arrow in the streams and also in the ocean. They used nets for fishing, too, and a snare with a bent handle with a loop on the end for small game, pig and chicken. Another method of catching wild pig was pitfalls. The natives assured him they could get all the pigs they wanted. Kenneth recorded the size of their fishnets and the materials they used to make the twine—heavy *vae* bark for the border rope and *aro* bark for the netting. Kenneth learned from a missionary that the natives of the interior spoke a different language from those living along the coast. They did not understand one another.

His biggest surprise came when he heard about a Tahitian in command of a small French naval vessel stationed in the New Hebrides. This Tahitian turned out to be his brother-in-law, Marii a Teai, from Papeete. Eventually they managed to arrange a reunion, and Marii caught up on news of Marguerite.

On October 24 Kenneth led a small expedition into the interior. "The Army was firing up there," he explained later. "People were living in the place. We wanted to find out where they were living and warn our side where not to fire."

With an upland guide from the mission, the party pushed along a steep path through heavy forest hung thick with vines. At almost forty-seven, Kenneth was by far the oldest in the group. But the others had not spent their lifetimes scrambling up cliffs, bulling through thorny lantana, and slogging over sharp-edged lava flows. He had no trouble keeping up except when he stopped to examine a new plant or watch a native in a tree shooting birds with a bow and arrow.

Halfway up the mountain they found a small village of four or five houses thatched with palm leaves and floored with hard-packed dirt, with fireplaces in the center. The women did not appear until friendly relations were established. The people maintained no contact with the shore. They had chickens, pigs, and dogs, and fished in mountain streams. Kenneth discovered that they spoke basic Malaya, which he could understand. "We went all the way to the top of the island," he said later. "It was an all day trip to get up there, very steep." But he returned with more information in his notebook.

On October 28 he started back to Honolulu. This time they went by way of an island symbol of war in the Pacific, Guadalcanal, which was in 1942 the scene of fighting as brutal as the world has ever seen. Its spectacular green peaks, rearing from the ocean, reminded Kenneth of Bora-Bora. They arrived at night at Tarawa, another historic scene of struggle, shadowy in the moonlight.

"We circled and circled," Kenneth wrote. "Could see red and other lights, reef wash. Ran into rain squalls which blotted everything out. Heard the rain on the metal of the plane. Finally we glided onto the smooth, hard, coral runway, hitting shallow sheets of water that lay on it from the rain."

When he stepped out of the plane he saw that the tops of the coconut trees were missing, having been blasted by artillery fire. There were burned-out barges and tanks on the beach and in the shallows of the reef, ghosts of violence under a pale moon. Behind the beach artillery shells had punched holes through the walls of a deserted, two-story, concrete Japanese blockhouse. They had a cold supper and flew on.

The plane landed again at Canton and then took off for Honolulu. Time dragged. It was more boring than a copra schooner. Kenneth rolled up in his blanket and tried to sleep. When he couldn't, he got out his diary and scribbled, "Two and one-half hours to Honolulu. My six weeks blackout of news of the family will be broken."

Chapter Thirty-four

Micronesia

Dr. George P. Murdock, Kenneth's advisor at Yale, showed up at the museum at noon on Thursday, November 9, 1944. He was a Yankee, about Kenneth's age, dynamic and forceful. The Emorys took him to dinner at the Halekulani. Pete Murdock was not, like Kenneth, an outdoor scientist, but rather a tough-minded student of cultures and a prolific writer with a flair for administration. He had temporarily given up his post at Yale to join the navy and write handbooks used to give military governments a frame of reference for dealing with natives of Pacific islands. He would end his naval career in command of the navy military government unit on Okinawa.

Murdock was already looking ahead to the end of the war. He reminded Kenneth that peace would bring new opportunities to American anthropologists in the Pacific, especially in Micronesia. Kenneth didn't have to be reminded. Micronesia, composed of clusters of tiny islands north of the equator in an ocean area as large as the United States, had been taken over first by the early Spaniards, then by the Germans until the end of World War I when Japan occupied the islands primarily for use as military bases. Americans had never been welcome. Micronesia was an empty shelf in museum libraries in the United States. Every anthropologist interested in the Pacific was eager to study the Micronesians who, with Polynesians and Melanesians, made up the three racial groups of Oceania.

Conversations similar to that between Kenneth and Murdoch may have taken place among other Pacific scholars during this period. Kenneth recalled that during his discussion with Murdock they dreamed up a plan to tackle Micronesia. Since the area was too big for the Bishop Museum or any other single institution to handle, why not organize a consortium of museums and universities, each to study a different Micronesian island group? For Kenneth it was a very exciting dinner.

But there was still a war to win. He lectured on survival through 1944, adapting the course to island conditions U.S. fighting men encountered as they moved away from the atolls. In January 1945,

Lieutenant General Robert C. Richardson cited Kenneth for his program, which had already trained 300,000 troops in survival techniques.

Rachel Emory died at Maluhia Hospital on February 2. No longer responsible for her care, Marguerite and Kenneth moved back to their own house in Dowsett Highlands.

About the same time Pete Murdock traveled through Hawaii, and they talked about Micronesia again. Kenneth's diary shows that he had lunch to discuss the same subject two weeks later with a group that included Dr. Douglas Oliver, a Harvard anthropologist, who had spent much of the war in Honolulu with the Board of Economic Warfare. Oliver had done fieldwork in New Guinea in 1937, and was writing a book on Pacific islands that would become a classic in its field. Along with Murdock, Oliver was focusing on Micronesia as a new challenge.

The luncheons with Oliver and others interested in the idea of joint work in Micronesia started up again in July. Kenneth's diary shows that Buck attended once. University of Hawaii professors from various disciplines showed up. On July 28, 1945, Kenneth wrote, "At my suggestion, Dr. Oliver, Dr. [Andrew] Lind [sociologist at the University of Hawaii], Dr. [John] Embree [anthropologist at the University of Hawaii], and I met to consider what recommendations we might make to our respective institutions for the shaping of postwar research."

The meetings took on new urgency when the atom bombs fell on Hiroshima and Nagasaki on August 6 and August 9. Japan surrendered less than a week later. By this time Kenneth had submitted his letter of resignation as a U.S. Army survival instructor, to become effective September 1, and was writing Yale about getting back to work on the dissertation for his Ph.D.

In October everything began to happen at once. Yale agreed to consider his dissertation even though it was tardy by five years. Oliver formulated a plan to study Micronesia. On October 11, 1945, Kenneth finished his own outline for *Planning Research in Micronesia* in support of Oliver. He wrote:

> I am in accord with Murdock, Oliver, and Embree that research in Micronesia should be cleared through an organization set up under the National Research Council. I think Oliver's plan forms an excellent basis . . . and believe that the Bishop Museum and the University of Hawaii could play a more brilliant part by working through such an organization than if they attempted to carry out the whole project alone . . .

Then a group at the University of Hawaii got permission from Admiral Nimitz to send four scientists sponsored by the U.S. Navy to Micronesia to survey conditions of fieldwork there. The group would include a botanist, a zoologist, a geologist, and an anthropologist. Paul S. Bachman, dean of faculties at the university, invited Kenneth to go along as the anthropologist.

There was nothing Kenneth wanted to do more. But he had the dissertation to write. He couldn't expect the long-suffering registrar at Yale to wait another year. Buck advised him to stay and get his degree. The University of Hawaii team left without him, and Kenneth felt like a student kept after school while his friends were out playing.

Yet his dissertation on Polynesian cultural comparisons by means of language soon engrossed him. He began to wonder if it might not be possible to work out a chronology for first settlement of islands in Polynesia. In December he began checking his comparisons with work done a quarter of a century earlier by William Churchill. On December 22 he wrote in his diary, "Worked 4½ hours on dissertation." The next day. "Put in five hours on dissertation." The day after Christmas, "Working full tilt on dissertation." On New Year's Eve, "Worked up to midnight on dissertation. Finished preliminary work on word comparison."

Kenneth worked through January 1946 on his word comparisons. By the end of the month he was typing up tables of word statistics. On February 3 he wrote exultantly in his diary, "On dissertation early in morning. Discovered could measure degree of differentiation in East Polynesian languages." The next day, "On calculation of degree of difference." Then he began to construct graphs. March passed in creative excitement as he worked out his conclusions. On April 8 he scribbled in his diary, "On relative time of branching off of East Polynesians and genealogical dates."

At last he began writing. By measuring the amount of change in his word lists using twenty-five years as a single generation in time, and adding the evidence of tradition and genealogies, Kenneth had arrived at dates for the migrations of the early Polynesians. It was a tour de force utilizing all evidence then available to take the elusive Polynesian out of mythology and put him within the context of history.

Kenneth estimated that the first Polynesians arrived in the Pacific about 500 B.C. and populated West Polynesia, Samoa, and Tonga. "Population pressure in West Polynesia is very likely to have been the cause of the migration . . . to Tahiti," he wrote. This migration took place about A.D. 200, he estimated. "Population pressure building up in Tahiti over about seven centuries is probably responsible for the sudden expansion to all points in [East Polynesia] . . ." he added. His summary gives the following chronology:

> Tahiti . . . sent an offshoot to the Marquesas [A.D. 900]. After a lapse of several centuries Tahitian culture then put out a branch in the direction of New Zealand [A.D. 1050] followed shortly by a branch to Hawaii [A.D. 1150]. About this time the Marquesan branch divided, sending an offshoot to far off Easter Island [A.D. 1150] followed a little later by one to Mangareva [A.D. 1250].
>
> Those early Tahitians who moved to the Marquesas possibly met some newly arrived West Polynesians, and those Tahitians who made the long voyage to Hawaii may have stopped at the Marquesas on the way, adding Marquesans to their passengers and crew. Or the Marquesans may have visited Hawaii early in its history. At least, we have good evidence of direct contact between Hawaii and the Marquesas . . .

By this time everybody at the museum was helping with the dissertation. Kenneth drafted Pat Bacon, the daughter of museum staffer Mary Pukui, to help type. Librarian Margaret Titcomb pitched in. Winifred helped make corrections while Titcomb proofread the manuscript. On Friday, April 19, 1946, it was done.

Three days later Kenneth received an invitation from Pete Murdock to a Pacific Science Conference scheduled for June in Washington, D.C., by the National Research Council. Kenneth's expenses would be paid by the Council. Delegates from major U.S. museums and universities would discuss how to undertake the scientific study of Micronesia, now being administered by the U.S. Navy. Buck had not been invited and felt slighted. Kenneth wired Murdock and Buck got an invitation.

As usual Kenneth did not shine at this high-level policy session. Oliver, who outlined the goals of the conference in an opening address, said later he does not really remember Kenneth being there. "Buck was very much in evidence at the conference as the grand old man of Polynesian anthropology and as a Maori," said Oliver. "He gave a chant which enchanted everyone. Kenneth doesn't stand out at those meetings."

Kenneth himself remembers asking that Bishop Museum be assigned Kapingamarangi, a Polynesian pinpoint among the atolls of lower Micronesia, for study. He also met with naval officials in Washington about using surplus military equipment. Oliver said no assignments were made at the conference and that the real work was done later by Dr. Harold J. Coolidge, who became director of the Pacific Science Board created by the conference. From Washington,

Kenneth went to New Haven, Connecticut, where he picked up his Ph.D. at a Yale graduation ceremony on June 26.

Back in Honolulu he returned to the hard reality of making a living without income from the military. Buck had raised his museum salary to $4,000 a year but that hardly covered the rise in grocery prices. Museum salaries had become a joke around town, Kenneth said later. There were no young college graduates eager to take jobs. Ed Bryan came back to the museum after the war over the strong objection of his wife who had to teach school to help support them.

The only way Kenneth could continue the work he loved was to find another part-time job. Kenneth said he was asked to teach by the dean at the University of Hawaii. Marguerite said it was she who suggested he teach. He said he didn't know how. "You learn," she answered. So he became a nighttime instructor in anthropology. His diary entry for September 24 reads, "Gave first lecture—course 252 —People of the Pacific. Twenty-nine in class."

To his surprise, he liked it. Marguerite said she went to the lectures because she wanted to do the driving. "You know, his mind was all over," she explained. "If he was driving, he would end up who knows where." She said she critiqued the lectures. Once she went to sleep and he came home discouraged because it had been a boring lecture. "No, no, Kenneth, I was tired," said Marguerite.

The students didn't go to sleep. Kenneth livened his lectures with tales from the atolls, demonstrations of weaving and fishhook manufacture, and movies of Tuamotuan dances. For him anthropology was more an adventure than a duty and he communicated that to the class. Female students responded as enthusiastically as the males. "It was something new, exciting," Kenneth said later. "I found out that people thought I was good. I was very pleased."

Coolidge, the new executive director of the Pacific Science Board, turned out to be a highly competent and wealthy New Englander with pipelines to money. His letters to Kenneth reflect the same relationship that had grown up between Pete Murdock and Kenneth, fondness and respect. Murdock wrote on December 4, "The latest news from Washington is that the Navy will probably come across with a substantial grant, plus transportation for an anthropological program to be begun 1947. . . "

What resulted was called the Coordinated Investigation of Micronesian Anthropology, CIMA, funded by a grant of $100,000 by the U.S. Navy, which administered Micronesia under a United Nations' trusteeship. Forty-two scientists—thirty-five anthropologists, four linguists, and three geographers—representing twenty-one institutions in the continental United States, the Territory of Hawaii, and

Australia, eventually participated. Their goal was to provide the navy with complete, accurate, and up-to-date information.

In December Kenneth submitted a proposal to the Pacific Science Board that Bishop Museum investigate remote Kapingamarangi. The party would include himself, Buck, and Dr. Sam Elbert, a linguist who had already paid a brief visit to the atoll via naval vessel. The proposal was accepted.

Early in 1947 the Pacific Science Board opened an office at Bishop Museum to assist scientists coming through on their way to Micronesia. Then surplus military equipment began to arrive. Kenneth wrote to Murdock on April 25, "The office equipment, laboratory and field equipment pouring into the Bishop Museum has been sorted by Leonard [Mason], Bryan and myself, working like stevedores. We had to transfer our huge skeleton collection to make room. The equipment is of excellent quality and we are going to be able to use all of it."

For Kenneth it was like Christmas. There were brand-new Bell & Howell motion picture cameras, wire sound recorders, Graflex cameras, and the latest in exposure meters. One of his students, Carroll Lathrop, had photographed navy training films during the war. He was also a natural handyman who could fix anything and knew all about where to find surplus equipment. Lathrop turned up with a portable gasoline generator capable of providing electricity on Kapingamarangi. Kenneth recruited him on the spot to come along and shoot movies on native life. Lathrop accepted.

The old fever had set in again: the urge to lose himself in the wastes of the Pacific, to find another island more remote than the last where the fragile culture of a fascinating people still clung tenaciously to its integrity. Kenneth would be fifty years old in November. But his love affair with the South Seas still filled him with magic.

Chapter Thirty-five

The Last Paradise

In some ways the Micronesia expedition was like a military operation. The scientists received bulletins dealing with passports, rations, equipment, expense accounts, and BOQ (bachelor officers' quarters) accommodations. The troops were to assemble in San Francisco, fly in military aircraft to Hawaii for their briefings, then head on to Guam. In Guam they would split up into companies and head for the staging areas to be outfitted, then separate and make their individual ways into the ocean wilderness like recruits bound for outlying forts in Indian country.

Loring Hudson, Kenneth's former survival training assistant, had gone ahead to line up equipment. He wrote from Guam on stationery headed United States Pacific Fleet, Commander Marianas:

> The Battle of Guam is not over yet. I'm fighting it every day in an effort to obtain needed supplies for CIMA at a minimum cost. The major food items we have not yet been able to locate include assorted jams and marmalade, rice, bouillon cubes, sea biscuit . . .
>
> I'll have a sea bag of gear, personal, for each person to pick up at Guam; sun helmet, sheath knife, poncho, mosquito net, mess kit, web belt, canteen, extra flashlight batteries, musette bag, sharpening stones, and other items . . .
>
> The BOQ [here] is not up to the one we used to stay in on Maui but it's next best. If you can manage, bring me three quarts of good Scotch for gifts to persons who have helped CIMA.

Kenneth's diary doesn't mention carrying Scotch, but it is full of the excitement he felt. Kapingamarangi was one of those improbable little places every anthropologist dreams about, an island frozen in time. Not until 1877 did the natives begin to have dealings with Europeans. The atoll is so tiny and remote that ships seldom called there. Under the Japanese the residents had been completely isolated from the outside. They were a tiny cul-de-sac of Polynesians, a virgin offshoot that had never been studied. After the Tuamotus, Kenneth was being given a second and final chance. He didn't intend to waste it.

Guam lies about two thousand miles west and a little south of

Honolulu. From there, Kenneth flew 570 miles southeast with thirteen other scientists to Truk, a craggy, jungle-covered island whose magnificent lagoon had served as a Japanese naval base. There they split up: four to Ponape (Pohnpei) in the east, and four from Yale to remain on Truk. The Bishop Museum party of four and a couple of tenderfeet from Columbia University boarded a landing craft now doing duty as a trading ship. For once Kenneth didn't get seasick. He started a journal, the most detailed he ever kept, to record the beginning of his adventure on Saturday, July 12, 1947.

The ugly vessel carried about fifty natives of Satawal Atoll in the Mortlock group on their way home after working for the navy on Guam. They had spent their wages on new outfits including shoes and jackets. "Their desire for clothes is almost pathetic," Kenneth wrote. "They were . . . dripping with perspiration although it was quite cool to me in my sandals." King David of Polynesian Kapingamarangi, who had come to Truk as a guest of the navy to accompany the scientists to his atoll, towered over the small Micronesians from Satawal.

An overnight voyage brought them to Satawal, a lush atoll teeming with vegetation. There the natives in their new clothes went ashore. The young scientists from Columbia, making their first fieldtrip, followed with hesitation, encouraged by the Bishop Museum veterans, Buck and Emory. The LCI (Landing Craft Infantry) remained overnight in the Satawal lagoon and sailed for Kapingamarangi at 5:30 A.M.

The ungainly craft pitched and rolled all day, plodding against a stiff head wind. They sighted Nukuoro at nightfall and signaled with a flashlight to leave word that the ship would be back in two days to pick up copra. The sea turned calm that night. At 11 A.M. on Tuesday, July 15, under an overcast sky, they sighted Kapingamarangi, little more than one hundred miles north of the equator, the westernmost outpost of Polynesia in the Pacific.

It was not at all like the dry, barren Tuamotus. Thick vegetation covered every islet of the atoll, a green necklace on the breast of an incredibly beautiful lagoon. Obviously there was plenty of rainfall. The captain of the LCI gingerly felt his way through a winding, narrow pass, then chugged eight miles across the lagoon to a thick cluster of thatched houses. A crowd had already gathered on the beach: some in *malos* (breechcloths), some in *lava lavas* (wraparounds), and others in European clothing. Kenneth saw one woman running along the shore while she struggled into a Mother Hubbard.

The museum party was given room in a large storehouse next to King David's quarters in luxury Kenneth had never known before on an atoll. He teamed up with gentle, scholarly Sam Elbert to work on legends and chants. Lathrop was to assist Buck by taking movies of canoe making, house building, and other activities, while Buck himself interviewed people about the use and manufacture of their tools. They set up their cots amid the clutter of equipment and provisions, and went to sleep.

When Kenneth awoke in the cool stillness of early morning, it was to a vast sense of peace. The village had come awake long ago. Neatly thatched houses, walls open to the breeze, were clustered at random in all directions under the coconut palms. In the houses Kenneth could see women, bare to the waist, combing their long hair. Babies rocked in hammocks kept in motion by strings pulled by the mothers. A few men hauled sleek, slender canoes from thatched sheds, hoisted lateen sails, and sailed off to fish.

By ones and twos the natives walked to the shallows of the lagoon and squatted companionably. Others not so old fashioned went to a communal outhouse built over the water. Kenneth saw that the toilet was new. He learned later that four U.S. warships had mistaken the original privy for a Japanese observation post and had bombarded it to kindling while the natives fled in terror.

Children passed on their way to and from the village well, bringing buckets of water for washing. Then they scattered to pick up leaves that had fallen during the night on the clean coral paving, which gave the village a park-like look. By this time the museum party was having a breakfast of coffee, cold taro, and fish left over from food brought them the night before. They watched middle-aged women set out by canoe, or by wading, to neighboring islets to weed, plant, and harvest taro. Others stayed at home and plaited mats and baskets.

As the days passed, Kenneth realized that he was witnessing a fully functioning traditional Polynesian society in the middle of the twentieth century. The Japanese had established small bases on two of the islets but had disrupted hardly at all the subsistence economy and cultural practices of the natives. Skills and customs that had become extinct in most of Polynesia were still used on Kapingamarangi: fishing by canoe, planting taro, thatching roofs, plaiting baskets, cooking in the *imu*, and dressing in the *malo*.

This traditional lifestyle supported five hundred people on land above the high tide mark that did not total more than six-tenths of a square mile. There was no crime. Nobody had stolen any of the tempting gadgets lying around the museum headquarters. The people of Kapingamarangi were courteous, hospitable, hard working, not quarrelsome, and superbly adjusted to their environment.

It was a classic lesson in survival. Kenneth wrote in his journal, "It is hard to think of anything which is better than what they already have. . . . Aside from good steel blades for their adzes, sharpening stones, some cigarets, soap, paper and pencil for their school, they really don't need anything [that requires money] except some medicine and some medical attention. . . . Were this a land of mosquitoes and flies there would be some excuse for covering the whole body with clothes. But we haven't seen a mosquito and the flies are few. . . . The natives are remarkably healthy. Their only affliction seems to be ringworm and this could be eradicated through a little medicine and education."

Yet the people of Kapingamarangi wanted to wear dresses and suits and shoes to church, to eat rice instead of taro, and to own sewing machines and metal cooking pots and perfume and corrugated iron roofs. They wanted to travel to Hawaii and America. The United States Commercial Company, authorized by the navy, traded with the natives and provided a market for island products: copra, mats, baskets, and curios. The most salable items at the moment were fancy woven belts decorated with seashells that sold for $1.25 apiece, although the price was going down. A person could weave from one to three belts a day. Kenneth wrote:

> Also, it is perfectly proper for men to weave these belts, and they can earn more money this way than they can at any other occupation. The adult inhabitants number 322 and they made 1,307 belts in the three weeks preceding the last boat. These sold at the old price of $1.50 apiece, and so netted $1,960.
>
> The belt business is so lucrative it threatens the upkeep of the village houses and canoes. Ordinarily the five-year renewal of the pandanus leaf roofing goes on steadily, a reroofing being tackled as a joint, community effort, about every ten days. Some fifty people participate in the work, each putting in an average of three hours. This includes the preparation of food by about a dozen women for the men who do the work.

It may have been his joy in sharing an elegant and natural way of life, before the taint of commercialism, that made Kenneth's stay on Kapingamarangi such a delight to him. Since those long ago expeditions to Haleakala and Lanai, he had never written about a place so enthusiastically. Maybe he felt comfortable with Elbert and Buck. Perhaps it was simply that he had at last found the South Seas of his dreams. He wrote in his journal:

> In all our sojourns among the Polynesians, we have never encountered quite so well behaved people as these. . . . The children are quiet and

obedient, yet they are rarely scolded and I am the only one in the party who has seen a child slapped by a parent. We attribute their good behavior to their happy, unsuppressed life.

As babies they must be the happiest in the world because a baby's cry is a rare thing on the island. This is not due to the lack of babies, but to the fact that they are rocked in their hammocks for hours, that whenever they are hungry they are fed. By all our rules this pampering should spoil them, but it doesn't.

Now, even more than before, Kenneth recorded the details of atoll living as a labor of love, as his benediction upon a people for whom he felt affection and respect. He and Sam dressed in the *pareu*, or *lava lava*, to encourage the natives to wear traditional clothing. The scientists atoned for an embarrassment of hospitality—gifts of more food than they could eat—by sharing with King David's family and offering tinned food in return.

Every day was an adventure. They feasted on fresh, raw tuna. Baked taro cut in small pieces, packed in a coconut cup, anointed with coconut cream and baked in a ground oven took the place of bread and crackers. Kenneth favored a pudding of grated swamp taro, *puraka*, which had been baked in the ground and then pounded with coconut cream. He devoured breadfruit dunked in grated coconut meat mixed with the water of immature nuts and cooked in a coconut shell, as well as whole chickens baked with vegetables in taro leaves.

Women did all of the cooking and used only coconut husk for fuel. Food preparation began by mid-morning and continued until about 2 P.M. when the heated stones were ready in ground ovens. Each parcel of food not baked in coconut shell had its own wrapping of taro or breadfruit leaves, neatly and methodically done. The whole lot went into plaited baskets. While the food cooked, the women usually bathed again. Everybody, with the exception of children, was in bed by 8 P.M.

"What amazed me was the absolute freedom and lack of supervision of the young people," Kenneth wrote in his journal. "Children are allowed to roam as much as they please, sleep where they please, the whole night. Their parents would not think of looking for them. And when the weather is clear and the moon is bright enough to discourage ghosts, everyone roams, except the tired people."

Yet young people on Kapinga were not encouraged to experiment sexually. Teenage boys and girls were not allowed to play and dance together as they did in the Tuamotus. The church, under King David's firm hand, forbade dancing and singing of songs other than hymns. The only time Kenneth saw male and female teenagers teasing each other was while Lathrop took movies as they sanded the coral pavement of the village. Kenneth wrote, "They became very excited and hilarious, playing all kinds of tricks on each other, and cutting loose to such an extent that the elders came out to frown. The taking of moving pictures undoubtedly stimulated them."

One of the girls had a seizure which the Kapingas termed *supe*, possession by a spirit. Lathrop was so alarmed seeing her writhe and groan on the ground that he ran for a sedative. The young men pried her mouth open and made her take it. She soon recovered and was not bothered after that. Then she began bringing Lathrop presents, claiming that the spirit was trying to get into her but could no longer do it. The same day another girl in a fit tried to fling herself into the ocean. Several men caught her in time.

There were other differences between Kapingamarangi and the Tuamotus. When Kenneth asked a woman for the name of her father, she gave him two names. It turned out that her mother had been the wife of two men at the same time. Kenneth learned that, before the arrival of Christianity, it was acceptable for a man to have more than one wife or a woman more than one husband. After Christianity was established, however, the Kapingas considered this pagan practice sinful. But the woman with two fathers was not at all embarrassed about it.

Kenneth said later that the Kapingas were less haughty and aggressive than the Tuamotuans. There were fewer arguments. The women were not so apt to wrangle as in the Tuamotus, where an enraged female, to show her utter contempt, would raise her buttocks to the adversary and pass wind. Also, the Kapingas were content to remain on their own atoll while the Tuamotuans still sailed between islands.

King David, however, had a thorough knowledge of the stars. One night he took Kenneth to the seaward shore where they could gaze into the eastern half of the sky. David pointed to the constellation Orion, and explained that Kapingas saw it as three canoes in a shed. Kenneth wrote:

> To form some of their constellations the natives of Kapingamarangi take a faint cluster of stars. To make others they select, for example, a brilliant star far to the north (Procyon), another star far to the south (Achernor), and a third (Sirius) on the eastern horizon. This makes Manu, a mighty bird with a crippled left wing.
>
> For them Delphinus represents a wooden bowl of the rain god Mairapa. When, in November, the bowl, which is supposed to be holding water,

begins to invert, the rainy season then begins. David knew all of the stars and constellations which the Kapingamarangi people have named and such stories as they have about them.

The new American administration in the Trust Territory of Micronesia had established a school on Kapingamarangi. Since the school was located next to the museum headquarters, Kenneth could not help but observe it. Koro, the Kapinga teacher, struggled valiantly to teach the students to read and write English although he didn't know much more than they did, having had only two months of schooling at Ponape and another at Truk.

The twenty-five students, aged six to sixteen, recited the alphabet and sentences like, "The student is diligent. Has the green grocer a monkey? Are there any universities?" Kenneth advised Koro to teach the students to read and write their own language correctly from Sam Elbert's Kapingamarangi-English dictionary and to devote an hour a day to singing. The next day, to Kenneth's delight, he heard the dull recitations broken by a native song that the children sang over and over with obvious joy.

Lathrop became a local hero because he could fix broken watches and sewing machines. One night he rigged a wire from the generator to an open space in the village and strung electric lightbulbs on the coconut trees. Five hundred natives, from babes in arms to bent old men, formed a closed circle several rows deep around the clearing. Kenneth turned on the sound recorder while two young men were talking. Then he played back their conversation. The voices caused a burst of excited laughter. From then it was easy. Kenneth wrote:

> Their chanting is so much like the Hawaiian that we could hardly believe our ears, and it evidently functions in much the same way. The first chant was about their ancestor Utamatua discovering the island. Dr. Buck ended the evening by chanting the Maori song of the Aotea canoe. This made a great hit with the people, bringing home to them their close kinship to Polynesia as little else could.

One night Kenneth and Sam strolled past the men's house, where the males of the village gathered, day or night, to weave kilts from *hau* bark on native looms, entirely men's work, and to plan fishing expeditions or communal projects in the village. The men were chanting. "We were entranced by the low, deep notes of their songs," Kenneth wrote.

Another day Buck and Lathrop went out to document sailing techniques. The expedition came back with fifty-three lobsters.

Kenneth did not see how anybody could cook fifty-three lobsters until the women of Hetata's household piled up coconut husk and lit them. The men heaped on coral pebbles. Half an hour later, the hot pebbles were spread out and the lobsters laid on top, the whole covered with mats and earth. Forty-five minutes later the lobsters were ready. Kenneth wrote, "We had a lobster apiece for supper and a lobster apiece for breakfast the next morning."

Kenneth took a census of the population. Then he cut his toe on coral and made the mistake of treating the cut with iodine. This fed the bits of coral left inside the cut. Native treatment finally healed him but he was off his feet for several weeks. While he was house-bound, he typed out the name, age, sex, religion, marital status, and place of residence for 410 of the 550 Kapingamarangi natives. Then he mapped Touhou, the islet of 12 acres where the village stood, including its 175 buildings and land boundaries. His lists and map became the foundation for a study of Kapingamarangi social organization.

As Kenneth's command of the language improved he was able to tackle the subject of government and religion. King David gave him his own genealogy as far back as his great-great-great grandparents on both sides, and a list of high priests, or *ariki*, who were elected for periods of five years. The list went back fifteen *ariki*. David, a devout member of the church, said he had formerly worshipped Uta-matua but now he worshipped Jehovah. Kenneth was amazed when he explored in back of the church. He found the upright slab, still standing, that had been Utamatua's back rest.

Kenneth wrote that the museum party had to endure the ordeal of going to church because the church people had showered them with gifts. An energetic resident of Nukuoro, Old Henry, had brought Christianity to the Kapingas in 1920 and had converted everybody. "Old Henry . . . holds forth rather gently," Kenneth wrote. "But Leo, son of the last native high priest in the heathen period, gives a regular New England fire and brimstone harangue. If you smoke . . . you are not regarded as a Christian, and in the census . . . you are classified among those who have no religion."

The months passed pleasantly with no effort: fishing expeditions, rambles to the other islets, a visit to Utamatua's old house site, a journey to watch canoe makers at work, and relaxed conversations about ancestors and gods and ghosts. Buck found such a wealth of material culture to document that he was afraid he wouldn't finish in the time they had allotted to Kapingamarangi.

Buck was the first to leave, chanting his farewell to natives with tears in their eyes. Sam Elbert went next. Kenneth stayed on with

Lathrop. As always, Kenneth's last three weeks were the busiest, a frantic burst of energy to make use of his rapidly increasing command of the language. Every day he moved closer to understanding. Still, when he came to his three-month deadline, it was not enough.

Nearly five hundred Kapingas were on the beach to see him off. They stepped forward to press into Kenneth's hand a shell or a dime or a woven belt. He and Lathrop boarded the LCI and the engines began to throb. The Kapinga boys on board leaped over the side making great splashes, then burst to the surface to wave. "A sailing canoe came out to see us off," Kenneth wrote, "clipping by our bow at probably 18 knots; its outrigger lifted 45 degrees out of the water."

He gazed at the neatly thatched houses, the white sand, the slender palms, and towering breadfruit trees as the voices of villagers in full song came across three hundred yards of water. He caught some of the words, "*Senisen ki ti mouri*—we are happy to be alive."

Chapter Thirty-six

An $18.35-a-day Scientist

There was irony in Kenneth's return to civilization. On Kapinga-marangi, the Polynesians supported themselves in dignity and comfort in spite of severely limited resources and deep isolation. In Honolulu, surrounded by limitless global wealth harnessed by modern technology, Kenneth constantly worried about how to pay his bills.

The $4,500 a year he got from the museum, even with his stipend from the university, simply didn't match the rising cost of living. His problem was not unique. Plantation laborers and dock workers all over Hawaii were organizing labor unions and striking for higher wages. But such action wouldn't do much good at the museum. In his annual report, Buck complained about "continued rising costs in operation and a decreasing income."

Museum buildings that were run down during the war went unrepaired. "We had a measly little staff," Kenneth recalled later. "Four or five of us rattling around in there." Linguist and Hawaiiana authority Mary Kawena Pukui did her translating while she worked at the reception desk. The post of curator had been filled by Buck's secretary during the war. Now Buck hired Lathrop, the Kapinga-marangi expedition handyman, who came cheap. Lathrop could take pictures and fix anything, but he was hardly an expert on the preservation of tattooing needles and fishhooks.

"Nobody came to see the exhibits," Kenneth recalled. "They hadn't been changed in years. I remember, people said, 'Who cares about that old stuff. Those Hawaiian days are over.' " Buck, deep in scholarly writing of which he produced a prodigious amount, had little patience for these details. His secretary handled much of the administrative work. Kenneth said she meddled in things that weren't her business. "Buck wasn't lazy," said Kenneth. "He was just too busy doing the things he liked to do."

The museum's most serious problem, in Kenneth's opinion, lay at the top with the trustee arrangment. Charles Reed Bishop, the founder, had designated the trustees of his Hawaiian wife's wealthy

Bishop Estate as trustees also of his own poorly endowed Bishop Museum. The Bishop Estate trustees were mandated to use income from the estate for operating the Kamehameha Schools for Hawaiian children. Bishop Museum, as it always had been, remained a step-child left to struggle along on its own resources. "The trustees really didn't take much interest in the museum," Kenneth said later.

To make ends meet, Marguerite tried her hand at the souvenir business. She was browsing one day in the Coconut Hut, a curio store located in a thick grove of palm trees on the corner of King and Ward streets, when the shopowner noticed her Tahitian jewelry. "He wanted to buy some," she said later. "I ordered from Marii; shells, *pareu* cloth, things like that. When it came, he gave me a bigger commission than I expected. I sold to him for two years."

On March 11, 1948, Kenneth received a letter from Dartmouth College inviting him to attend the June 13 graduation and receive an honorary Doctorate of Science. At the time Kenneth could hardly afford to pay for the groceries, certainly not a roundtrip ticket to New England. Two months later he wrote in his diary, "To bank to borrow $1,500 for house repainting." Fortunately, the invitation was good for several years. Maybe he could get to Hanover before it expired.

Low pay did not mean less work. Besides preparing his lectures for class, he spent the year writing up the Kapingamarangi material. Then he got appointed to The Advisory Committee on Education for Guam and the Trust Territory [Micronesia]. That meant endless meetings and a quick trip in August to Majuro Atoll in the Marshall Islands.

The committee recommended that the administration work toward helping Pacific natives be self-supporting and self-governing. Committee members unanimously opposed a complete assimilation of the American way of life because it had not evolved under the conditions Micronesians must meet. Kenneth's committee report concluded, "The educational assistance given the islanders . . . will be judged successful in so far as it results in a reasonably secure, comfortable and satisfying life for them, rather than the degree to which their attainments or standards match ours."

All year he and Marguerite had scrimped and made do with less and fretted over unpaid bills. He could think of only one way to make enough money to live decently. That was to become a full professor at the university. It would mean teaching daytime classes, which would cut into his museum work schedule. But it would add more than $2,000 a year to his salary. Here is how he put it to Buck in a letter dated December 1, 1948:

The department of anthropology at the University of Hawaii wants me to give a day course on Polynesian culture . . . to follow through . . . on my twice-weekly evening lectures on the peoples of Oceania . . .

If you and the trustees would be willing to release me three hours a week during the university sessions for these lectures, allowing me another three hours a week which I would probably need in preparing . . . the lectures, then this course could be presented . . . allowing me to have an increase in salary which I desperately need if I am to meet for myself and three dependents the now bare cost of living . . .

I would be willing to accept a reduction of from $4,500 to $4,000. . . . On the other hand I would ask that no objection be given to the university paying me . . . the regular rate for one of my university status. This is higher than the museum rate of pay. . . . While we [at Bishop Museum] are in the predicament of not being able to offer to our scientists what universities are offering, this is the solution I would submit in my case, a solution which would enable me to stay with the museum and survive . . .

On Friday, December 17, Kenneth wrote in his diary, "Trustees to vote on my university job." On December 22, "My job with the university at $2,410, half time, approved by museum." But not without sacrifice. The trustees got out their pencils and scratch pads to make sure Kenneth with his new affluence did not cheat them. They divided his salary by his working hours to assess his value: $18.35 per working day, $9.18 per half day. This value would be deducted from his salary every half or whole day he devoted to teaching. He would, therefore, report such absences to the director's secretary who would be in charge henceforth of making salary deductions for university professors employed at the museum.

Kenneth's salary increase may have jogged his memory about other things the museum hadn't done for him. In 1949 he put together a plan for an extended leave that would take him to Dartmouth in June where he would pick up his honorary doctorate, then on to Europe for updating his study of museum collections. The trustees gave him three weeks to become an honorary doctor of science, but turned down the trip to Europe. He and Marguerite had to sell the Buick so she could fly on to Paris and visit relatives while he stayed behind at Dartmouth.

He saw many of his old classmates including Ralph Miller, now a medical doctor. Kenneth told Miller he expected to return to Kapingamarangi in about a year. How about coming along? The Kapingas needed medical attention and Kenneth needed company. Miller began making plans to do a parasitological study in Micronesia.

In one way his appearance as a scientific celebrity proved an embarrassment. Students came up and asked, "What are the opportunities as Bishop Museum?" How should he answer? There weren't any opportunities. The museum could hardly pay its present staff. Faculty members asked about museum plans for the postwar period. And what the museum was doing to cope with the common problem of rising costs. Kenneth didn't know what to say. How could he admit the museum wasn't doing much of anything.

After his return to Honolulu a correspondence sprang up between Kenneth and a young Swedish anthropologist, Bengt Danielsson, who was interested in the Tuamotus. He had sailed with Norwegian anthropologist Thor Heyerdahl in 1947 from Peru to Raroia in the Tuamotus on the balsa log raft, *Kon Tiki*, to prove that Peruvians in pre-Inca times could have settled Polynesia by drifting from South America. Danielsson did not promote this theory, but he did want to return to the Tuamotus for field work. He wrote to Kenneth who advised and encouraged him.

Meanwhile the sorry state of Bishop Museum preyed on Kenneth's conscience. On his own initiative, apparently, he drafted a statement on policy for the lackadaisical trustees, although the indications are he showed it to only one trustee, Frank Midkiff, an old friend. Kenneth offered to work with the director and the trustees to bring the museum out of its doldrums. It appears that nothing much came of this.

Most important of all in 1949, Kenneth signed up to teach a new course at the university in archaeology. A great deal came of this. So much in fact that the unheralded course started one of the most exciting and unexpected sequences in the entire scientific study of the Pacific. Later Kenneth could not remember the exact chronology because he began digging in caves about the same time. On August 5 a Hawaiian named Hanohano took him in a sampan on Kauai to the uninhabited valley of Kalalau. The next day Kenneth wrote in his diary, "Located a bluff shelter to excavate. Excavated A.M."

Did the request to teach a course in archaeology stimulate Kenneth to dig so he could lecture from first-hand experience? He didn't remember it that way. "No, I was digging before that," he said. "I think what I was finding stimulated the university to ask me to give a course in archaeology."

In any event, dirt archaeology, or digging to find remnants of past cultures, had never been seriously attempted before in the Pacific. Every scientist knew that it was a waste of time to dig on tropical islands. This was an article of faith, an accepted dogma for many wise and irrefutable reasons. In the first place, Pacific island cultures were too young to leave stratified remains; that is, deposits in the earth that went back through time. Also, hurricanes and tidal waves destroyed whatever may have been left. Besides, the tropical dampness rusted and rotted all but stone artifacts of which museums had plenty already.

The best reason for not wasting good money on digging in the Pacific was the lack of pottery, the key upon which archaeologists all over the world relied for constructing chronological sequences. Older and cruder forms of pottery were found lower down in the dig, newer and more sophisticated forms higher up. Even with pottery, the dates were all relative. Without pottery, how could you date anything? Every archaeologist knew there was no pottery on Pacific islands.

Kenneth had heard all this. Yet he found artifacts buried in the dirt floor of the cave on Kauai. Obviously, Hawaiians in the dim past had used the cave as a shelter. Then he speculated that such caves would be natural living places for people on first arrival. Did this idea come from a book? "No, just by the nature of things," he said. "In these valleys the first people that came had no houses. They would use these shelters at first and leave things they owned. Later they would use the caves as temporary shelters, like camp sites. So the shelters would take us back to the very beginning of the occupation of the valleys."

He had always believed in teaching by example. What he needed was a cave his students could dig in. Then he heard about a shelter cave in somebody's back yard in Kuliouou Valley on Oahu, only six or seven miles from the university and near the beach—a perfect place for early Hawaiians to set up housekeeping. A couple of archaeology buffs had scratched around in the cave before the war. One of them showed Kenneth the artifacts he had dug up. Kenneth got permission for his class to dig there.

Eleven students started in February, 1950, using sifting screens Lathrop nailed together. Kenneth showed the students how to carefully measure out the floor of the cave in three-foot grids, then mark off each grid into one-foot squares. With garden trowels the students gingerly dug down in the one-foot squares, spaded the dry dirt into the screens, and sifted it like prospectors panning for gold.

Right away they began finding things: scraps of twine, sea shells both broken and whole, bones of birds, fish, dogs, and rats, discarded pieces of *awa* root used in making a narcotic drink, scraps of *tapa* or paper bark, shreds of netting, halves of oily kukui nut shells, pieces of wood bowls, tatters of matting, and ash and charcoal from fires. The students saved it all, keeping the items from one square separate from that of the other squares. At each six-inch level, the students began a new collection for each square. Such material they called midden.

Not all of what they found was rubbish. Pounders for making *poi* turned up, adzes for carving bowls, dye cups for tinting *tapa*, ornaments, and fishhooks. The fishhooks interested Kenneth most of all. They were the most revealing signature of the people who had used the cave.

He used the artifacts in his lectures about the technology of early Hawaiians. By putting the rubbish and the artifacts in association, he drew a picture of the cave's residents: people who fished and grew *awa*, sugar cane, and taro—from which they pounded *poi*; who ate shellfish and birds and dogs; slept on mats; stored food and water in wooden bowls that they hung in nets to keep them out of the reach of rats; who lit the cave with *kukui* nut torches; and who wore ornaments and *tapa* cloth decorated with natural dyes.

An abundance of bird bones at the bottom strata indicated that the earliest inhabitants lived off birds at first. This was because they had not had time to grow crops and because birds were plentiful and tame, never having been hunted before.

It was all tremendously exciting, especially for the students. They couldn't wait for the Saturday afternoon digs. "Excavated all P.M. at Kuliouou," Kenneth wrote on Saturday, March 18. "Found one fishhook, a coral adz and a regular adz." Saturday, April 1, "P.M. excavated, found large adz. Then whole group to Hanauma Bay for picnic." Kenneth became as eager as his students. He found himself driving out to Kuliouou to dig during the week: "Wednesday, April 26. To shelter with Hudson, dug for two hours."

Because Kenneth had never before conducted a systematic dig he learned as he went along, reading books and articles about dirt archaeology. An article about a new technique called carbon dating by Dr. W. F. Libby of the Institute for Nuclear Studies at the University of Chicago especially piqued his interest. Libby was dating samples of charcoal by measuring its radioactivity. News of the technique had hit the archaeological world like a bombshell. For the first time it was possible to fix a historical date on things found below ground. Libby asked in the article for charcoal samples.

By this time, Kenneth's students had collected more than two hundred artifacts and had dug down by six-inch increments in one place to the sterile floor of the cave. That meant they had gone back from the present to first occupation. And the students had dug into a fireplace at the lowest level. Why not send in a sample of the charcoal and see if Libby could date the first occupation of a shelter cave in Hawaii?

Amidst this flurry of activity, the Pacific Science Board approved for Kenneth a second visit of two and one-half months to Kapingamarangi. He wired Miller, who put his practice in New England on hold and came out to join the expedition. There was just time to give one of his students, Yolanda de Bisschop, a sample of charcoal with instructions to pack it carefully and mail it to Chicago. Kenneth and his friend boarded a navy aircraft on June 1, 1950, and set out on their new adventure.

Chapter Thirty-seven

Castaway
in Paradise

Low-slung sailing canoes raced out from Kapingamarangi to greet the station ship. Kenneth climbed down into a whaleboat. A canoe threw over a towing line and they sped through the pass. Ralph Miller followed in the village boat towed by two canoes. King David's son, Hetata, stood in greeting on the foundation of a coral pier under construction, something new.

King David was dead, another change. They went with Hetata to visit his grave, then stowed their belongings in the house they would occupy. Villagers were intent on selling mats, wooden bowls, and graters to an agent for the Island Trading Company. They did $1,600 worth of business before the ship sailed the next day. It seemed to Kenneth that more of them had switched to wearing European clothing.

But the charming, cheerful, immaculate village was as Kenneth remembered it, thatched houses scattered spontaneously in the dappled shade of graceful coconut palms. He changed into his *pareu*. Once more he had become Keneti. He wrote in his journal dated June 17, 1950, the day of their arrival, "I sat with some of the group on mats in front of Hetata's house. A half moon and stars shown through the breadfruit and broad banana leaves. Slept soundly on a cot in my place in King David's house. It was wonderful to listen to the surf again and to know we are here."

Ralph Miller, whom Kenneth called Ruff, began taking blood samples. In his thatched laboratory he worked up blood types for comparison with Polynesians on other islands. His reputation as a doctor and dentist quickly spread. The fourth day of their stay he pulled ten teeth.

Kenneth, in his soft-spoken way, renewed old friendships to pick up the threads of island life. On July 21 he wrote, "Made rounds of the south part of the village with Hetata, noting new houses. Tereh was looking fine, making two paddles. Old Wehieume, fortunately, is spry. Simoni is making a new canoe, nearly finished. . . . Took first moving pictures of fourteen year old girl, Maria, at Keweti's pounding pandanus leaf. . . . Sat in men's house for a while talking with Tieseu and Tuisi and Tirongorongo."

The purposeful but relaxed flow of village activity carried the visitors effortlessly along. Food flowed in—unsolicited gift exchanges for a tooth pulled, a broken arm set, a photo taken, or merely a share of surplus. At Dartmouth, Kenneth on his ukulele had harmonized with Ruff on his harmonica. They took up their duets again in the evenings to the delight of their neighbors who began learning the songs.

For Kenneth, as usual, information came in unexpected ways. On Thursday, June 29, he wrote: "In the forenoon I went *ngeiha* [down or northward] for a stroll. Heard Marakarita chanting in her house. She was doing this to lull the child of Eunice to sleep. I had her dictate half the chant to me. Then we talked about the price of mats, etc. Returned at noon." One day Ruff found a child with type B blood, unusual in Polynesians. Sure enough he turned out to be the son of a Micronesian. In learning about this from the child's grandfather, Kenneth also discovered a term for in-law that he had never recognized before.

The days passed in pleasant, profitable work. Miller began taking stool samples. Kenneth developed pictures. On Saturday, July 15, he wrote, "Heard that last night the men chanted. . . . They worked late into the night on community fish net of coconut fibre, using the Coleman lamp of Tuiai [the new chief]. Each man has been assessed about twenty or thirty fathoms of [hand made] twine . . ."

The first fishing expedition with the new net took place two days later. Kenneth and Ruff got up at 5 A.M. to go along. A fleet of thirteen long, narrow sailing canoes with outriggers made a festive sight as they glided over the lagoon like seabirds low on the water. The air was cool and crisp with dawn, which would soon give way under the sun's brassy heat. Forty-three fishermen sailed in the expedition. Still sleepy, they handled the steering paddles and the booms of the sails with casual competence. Kenneth, protecting his movie camera from the spray, was wide awake.

There was little conversation as the canoes sailed to a shallow part of the lagoon. The community fishnet unfolded in sections from the lead canoe. Working in thigh-deep water, men placed a length of net parallel to shore and another length at an angle into the lagoon to form a V, with a bag or trap at the point of the V. Then they added sections to extend the arms of the V. Chunks of coral found on the lagoon bottom held down the lower edge of the net.

When the net was in place, the canoes swept along the open end of the V and dropped off fishermen armed with poles and paddles. Then things got lively as they marched forward, beating the water and driving the fish into the V. Those on the ends of the line closed the net behind them. Everybody grew more excited as fish of all sizes and colors threshed in the narrowing V, the fishermen shouting and splashing to drive them into the trap. The contents of the trap filled a canoe.

Working steadily toward the pass they set the net ten times that morning during low tide. The fishermen set the net quickly to get as many settings as possible before the tide turned. A long net, instead of one in sections, would have been heavier and more clumsy to handle. Sinkers on the net would also have made it too heavy. Besides, there was plenty of coral on the lagoon bottom to anchor the net. Kenneth took 120 feet of motion picture film.

The expedition returned to Touhou islet and the catch was distributed among the fishermen; fish of equal size placed in piles one by one, two by two, or five by five, one pile for each fisherman. Odd numbers of fish went to the chief, to Kenneth and Ruff as guests, and to the owners of the ropes used.

These fishing expeditions sometimes provided patients for Ruff because young men tended to get overexuberant and cut themselves on coral. Ruff did the same thing, yet his foot wouldn't heal. Kenneth wrote later:

> Having an M.D. along, I felt pretty secure until I saw him using penicillin injections on himself to try to stop a bad leg infection from a coral cut, with some doubt that this might save his life.
>
> We were told of a Frenchman who died on Nukuoro [180 miles to the north] from a leg infection. So every time a scratch started to become inflamed, we attended to it as if it was a serious injury. We found that after we had developed some immunity, if we simply kept a cut clean, sealing it with adhesive tape, it would quickly heal.

The dynamics of atoll life engulfed them so subtly they were hardly aware of the adaptation. For weeks Kenneth worried about a drought, because they needed rainwater in their tank for Ruff's laboratory and Kenneth's developing. But the heavens always opened in time to provide a fresh supply. Ata, their next door neighbor, owned an old phonograph with scratchy records that he sometimes played for hours. It set Kenneth's teeth on edge. But the rules of courtesy did not permit one to complain. So during those periods Kenneth would find something to do on another islet.

Every time a mother was about to give birth someone came running for Ruff. Kenneth usually went with him and they were invariably too late. Yet the mothers seemed grateful to have the doctor tell them everything was all right. Kenneth wrote:

We would arrive one to five minutes after the child was born, but we saw the cutting of the navel cord, the washing of the baby with coconut cream, the forced feeding of the mother to give her strength.

While we learned about their procedures, they learned about ours. Dr. Miller found very little he would wish to alter in theirs, and marveled at the ease and simplicity with which they went through this and all events.

This intimate interaction permitted Kenneth to go deeper than he had before into the complex relationships among his Polynesian hosts. At the men's house Rimari gave him the magic for detecting a thief. At Werua islet a new father sketched the ceremony at the birth of the first child. At the village meetings Kenneth observed how villagers governed themselves.

On August 3, leadership of the newly elected chief was put to test. By order of the civil administration at Ponape (Pohnpei), he had installed a ballot box at the men's house where all adults of both sexes over age fifteen voted by secret ballot. Then the ballots were counted. This made the chief, Tuiai, very nervous.

The ballot counters reported more votes than people because some of the youngsters had voted as a joke. Thereupon Tuiai ordered the people to vote again but sign their names to the ballots. Nearly everybody voted for him. Those who did not objected. This was not the secret ballot required by the administration. Tuiai wanted to know how else they could make sure someone didn't cast more than one ballot.

No one seemed to have a good answer so they decided to vote their own way. Rikeneti, the scribe, simply called out to each one and asked whom he wanted to be chief. They gave either Tuiai's name or said *Hakari*—no opinion. Tuiai was thereby reelected, which made him feel so relieved that he broke into tears and made a speech about the burdens of being chief.

He told about trying to cope with the new American laws, and the price of copra being changed from kilos to pounds. He said they badly needed a jail and that the chiefs before him didn't have it much better. For example, Tawehi had to do what the Japanese wanted, not what the people wanted. David had been a good chief because he was descended from a family of chiefs. The meeting came to an abrupt end at 10 A.M. when the cry went up, "*Waka pari*," (ship), and everybody ran for the shore.

The Island Trading Company's small, dirty, underpowered boat, the *Perenkita*, was heaving to off the pass on her maiden voyage, the first visitor from the outside since June 17. But she carried no letters for Kenneth, only an order for mats and grater stools, and grave news that war had broken out in Korea. U.S. forces were leading a United Nations counterattack against an invasion of South Korea by Communists in North Korea. Kenneth was more concerned with life on the atoll. He dashed off a six-page report that ended as follows:

> Each day is so full of interest and rendered so agreeable by the readiness of everyone to help us that it is too short. The dreaded day of departure, September 3, is approaching with headlong speed.
> With all of our activity . . . we do not feel we are pressed for time, which of course we are. I believe this is because of the lack of harassment when there are no wrist watches to look at, no people rushing as if to catch a train, no sound of trucks, airplanes, radios, whistles. This island and all who dwell upon it are continually in the grip of a deep sense of peace.

The days passed too quickly. Kenneth and Ruff told time by the sun, because their alarm clock fell on the floor and stopped working. Both men tried to speed up their work in order to be finished by September 3. Yet the villagers would not be hurried. "Ready to work on chants with Alfred but he went off to Werua to work on grater stools," Kenneth wrote on Thursday, August 17. Thank goodness he still had two weeks.

Twenty-four hours later his precious treasure of time suddenly disappeared. The station ship appeared ahead of schedule off the pass with supplies for the atoll. A navy administrator on board explained that everything was topsyturvy now because of the war in Korea. China and Russia might enter the fighting and turn it into a global conflict. There was no telling what would happen in this part of the world. The next station ship would not return to Kapingamarangi for at least two months.

"But to haul up now would be tragic," Kenneth wrote in his journal. The final days of an expedition were always the most productive. In two weeks of concentrated work, now that his goals were defined and his informants lined up, he could accomplish more than he had in the first two months. If he stopped now he would go away with hundreds of unasked questions. And they would never be answered because this was his last chance.

The Ponape director of the Island Trading Company told Kenneth he could send the little *Perenkita* back in two and one-half to three weeks if he wanted stay. Kenneth grasped eagerly at the opportunity. "The war in Korea introduces an element of grave anxiety," he wrote. "But we must not be panicked into dropping such an opportunity that has come to me only this once—getting further than I ever did before into really sound, thorough information on matters Polynesian." The station ship sailed away and Kenneth paddled back in the dark through the pass.

"Happy to wake up in Kapinga," he wrote the next day. He went to work revising his land-use map of the islets. Then the reaction set in. Was his decision to remain on the isolated atoll heroic or foolhardy? His experience in the Tuamotus told him how many things could go wrong. He had not considered his family until now. What if the *Perenkita* did not come? Ruff and he would be marooned until mid-November when the next station ship was due. The fall term at the university opened in September. He might miss the whole semester.

"A bit blue today, scared over the uncertainties," Kenneth wrote on August 22. But the next day Rimari and Tomoki gave him a *tauaroho*, chant of affection, for the god Mongotohoro. "I asked them to chant it first," Kenneth wrote. "It took them nearly an hour. We gave them lunch, after which I settled down to taking the chant on a typewriter. It took at least three hours—over thirty verses and twelve typewritten pages."

The weather kicked up into rain storms. Ruff began packing. Hetata announced a feast for their departure. But the tiny *Perenkita* would not put to sea in weather like this. On Friday, August 25, Kenneth wrote, "Realizing now the gravity of the risk we have taken . . . should the boat break down or war burst upon us." Nights were the worst. During the day, he was too busy to worry. By August 30, they had only a week of food supplies left.

"A week from today I will know if we won our gamble," he wrote on September 1. "This afternoon over to Werua to finish the mapping of the taro fields. Everyone is preparing breadfruit paste with the surplus of breadfruit." The preparation of breadfruit paste impressed on him again his isolation. This was food stored against time of famine. Still the wind blew strong in the wrong direction.

A new worry beset him. He should have sent his film on the station ship. In this heat and humidity it might spoil if they had to wait too long on the atoll. The brutal wind discouraged him. By this time it was September 4. He visited the school teacher and "tried to impress on him the importance of having school children wear *seru* [wraparounds] and that they must not smoke."

"Had a restless dreamful night, anxiety about the boat is great," he wrote on September 6. "Delighted to find the school children today . . . all in *serus*." September 7 dawned, the day he hoped the *Perenkita* would appear. It didn't. Kenneth tried to be optimistic: "On calm reflection I see that it could be reasonable to expect [the vessel] to have left Ponape on the 4th, Monday, be at Ngatik the 5th, sail Ngatik the 6th, be at Nukuoro today, sail from Nukuoro tomorrow, and be here Saturday before noon. . . . So there is no reason for real concern for another two days." He could still avoid losing a semester at the university and the loss of his film.

Saturday, September 9, passed and there was no ship. Canoeloads of breadfruit arrived on Touhou islet to be cooked and pounded for preservation. Kenneth scribbled in his journal, "Well, it looks as if I have lost the gamble. What now, Keneti? Hope is fading but I have been trying to prepare myself for such an eventuality. All I can do is throw myself into my work and wait—wait—pray that all is well with the family." He made a circuit of the village before he went to bed. Then he settled down against a coconut tree and watched the little lights in the thatched houses where people were eating, weaving, and reading. For a long time he sat facing the sea.

For two days he was plunged in the blues. Then the cruel wind moderated. His spirits lifted. "Slept peacefully, more peacefully than for days," he wrote on Tuesday, September 12. "I have . . . decided to look upon this possible set back as an opportunity. It gives me a unique one here. I can sail into the old lore, and make more careful observations. I can write up my material much better here." Tereki and Alfred came to help with chants. Ruff pulled a tooth.

Gifts of food eked out their dwindling supply of rice and corned beef. Information flowed in at a faster pace. One day Kenneth and Ruff borrowed a canoe to paddle to Torongahae islet. There they found thirteen men carving a twenty-three-foot canoe and sixteen more carving another canoe twenty-seven feet long, both of wood from the breadfruit tree. Women cooked a large pig, breadfruit, and taro for the workers. Kenneth stayed to shoot movies. The men finished the canoe hulls that day. The women fed Ruff and Kenneth.

"Rimi gave us a bunch of bananas," Kenneth wrote on Friday, September 15. "People are terribly nice. I am not a bit bored with Ruff, fortunately. . . . The people are on the verandah tonight playing the ukulele. This was a great present we brought them. Ralph broke out his harmonica for a while. We are in fine shape."

Ruff constructed a calendar through November. "We are resigned now to sixty days more," Kenneth wrote on September 19. "We bought out the store; thirty-five pounds of rice, eight tins of corned beef. All would be well were it not for anxiety over the family at home."

When it became obvious that Kenneth and Ruff were marooned on the atoll with inadequate food supplies, the natives took matters into their own hands. On Saturday, September 23, Kenneth wrote, "The people are going to feed us starting tomorrow taking turns!" Every day one of the forty-two families on the atoll would provide food. The next morning the first contribution arrived: a bunch of ripe bananas, two chickens baked in the ground oven, a large leaf package of taro cooked in coconut cream, and three coconut shells, hot from the oven, stuffed with sliced breadfruit and grated coconut meat.

For Kenneth there could be no finer expression of the warmth and hospitality of his Polynesian hosts. He wondered if people of cultures more modern and affluent would respond so generously to a stranger's plight. What if he were marooned and destitute for two months in Chicago or London or Moscow or Canton?

He recorded the breadfruit celebration. Now he was getting his first sex chants, then a whale chant. "Day went swiftly and pleasantly," he wrote on October 1. "Two chickens from Manuere, six eggs for breakfast, one chicken left over from yesterday." The next day he stumbled onto authors of chants and took down their compositions. "A rare experience," he wrote exultantly. "Ralph works so hard with his microscope each day that he goes to bed at 7:30."

On October 7 there was a great stir in the village when someone in a canoe on the lagoon waved a kilt, the traditional signal for a ship. "We . . . gave no credence to it beyond holding judgement in reserve," Kenneth wrote. "We did, however, hurry back and I had mingled thoughts of joy and sadness [when the report proved false]. Now that we have overstepped the bounds, I want to finish my work."

By October he had translated nine whale chants. He was getting chants about the arrival of the first sailing ships, the first steamer, burials, sacred canoes, fishing, cult houses, and World War II. "Keweti and I worked alone all morning," he wrote in his journal. "It is slow, tough work digging out the meaning of the chants, but here we have the thoughts and the value systems of the people."

On Kapingamarangi Kenneth found Purslane (pig weed) the wild salad greens he had recommended to castaways of World War II. Since Ruff and he had become burdens on their neighbors, why not feed themselves? He was not aware that the Kapingas looked upon the plant as rubbish because they had never tried it. When they saw Kenneth picking it and eating it, they were horrified. Their guests were not getting enough to eat. More food poured in.

Kenneth learned that the hospitality of his hosts was not affected by a drought that worried all of them. In fact, sharing was a technique of survival. But it did not help when there were more people than the island was able to support. Hetata explained that the population was now at its maximum at about five hundred. Migration to Ponape or some other island would be the only way to handle an increase.

"This ends the second week of this month," he wrote on October 14. "Knowledge comes flowing in. Keweti came around again, faithfully, this morning. We had it alone and quiet till 11 o'clock. Discovered terms for in-laws of the opposite sex, same as in Hawaii. One more chant for funerals. Data on coconut offerings at Hereu." On October 18 he added, "The time is beginning to be excitingly short."

The more he learned the more he realized he didn't know. "Chant of rope fishing completed at last," he wrote on October 21. "Sex chant of Tomoki almost finished." On October 26: "Sanded paths today. Typed out chant of first steamer. Had an hour with Tokiroti, the priest of the north."

Hetata always took his evening meal with Kenneth and Ruff. Over coffee as long as it lasted, then over a coconut, they talked about anything and everything: the meaning of dreams, when it would rain, who would be fishing tomorrow, what should be done if a bearded Russian stepped ashore from a submarine. Their isolation made the outside world mysterious.

But there was no answer to the mysteries. At 5 A.M. on October 28 the cry went up, "*Waka pari*" (ship). Kenneth rushed out to look. There were lights in the predawn darkness on the eastern horizon. Some thought they must be Japanese fishing boats. Then more lights appeared. Ruff ran for his binoculars. He saw two lights on one boat. Hetata saw green lights. It must be a convoy. But if there was war with Russia, ships would be blacked out. Was the war with Korea over? Nobody knew the answers as the lights faded away.

On November 3, Kenneth took down three chants from Tomoki. "Had breadfruit yesterday, fresh, ripe, for the first time in about seven or eight weeks," he wrote. On November 6 he and Hetata counted the pigs on Werua, 109 adults and 40 sucklings. Days of despondency alternated with productive days. He and Ruff ate their last three tins of corned beef on November 22, 1950. Twenty-five of his Kapinga neighbors gave Kenneth a birthday party the next day. He was fifty-three.

On Friday, November 24, Kenneth was coming up the beach from his daily afternoon swim when the cry arose, "*Waka pari*." This time it was not a false alarm. The station ship nosed around bushy Werua islet. Kenneth sailed out with Hetata in Koro's canoe to meet it. Answers to his questions eased his mind about the war. But he was terribly impatient to get home.

Two nights later, Kenneth had packed and was ready to sail in the morning. He waded out on the reef and stood on the point nearest Hawaii. Then he took a last long look at Kapinga, the island that had given him so much.

"Moon to the right, Canopus to the left," he wrote when he returned to village. "Orion over Touhou: the three canoes in their shed. All's well."

PART SEVEN

BURIED TREASURE

Chapter Thirty-eight

The First
Carbon Date

Kenneth promised Marguerite when he returned to Honolulu that he would never again subject himself to the risks he had taken on Kapingamarangi. Indeed, there was no more need to endure the hardships he had survived on so many remote islands because the islands were becoming less and less remote.

The Stratocruisers of Pan American World Airways flew from California to Hawaii in nine and a half hours. The distance between Hawaii and Tahiti, which boasted a World War II airstrip on Bora-Bora, had shrunk from a month roundtrip to two days one-way. Airplanes linked Samoa, Fiji, New Zealand, and Australia to Asia and the United States.

Kapingamarangi had been an improbable survival of the old culture, a precious backwater that was already in the midst of change. Spry but aging Vehiem, wife of the last pagan priest, had died before Kenneth could talk to her. King David was gone. The old values were giving way to new ones that promised greater rewards in a world of tin roofs, outboard motors, and store-bought clothing. In twenty years, or more like ten, memories would fade. Kenneth's had been a salvage operation, a last-minute recording of the way it had been.

It was far too late now for even last-minute recordings on better-known islands that had been curiosities only two hundred years ago: exotic showcases of human versatility, places that had excited the interest of Captain James Cook and Charles Darwin and Jean Jacques Rousseau. These islands were no longer part of another world. They lived in the present. Polynesians were adapting themselves to money and Christianity and the automobile and the eight-hour day like everybody else because they could not do otherwise and survive.

In a way, Kenneth had outlived his usefulness. His brand of anthropology had gone out of date. There were no more sages from whom he could learn about the ancient religion. Suburbs were being built over the old temples. He had no inclination to measure plywood canoes. By this time he was more familiar with the old chants than most Polynesians.

Of course, there was plenty of work for anthropologists to do in the Pacific: new immigrant groups to study, political systems to compare, cultural change to measure in all its complexity, the dynamics of island economies to understand. But the classic mysteries that had always motivated Kenneth—when and where the Polynesians came from and how did they got there—seemed a dead issue because the evidence was all in. The witnesses were dead. The clues had long since been found and evaluated. Kenneth was a pioneer whose pioneering days were over. Or were they?

On February 19, 1951, Buck called Kenneth to his office and read aloud a letter just received from Chicago. Libby had dated Kenneth's sample of charcoal from the cave at Kuliouou at A.D. 1004, plus or minus 180 years. It was the first carbon date for Polynesia. "Boy, was I excited," said Kenneth later. "Immediately it opened a whole new vista of possibilities."

Here was a tool that could place prehistoric events in time more precisely than pottery or language change or genealogies. Now he knew for certain when the first Hawaiians had inhabited the Kuliouou cave. That knowledge provided an indication of when Polynesians had settled the island. Could other digs on other islands yield the same kind of information? For the first time he would be able to accurately track the movements of the old Polynesians.

To him it was a miracle as improbable as the one that had turned him into an ethnologist when he didn't even know what an ethnologist was. Just when the irreplaceable store of traditional Polynesian knowledge had vanished forever, he had found a new, untapped fund of information. All these years the clues had lain underground. There was no way of knowing what secrets other caves would yield, no way of knowing where other secrets were buried. Finding them could take a lifetime. His work had only begun.

The historic carbon date and the cave in Kuliouou attracted newspaper publicity. Kenneth told an *Advertiser* reporter that the new method was more accurate for measuring time than genealogies of unknown authenticity for which there was no way of knowing the length of each generation. He added, "This marks a tremendous advance and opens up unlimited possibilities of establishing the beginning and course of history on our islands in the Pacific.

"When this [excavation] is completed it will be possible to describe many aspects of the life of ancient Hawaii as it went on at Kuliouou from the beginning until the arrival of Captain Cook. We know that the people who first lived in the Kuliouou shelter were

Polynesian because their fishhooks and adzes were typically Polynesian. The adzes are typical of those used in ancient Tahiti and in the Marquesas Islands. Since the first occupation, changes in most of the articles represented in the shelter and in the food habits were slight . . ."

The cave became a bonanza of surprises. The students found a skeleton, then a bowling stone, and fishhooks in many shapes and sizes. One afternoon one of the students picked a long sliver of bone from her sifting screen and asked, "What's this?" "It's a tattooing needle," Kenneth answered in astonishment. He recognized the artifact from those he had seen in museums. Artists who sailed with early European explorers had sketched tattooed Hawaiians, and Kenneth had found a tattooed corpse in a burial cave. But nobody had ever seen a Hawaiian tattooing needle. It was like finding Michelangelo's paintbrush.

The wealth of information coming out of the Kuliouou cave turned Kenneth's restless energy in a new direction. He warned *The Advertiser* reporter: "A record of the past lies buried on many a site on Oahu and the other islands. It takes only a few strokes of a shovel to completely destroy this record. . . . If anyone has come across what he believes is a site which would reveal evidence of the past, please report it to the Bishop Museum or to the department of anthropology at the University of Hawaii."

As usual, Kenneth was not content to wait for the reports to come in. News of his Kuliouou cave discoveries had spread like wildfire among Hawaii's sizable population of history buffs. Kenneth became their hero, leading them to new adventures. On February 22 amateur anthropologists from all the islands met at Iolani Palace on invitation from the Pacific Science Board of the U.S. Science Council. They formed the Hawaii Conservation Council, of which a Sites Committee became the driving force with Kenneth in the driver's seat.

Most of the committee members were women, some of them matrons of the highest social standing, all eager to learn about fishhooks and adzes and tattooing needles. Kenneth formed them into battalions on each island to defend archaeological sites from pot hunters, and to find new sites.

His chief of command was Alice Spalding Bowen, president of the Outdoor Circle, a militant and capable group of women married to the most important men in town. The Outdoor Circle had established its clout by browbeating America's most powerful corporations into taking down the billboards that advertised their products in Hawaii.

On Oahu the regimental commander was Mrs. Richard L. "Cappy" Summers, a Cooke of the prominent missionary and Big Five family. Cappy Summers had started as one of Kenneth's brightest and most dedicated students. She was also president of the Lanikai Outdoor Circle on Windward Oahu. Her troops immediately set out into the boondocks and located the Ulupo agricultural *heiau*, the clearing of which became the first conservation project of the Sites Committee.

Even better organized was the division on Molokai led by Mrs. George P. (Sophie) Cooke, wife of the rancher who owned half of the island. She not only had the cowboys clear the sites but also paint signs to mark them like tourist attractions. Then she drew a map showing all the points of interest.

Kauai was slower getting started under Eric A. Knudsen, and Maui, where Inez Ashdown was in command, really never did get off the ground. On the island of Hawaii, Homer Hayes, Jr. and his troops performed the most spectacular feat of all. They saved the ruins of a *heiau* in Kona by persuading the Territorial Department of Public Works to realign a new road.

Kenneth provided the inspiration for this crusade, constantly dashing off to address a sites committee on one island or a historical society on another. It was about this time that Marguerite began to complain of neglect. She probably had good reason, because Kenneth was spending more time with his students and the volunteers than with her. But there wasn't much he could do about it.

At the museum, things were going steadily downhill. Illness, apparently cancer, was sapping Buck's energy. Elwood Zimmerman, the entomologist, had already asked Kenneth to support his bid to become director. Kenneth was more interested in a new project he had started with the help of volunteers, rerecording on wire the chants originally recorded on fragile dictaphone cylinders. Margaret Mead came to dinner again. Raymond Firth visited the museum, deeply interested, like Mead, in the new carbon date and the discoveries in Kuliouou cave.

His university classes gave Kenneth a great deal of satisfaction. By this time he didn't have to set up his slide projector, or even unload it from his car. Students, usually young women, were happy to do it for him. He had a way of turning dust-dry archaeology into adventure. One of his best students, Mary Stacey, went to Kauai to catalogue artifacts in collections there. She was one of a growing number of young people in his classes who wanted to make anthropology a career.

Toward the end of the year, the Sites Committee identified

another *heiau*, a medical temple, for preservation on top of Aiea Heights overlooking Pearl Harbor. Then the Pan-Pacific Surgical Congress scheduled a conference in Hawaii. Dr. Nils P. Larsen, a student of traditional Hawaiian medicine, talked congress officials into rededicating the old temple as part of the conference program.

That is why Kenneth found himself on Aiea Heights with Kamehameha Schools teacher Don Mitchell and his students on Sunday, November 11. They cut back the underbrush. Nearly one thousand people attended the rededication on Thursday to witness the rites of purification. All the doctors were sprinkled with saltwater from strips of *olena* fiber.

Although weak and unsteady, Buck spoke in his commanding voice. He described the skills of ancient Hawaiian medical *kahuna*s. Then he chanted. As usual, his imposing presence and the eloquent beauty of the chant, a kind of music in prose, held the audience silent. "When he finished a breeze came and the trees rustled," Marguerite remembered later. "And from somewhere it rained, a shower. The gods were *present!*"

It was the last time Buck chanted. A week later Kenneth wrote in his diary, "Dr. Buck in hospital since Saturday with pneumonia." On Saturday, December 1: "Dr. Buck died at 2:30 P.M."

Chapter Thirty-nine

Fishing Shelters at Moomomi

The death of Sir Peter Buck in late 1951 found Bishop Museum at its lowest point since the first precarious days when William Tufts Brigham fought to save it from becoming a trophy room for the Kamehameha Schools. In spite of its international reputation, the institution was in financial chaos: an atomic-age museum with a horse-and-buggy budget.

An endowment of $30,000 and a small income from land holdings did not meet expenses at post-World War II prices. Buck's scholarly reputation had not translated into financial support. He had considered it beneath him to scramble for funds and treated mainland foundations with olympian condescension. In his last years his secretary was running the business end of the museum.

Kenneth felt the trustees had drifted into a state of ennui. They were either unaware of or didn't care about the sorry condition of the buildings and the lack of direction for scientific research. Buck's death caught them flat-footed. Dr. Charles H. Edmonson, the zoologist, became acting director as senior member of the staff. Both Kenneth and Ed Bryan felt Edmonson was an ineffectual fuddy-dud. Other colleagues said Edmonson, who was elderly and reserved, was not suited to administration but he did the best he could in a difficult situation.

Neither the director nor the trustees were much interested in public support, Kenneth said. Most people assumed the museum was funded by Bishop Estate or owned by the government. In any case, it had become a dull, stuffy place with the same old canoes on display. The life-sized whale hanging in Hawaii Hall was about the only attraction children cared about, Kenneth said.

For Kenneth, Buck's death came as a disaster. The loss of a dear personal friend and long-time colleague pained him as much as what he saw happening to the museum. He learned about Buck's death through a solicitous phone call from entomologist Elwood Zimmerman, who asked for support in his bid to become director. But Zimmerman, Kenneth had decided, was no better an administrator than Buck had been. The museum was about to slide into mediocrity.

After the phone call Kenneth immediately penned a letter to Pete Murdock at Yale. Yale and Bishop Museum had worked in partnership since the 1920s. Now, if ever, the museum needed Yale's support. Kenneth wrote hastily:

> Zimmerman just called me to say that Peter Buck has just passed away at the hospital. We are without a leader and without provision for the future.
>
> I know that you and the Yale Committee will offer its services to the museum, to steer it back to its role as a scientific institution in the forefront of Pacific research . . . I hasten this off to you.

Murdock wrote back to explain that Ira Hiscock, chairman of Yale's Bishop Museum Committee, was away attending a World Health Organization meeting in Geneva, Switzerland. Kenneth might write him there if it was urgent but it might be wiser to wait for initiative from museum trustees. Kenneth didn't wait. On December 18 he wrote to Hiscock in Switzerland:

> We are not at all adequately meeting our potential service to the island community or science [either] in the eyes of the island people [or] those engaged in Pacific research. . . . We will not be able to [do this] solely on our original endowment . . . without considerable reorientation of policy . . . and the enlargement and reorganization of the staff.

Kenneth explained that while the museum's original endowment no longer met its financial needs, there was plenty of potential for support from individuals, government, and institutions if somebody just made the right approach. He added that the job called for training, experience, and ability that nobody on the museum's dwindling staff possessed.

To Murdock he pleaded, "The best move might be to seek the temporary loan of someone who, because of his wide experience, training and good judgement, could step in to redetermine the museum's policy and to reset the organization . . . I have in mind someone like yourself or Alex Spoehr [at the Chicago Natural History Museum]."

Murdock wrote back, "According to present plans, I shall probably be arriving in Honolulu on the morning of the 8th [January 1952] and [will be] leaving [for Tokyo] in the afternoon or evening of the 10th. I have been commissioned by Yale to look into the Bishop Museum situation and report back to our administration. Can I call on you for help?"

What Murdock wanted was for Kenneth to set up a conference with members of the Bishop Museum staff, a meeting with the trustees, an interview with University of Hawaii president Gregg Sinclair, and an informal gathering of influential Yale alumni in Honolulu. Kenneth went right to work.

George Collins, president of the trustees, seemed grateful for the interest Yale was showing. But Sinclair at the university saw an opportunity for empire-building. "Maybe now is the time for the University of Hawaii to take over the museum," he suggested to Kenneth. To counteract this move, Kenneth enlisted the support of university anthropologist Leonard Mason, who believed the museum should preserve its independence.

On New Year's Eve, 1952, Kenneth didn't sleep well. Tingling sensations in his arms and legs worried him. Two days later he went to see a doctor who told him he was suffering from nervous tension. On January 5 he drafted a statement for the trustees about changes necessary at the museum: a vigorous bid for private and public support, a drive to enlist volunteer help, and better use of the scientific staff with salaries equal to those at the University of Hawaii.

Pete Murdock arrived on Tuesday, January 8, for his whirlwind round of meetings. Then he flew on to Japan and back to Yale. What he found in Honolulu appalled him. He later told an anthropology colleague that he wondered at first if the museum was really worth saving. The decisive factor in his mind was the dedication and competence of the staff, in particular Kenneth Emory and a few others including Margaret Titcomb who had single handedly built the Bishop Museum library.

The Yale Committee voted to send Murdock back to Honolulu to see what he could do about getting the museum back on track. Murdock very quickly demonstrated his formidable organizational skills. Starting with Yale alumni, he brought together community leaders interested in saving the museum. Quite a few were drafted from Kenneth's Sites Committee. They became the Bishop Museum Association, a fund-raising group led first by Ernest Kai, then by Valdemar Knudsen. Next Murdock went to the local foundations to explain that if the museum were to survive it needed a modest kitty to allow some initial operating room. The foundations responded. Finally, Murdock impressed on the trustees their need for a director with experience in museum administration and, hopefully, who was a Pacific specialist. The search began.

After Murdock went back to Yale, the trustees approved the appointment of a new acting director, Ed Bryan, the energetic curator of collections, founder of a clearing house at the museum for scientific information about the Pacific, and man of all work. Buck's secretary immediately quit. When asked why, Bryan answered, "She knew that, under me, she couldn't get away with the things she had been doing." A petition circulated at the museum to bring the secretary back. The petition failed and the problem was put to rest.

Kenneth said later that several people urged him to take the directorship. He told them he was not interested in administration and, besides, he had too much to do in his own field. The latter can be classed as a dramatic understatement. His discoveries in the cave at Kuliouou were attracting wide attention, a lot more volunteers, and constant demands on his time.

Newspaper reporters, dignitaries, and visiting scientists wanted to see the cave. In May 1952, the Junior League turned up at the museum for a lesson in archaeology. In July a new volunteer, Dorothy Barrère, brought Honolulu Symphony conductor George Barati around to hear Polynesian chants. Martha Beckwith, translator of Hawaiian legends, wrote from Berkeley for Kenneth's advice on a book about King Kalakaua, *Last King of Paradise*, by Honolulu author Kathleen Mellen.

"Do you regard it as entirely accurate in detail?" Beckwith wanted to know. "Was it possible for the king to pray his two sisters . . . to death in that public manner at a time when *kahuna anaana* practices [praying to death] were being outlawed? I recall visiting the women's ward in the prison in Honolulu and having a pretty young woman pointed out to me as accused of such practices on Kauai. That was in 1893 or '94."

Kenneth's new role as oracle did not change his hand-me-down quarters at the museum. He operated from a cubbyhole equipped with a battered typewriter and some filing cabinets. He did, however, get an assistant. Mary Stacey was now working on her Kauai material under his direction and helping with paperwork. But he wasn't in the office very much. On July 18 he went to Kauai with Murdock and Coolidge, of the Pacific Science Board, and Atherton Richards, a new trustee, to look at a site in Nualolo Kai Valley on the rugged and inaccessible Napali Coast. From there he hopped over to Maui to speak before a Historical Society meeting. The following month he was on Molokai. In the meantime he helped Bengt Danielsson in Sweden get an assignment from the Pacific Science Board in Washington to do fieldwork at Raroia in the Tuamotus.

The main thrust of all this frenetic activity remained dirt archaeology. Kenneth was like a bloodhound on a scent, sniffing for his next site. "You inquire around among the island people and if you're lucky you run across shelter caves and bluff shelters nobody has disturbed," he told a reporter that summer. He sent graduate student William Bonk and anthropology senior Ronald Brown to explore on Molokai. They found four shelters at Moomomi Beach and two more also on the west end of the island. The Kauai site showed possibilities, but Molokai was more accessible and the help Sophie Cooke promised made the sites at Moomomi Beach look extremely attractive.

Kenneth decided on Molokai in August. His students were so eager to go that they agreed to pay their own air fares and $1.50 a day for food. Sophie Cooke would provide keys to the ranch gates that kept out intruders, a Jeep for hauling equipment and supplies over red-dirt ranch roads to the beach, and moral support. But he couldn't very well ask her to buy equipment and pay the small salary of Bonk who would be in charge of the dig. So Kenneth appealed to the local McInerny Foundation, the most versatile of Honolulu's grant-giving charities. McInerny gave him $1,225.

Kenneth said later one of his goals on Molokai was to build up a collection for establishing an age sequence for artifacts. There was little such information for the museum's present artifact collection. But, unlike artifacts found scattered on the ground, excavated artifacts appeared in time sequence. The archaeologist could follow changes in their shapes as they evolved. If Kenneth and his students could assign distinctive artifacts to their geographical locations and their periods in prehistory, all artifacts would become more meaningful. Besides, artifacts dug up on Molokai might indicate settlement by a different group than the pioneers on Oahu. This would be valuable information.

He told a reporter, "We think it is possible that some of the islands were settled quite a while before the others and that the different islands may have been settled by different migrations." Hawaiians on Kauai, for example, used ring-shaped *poi* pounders and stirrup-shaped grinders found on none of the other islands.

Marguerite refused to be left behind, although she preferred a comfortable hotel to a tent on the beach. Besides, camping out wasn't Parisian. "I was not trained for it," she said daintily. "I didn't know anybody in France who did things like that. You know, it was a hardship for me. All that for the sight of this little fishhook."

Kenneth's students excavated four shelters in back of Moomomi's lonely, sweeping, wind-carved beach. The shelters told a somewhat different story than the cave at Kuliouou on Oahu. At Moomomi the students found pieces of gourds and gourd seeds. Kenneth told a *Star-Bulletin* reporter that gourds on Molokai must have been a big vegetable item in the diet at an early date, before the time of Christopher Columbus, because the gourds were found a foot from the lowest level of human habitation.

The students found no taro pounders for making *poi*, the universal Hawaiian food, apparently because the parched west end of Molokai was too dry for growing taro. People living in the shelters made up for the lack of *poi* by feasting on fish, birds, and chickens. Slivers of the bones were found all through the dirt floors of the shelters. There were also bones of dogs and pigs but not, as in the Kuliouou cave, at the lowest levels. That meant the colonists of Molokai probably didn't have dogs and pigs at the beginning.

Among the more interesting finds at Moomomi Beach were fish gorges—small oblong objects that entered a fish's mouth and then turned sideways after being swallowed, holding the fish at the end of the line. At Moomomi, the students dug up fishhooks made of shell, bone, turtle shell, and even turtle bone. In association with the hooks were stone sinkers and tools for making hooks: coral files, bone awls, and drill points. Also fish lines and fishnets.

There were many other tools: adzes, hammers, knives, pestles, and shark's teeth together with hair clippings, which indicated that shark's teeth were used for cutting hair. Scraps of *tapa* turned up in the debris. The oldest wooden artifact dug up was a heavy hardwood beater used for making *tapa.*

The pervasive presence of *opihi* (limpet), *pipipi* (periwinkle), cowry, and other seashells testified to their use in the diet. "One of the things you can tell just by sorting is the comparative amount of the different kinds of shellfish the old Hawaiians ate," Kenneth reported. "More interesting and less obvious is the way shell distribution can indicate where political boundaries were drawn. If you fail to find *opihi* shells on a coast that has plenty of *opihi*, you're safe in betting there was an uncrossable political boundary between that shelter and the coast."

From Molokai, Kenneth went to the Kona Coast on Hawaii to lecture at a three-day teacher's workshop on Hawaiian culture sponsored by the Kona Education Association at Kealakekua, a village above the bay where Captain Cook was killed. The workshop, as well as the newspaper headlines it produced, reflected a growing interest in Hawaiiana largely as a result of Kenneth's discoveries. Teachers stumbled over lava flows to see petroglyphs, squirmed through scratchy lantana and thorny *kiawe* to view Hawaiian ruins, and generally had a marvelous time.

The workshop inspired *Star-Bulletin* columnist Clarice Taylor to write a long series about Kenneth's adventures. She wrote, "Dr.

Emory is now being recognized by fellow scientists as the greatest living Polynesian ethnologist. He is in constant demand by groups in Hawaii . . . and visiting scientists to the Pacific who prepare themselves for work in the Pacific at Bishop Museum."

His squad of volunteers had become an army. By the end of the year they had excavated fifty-six burial caves on the windward side of Oahu, excavated a bluff shelter at Hanauma Bay out beyond Koko Head, were about half-finished with the excavation of Kuliouou cave, had dug in eight sites on Molokai, and had scouted for new sites on Kauai, Oahu, Molokai, Maui, and Hawaii. And there was still the site at Nualolo Kai on Kauai, house platforms under a great overhanging bluff. Kenneth couldn't wait to get started.

Chapter Forty

Yosi Sinoto

Dr. Alexander Spoehr arrived with his family in Honolulu on the evening of Friday, January 23, 1953 to begin his post as new director of the Bishop Museum. Spoehr came from the Chicago Natural History Museum, where he had been curator of oceanic ethnology. He was an anthropologist with wide experience in the Pacific, had obtained two radio carbon dates for Micronesia, and brought to his assignment experience as a museum administrator. His wife, Anne, was a professional museum exhibit designer. Kenneth and a welcoming party met the plane for what turned out to be a new era at Bishop Museum.

Spoehr said later he and his wife came out as an adventure. He added, "No completely sane man would have taken over the directorship of a museum in the situation Bishop found itself, especially if Murdock had not gotten things started." At least there was no way to go but up.

"The maintenance man had $150 a year to maintain the place when I arrived," Spoehr recalled. "You can imagine the deferred maintenance that had piled up. The exhibits hadn't been changed since about 1920." When janitors scrubbed the dirt of decades off the floor of Hawaii Hall, the main exhibit space, they found beautiful terrazzo tile. The Handys were back in Hawaii and had set up housekeeping upstairs at the museum. Spoehr said one of his first unpleasant duties was to ask them to find other quarters.

He assembled a grand display of *kahili*s to announce the new regime. *Kahili*s are oversized royal fly chasers, great cylindrical arrangements of brightly colored feathers riding atop stately wooden poles. In prehistoric times, they were carried before the chief as symbols of his sacred power when he walked among his subjects. In historic days of Hawaiian royalty, *kahili*s flanked the king's and queen's thrones at Iolani Palace. The *kahili*s at Bishop Museum had passed from the Kamehameha dynasty through Princess Bernice Pauahi, wife of Charles Reed Bishop.

"We had loads of *kahili*s," Kenneth recalled later. "Some of them were so old they had names. But they were getting lousy and looked pretty sad. They had to be rehabilitated." Volunteers came in to work over the feathers. Hawaii senator Flora Hayes sent women to help. New museum receptionist Martha Hohu brought in her friends. The *kahili*s had to be taken apart and reassembled, the feathers tied to wooden spokes. Women sat all over Hawaii Hall putting the *kahili*s back together.

For the grand opening Marguerite helped with flower arrangements. She said the *kahili* display turned out to be a big success. Meanwhile Anne Spoehr designed new exhibits and the Bishop Museum Association, headed by attorney Ernest Kai and his wife, Peggy, raised money to pay for them. They opened a small bookstore where "Wild Bill" Anderson's daughter, Marion, now an anthropology student, volunteered one day a week as clerk. The Outdoor Circle landscaped the museum grounds. Later, the Museum Association turned the courtyard into a display of endemic plants and monumental stone artifacts. Museum attendance immediately took an upturn.

Dr. J. Linsley Gressitt replaced Zimmerman in entomology. Gressitt initiated innovative research that would bring his department international recognition in the world of insect research during the next decade. Spoehr lobbied for and received an appropriation of $25,000 from the territorial legislature to carry the museum through 1953. He built a second exhibit space and filled it during Aloha Week with the museum's rare feather cloaks. Ten thousand people came to see the exhibit.

The trustees also brought on young George Vanderbilt, heir to a fortune, as a new member. This proved a mixed blessing because Vanderbilt, according to Kenneth's diary, once turned up drunk at a trustee's meeting. Marguerite, however, considered "Georgie a nice boy." He hosted a local television program about things cultural and scientific at the museum, and promoted Hawaiiana in general.

The new director inherited one more Pete Murdock miracle, a venture called the Tri-Institutional Pacific Program (TRIPP), which was cosponsored by Yale, the University of Hawaii, and Bishop Museum. Funding of $200,000—half to the University and half to the museum—came from the Carnegie Corporation. The money paid for a five-year research program, extended to ten, in the nature of cultural change on Pacific islands.

Meanwhile, Kenneth continued to be the darling of anthropology. The McInerny Foundation distribution committee was so pleased with his excavations on Molokai that they granted $1,500 for another dig in 1953. Kenneth had his eye on Kauai until Amy

Greenwell, a volunteer on the island of Hawaii, asked him to look at her collection of artifacts in Kona. Kenneth studied one fishhook after another. They were a type he had never seen before.

"Where did you get these?" he asked.

"At South Point," she answered. "I found them in an eroding sand dune."

South Point is a barren, windswept promontory nearer to Tahiti than any other place in Hawaii. Converging currents make it a sports fisherman's paradise and a small boatman's nightmare. Holes chipped into black lava along the rocky shoreline testify that Hawaiians once moored canoes there. Kenneth hurried to South Point. He found what could have been a small fishing village covered over with sand. Waves were washing fishhooks out of the dune.

Here was the site of his next dig. If only there weren't so many other things to do. He had class lectures to prepare, visitors to greet at the museum, letters to answer, meetings to attend. He never seemed to find the time to get at his manuscript on the Kuliouou dig. On top of all this, Marguerite and he quarreled a lot now.

Spoehr kept after him until he produced a five-year plan for anthropology. "It was an excellent plan," the director said later. He added, "Kenneth does not write easily. It was always difficult for him to write reports. Another weakness is a tendency to try to do too much at one time. His interests are so broad and varied that he tends to get distracted. So those who really like him and who work with him are always having to pull Kenneth back on the main track." Spoehr said he felt a responsibility as director to give his popular and talented anthropologist the support he had not had before. He raised Kenneth's salary and encouraged him to cut back on teaching so he could devote more time to research.

The South Point dig began on August 28 with Bill Bonk in charge of the volunteers. They moved into an empty Coast Guard lighthouse station considerably more luxurious than the tents at Moomomi Beach. The sand dune site at South Point was called Puu Alii, which means hill of chiefs. Kenneth, Marguerite, and Tiare stayed for a week. During that time, Marguerite helped cook. "Those students had such terrific appetites," she marveled. "You would think they hadn't eaten for months. They were the first ones to be there and scooped the whole thing."

The Emorys went back to Honolulu after a week so Kenneth could begin a new teaching semester at the university. He returned in October to check on progress and end the dig. By that time, the volunteers had stripped away six feet of sand to reveal an ancient and long-occupied houseyard, sixty by sixty feet. The floor of the yard had accumulated six to twelve inches of fish bones, shells, pebbles, ashes, and earth. Amid the debris, diggers found files of coral and pencil urchin spine used in the manufacture of fishhooks; many hooks in the making; finished hooks; and parts of broken hooks. The shape of those hooks intrigued Kenneth. They were different from those in the cave at Kuliouou. Did they represent a period before A.D. 1004, or merely a local variation?

Bonk and his crew also found a cave shelter, called Kamakalai, half a mile inland. They dug a test trench there during Kenneth's second visit. There wasn't time for more. During Christmas vacation, Kenneth went back with another crew of volunteers and worked through the New Year. After all this, only one-sixth of the large dune site had been excavated. It was like digging for gold. He never knew when they might strike the mother lode.

Kenneth started 1954 at the same headlong pace he ended 1953. Mary Stacey became Spoehr's secretary, so Eleanor Anderson, principal of a business college, volunteered to do Kenneth's typing. He kept making starts on his Kapingamarangi report, but spent more time editing the motion picture film he'd shot on the atoll. In April he finished his proposal to McInerny Foundation for support of his five-year plan. "McInerny granted $3,000 for archaeology [this year]," he wrote in his diary on April 28. In May he took Marguerite to the movies *From Here to Eternity* and *Stalag 17*.

By summer he was deep into his Kapingamarangi manuscript. "All A.M. trying to finish Kapinga," he wrote on Sunday, June 27. But the South Point dig intruded in July. His diary bristles with references to hieroglyphics identifying the squares that marked off Puu Alii. "Dug the bottom twelve inches of J13 before breakfast," he wrote on July 5. He couldn't stay in one place. That afternoon he visited Amy Greenwell, then spent two hours in Ohia cave near Kailua. The next few days saw him exploring the Thurston lava tube at the volcano, excavating square G9 at a cave in Kahaluu, and making a rich haul of fishhooks at the Ohia cave.

On Saturday, July 10, he drove to Kona airport to pick up a young archaeologist from Japan enroute to the University of California at Berkeley. The student, Yosihiko Sinoto, wanted to see the South Point dig while he was between oceanliners. But he didn't get off the plane at Kona Airport. Kenneth waited for the next flight. He had no way of knowing that he was soon to learn a lot more about archaeology.

Because of a language problem Yosi Sinoto did not make it to Kona. He didn't speak English very well. His sponsor in America, Peter Throckmorton, who became interested in anthropology while serving with the U.S. Army in Japan, had dropped him off at the Honolulu airport and told him to take the Kona plane. Yosi interpreted this as, "Take the corner plane." But he couldn't find an airplane in a corner. Confused, he boarded the wrong flight and ended up in Hilo on the opposite side of Hawaii from Kona.

At Hilo, he disembarked and saw a lot of people waving at him. They turned out to be Filipino taxi drivers looking for fares. There was no sign of the distinguished Dr. Kenneth Emory. Yosi went to an airport security guard and explained that he was supposed to meet an archaeologist who was digging at a place called South Point. "*South Point*, that's almost a hundred miles from here," the guard said suspiciously.

Then Yosi remembered that a reporter from the *Times*, a Japanese-language newspaper in Honolulu, had interviewed him in his own tongue. Maybe there was a branch office in Hilo. Sure enough, he found the *Times* listed in the phone book. Yosi phoned, and a Japanese-speaking reporter came racing to the airport. He told Yosi that there are three airports on the island, and began calling the other two. At Kona he got Dr. Emory on the line. Kenneth gave instructions to put Yosi on the jitney that came as far as Naalehu, a plantation town near South Point. He should wait there, "And tell the driver to let Yosi off at Mr. Takemoto's place."

The jitney detoured through Puna and stopped at every general store and filling station along the highway to take on and let off passengers. It took Yosi two hours to get to Naalehu. The ride gave him an excellent anthropological introduction to the local population and his first brush with pidgin English. It turned out that Mr. Takemoto was the postmaster. Yosi waited half an hour, then Kenneth came.

"He was with some students," Yosi recalled later. "I thought when I look at him, yes, he is a scholar and an academic person." What Kenneth saw was a small, slender, dark-haired, very young thirty-year-old man wearing black, horn-rimmed glasses. They got into the car and drove eighteen miles to South Point.

Kenneth knew only that his guest had worked as a student assistant for a distinguished archaeologist in Japan and that his father was a plant geneticist at the Imperial University of Tokyo. Years later, Kenneth remembered that day:

> When we got to South Point, Yosi took out a silk scarf like a package to carry things. His field kit was in the scarf. He had his little brush and things. Oh, my! He was ready to go to work. He was good! I was immediately impressed with his training.

Yosi said he had planned to stay in Hawaii a month between ships and that he didn't know anything about Polynesian artifacts. However, he was familiar with fishhooks, arrowheads, knives, and harpoons made of boar tusks, as well as stone implements, which he had helped excavate in the shell mounds at Ubayama that dated back to the early Joman era from 8000 B.C. to 500 B.C. in Japan.

After a few days, Kenneth asked him to map the Puu Alii site, which was becoming more complicated than Kenneth's students had anticipated. The paved floor of the houseyard now revealed corner post holes of many houses, stone seats, fireplaces, ground ovens, and grindstones and stone anvils where fishhooks had been manufactured. Yosi said he drew the map and, after about ten days on the site, announced he'd better start back.

Kenneth didn't want him to go. Yosi carried out Kenneth's orders quickly and with surer competence than anyone else on the site. Although he didn't have a degree, he was more experienced than the other students. He would make an ideal assistant. Every time Yosi tried to leave, Kenneth urged him to stay: "No, no, no, no. You stay here and we will take care of you while you go to the University of Hawaii. I'll get you a job at the museum." Marguerite said later, "Poor Yosi. Kenneth kidnapped him."

Yosi was torn. In California there was Dr. Chaney, his father's friend, a famous paleontologist who had discovered the sequoia alive in China and who had arranged Yosi's admission into Berkeley. But here he had already made friends. He felt at home. There was Dr. Emory to teach him and plenty of digging to do. Enrollment at the University of Hawaii totaled four thousand, compared to forty thousand at Berkeley. He'd be buried there. So he decided to stay one semester. It may have been Kenneth's promise to look after him that tipped the scales for Yosi. His total wealth consisted of $150 in traveler's checks and a new Nikon camera.

Kenneth's interest went deeper than charity. He said later that Yosi's excavating techniques were more sophisticated and up-to-date than his own: "I didn't want him to go to the University of California. He was the best archaeologist I had. I had to train all the others myself."

Yosi had been much too polite to criticize, but he admitted later that the South Point dig dismayed him: "Frankly, I thought it was a terrible excavation. Terrible excavation. Not digging but destroying the site." He said the students were digging three-foot-square holes here and there by three-inch increments that had no relation to the cultural layers they were uncovering. Material from one cultural layer got mixed with another. When the diggers finished they would be unable to determine which cultural layer the artifacts came from.

This problem came about because the strata uncovered were not level. These strata, or cultural layers, dipped and rose like contours of the countryside. Yosi explained that he had been taught first to put down test pits to locate where the excavation should take place, then strip away one cultural layer at a time by following its contour. This way, material from each cultural layer could be kept apart from the other cultural layers. What emerged was a time sequence that yielded the maximum amount of information.

Because Yosi had no place to stay in Honolulu and no money for rent, he worked at the dig until the fall semester began, living in the abandoned Coast Guard lighthouse station. It was a lonely time for him. South Point is a bleak place—parched grassland turning into black lava where the land juts into the turbulent sea, ten miles from the nearest highway. His wife had remained behind in Japan. "Three months," he said later. "I was there for three months."

When school began Kenneth enrolled Yosi at the university and put him to work part-time as his assistant at the museum. The new student rented a room near the university in a big house that was overrun by the landlady's cats. Yosi, as a foreign student, had to study English. The teacher gave him various topics to write compositions about. One assignment Yosi received was to write about where he lived. He wrote a very nice composition about the "Cat House." It was some time before he understood why the other students thought it was funny.

He proved as versatile at the museum as Kenneth had been as a beginner. He sorted artifacts and catalogued them, took pictures and developed photos, and drew maps. Kenneth refused to let him go at the end of the semester, and wanted to put him in charge of the South Point dig over Christmas vacation.

"I told him I would go if I could do it my way," Yosi recalled later. So he went to South Point and dug by cultural layers, taking photographs to illustrate the technique. He also helped map new shelters to the north of South Point in an area called Waiahukini where Kamehameha I had lived as a boy. On Yosi's return to Honolulu, he showed his teacher the color slides of cultural layers. Kenneth got the point right away. He said later he was very impressed and even more determined to keep Yosi.

The two men developed a father-son relationship. Kenneth depended more and more on his assistant, championed his interests, and watched him develop with growing pride. Yosi treated Kenneth with unfailing respect, deferred to his wisdom, and overlooked his failings.

By May 22, 1954, Kenneth had completed 517½ pages of his Kapingamarangi manuscript. During the same year he moved his office to the second floor of Kunia Hall. What the quarters lacked in luxury they made up in space, necessary because Kenneth's office also did duty as the anthropology laboratory. Besides Kenneth's filing cabinets, map case, and desk, as well as work space for Yosi, there was a long table where students could sort artifacts, and another in the hall when the work spilled over. Marguerite hung some petroglyph rubbings on the cement walls to make it look less like a warehouse.

The McInerny Foundation granted another $3,000 in 1955. With plenty of student volunteers now, Kenneth pursued two objectives that year. At South Point, Yosi and Bonk and the volunteers excavated in a shelter they called H-8 at Waiahukini. From the start they used Yosi's method of first digging test pits, then going down by cultural layers.

Next, everybody joined Kenneth for an expedition to the northwest coast of the island in the Kohala district to survey archaeological sites along the route of a proposed state highway. They worked out of a comfortable beach home owned by Hilo resident Annabelle Ruddle, another of Kenneth's fans. Yosi hiked through the boondocks and located three or four shelters in collapsed lava tubes where he found fishhooks. Kenneth spent a great deal of his time talking to local residents getting legends about the area. But the biggest excitement came from petroglyph discoveries, because hardly anybody had bothered to look for them in this wilderness before.

The beach house stood on the edge of the wilderness, just beyond where the road ended in Puako Village. Here the weekend cottages of nonresidents and the homes of Kohala fishermen were strung out along a lava rock shore. Beyond Puako for thirty miles to Kailua there was nothing but bare lava. An old Hawaiian trail followed the coast past pristine beaches marked with clumps of tall, shaggy coconut palms and, in some places, a few beach houses. The beaches were given musical names: Anaehoomalu, Keawaiki, Kiholo, Maniniowale, and Makalawena.

At Anaehoomalu, three acres of Hawaiian rock carvings straddled the new highway route. One job of the expedition was to document these pictures in the stone. Mrs. Ruddle knew of another petroglyph field a quarter of a mile inland from her place at Paniau. There was a long curving stick figure like an enormous centipede. Kenneth said it represented an army of marching men.

They always made the four-mile hike to Anaehoomalu in the cool of early morning. Along the way they spotted more petroglyphs, which appeared to occur at intervals as if marking reststops for travelers. Missionary William Ellis in 1823 had noticed the same thing and had asked about it. The Hawaiians told him the carvings were made to leave a record. Circles represented trips around the island. Dots inside the circles, or several concentric circles, told how many were in the party.

There were other figures Kenneth had never seen before. One day two *kamaaina*s, Jack Paulo and Ishiro Goto, led him and his band farther inland through *kiawe* trees beyond the centipede to another petroglyph field covering a bulge of lava, which Yosi called "maternity hill." The students scattered like children on an Easter egg hunt and quickly found more petroglyphs. They were buried under leaves and fallen branches. The next day the students brought brooms and rakes. By the time they finished, they had uncovered five acres of petroglyphs.

It was a Stone Age art gallery: stick figures of canoes with sails, men holding paddles, praying figures, weird representations of humans that looked like ghosts, dogs, chickens, turtles, lizards, crabs, fledgling birds, and fishhooks. Kenneth interpreted these figures as signatures, the *aumakua*s or guardian spirits of the people who had chipped the images in the hope of insuring a safe journey.

Some of the petroglyphs were simply childish stick figures. Others were more realistic, having triangular chests. Still others depicted bulging biceps and calves similar to carved wooden idols— apparently the work of a later time by artists with improved techniques. There were other abstract figures that Kenneth, unable to step back into the mind of an ancient Hawaiian by the side of the trail, didn't try to interpret. Each petroglyph had to be chalked and then sketched or photographed.

In 1956 excavation continued at Waiahukini near South Point. The shelter called H-8 produced a wealth of fishhooks, also carbon samples. The diggers found three cultural layers and this time there was no doubt about which layers the artifacts came from. Between expeditions, excavated bones and rocks and shells had to be sorted and weighed, and artifacts had to be catalogued. In March of 1956 Kenneth took up his Kuliouou report again. He became quite interested in bones. Amy Greenwell came in to help. Kenneth explained later that the Hawaiians living in the cave shelter used dog bones to make instruments. "There was something about the jaw, the whole jaw," he said. "They'd make it into a knife, maybe by putting a shark's tooth into it. . . . There were also tattooing needles made from albatross bones, the biggest ones. These objects had to be described."

On July 5, 1956, Kenneth wrote in his diary, "Yosi and I deep in representing quantitatives." The next day: "Did turtle bones."

"Quantitatives" was the term used to describe the weighing of material from the excavation. There were so many shells and bones of different sizes that counting them would have been meaningless. So they were weighed instead to measure the consumption of birds or shellfish or dogs or turtles in a given period. The weight of accumulated shells and bones provided information, based on food consumed, about the number of people who inhabited the shelters.

At home Kenneth and Marguerite still quarreled a good deal. She felt neglected and he felt misunderstood. In August, he began sorting and classifying fishhooks with Yosi. When the fall semester started, he got a sore throat. By September 14 his laryngitis was "rather bad." The next day he went to see a doctor. "He frightened me by saying I could lose my voice if I don't stop talking," Kenneth wrote in his diary.

He stayed at home for a few days and tried to avoid using his voice. On September 22 he wrote, "The doctor's report gave me grave concern about my voice . . ." The next day: "Face a grim problem, not knowing how much my voice has been damaged. Tried it today. Quickly tired, does not sound normal."

Kenneth became depressed. Since he lived on enthusiasm, the blue mood made his laryngitis worse. Eleanor Anderson read his lectures to the class. He stayed at home and moped. "After a week of voice silence, my hopes were rather high that today would see marked improvement," he wrote on Sunday, September 30. "But no. It is hard not to be discouraged."

A week later he saw another doctor who assured him he didn't have throat cancer or some other fatal disease. All he'd done was strain his vocal cords. Kenneth wrote, "The terrible bug-a-boo of throat tuberculosis or cancer is rubbed out and today I used my voice cautiously . . . I am vastly encouraged. Gave lecture at U.H." Within a week he was back to normal and working on a contract to survey the City of Refuge on Hawaii for the National Park Service.

Chapter Forty-one

Fishhooks and Hurricanes

Kenneth taught his field-methods class how to conduct an expedition by describing his own experiences: voyaging on board the *Kaimiloa*, atoll hopping through the Tuamotus, and being marooned on Kapingamarangi. Yosi became not only an apt but an appreciative student. He said later that he learned things from Kenneth that he could not get out of books and that most professors don't teach.

"When I learn from a professor, I want to know from first hand experience, not from books," Yosi explained. "In that sense, Dr. Emory is the most experienced one in the area of Oceania, Polynesia. I still vividly remember, because many times [during my own expeditions] I encountered different problems and always what Kenneth taught me was very useful. He called it entrée to a place. How to deal with people when you start work. One thing is you have to be with them, not act superior to them. And to learn their language. And to give the impression that you want to learn from them."

By this time Bishop Museum expeditions had dug up thousands of fishhooks. There were more than 1,600 hooks or fragments from the Puu Alii site. Waiahukini, by the end of the decade, produced 5,000. Clearly here was a signature of the Polynesians, as common as pottery to the Mesopotamians or Egyptians, that might be used by archaeologists in the Pacific to provide chronology. Yet no one, before Kenneth began digging, could have conceived of so revolutionary an idea.

Who actually thought of it first is not clear. The public attributed it to Kenneth although he later refused to take credit for originating the concept. Spoehr said, "I would doubt that it was a terribly new idea to Kenneth. He could have an overall vision." Yosi thought of it right away. He said he remembers asking Kenneth soon after he arrived at South Point, "Where's the pottery?" In his previous digs, potsherds in the cultural strata had provided a chronology in each site and a means of comparing the chronology of one site with another. Kenneth said the Hawaiians did not have pottery.

"Then what other object, diagnostic artifact, can be used to date the site, at least comparatively with other sites?" Yosi asked. Kenneth explained that they had been digging for only three years and had not yet found a substitute for pottery. Yosi went to work on fishhooks with Kenneth's encouragement. Kenneth's diary shows that he also worked with fishhooks when he had time.

It was a gargantuan task. A volunteer couple, Ivan and Dorothy Rainwater, had already done some work on separating the fishhooks into types: hooks with the barb inside, hooks with the barb outside, straight-shanked hooks with a curved point, curved-shanked hooks with a straight point, one-piece hooks, two-piece hooks, hooks lashed to a knob, hooks lashed to a notch.

For Yosi, this was a beginning. He went through the fishhooks one by one until he had listed sixty-five different types. He could see that those from the Puu Alii site at South Point fell into a different general classification than those from the cave shelter, Kamakalai, farther inland. If the changes in hook shapes represented an evolution in time, which types were older and which more recent?

It wasn't until he had in hand fishhooks from the Waiahukini site that he could make sense of it. Each cultural strata produced a different type of hook. Fishhooks from the top layer looked like the hooks in Kamakalai cave. Fishhooks from the bottom layer were like those from the Puu Alii dune site. Fishhooks in the middle layer formed a transition between the older and newer hooks. A new clue turned up. Captain Cook in the early 1870s had brought some fishhooks back from Tahiti. The hooks in that collection, now in the British Museum, were similar to those in the bottom layer of Waiahukini and from Puu Alii. It seemed clear that early Hawaiian hooks were Tahitian types. Later the hooks were adapted to local conditions.

Yosi now had to test the theory. Would the thousands of fishhooks at the museum fall into the proper categories? To find out, Yosi invented what he called the "poor man's IBM." For each fishhook he worked up a punch card. Along the top of the card he punched a hole or cut a slot for each descriptive feature of the hook. By the time he finished he had punched 3,500 cards and filed them in boxes.

Then he began exploring the relationships between the hooks. To assemble quickly all the hooks with outer barbs, for example, he ran a slim metal rod through the proper hole in the batches of cards, then lifted. Those with outer barb holes came up with the rod. All the other cards, with open notches instead of outer barb holes, stayed in the box. In this way, like a computer, he could quickly assemble hooks from any site and of any description for comparison. When he wasn't sure about something he consulted Bonk or Kenneth.

There was plenty of work to do for everyone. The year 1957 began with a survey of the City of Refuge at Honaunau on the Kona Coast of Hawaii. By this time the pattern of such Bishop Museum expeditions had changed considerably from twenty years ago when Kenneth would have gone out by himself. Now he headed a team. His most important role was to plan the work and direct it, although he was no more able to resist digging and measuring and interviewing than he could stop breathing.

In November he would be sixty years old. His diary indicates that hardship didn't slow him down. He hiked all day over raw lava under a blistering sun, slept in a tent, and got up at dawn. He was constantly greeting visitors. Thursday, January 31, went like this: "Sinoto surveyed trail to Kiilae. [Bill] Bonk, [Haley] Cox and I went to . . . site in Kiilae. [Ivan] Rainwater, A[my] Greenwell worked H-50. M[argaret] T[itcomb], Mrs. Betty Black came by to photograph. M[arguerite] Emory joined us at breakfast time. Iolani [Luahine] brought her over. Partly overcast."

Caving provided the biggest thrill. The Kona Coast is laced with lava tubes, some of which extend for miles between mountain and shore. Some were used as refuges by the people of old. Kenneth's diary mentions three or four refuge caves known to local residents, as well as burial caves. They had to be explored and he went into all of them.

Yosi remembered a refuge cave in which Homer Hayes of Kona had found huge shark hooks. Kenneth went in with Yosi and Mazie Cameron, a student volunteer. Each followed a separate branch of the cave. Mazie found a bone fishhook in a flat corner where the ceiling was so low she had to crawl. She called to Yosi who examined the hook, then dug in the dust with his fingers. "We found over sixty fishhooks," he said. "Most of them complete. I never experienced an encounter such as that. They looked like just one person made it. Which means [we found the] fishhook maker's storage area. . . . Amazing. Most beautiful fishhooks I ever saw."

Back at the museum the writing of reports and mapping began. The City of Refuge area was to become a national park, and the National Park Service had contracted to find out how the site was used, by whom, its history, government, religion, housing accommodations, diet, fishing and farming practices, and as much other data as the Bishop Museum team could produce.

Dirt archaeology now generated most of the new information about the people of old. But there were still other sources out of the past that revealed secrets and created mysteries. On April 11, 1957, with visiting anthropologist Charles E. Snow, Kenneth examined one of the museum's most valuable possessions, the woven sennit casket of a chief of legendary times, Liloa.

The casket was composed of a container—an elaborate basket—in the shape of a head with ears, eyes, nose, and mouth, and a torso without arms or legs. The head and torso were nearly three feet long and twelve inches wide at the shoulders, large enough to contain the bones of the trunk and limbs. At one time the casket had been x-rayed to reveal bones as well as some foreign objects inside. The bottom had become frayed where the weaving closed, leaving a small hole. Kenneth and Snow, who was doing a study of skeletonal material at the museum, decided to remove the objects through the hole and examine them.

Since Yosi's hand was the smallest, he reached in and took out what was inside. In addition to bones, the casket held several beautiful ornaments of turtle shell, pig tusk, and whale tooth. There was also a piece of metal, like a square nail about five inches long, attached to a wooden handle. The weapon resembled a dagger or an ice pick. Finally, Yosi removed a *malo*, or loin cloth, five or six inches wide and about eight feet long in many layers. The fabric was woven and sewed with thread. These objects had been placed in the casket as the prized possessions of a very sacred and important chief.

Where had the mysterious iron dagger and woven *malo* come from? The Hawaiians before contact with Cook did not produce either iron or woven cloth. And they did not sew. The large nail might have drifted to the islands in a piece of wreckage, a ship's timber. The fabric might have been part of a sail of a ship wrecked at Hawaii, or cloth in the cargo. Yet there is no record of such a ship before Cook, only myths of Spanish galleons. The materials went back into the casket and the mysteries remained unsolved.

On August 12 Kenneth wrote in his diary, "We have decided to work up fishhooks together; Yosi, Bonk & self." On October 7 a carbon date for Waiahukini at South Point arrived from the University of Michigan's Randall Laboratory of Physics. The date was A.D. 957. Kenneth told newspaper reporters, "This [date] doesn't mean it was the first of all settlements for the entire island . . . When you allow for a period for the establishment of the Hawaiian population, indications are the first arrivals of the Hawaiian ancestors were in 750 A.D."

Three days later Kenneth wrote, "Yosi has worked out correlation between fishhook sites." It had taken him three years to compile the data and he was still at it. Kenneth began to write up the results. With interruptions, it was slow going.

He dreamed about digging in Tahiti. But there was too much to do at home first. Material from seventeen excavations had to be processed. A museum party spent two weeks in 1957 at one of the most important sites discovered on Kauai. They were shocked to find it vandalized. Only a small patch of floor in the shelter had not been spaded into chaos. Kenneth spent weeks lobbying in the legislature to get a law passed protecting archaeological sites.

Because the pot hunters were so active on Kauai, he targeted Nualolo Kai on Kauai's Napali Coast for excavation in 1958. Meanwhile, Yosi graduated in June and became Kenneth's full-time assistant. Now he could bring his wife to Hawaii. That meant looking for a place to live.

A report came from Hawaii that goat hunters had found Kamehameha's burial cave in the cliff above Kealakekua Bay. Kenneth dashed to Hawaii for a look and found plenty of bones but not, he decided, those of Kamehameha. He was working full tilt on the fishhook paper now.

At least he got some help with paperwork. Marion Kelly, the now-married daughter of "Wild Bill" Anderson, came to work as Kenneth's full-time secretary in 1958. Volunteer typist Eleanor Anderson moved into Spoehr's office as the director's secretary. Marion said, "Kenneth did a lot of his own typing with two fingers. Yosi was there a lot. I typed manuscripts and outgoing letters. After a few days I got a terrible pain in my back. I tried to see if the typewriter was too high or too low. Finally I took the pad off the chair. There was no seat in it, just a hole."

The Nualolo Kai dig began on July 29. This time the workers could not drive to the site. Tents, sleeping bags, stoves, pots and pans, provisions, and excavation equipment had to be loaded into a boat on the beach, dragged into the water, and taken ten miles up a cliffbound, uninhabited coastline to the valley. This had to be done early in the morning before the wind came up and the sea got rough. Sometimes it got rough anyway.

Like Kenneth's other digs, this one became a training course for the new generation of anthropologists. Yosi and Bonk were there, also Ben Finney, an ardent surfer turned archaeologist, and Roger Green from Harvard. Finney would later become an authority on Polynesian navigation and chairman of anthropology at the University of Hawaii. Green's work on Mangareva, Moorea, and Samoa would make him one of the leading archaeologists in the Pacific.

Also, a member of the press turned up as Kenneth's guest to describe the romance of digging for Stone Age artifacts in an uninhabited valley. The reporter explained to his readers that the only land route out of Nualolo Kai was a footpath. Here's how he described it from an out-of-print archaeology report:

> It starts around the base of the bluff . . . and runs for 30 feet or more on a narrow ledge sharply overhung by a cliff about 20 feet above the ocean. At the end of this [ledge] a rope ladder leads [up] to a ledge 25 feet above it. The bulge in the cliff makes the ladder hang out over the sea. The ladder is fastened [at the top] into four rings cut through the solid rock for that purpose. . . . From the top of the ladder a series of notched steps and finger grips have been cut that lead to a narrow trail that runs up to the top of the bluff [and into the next valley]. The notches and finger grips have been worn smooth by ancient usage.

The rope ladder, last replaced in 1922 by a hunting party, had rotted away. Now the sea provided the only access to the valley. The reporter described the voyage:

> At 4:30 A.M., while the night was still deep, we drove to a black sand beach near the sugar plantation village of Kekaha where Jim Bal, a graying plantation supervisor, put his boat in the surging water. The boat is small, a 16-footer with an outboard motor. It rode like a match stick on the angry ocean that morning. But Jim, with the blood of seafaring Hawaiians in his veins, calmly chewed a dead cigar and steered up and down along the line of breakers, looking for an opening in the marching surf. When it came, he darted through into the open, rolling sea.
>
> An hour and a half later, after a bone-jarring ride along that spectacularly rugged coastline, Jim eased the boat through a hole in the reef and anchored in a quiet lagoon that shelters a half mile strip of white sand beach. It is the same lagoon, protected by a circling reef, that provided the ancient Hawaiians with the only safe canoe anchorage along the Napali Coast, a fact which accounts in part for the traces of former habitation here.
>
> The valley has changed little since the old Hawaiians lived here. . . . Nualolo-kai is about half a mile across and a quarter of a mile deep. It is completely enclosed on the land side by a semicircle of sheer, black cliffs. At night if you happen to walk in front of the camp fire, your shadow is projected to a height of 800 feet on those towering walls.

The archaeologists dug under a cliff overhang where Hawaiians had erected their houses on terraces that gradually built up over the centuries on the accumulation of debris. Sand and chips of rock falling from the cliff above added to the build up. The diggers went down through eight feet of cultural material.

By this time the student archaeologists had resigned themselves to Kenneth's habit of getting up with the sun. "He goes to bed early," Yosi explained. "We get up 6, 6:30. But Kenneth gets up at 4 o'clock. Then he wants to make coffee and he lights the stove. [In a] Tent is not so bad. But inside a building like at South Point, terrible racket. Nobody can sleep."

That year, 1958, Frank Stimson died. It happened not long after Kenneth had written a long critique for the *American Anthropologist* about Stimson's last book, warning readers to beware of altered material. Bengt Danielsson wrote from Tahiti about Stimson whom he had come to know well. Danielsson was also grateful to Kenneth for his help and advice, and admired his work. Now he offered some gentle advice of his own about the long-standing feud with Stimson:

> As I am an old subscriber to the *American Anthropologist* I had already read your review of Stimson's last book long before you sent me a photo-static copy of it. Of course, you are right. But frankly speaking I think that you have lost too much time and energy on this feud. As it is now, you can certainly calmly rest your case and let coming generations of anthropologists write the final verdict.

Kenneth handed in the fishhook manuscript in October. It was signed by himself, Yosi, and Bonk. The paper described for the first time how archaeologists on Polynesian islands could use fishhooks as tracers in their digs. He began writing about tattoo needles in November.

The year 1959 brought statehood for Hawaii on March 12, and with statehood a super-heated economic boom. Hotels began to sprout like mushrooms. A preview of the new era came on April 20 when Lyle L. Guslander, president of Island Holidays resort chain, announced construction of a 105-room hotel on Kamakahonu Beach in Kailua on the Kona Coast. "My letter to *The Advertiser* appeared on Kamakahonu," Kenneth wrote in his diary on April 22. So began his first battle with a developer.

Kailua, a Waikiki in miniature, was a chiefly fishing village turned resort destination. In the early-nineteenth century the aging Kamehameha I had returned there to end his battle-studded career as conqueror of all the islands. He built his thatched compound on a charming, sandy cove called Kamakahonu Bay: a house for himself, houses for his wives, a storehouse for his wealth, and houses for his royal court. On the black lava point he rebuilt a temple to Lono, god of peace and agriculture. There he died in 1819 just one year before the first missionaries brought a new god to Hawaii.

The $750,000 hotel was to be built hard on the beach, would boast the island's first elevator, and would provide jobs in a depressed economy. It would replace a lumberyard now being operated near the site. Hotelman Guslander promised to give public access to the beach and to preserve the *heiau*, all that remained standing of the old place.

Kenneth and others knew that the old house foundations were also still in place. They must not be destroyed by careless development. Old Kamehameha's deceptively unassuming "palace" was among the most important sites in Hawaii's history, not the least because it projected the values of another culture. It had been earmarked in plans of the territorial government as a park but, as usual, there wasn't enough money to buy the land. Kenneth believed that Kamakahonu should be restored as it had been in the days of Kamehameha, not commercialized and overrun by beach concessions.

In the days that followed, Kenneth became a spokesman for the Conservation Council and its Sites Committee. He buttonholed his childhood playmate, Lorrin P. Thurston, now publisher of *The Advertiser.* He appeared before legislative committees. Yosi helped him draft a map of Kamakahonu to appear in the Sunday paper, so that people could see where Kamehameha's house had been, as well as those of his wives. He raced off to Kona to make speeches there. He met endlessly with Guslander, the developer; with officers of Amfac, the Big Five firm that owned the land; and with members of the press, the Sites Committee, and Kona people. Over and over he proposed that the hotel be moved one hundred feet back to preserve the integrity of the ruins.

The territorial legislature passed a concurrent resolution asking the governor to turn Kamakahonu into a park. But the lawmakers failed to provide any money. Then the Hawaiian Civic Club in Kona voted forty-seven to twenty-seven on a compromise permitting construction of the hotel but demanding public access to the beach and a guarantee of eventual restoration of the *heiau.* Legislators appropriated $200,000 to buy an easement on which the public could walk to the beach, and developer Guslander promised that his hotel would not infringe within fifty feet of the high-water mark. At least the ruins of Kamehameha's old living compound remained intact.

In July Kenneth got a letter with a startling new date of settlement for the island of Hawaii based on a carbon sample from Puu Alii at South Point. Professor H. de Vries of the Physical Laboratory, University of Groningen, the Netherlands, put the date at A.D. 124, eight hundred years earlier than any date received before.

Kenneth announced the date cautiously. He told reporters the carbon probably came from a campfire made by sporadic campers, wandering fishermen, or even by castaways. The date did indicate that

South Point was the first place inhabited in Hawaii, he said. The truth was he didn't know exactly what to make of the new date.

In fact the carbon dates now flowing in for South Point had become as much a frustration as a help. Several dates for South Point indicated an occupation of only two hundred and fifty years. The fishhooks found there showed that couldn't be right. Kenneth had not bothered to announce those dates. He had accepted three dates that came in later: A.D. 1380 and A.D. 1270 from the bottom of the site, and A.D. 1420 from near the middle. That squared rather well with the fishhooks.

So did the A.D. 950 date for Waiahukini. Then came another date for Waiahukini, A.D. 1860. Parts of another sample from the same site were given a date of A.D. 1230 by the laboratory in Michigan and a date of A.D. 1660 by the laboratory in Holland. Now he had received a date for Puu Alii of A.D. 124. Something had gone wrong. It had to be contamination of the samples, and perhaps differences in dating techniques.

Yet the carbon dates and the fishhooks were providing a window into the past that had been shuttered before. Kenneth was comfortable with the A.D. 950 date from the bottom cultural layer at Waiahukini where the fishhooks were barbed with early Tahitian notched bases. The next level produced a transition to fishhooks with knobbed bases, a later Hawaiian development. This level also produced a carbon date of A.D. 1230 which Kenneth accepted.

The fishhooks from Puu Alii had the Tahitian style—notched bases. It seemed clear that this early fishing settlement had phased out before the later, Hawaiian-style knobbed hooks had come in. Sand had covered the site and Hawaiians had buried their dead in the dune. Why had Hawaiians deserted such a long-established fishing base? Was it a change in the climate? Why must new information always lead to more questions?

At least the excavations yielded hard evidence, first-hand testimony from the people themselves rather than mythological symbolism. That testimony formed a picture, clearer than it had ever been, of the first Hawaiians: where they came from and how they got to Hawaii. Kenneth spoke to Honolulu's prestigious Social Science Association:

> Going back to a thouand years ago . . . we find that . . . our island inhabitants possessed the pig and the dog. I think it is safe to assume that . . . they had also introduced many if not all of the numerous domesticated plants, such as the taro, banana, sugar cane, yam, breadfruit, and paper mulberry which were here when Captain Cook came

. . . When we have evidence of the first appearance of the poi pounder, we will have a clue as to when taro was introduced.

The stone adzes of this early period are identical in types to stone adzes found in Tahiti. Also in Tahiti occur all the domesticated plants and animals which were introduced to ancient Hawaii. Because the language, physical types and culture of the Hawaiians are very closely allied to the Tahitian equivalents . . . we are convinced the ancestors of the Hawaiians came from the Society Islands, to which Tahiti, the largest island, often gives its name . . .

What impressed me and my fellow archaeologists as we observe the artifacts left behind by the people of the earliest period in Hawaii, is . . . [that] they seemed already to have had everything. It looks as if the Hawaiian Islands were first settled by a rather large and remarkably well equipped expedition bent on finding a new home. Such an expedition could only be organized by a powerful chief . . .

How did these people find Hawaii's isolated islands two thousand miles to the north? Rhodes scholar and old Pacific hand Andrew Sharp in New Zealand had recently published a book, *Ancient Voyagers in the Pacific*, promoting the theory that Polynesian voyages of discovery and settlement were accidents. Sharp argued that a Stone Age people could not have sailed in primitive outrigger canoes against against winds and currents. Nor could they have purposefully found their way over such incredible distances. Kenneth disagreed that the Polynesians could not find their way back once they had discovered a new island:

The first band of settlers would have had an excellent idea of the location of the islands from which they came. There probably was a very strong desire to send back their vessel to tell those left behind of their magnificent discovery. . . . If an attempt were made while some who had accompanied the first voyage were still living to guide them, I believe it quite possible for them to have returned to Tahiti and to have made their way back to Hawaii . . .

I am willing to give those early Polynesians who were out hunting for new homes . . . more navigational credit than Andrew Sharp does . . . The odds may have been against them . . . but if they sailed south they were bound to hit islands whose inhabitants would know where the Society Islands lay, and in sailing north again, they could not miss the 1,500-mile chain of Hawaiian Islands. But, once the connection . . . was broken by the dying out of all those who had made the trip, it would be exceedingly difficult to renew it.

Hawaii was not the only island in the Pacific producing carbon dates. Kenneth's discoveries in the Kuliouou cave had encouraged archaeologists to dig into the earth on islands spread all across that vast ocean, especially in Polynesia. Jack Golson of Auckland University in New Zealand was excavating in Tonga and Samoa. Robert Suggs of the American Museum of Natural History was in the Marquesas. The same institution was sponsoring Roger Green in Mangareva. The University of Chile had sent Thomas S. Barthel and R. Vargas to Easter Island. In New Zealand, H. D. Skinner rivaled Kenneth as an archaeological pioneer.

They were the crest of a new wave. Other expeditions were sure to follow. Roger Green already had his eye on Moorea in the Societies. Kenneth couldn't wait to get back to Tahiti. But the excavation at Nualolo Kai had to be finished first. In the summer of 1959 the digging crew returned to the shadow of the cliffs. Kenneth flitted in and out: part archaeologist, part tour conductor, part administrator, and always enthusiastic. He ferried in supplies, escorted visitors, and joined in the excavation. But not for long. He couldn't stay still.

Seven people were in the valley on Wednesday, August 5, when Hurricane Dot loomed over the horizon. Kenneth had planned to send a boat with fresh supplies, but by that time the ocean was too rough. He commandeered a local pilot, Joe Prigge, and loaded the small plane with six loaves of bread, two pounds of meat, tinned goods, fifty pounds of ice, and a copy of *The Advertiser* showing the route of the storm.

Members of the expedition in Nualolo Kai watched in amazement as the airplane dive-bombed the valley. Kenneth described the flight to a reporter: "Ice water kept dripping down my neck. Every time we hit an air pocket the ice slipped and banged me on the head. Prigge wasn't too sure we could get in and out of the valley because of the wind. He turned the nose down and dove. We skimmed the tops of the weeds."

Bonk was in charge of the expedition. Pauline King, one of Kenneth's students, had charge of the camp. They pulled their boat high up on the beach, put the archaeological specimens into canvas bags, tied them down under the cliffs, and waited. When the hurricane didn't hit Wednesday night, they thought it had missed them.

It struck at 2 P.M. on Thursday while they were sitting in the biggest tent. It collapsed over their heads. The wind shredded another tent. They managed to flatten and save the other two, then spent the night under the cliffs. Kenneth said he was most worried about their water supply. But the heavy rains provided plenty of fresh water from waterfalls and instant streams.

Chapter Forty-two

Disappointment in Tahiti

Once more Kenneth waited for his first glimpse of Tahiti. As dawn broke over the empty ocean he gazed out of the blurred airplane window and searched for an island. It was Easter Sunday, April 17, 1960. Yosi occupied the seat beside him, eager and expectant. Would Yosi's introduction to the South Seas mean to him what it had to Kenneth on that long ago New Year's morning when he watched his first sunrise over Papeete from the deck of the *Kaimiloa*?

This time they would land at Bora-Bora where there was an airstrip. This time, also, Kenneth carried a burden of responsibility he had not felt during that first, carefree visit. It was probably his own fault. Perhaps he should not have shared his optimism with newspaper reporters about digging in Tahiti. He had told them that he would be amazed if he didn't find a link between Tahiti and Hawaii. The only other possibility was the Marquesas.

He had also been specific about other questions he expected his excavations to answer. How long has Tahiti been inhabited? What did the first inhabitants bring in the way of artifacts, plants, and animals? What changes in cultural content occurred and at what periods? All this had appeared in the press in Honolulu and in the *Christian Science Monitor*, along with his guess that Tahiti and the Marquesas had been settled about 300 or 400 B.C. His guess was based on a recent carbon date establishing occupation in the Marquesas by 124 B.C. But now he had to find the sites in Tahiti to prove it.

If he failed, he could blame no one but himself. He already owed a great deal to Bengt Danielsson, now a permanent Tahiti resident, for smoothing and guiding his way through the pitfalls of French colonial bureaucracy. Spoehr had scratched together the last of the Tri-Institutional Pacific Program money to send this expedition to the Society Islands for five months. Nobody had ever gone underground in Tahiti before. Kenneth was enthusiastic. He couldn't help it. The sites had to be there.

The jagged, fairy-tale skyline of Bora-Bora rose from the ocean. On a sand spit on the reef, the airstrip looked no bigger than the deck of an aircraft carrier. They landed with a roar on the hard-packed coral. Then a launch took them to Bora-Bora.

It was almost as festive as a steamer arrival. Little tables, lined up on the beach, were covered with grass skirts and shell headbands and conch shells for sale. The girls behind the tables wore flowers in their hair. And no shoes. Somebody was playing Tahitian music in the small terminal constructed of woven bamboo wall paneling and roof thatch. Tentatively, Kenneth tried his Tahitian for the first time in twenty-six years. Yosi said later, "In no time at all his Tahitian came back and he started talking. I was really amazed at Kenneth. He was very good."

Then they boarded a flying boat in the lagoon. The plane lumbered from the water like a giant albatross and droned away toward Tahiti. They landed there amid great fans of spray. Kenneth waited impatiently for a glimpse of Papeete. It really hadn't changed much. If anything, the stores across the drowsy, narrow street from the quay looked more colorful in their blue and white and pink paint. And the boats tied up along the waterfront were smart cruising yachts, not frowzy copra schooners. There was still a gay, impudent, French-Tahitian air about the place.

His old friend Bertrand Jaunez, affluent patron of things scientific, met them in elegant casual attire with impeccable manners and warm hospitality. They were to be guests at his beach estate some ten miles from Papeete. The ride made Kenneth feel even better about coming back. More cottages were thatched now than before. There was the same careless beauty, a natural clutter everywhere of coconuts and canoes and palm fronds and pigs and flower-beds bordered in white coral. The exquisite pastels of the lagoon and the bold statement of the skyline still framed it all.

A change he didn't appreciate was the increased arrogance of French officials. Thank God for Bengt Danielsson. On Bengt's advice, Kenneth had written to the colonial administration in France suggesting that the government assign a French archaeologist to the expedition. The man was supposed to be on his way. So far, Bishop Museum had maintained friendly diplomatic relations with the French. Marguerite, with her family connections, would soon arrive to help keep it that way.

Now they must find a site and begin digging. This, too, had become more complicated: in the old days, Kenneth had gone to the chief of a district for permission to scout for maraes, but now there were hundreds of individual landowners to deal with. He enlisted the aid of Aurora Natua, the museum librarian and curator in Papeete, who had an encyclopedic knowledge of Tahitian families, genealogies, and island history. Since she could barely support herself on the pittance she received from the museum, Aurora welcomed the chance to make a little extra money.

They started along the coast, Aurora and Yosi and Kenneth, looking for shelters similar to those that had produced such rich hauls in Hawaii. They found none on the coast. In Tahiti the mountains stood far back from the beaches with a broad coastal plain in between. The shelters in the mountains were wet and uninhabitable.

Day after day they slogged along the coast on foot under a blazing sun in a dreary, fruitless expenditure of energy, searching for some trace of ancient habitation. They combed eroded beach banks and river mouths, where the people of old might have settled, for telltale traces of buried artifacts. There was simply nothing: no hint, no clue, not a single coral file or unfinished bone fishhook. It was hard not to be discouraged.

"They don't have squid lures, *ulumaika*s [bowling stones], or hammer stones with grip marks, or pointed sling stones, which are of some help in Hawaii," Kenneth wrote to Marion Kelly after ten frustrating days. "We are going to go after burial caves, and that is a slow, tough business. The brush here is clogged with lantana and *aeho* grass, and after 10 A.M. it is insufferably hot. My hope is that some of these burial caves have a floor of some depth and that they will go back a long way in time."

The social side of their visit helped keep Kenneth going. "I get along famously with the Tahitians," he wrote. There were hotel floorshows to see. One night the dancers used bamboo torches, which set fire to the headdresses of two *wahine*s (women). The Danielssons entertained him and Yosi. Bengt had a little pig ready to roast for Marguerite's arrival. An auto dealer rented them a brand new Citroen for driving into town. Kenneth lectured to the Papeete Rotary Club.

But the sites Kenneth had been so confident of finding eluded them. In May they heard about a secret collection of artifacts on the other end of the island at Taravao. "We arrived at a nice little house overlooking the deeply indented lagoon there," Kenneth wrote. "The collector was a Monsieur [Henri] Picard, age 54, a pleasant half-cast staying with his brother. . . . Laid out on the floor were hundreds of stones . . . and at one end of the house boxes and boxes piled up, filled to the hilt. We quickly found that among the huge accumulation were many fine and remarkable specimens."

If they could not dig artifacts out of the ground at least here was a chance to buy them. Roger Green arrived to work on nearby

Moorea. He had completed a successful dig on Mangareva where he found that all fishhooks were manufactured from mother-of-pearl. They were filed into shape with odd pieces of dyke rock and whatever sections of branch coral came to hand. That could explained why the Tahitians did not leave behind the distinctively shaped files so common in Hawaii.

Kenneth, as usual, refused to be discouraged. He wrote home, "The very fact that files for shaping hooks are not lying about is significant." Now he and Yosi knew they must look for pieces of pearl-shell hooks. The natural place to search would be behind passes in the reef where fishermen would store their canoes and manufacture fishhooks. This idea produced no better results than before. Three weeks passed. They hadn't found a hint of ancient habitation.

Meanwhile diplomatic relations remained sensitive. Roger Green's entire collection of artifacts from Mangareva for the American Museum of Natural History might have been impounded at the Papeete Museum if Bengt had not stroked ruffled feathers. In a letter home, Kenneth blamed "the manner in which the expedition was set on foot." He added, "I only wish the spirit of cooperation which exists between Green and me existed between Harry Shapiro [chairman of anthropology at the American Museum of Natural History] and me." To avoid a similar disaster, Kenneth had already donated Bishop Museum artifacts to the Papeete Museum.

Collector Picard offered a ray of hope by telling Kenneth the location of burial caves from which he had taken stones. Picard had also found two large adz workshops on Raiatea. Kenneth asked Spoehr's permission to offer $1,650 for the collection of 1,250 artifacts.

Marguerite arrived and a round of reunions began. Poor Yosi, who did not understand French or Tahitian, had to sit through hours of animated chitchat about marriages and divorces and births and deaths and nieces and nephews and considered opinions about new houses and old flames. Worse still, when he was at home with the Emorys Marguerite took full advantage of his obligatory attention because Kenneth didn't listen.

Kenneth wrote home on May 17, "Marguerite is in her element. At the Pearson party the night before, four Frenchmen got going on politics and Yosi just burst out laughing. When asked why, he said this was the first time Mrs. Emory could not get a word in edgewise since her arrival in Tahiti." But it wasn't all boring for Yosi. During a party in the bosom of Marguerite's extended family her nieces gave him a hour's lesson in Tahitian dancing. "He is doing fine," Kenneth wrote.

He and Yosi expanded their search into the valleys. On April 22 they found a promising shelter located on the outskirts of Papeete on Taharaa Hill. Negotiations for permission to dig began, Kenneth's job. When Henri Picard saw the shelter he took Kenneth to a shelter he remembered at Tautira. There Kenneth found a grooved grind stone, a pounder, and a nice hammer stone. Then news came of another shelter in the rugged cliff coastline beyond Tautira.

The strenuous pace told on Kenneth. He was, after all, sixty-two years old. On May 6, he wrote in his diary, "Slight dizzy spell again." The next day, "Little dizzy when I woke." The day after, "Dizzy and nauseated." He slowed down for a few days, then dickered for the Picard collection and caught a cold. On Saturday, June 4, they began digging at Taharaa Hill. On Sunday, Kenneth wrote, "Down four feet. Nothing." On Monday, "Dug to seven feet, three inches. Nothing but human bones."

Kenneth wrote home, "We determined for certain that what would have been an ideal shelter in Hawaii was not used in Tahiti, probably because vegetation offered abundant shade . . . and material for shelter." The first inhabitatants must have camped on the coastal plain. By this time those sites might be covered over by coconut plantations or beach estates. In desperation, Kenneth followed a bulldozer on a construction site to see if artifacts turned up.

The French archaeologist Pierre Verin made his appearance. He was a rather soft-looking young man who had worked in Madagascar. He seemed eager and competent. Kenneth took him on an official round of visits, then they all went by canoe to the back side of Tahiti where they dug in another shelter. They found nothing, although bananas, breadfruit, and taro grew luxuriously outside the cave.

Discouraged, Kenneth sent Verin with Yosi to prospect Moorea. Yosi came back with an enthusiastic report. He said he was riding his bicycle past a drainage ditch on July 1. A gleam caught his eye. When he went back he found a pearl-shell fishhook. He widened his search and found pieces of broken hooks. The place was called Maatea. Yosi wanted to dig there.

On July 7 Kenneth went to Moorea to see for himself. Yosi met him and proudly showed his site. The next day Kenneth bicycled around the island and spent the night with Med Kellum. Roger Green took Kenneth on a tour of his own sites in Kellum's valley. "He has done a remarkable job of locating, clearing, mapping structures and [has] made very significant discoveries," Kenneth wrote.

By the time he returned to Tahiti his voice had almost given out. A doctor told him to stay in bed and rest his throat. Pierre Verin went to prospect on Raiatea. Yosi was busy on Moorea. Kenneth had a bad case of diarrhea and had to stay behind. His throat was no better. "Desperately discouraged," he wrote on July 18. With no telephone communication he was out of touch with the expedition. Then his optimism surfaced again. This was a good chance to rest, get his throat in shape, clean up the correspondence, go over accounts, and plan their next moves.

Yosi and Verin set off for another look at Raiatea. Kenneth and Aurora took Marguerite to Bora-Bora for her return flight on July 28 to Honolulu. Then Aurora's relatives took in Aurora and Kenneth as well. Among the Tahitians, he was Keneti again. In spite of a cold, he went exploring: *maraes, motus,* and backyards full of sandcrab holes. "Tired and sad, throat coarse," he wrote in his diary on August 4.

His mood picked up when he flew to Raiatea to check in with his expedition. Yosi, it turned out, was on nearby Tahaa. Kenneth rented a speed boat and caught up with his tireless assistant. Yosi had found the best fishhook yet. During their half-hour's visit he assured Kenneth that Tahaa showed excellent promise. Kenneth returned to Raiatea on August 8 to await the Bermuda flying boat enroute to Tahiti. The plane was overbooked and Kenneth got left behind in spite of reservations made three weeks in advance. The pilot promised to pick him up the next day.

That afternoon Kenneth wandered out on a sandy point beyond Uturoa, the capital of the island. There he found a prehistoric fishhook factory. "In the hour before sunset, we assembled a nice little collection of hooks and blanks and files. It seemed like old times again," he wrote with rekindled vigor.

The next morning, although the airplane was due in a few hours, he hired a canoe with an outboard motor for a quick trip to two islets flanking the pass. The starting cord broke before the engine got going. Then the outboard engine stopped on the way because of dirt in the gas line. But one of the islets repaid Kenneth for the inconvenience. In twenty minutes ashore he filled a paper sack with spalls (adz fragments), adz blanks, several broken adzes, and a complete adz. The entire islet had been a workshop for an adz maker. The outboard motor stopped again on the last mile back. Kenneth arrived at the plane with a scant five minutes to spare and his self-confidence immeasurably restored.

Now he knew they were on the right track. A fruitless visit to tiny Maupiti didn't discourage him. The sites were there. But his time had expired. They would have to go back. In a letter of thanks to Bertrand Juanez and his wife, Kenneth wrote:

> At the end of these five months we are just beginning to get good results. . . . We have completely circled Moorea, Raiatea, Tahaa, Mau-

piti, Bora Bora, each island twice. In our prospecting we have come across numerous *maraes* unknown to us before, many excellent ones, imposing and in a good state of preservation. . . . In time and by luck and accident we are bound to stumble onto rich spots. . . . But oh it is slow compared with the several rich strikes we were lucky enough to have [made] in Hawaii and with the Mangareva site worked by Roger Green.

Kenneth could only tell reporters when he landed at Honolulu on September 14, 1960, that "Fishhooks and adzes are the clues. We found exactly what we had hoped. But we stumbled upon it at the last minute. . . . It will take another expedition to unfold the whole story." Yosi headed for Japan and work on a doctorate. Spoehr titled his own annual report for the museum that year, *Work Half Done.* Kenneth felt the same way. He had made only a start in Tahiti. But another expedition would take funding.

In any event he would wait until Yosi returned. News from Japan made him furious. The Imperial University of Tokyo had rejected Yosi's application for study because he was too young at thirty-five to be a doctor of anthropology. But the University of Hokkaido accepted him.

There was another reason why Kenneth did not feel pressed to return to Tahiti in 1961. The Pacific Science Congress would meet in Honolulu for the first time since 1920 when Kenneth had been its errand boy. He couldn't be away for an event like that. Both Kenneth and Spoehr recognized an opportunity to assume leadership for archaeology in the Pacific.

An irritation in his throat nagged at him. He had surgery in February and felt better. "Dr. Wright said no trace of cancer in spot removed," he wrote in his diary on February 11, 1961. "Also examined throat well, nothing serious to worry about. Very happy."

He put together a slide lecture on Tahiti for the Bishop Museum Association and Marguerite left for California to visit their first grandson. On May 17 Yosi returned and, a month later, set off for Tahiti by himself to dig on Moorea. Kenneth put together a paper on language for the congress.

The congress met in August and the press made a lot about the opposing theories of Norway's Thor Heyerdahl and Hawaii's Kenneth Emory on the origin of the Polynesians. A confrontation between the two men never came off. Kenneth and Heyerdahl appeared together on a radio show but did not lock horns. Instead they agreed to disagree about where the Polynesians came from; Heyerdahl insisting they approached the islands from the east, Emory equally sure they came from the west.

To honor the memory of Gregory, the Bishop Museum established a Herbert E. Gregory medal to be awarded for distinguished service to science in the Pacific. The first winner was A. P. Elkin, professor emeritus of anthropology at the University of Sydney, for his research in Melanesia and Australia.

Kenneth spent a lot of his time meeting with a committee called to organize archaeological research in the Pacific. Quite a few people were in the field already, including Roger Green for the University of Auckland in New Zealand, Roger Duff as director of the Canterbury Museum in Christchurch, Heyerdahl's *Kon Tiki* Museum in Norway, Kenneth Emory and Yosi Sinoto for the Bishop Museum, and Pierre Verin for the Papeete Museum. It would be better if they didn't compete and overlap.

The committee hammered out a resolution, which the congress passed, calling for a coordinated plan for archaeological research. Sites were to be pinpointed in Polynesia, Micronesia, and Melanesia, funds were to be solicited for digging, and the work was to be divided among interested institutions.

About the same time Spoehr introduced Kenneth to an official of the National Science Foundation, now the largest source of scientific funding in the country. The man was very interested in Kenneth's digs. By the time the congress closed and the last delegate was taken to the airport, Kenneth was exhausted. But the next day he and Marion Kelly went to work on a proposal to the National Science Foundation for a five-year archaeological program in Polynesia. "All our effort is on preparing proposal," he wrote in his diary on September 18.

A month later, Spoehr resigned from his post at the Bishop Museum to become chancellor of the recently established East-West Center at the University of Hawaii. The trustees of Bishop Museum announced a new director, Dr. Roland Force of the Chicago Natural History Museum. He was an anthropologist with another degree in education. Articulate, poised, and handsome, Force had worked widely in the Pacific.

Marion Kelly and Yosi later recalled their nervousness about the request for grant funds. "It takes about six months to get an answer. It was very exciting," said Yosi. They didn't have to wait six months. On December 14, Kenneth scribbled in his diary, "News came of National Science Foundation grant! They are giving the entire $79,000." The grant was for three years and named Bishop Museum as the administrative institution and Kenneth the principal investigator. Now he was ready to go back to Tahiti.

Chapter Forty-three

The Great Discovery

Kenneth never contradicted critics who complained that he didn't write enough. His friends were the most insistent. "You have so much knowledge in your head," they said over and over. "If you don't put it down, it will be lost." What most of them meant was that he did not write like he talked.

Kenneth enjoyed conversation as an adventure. Drawing from a lifetime of bold undertakings his mind could leap from one idea to another in free association to both entertain as well as instruct. Writing was work for a faceless, unforgiving multitude; an obligation to the scientists of the future. It permitted no margin for error and no room for humor. This may be why so much of his time went into preparing lectures and slide shows before live audiences. As his reputation grew and people listened with increasing attention, Kenneth tended to talk more and write less.

Yet every now and again he was taken by the urge to put it down on paper. Then he would resolutely sweep away distractions and put himself on a schedule that lasted as long as most people stay on diets. Such an urge came over him after the Science Congress. He would write the epic story of the origin of the Hawaiians. To accomplish this he set aside two morning hours to devote to writing in his new private office.

This spartan regime coincided early in 1962 with the phasing out of his university classes because, in November, he would reach the teaching retirement age of 65. Kenneth pecked away with four fingers on his typewriter through January and February. Yet the distractions did not go away. On February 22, Yosi's father called with the news that his son had received his doctorate of science. That day Yosi was returning from Maui. Kenneth raced out to buy a big red carnation lei. He drove Kazuko to the airport and they surprised Yosi with the news.

Kenneth came down with the flu. Then he had to help entertain members of the legislature at the museum in a bid for appropriations. In March he made a trip to Hawaii for a ceremony at the new City of Refuge National Park. He worked furiously on his paper about origins, while his energetic assistant constructed four large boxes in which to ship their equipment and supplies for the next Tahiti expedition. Yosi built shelves and drawers in the boxes so they could be used as cabinets in the field. Kenneth stashed a supply of chocolate bars in with the trowels and sifting screens.

The boxes, painted bright orange for easy identification, went south in a steamer while Kenneth pounded on the typewriter. On April 26 he finished the manuscript on Hawaiian origins. Three weeks later, on May 16, 1962, museum director Force shook his hand at the airport and he boarded a jetliner to join Yosi in Tahiti.

There the precious boxes had disappeared somewhere between the airplane and the customs office. Tracing the boxes required a lot of diplomatic negotiation, which went nowhere until Yosi spotted a customs official sitting on one of the boxes at the warehouse while he scribbled at a desk. With this clue they found the other boxes. The boxes then had to be opened, at which point the customs officials found Kenneth's contraband chocolate bars on which no duty had been paid. More diplomatic negotiations followed in both French and Tahitian before the boxes cleared customs.

Kenneth's plan was to dig at several likely spots that were discovered in 1960. But they had hardly finished unpacking when a more exciting discovery walked in off the street. Or rather the discovery met Yosi walking down Pomare Boulevard in Papeete. He was out for an evening stroll on May 20 when a voice called, "Tapone," which is Tahitian for "Japan," Yosi being one of the rare Japanese on the island. He turned and found a man named Bruno Schmidt hurrying after him.

Yosi had met the man in 1960 on tiny Maupiti Island where Schmidt was then engaged as a paramedic in charge of the dispensary, there being no medical doctor on the island. Schmidt had displayed interest in prehistory and the museum's search for ancient artifacts. Now, it turned out, he was on assignment to Mangareva and was waiting at a relative's house for the boat.

Schmidt insisted that Yosi come and look at some objects he had brought from Maupiti. The strange artifacts were packed away in his trunk. Yosi trotted obligingly along. Schmidt explained that the objects had been dug up by a man who was planting watermelons on a *motu* (small island) on the reef. It turned out that large watermelons were commanding more than $20 apiece in the market at Papeete, so watermelon planting had become the rage at Maupiti. However there was no soil on the *motu*. The watermelon planter had to dig holes in the sand and fill them with dirt brought from the main island. He was digging such a hole when he struck a human skull and other objects unrecognizable to him. Since he had no use for the objects, he gave them to Schmidt.

In the dim light of a kerosene lantern, Schmidt laid his treasures out on a wooden table. "That was one of the really exciting moments of my life," Yosi said later. "I could hardly believe it. There were two adzes of the old, archaic form. With them was a whale tooth pendant which was known only from the early Maori culture. At that time this pendant was known only from New Zealand. Here there are two of them from Tahiti."

Yosi hurried to tell Kenneth. They both knew that the early Maoris placed offerings of such objects in their burials. These artifacts could be proof of Peter Buck's theory and the Maori legend that the Maoris began their voyages of migration from the great *marae* of Taputapuatea at Opoa, Raiatea. Kenneth went with Yosi to Schmidt's house on May 22 to see for himself. No doubt about it, they had discovered artifacts never found before in Tahiti.

"Dr. Emory, I must go to Maupiti right away," Yosi insisted.

About two weeks later Kenneth sent Yosi to Maupiti, along with Aurora Natua to act as an interpreter. They picked up Tihoti Russell, Yosi's assistant, on Raiatea. When they returned to Papeete on June 19 they had an amazing tale that rivaled Kenneth's own adventures in 1926. Yosi said they boarded the boat that sailed once every two weeks to Maupiti, found the *motu*, and, after a false start, located the burial that was to become a watermelon patch. With permission from the watermelon grower, Yosi excavated the rest of the skeleton. On the chest he found more adzes of the early type, more whale-tooth pendants, and some bonito hooks. It was Yosi's first big discovery. He wrote in his diary on June 16, 1962, with understandable enthusiasm, "This is the greatest day of archaeological study in the Society Islands."

Then disaster struck. It turned out that the watermelon grower didn't own the land. He was merely the son of the landowner who took a decidedly negative view of strangers who made off with valuable objects found on his property. This happened the night before the boat was to return to Bora-Bora. Unless Yosi could bring back the artifacts as proof, who would believe he had set archaeology in Tahiti on a new course?

To give himself time he negotiated with the captain of the boat for a longer stay. The captain demanded 300 francs per day to remain on Maupiti. At 88 francs per dollar, this came to $3.45 in U.S. currency. "What?" said Yosi, surprised that the figure was so low. The captain, assuming that he had overreached himself, came down to $2.45 per day. Yosi accepted gratefully.

The next morning negotiations began with four or five elderly relatives of the watermelon grower in a shack near the jetty. Aurora and Tihoti acted as interpreters. The elders said they could not allow Yosi to take the artifacts away because he would sell them to make money. He explained their importance to the history of the island and assured the elders that his wish was to preserve the artifacts for study by future scholars in the museum at Papeete. If the artifacts remained on Maupiti, they would be sold by younger members of the family to tourists and, therefore, lost to Polynesia.

"They are our artifacts," said the spokesman. "If they stay in the Papeete Museum, we will have to pay to see them."

"You will not pay," Yosi countered. "I will bring a free pass for every member of your family."

The elders finally agreed to let Yosi take the artifacts to Papeete on loan. Then he, Aurora, and Tihoti boarded the boat and sailed to Bora-Bora where a gendarme met them at the pier and escorted them to the police station as suspects in a theft on Raiatea. Yosi couldn't believe it. Nevertheless, he had to admit that they had stayed with a Tahitian family in Raiatea enroute to Maupiti from Papeete. It turned out money was missing from this house. The gendarmes suspected Tihoti Russell, Yosi's assistant on Raiatea, of the theft. They searched his duffel bag.

Aurora flew into an indignant rage. Yosi refused to give permission to have his luggage searched. The situation had become sticky when the Bermuda flying boat from Raiatea arrived. A daughter of the family who had been robbed walked off the plane. The gendarmes questioned her and received answers different from those she had given to police on Raiatea. Under more questioning she confessed that she had stolen the money to get away from her father.

The next day Yosi's wife and son, Kazuko and little Aki, arrived to join him. Kenneth accompanied them with a mountain of luggage to Moorea where he saw them comfortably settled in a one-room, thatched Tahitian house on the beach five minutes from the dig. Then he returned to Papeete. A chicken promptly selected Yosi's bed as her nest. She laid a very fresh egg there every morning. Kazuko pressed their clothes with a charcoal flatiron. Aki raised a pet pig. Their only concession to technology was a small kerosene refrigerator. When Kenneth and Aurora came to visit, there was hardly room in the house to take a deep breath.

The dig produced more pieces to the puzzle Kenneth had spent his lifetime fitting together. Yosi found the first articulated, or complete, dog skeleton from prehistoric Tahiti, at last providing an opportunity to study an animal the Polynesians had carried on their migrations. The dog skeleton was found with human bones under the cornerstone of a *marae* close to what Yosi determined to be a small fishing village, supporting a tradition that human sacrifices were placed beneath the foundations of temples. Yosi also found fishhooks, which expanded the usefulness of the work already done with hooks in Hawaii.

On July 7, 1962, while Yosi dug up Tahiti's past on Moorea, Kenneth flew back to Hawaii for a three-week stay. There he discovered that director Force had proclaimed a new edict requiring staff members, including department heads, to clear all decisions through the head office. There was considerable grumbling about this because, under Spoehr, staffers had received assignments then completed them their own way. Spoehr had kept in touch with work in progress by eating his brown-bag lunch with everybody else under the *hau* tree in the courtyard. Force, on the other hand, believed in receiving memorandums to keep him informed of what was happening in the departments. A daily blizzard of memorandums had to be approved or rejected before work could proceed.

The first thing Kenneth did on arrival was write a memo asking permission to tell a reporter from the *New York Times* about the discoveries in Tahiti. He told the press that the artifacts found on Maupiti were unmistakable proof that the ancestors of New Zealand's Maoris came from the Society Islands. Kenneth added that the find of early Tahitian artifacts also had significant implications for Hawaii. He stated: "It indicates that Hawaii did not share in this early phase of Tahiti, but a later phase of it," he said. The earliest people in Hawaii used fishhooks and ornaments more closely resembling those found in the early phases of Marquesan settlement. It was not until the 11th or 12th century that fishhook forms in Hawaii merged with those then in use in Tahiti." He said this may have been the time Tahitian chiefs arrived in Hawaii. According to the evidence, "Hawaiian culture, then, would have a multiple origin . . . the first settlers coming from the Marquesas; later settlers coming from Tahiti."

Meanwhile Kenneth led another expedition into Haleakala Crater for the National Park Service. "Dug three squares at Bubble Cave," he wrote in his diary on Wednesday, July 18. On July 20, "Up to summit one. Dug fire place." On July 21, "Hiked up out of the crater in less than two hours." Marion Kelly, who went along, described later what it was like tramping with her 69-year-old boss in the wilderness at an elevation of ten thousand feet:

We walked and walked to find the Pililani Highway [which Kenneth remembered from 1920] . . . From there we walked [halfway across the crater] to Holua Cabin and met the State Fish & Game people who were fencing in an area for a shipment of *nene* [a nearly extinct species of Hawaiian goose] which were arriving the next week from a private zoo in England. Then it took us two hours—we'd been up since 3:30—to hike that switchback trail. And that's a day in the field with Kenneth.

The expedition gave him solid satisfaction for a number of reasons. "Certain odd platforms I had tentatively identified as shrines [in 1920] I could now positively say were such," he wrote later. "A cliff shelter which offered protection against sun, rain, snow yielded from the bottom of its floor deposit charcoal which gave a radiocarbon date of A.D. 800 indicating that, as early as this, Maui was inhabited. This shelter was adjacent to the only spring for miles which explains its constant use."

His mission in Hawaii accomplished, Kenneth boarded a plane on August 1, 1962, for Papeete where his routine of island hopping continued: Moorea to check on Yosi's dig, Bora-Bora for a survey of *marae*s, and Raiatea to make final preparations for excavation at Taputapuatea. He helped Yosi close his dig at Afareaitu on August 20, and they all shifted location to Raiatea.

It was there that Yosi in 1960 had discovered Tihoti Russell, a skinny, hard-drinking, fun-loving part-Tahitian with a knack for finding artifacts. Tihoti had brought around a batch of pearl-shell fishhooks he picked up by an old native well near the great *marae*. Now Kenneth intended to excavate in the well area and to restore the famous temple itself, the place Peter Buck had considered his ancestral home.

There was no road from Uturoa, the drowsy capital of Raiatea, to the district of Opoa where Marae Taputapuatea stood crumbling in silent mystery. The whole party went by boat inside the reef along a shore guarded by tropical mountains. Kenneth installed Yosi and his family in a cottage on the lagoon, then returned to Papeete to come back later for a longer stay.

Yosi hired workers and began to dig. He found nothing of interest around the well, but restoration of the great *marae* revealed that it had been built upon a smaller one. And his tireless exploration of the overgrown temple area uncovered a whole complex of ruins of which the great *marae* was only one. He found smaller temples, an archery platform, and a chief's council platform. Near the council platform he excavated a refuse pit in which he dug up many burned and chewed pig, dog, and human bones. The remains indicated that some of the ancient Tahitians had eaten human flesh. Similar platforms had been found in the Marquesas and Kenneth had recorded one at Huahine and another in the Tuamotus.

August passed into September. The team broke camp at Opoa. Their next stop was Maupiti via Bora-Bora. The flying boat that carried passengers to Bora-Bora kept to a reasonably dependable schedule. But the little motor launch that put-putted once every two weeks from Bora-Bora to Maupiti made no such claims. "We were in a state of complete uncertainty until 12 [noon] when *Manuia* showed up," Kenneth wrote in his diary on Friday, September 21. The expedition piled its baggage on deck with the baskets and mats of Tahitian passengers, and off they went.

The first order of business on Maupiti was negotiation with family elders of the watermelon planter for disposition of the artifacts to be discovered. Kenneth wrote in his diary, "The whole day [spent] bringing the owners of the land before the *tavana* [village chief]. They finally agreed to give the things to the Papeete Museum." Yosi handed out the free passes he had promised. The agreement became the primary accomplishment of their whirlwind tour of Maupiti.

Yosi also found another burial, without offerings, from a later period. Tihoti combed the island for artifacts and Kenneth developed a boil on his backside, which made sitting down a purgatory. Pricking it started an infection. He returned to Papeete an invalid. The doctor gave him a shot of penicillin, assumed a grave expression, and hoped he would not have to operate. During this tribulation Aurora received word from the Papeete Museum that her appointment was not to be renewed.

The boil healed in time for Kenneth to sit down all the way back to Honolulu on October 19, 1962, while Yosi returned by way of Samoa. Kenneth worried about how to keep the indispensable Aurora afloat. To make matters worse Marguerite had gone off to visit Tiare, who was working in Virginia, so Kenneth rattled around alone at home. Kazuko came over sometimes to cook dinner.

However, the rapid flow of events left Kenneth little time to feel sorry for himself. Yosi returned from prospecting in American Samoa. He reported that New Zealand archaeologists were doing such a fine job in Western Samoa that there was no need for Bishop Museum to compete in the same archipelago. He suggested the money be spent on excavating in the Marquesas.

About the same time a letter arrived from the Gakushuin University Radiocarbon Dating Laboratory in Tokyo supporting the A.D. 124 date for occupation of South Point on the island of Hawaii. On December 3, Kenneth told members of the Social Science Association what that probably meant: "We are bracing ourselves now for dates that will push the time of man in Polynesia further and further back," he said. "They [Gakushuin University] have just given us a reading on pieces of charcoal which we took from a hearth at South

Point. It dates 2250 years before present, which would extend the occupation of South Point back to 288 B.C. . . . Lest we become unjustifiably excited about these early South Point dates, let us caution ourselves with the fact that we are getting some erratic results in the eleven radiocarbon dates so far run on the site."

Early in 1963 Kenneth found a way to keep Aurora on at the Papeete Museum. The friends he had accumulated in Tahiti included a couple of sophisticated New England beachcombers from Windmill Hill in Putney, Vermont, Edward H. Dodd and his wife, Camille. When the rigors of his publishing house, Dodd, Mead & Company of New York, became too much for him, Ed Dodd escaped to the South Seas. His discovery of Keneti, by now a legend in the Pacific, delighted him and led to correspondence.

Kenneth kept Dodd, a knowledgeable anthropology buff, abreast of his lastest discoveries. The impending loss of the indispensable Aurora Natua, all because of the lack of money to pay her miniscule salary, naturally came up. Dodd insisted he be allowed to help because it was exactly the kind of personal and effective giving he preferred. So began an annual anonymous contribution of $1,000, which subsidized Aurora's labors for Bishop Museum.

The same thing had happened before. A federal judge's wife in Honolulu, Francesca Wiig, had paid the first year of Marion Kelly's salary so that Kenneth could have a full-time secretary, then had quietly continued to support other projects for which there was no money. A businessman, Atherton Richards, donated anonymously to the anthropology department. In both Hawaii and Tahiti Kenneth constantly benefited from free transportation, housing, supplies, and information. Like Dodd, people helped Kenneth because it was fun and exciting and it made them feel useful.

By this time a return to Maupiti had become the goal of both Kenneth and Yosi. They would remain for at least a month, enough time to do test digs and a controlled excavation. On May 17, 1963, at 2:30 A.M., they embarked again at Bora-Bora for the most remote island in the Tahitian chain. Once more they found themselves on board the *Manuia*, an old and weatherbeaten motor launch about thirty-five feet long. Everyone stayed on deck because the entire space below was reserved for the engine and cargo: supplies for Maupiti going out and sacks of copra and watermelons coming back.

The passage had lost none of its excitement since the first time Kenneth made it in 1926. Most of the passengers got seasick. When the *Manuia* wallowed into the Maupiti Pass at 7:30 A.M., the current was boiling out. The captain circled a few times before attempting the dangerous passage through the reef.

Kenneth calmly sat through the ordeal. Yosi recalled later that a crew member leaned with all his strength on a steering oar to help the captain at the wheel hold the *Manuia* against the powerful current. The crewman leaned so hard the steering oar broke. Yosi, who was sitting on the rail, watched the reef slide by the hull with only a foot or two to spare.

A village, divided into Mormon and Protestant sections, straggled along the shore inside the reef. Kenneth found lodging with one family, Yosi with another. Maupiti, with a population of about 350, was still innocent of policemen and automobiles. The supply of beer usually ran out before the next arrival of the *Manuia* replenished it. Yosi paid his workers in *pareu* cloth and the latest Japanese rotating fishhooks, unavailable even in Papeete.

He launched his test digs on the *motu* while Kenneth looked after the diplomatic end of the expedition and checked out *maraes*. This time Yosi dug exploratory trenches radiating from the burial already discovered. Before the first day ended he had found adzes, and the next day he found fishhooks. They spent a week systematically probing in the palm grove.

On Monday, May 27, they hit a whale-tooth pendant, and on May 28 the burial of a short-statured male, probably a chief because of the pearl-shell ornament resting on his chest. Adzes and pearl-shell scrapers nestled near the skeleton. Kenneth helped take measurements of the bones, which then were reburied. The trenches turned up one burial after another, fifteen in all, with artifacts that firmly established the link between Tahiti and New Zealand.

This confirmation of the old legends made the whole year's work worthwhile. But it was not accomplished without a more painful lesson in the history of Maupiti. The inelegant *Manuia* was scheduled to arrive on Friday, May 23, 1963, with fifty-two Mormons returning from the dedication of a new church on Huahine. Kenneth and Yosi were having breakfast in front of Mahuta's house at 7:30 A.M. when the overloaded vessel appeared off the reef. A few minutes later someone beat frantically on a bicycle rim that hung from a tree in the village and served as a call to summon the people.

Kenneth and Yosi hurried to the village center where they saw that the *Manuia* had capsized in the pass. They watched helpless as people launched canoes and ran to an islet off the pass. Yosi grabbed his camera and went along. He shot a photo of the little vessel bottom up on the reef. Survivors clung to wreckage as the current swept them to sea. Others, trying to swim over the jagged reef, were being gashed on the coral. Someone brought an axe and chopped through the hull of the *Manuia* to release bleeding survivors trapped underneath.

Kenneth and Yosi wanted to help. But what could they do? The nurse who ran Maupiti's tiny dispensary had been on board the wrecked boat. Yosi ran for the little medical kit he had packed with the museum supplies. He and Kenneth bandaged coral cuts. Some of the wounded badly needed expert medical attention. But no one except the nurse knew how to operate the radio. Yosi found a teen-age boy who had watched the nurse make her daily noon broadcasts. The boy sent out a call for an airplane to search the ocean for survivors. Several hours later they heard the sound of an engine. Two days later a French warship arrived to take the wounded on board. Yosi's photograph of the capsized *Manuia* appeared in a Papeete newspaper.

Fifteen people drowned in the disaster. With no facilities for embalming, the bodies were buried next day. In the Mormon section of the village, nearly every house was in mourning. Families dug the graves in their front yards. "It was a terrible sight," Yosi recalled later. Kenneth and Yosi went from house to house attending each funeral and recording the *himenes* (hymns).

The burial of the dead did not end the impact of the disaster. People on Maupiti depended heavily on food brought by the supply vessel. Everybody ran out of rice and sugar. Nobody had cigarettes to smoke. Because of the food shortage Yosi had to let his workers off early every day to catch fish. Divers went down in the pass to bring up the *Manuia*'s cargo: canned goods, tools, household items, and so forth. The divers also found more than one hundred archaic adzes, proof that the canoes of the ancients had also capsized in the dangerous pass.

Kenneth and Yosi began the job of measuring, recording, and photographing the adzes. It was a treasure of artifacts that must be preserved. Negotiations with the village *tavana* (chief) were underway when an old woman, who had lost a son-in-law and a grandson in the *Manuia* disaster, dreamed that the adzes must be returned to the pass, otherwise the village would suffer more bad luck. The next day another woman reported having the same dream. Not to be outdone, old women all over the village dreamed about adzes and bad luck.

The *tavana*, recognizing the force of public opinion, ruled that the adzes must be thrown back. "Yosi and I went to see [the] people who had [the] dream," Kenneth wrote in his diary on June 6. It didn't help. The adzes were dumped back into the pass. Yosi said, "I know what happened later, not right away, those boys [divers] went back [to the pass] and took the adzes and started selling them to tourists. Probably all gone now. We have only the records and the photographs."

Kenneth turned his attention next to his favorite Tahitian island,

Bora-Bora. A Honolulu newspaperman found him there in October, pedaling his bicycle along a dirt road outside Vaitape, the principal village. In view of his grey hair and hawk face, people on the island called him "The Old One." Yosi had gone to scout sites in the Marquesas. The reporter wrote:

> His [Kenneth's] headquarters are a tiny room in a thatched house. His chief assistant is an intelligent, small, wiry woman named Tetua, friend of James Michener during World War II. . . . The luxurious Bora Bora Hotel, five miles from the village, has made little change in the way of life here. The 1,800 inhabitants of the island drive fifteen cars, attend one movie theater, support three schools and spend most of their time farming or fishing.
>
> As usual, I found Emory hard at work reconstructing the past. And on this most dramatically beautiful of all the South Sea islands he is making startling progress. During the past three months, using funds he'd scrounged from all sorts of people, Emory and his gang of industrious Polynesian helpers have restored nearly half a dozen *maraes* on the island. It's the first time any such work has been attempted on Bora Bora."

A clue as to where Kenneth got the money appeared in his diary on July 11 during a quick trip back to Honolulu, "Francesca [Wiig] is giving $4,000." From August to October, the diary details the restoration of *maraes;* clearing away undergrowth and resetting fallen slabs of limestone.

"Started clearing Marae Taianapa," he wrote on Thursday, September 18, 1963. On September 24, "With pulleys we erected two fallen slabs, straightened three leaning over." On September 30, "Seven men on Taianapa till 6 P.M. Erected four slabs." On October 3, "Seven men on Taianapa again. Cemented first [broken] slab. Put up about five back slabs. Removed tree . . ." On October 8, "To Taianapa P.M. Grand work. Only two front slabs and five or six [in] back to put up." Workmen mended the last slab of this temple on October 19. Kenneth put up a sign and proudly conducted tours for visitors. He felt as if he had in a small way repaid the Tahitians for the secrets their islands had divulged to him.

The successful and satisfying Tahiti expedition ended on October 26 when Kenneth returned to Honolulu on a South Pacific Airlines jet to prepare for a meeting of the American Anthropological Association in San Francisco. More good news arrived when Yosi returned from the Marquesas. With the luck and persistence and keen observation that had paid off so often for Kenneth, Yosi had stumbled upon a promising site that resembled the pivotal South Point dig.

The site was located at a place called Uahuka, where the tidal wave of 1960, associated with the earthquake in Chile, had washed artifacts out of a sand dune. Yosi was in a fever to begin digging. But San Francisco came first.

Kenneth and Yosi, along with Marion Kelly, prepared Kenneth's slide lecture for the November conference. They all remembered it later as a triumph. "It was the first time scientists heard about our discoveries in Tahiti," said Kelly. The lecture, a detailed review of his archaeological discoveries, was a highlight of the meeting and the crowning achievement of his long career.

Kenneth put to rest any doubt that the early people of Tahiti, the Marquesas, the Tuamotus, and Easter Island came from a culture different from that of Polynesians of the west—Samoa and Tonga. It was from Samoa and Tonga that Tahiti and the Marquesas were settled, he said.

As for Thor Heyerdahl's theory that Polynesia was first peopled from the Americas, he termed it "zealous excess" that should not prejudice researchers against a continued search for such influences. Kenneth said occupants of a raft from Peru could have reached Easter Island and possibly exerted an influence there. The South American sweet potato is established at Easter Island and found its way to distant Hawaii and New Zealand. Yet the culture on these islands is overwhelmingly Polynesian.

Kenneth said the newly discovered burials on Maupiti established the link between Tahiti and New Zealand, and at the same time indicated that Hawaii was first settled from the Marquesas. Kenneth ticked off the evidence like clues in a mystery novel: fishhooks, whale-tooth necklaces, tattooing needles, octopus lure sinkers, and adzes from sites on all the islands and all established in time. Kenneth concluded with a revised timetable of migrations. He told his audience, "It would seem that this was the primary settlement pattern of East Polynesia: (1) From West Polynesia [Tonga and Samoa] to the Marquesas, (2) then to Tahiti, (3) then to Easter Island, (4) then to Hawaii from the Marquesas, (5) then to New Zealand from Tahiti, and finally (6) to Hawaii from Tahiti."

In those brief words he summed what he had come to call the Polynesian quest, which began in 1920 when he caught fire at the first Pacific Scientific Congress. He had been on the trail for forty-three years. The mystery had led him to islands and atolls where no anthropologist had been before. No one knew the elusive Polynesians better than he: their gods, their language, their dances, their chants, their tools, their architecture, their medicine, their ships, their dress, their food, the warmth of their hospitality and the social complexities it entailed. He had fit more pieces of the puzzle together than any scientist before him. To Kenneth, nothing meant more or had cost him so much. Yet this landmark paper, like all his others, was as dry and unemotional as a treasurer's report.

At the banquet that ended the conference, Margaret Mead invited Kenneth and Marquerite to sit at her table. Director Force was impressed. He said later, "Margaret Mead was a master at emasculating male anthropologists. But she always was solicitous of Kenneth."

Chapter Forty-four

A Living Legend

The years passed but Kenneth did not grow old. He seemed as age-less and indestructible as Diamond Head or the whale that hung from the ceiling of Hawaii Hall at Bishop Museum. To many people, including journalists and his former students, he *was* the museum. Stories about him acquired a patina and became little legends.

Every morning before going to work he strung a few leis from the fragrant orange blossoms of the *puakenikeni* tree growing in his backyard. He brought the leis to the museum and draped them on ladies who took his fancy. With each lei went a kiss. Secretaries, matronly volunteer guides, visitors—all were candidates for a lei and a kiss and they loved it.

At the museum he was surrounded by former students: Yosi, Marion Kelly, Dorothy Barrère, Cappy Summers, and Elspeth Sterling. Each had a favorite Kenneth Emory story about exploring a cave with him, or about the whistle he always carried in the wilderness, or about his weakness for chocolate bars, or about his habit of getting up with the roosters, or about his absolute disregard for hardship. They arranged a little birthday party for him every year, the annual social event of the anthropology department.

To the public he had become the source, the font, the final authority on prehistoric Polynesia. Telephone callers, to the despair of his secretary, constantly tapped his encyclopedic knowledge of things Hawaiian and encouraged his tendency to do too many things at once. Marion Kelly recalled later:

> Every year was a busy year for Kenneth. There was constantly something going on because he got truly excited about things. He'd get a phone call. Then he would pop up and go across the room and look through some past research material and locate a site somebody asked about and then make arrangements to go see it.
>
> I remember one time when Jo Bekin had been to Maui and had taken pictures of the Olowalu petroglyphs. She was so proud of the photos and insisted on showing them to Kenneth because she was helping him in the

anthropology department. He looked at the pictures and suddenly said, "Something's missing, something's missing. Let me get my slides."

He got his slides, and, sure enough, one of the petroglyphs had been chipped out and stolen. Kenneth went to the phone and called someone on Maui. There was a lot of publicity about the stolen petroglyph. Finally, it was returned, placed on the steps of the Wailuku [Maui] Museum. Then one of the sugar companies and a community organization got some funds together and constructed a walkway so people can view the petroglyphs without climbing over them. That's Kenneth. He recognized right away that a petroglyph was missing because he was so familiar with them.

Some of the younger archaeologists felt he was out of date. They lamented to each other his failure to write a site report for the historic first dig in Kuliouou Valley and for other excavations he headed. A site report is the careful documentation of the dig, step by step, as it is carried out. The work is boring, systematic, and meticulous—but crucial. Once the dig is finished, it is destroyed. The site lives only in the report from which other archaeologists can fit all the pieces back together, study their relationships to each other and to other digs, and draw meanings. Without a good site report, nobody else can interpret it.

Kenneth's horse-and-buggy digging techniques led one of the new breed at the museum to write a sharp criticism. This brought upon the young archaeologist's head the wrath of Marion Kelly, who had a new post as editor of anthropology department publications. "It's not fair to criticize Kenneth for being the way he is," she blazed. "He comes from a different time. Just remember, when you criticize his early digs, that without him there wouldn't be any digs at all." Yosi also made excuses for Kenneth. And Spoehr later smiled indulgently at his old colleague's failings.

Kenneth enjoyed his role as The Omnipotent One. Yosi did the fieldwork now, while Kenneth became more of a gardener who dug now and then. As head of the department Kenneth announced Yosi's discoveries and basked in them, like the superb excavation at Uahuka in the Marquesas in 1964 and 1965 that became a timetable against which all other elements of East Polynesian culture are measured. The dig sliced through the complete cultural history of the Marquesas from first settlement to the present. It was a textbook excavation.

Yosi had too much affection for Kenneth to complain about his monopoly of the spotlight. "I was doing what I wanted to do," Yosi explained. And Kenneth supported his assistant when he needed it. Such an occasion arose in 1965. An anthropologist from the Midwest asked Yosi to follow up on his discovery of pottery in the Marquesas the year before. The anthropologist wanted the information for a paper he was to give before the Pacific Science Congress in Moscow.

When Yosi arrived at the dig, a Marquesan worker confessed that he had played a joke on the Midwest anthropologist by making pottery on the spot and planting it in the dig. There was no time before the Moscow conference to write a letter from the remote Marquesas. Yosi radioed the anthropologist that the pottery was a hoax. The anthropologist assumed that Yosi wanted to save the discovery of pottery in the Marquesas for himself. Furious, he cabled Force at Bishop Museum who immediately went to Kenneth. Bewildered but loyal, Kenneth assured Force that Yosi was incapable of jealousy. The Midwest anthropologist eventually apologized when he realized he had been saved from making a fool of himself at the conference.

The Emory legend took shape in bits and pieces fitted together by journalists, museum volunteers, and friends and former students. Part of the legend was Kenneth's happy-go-lucky attitude behind the wheel of an automobile. He tended to shift into low gear going down a hill and choose the high gear for pulling up a slope, which stalled the engine. Kenneth would drive by a bakery, feel a sudden craving for sweet rolls, and make a left turn in the face of oncoming traffic. He became so interested in conversation that he forgot where he was going. The friends who knew him best preferred not to ride with him.

Marguerite was just as famous for being late. She took a regal, nonchalant attitude toward the passage of time, which created havoc even with Kenneth's haphazard social schedule. In desperation he set the clocks in their house ahead an hour. It made no difference to Marguerite because she did not look at clocks.

Pat Bacon, Kenneth's secretary after Marion Kelly, described how they almost missed a flight to Japan for the Pacific Science Congress in Tokyo in 1966. "Everybody was ready to go but Marguerite," said Bacon. "A fellow passenger they were picking up kept calling every five minutes. They finally picked him up with forty-five minutes to spare. On the way to the airport, Marguerite said, 'Oh, we have to go back. I forgot the book I as reading.' Their passenger pleaded with her to buy magazines at the airport. Then Marguerite said, 'My earrings. I left them on the table.' The worried passenger promised to replace her jewelry in Japan. He'll never forget that trip."

Nobody can remember who thought of surprising Kenneth with a special gift for his seventieth birthday, November 22, 1967. The idea took root and grew and blossomed like an exotic flower amid the clutter of rocks and bones in the anthropology department. The gift would be a book written in his honor by his friends around the world. Margaret Mead at the American Museum of Natural History promised to submit an article. So did Raymond Firth at the London School of Economics. Douglas Oliver from Harvard also contributed.

The list became a who's who in Pacific anthropology. A manuscript came from H. D. Skinner, the New Zealand pioneer, as well as one from Mary Kawena Pukui, the long-time Hawaiian scholar in Honolulu. Bengt Danielsson in Tahiti promised to write the introduction. Roland Force, Bishop Museum director, and Alexander Spoehr, former director, contributed articles. The young breed wrote pieces: Roger Green, Janet Davidson, Alan Howard, Ben Finney, and Adrienne L. Kaeppler. Kenneth's students added to the list: Dorothy Barrère, Yosihiko Sinoto, and Marion Kelly. They titled the book *Polynesian Culture History, Essays in Honor of Kenneth P. Emory.*

The museum trustees, with an eye toward Kenneth's retirement, arranged another gift—the John Ledyard Distinguished Chair in Culture History at Bishop Museum, of which Kenneth would be the first occupant. All these plans, of course, had to be accomplished in secret and kept from the most curious mind at the museum. To throw Kenneth off the scent, the ladies in anthropology invited him and Marguerite to the usual staff birthday party and, as usual, Marguerite was late. She and Kenneth arrived to find the museum overflowing with people. He, of course, had a marvelous time.

And he refused to slow down. With the tourist industry in full boom, Kenneth applied his energies to contract archaeology for construction companies building new resorts. In his battle to save old Hawaiian sites, he threw himself in the path of a bulldozer at Keauhou on the Kona Coast of the Big Island.

Yosi became chairman of the anthropology department in 1970, and Kenneth took the title of senior anthropologist. At seventy-three, he continued to fight for the preservation of Hawaii's Polynesian heritage. In 1974, a developer agreed to reconstruct Kamehameha's living quarters at Kamakahonu in Kailua, Kona, ending Kenneth's battle of almost twenty years to save the site. In 1975 Kenneth became adviser to the Polynesian Voyaging Society, a group dedicated to building a sixty-foot replica of a Polynesian voyaging canoe to be sailed on the ancient migration route to Tahiti without benefit of compass or sextant. The canoe, navigated by stars and the set of the waves, reached Tahiti in 1976, demonstrating that ancient Polynesians could have done the same. Kenneth greeted the crew in

Papeete, as proud of their accomplishment as if he had made the voyage himself.

By the time he turned eighty, he was wearing a pacemaker to control an irregular pulse beat. Every morning he appeared at the museum, distributed his *puakenikeni* leis, worked on unfinished manuscripts or upcoming lectures, and took calls for information about things nobody but himself could answer. He was as familiar and well known a part of the museum as fishhooks and stone adzes.

Frail, his white hair thinning and his hawk face creased with wrinkles, still shy and quick to laugh, he lived among people who admired and respected him. And he thrived on it. Each birthday produced a new recounting in the newspapers of his adventures and scientific discoveries. There had been so many they seemed inexhaustible. In 1983 delegates to the Pacific Science Congress assembled in New Zealand where he received the Gregory Medal for Distinguished Service to Pacific Science. That was sixty-three years from the time he had served as errand boy for the first congress.

In 1984 he received Hawaii's highest cultural honor, the Governor's Award for Distinguished Achievement in Culture, the Arts and Humanities. In 1985 more than five hundred people met at the Sheraton Waikiki Hotel to hear speakers once more review his achievements. A heart attack put Kenneth in the hospital seven days before the dinner. He fought his way out of intensive care and demanded to attend the party. His doctor finally gave in. But the hospital made the doctor sign a paper accepting responsibility if Kenneth expired on the way.

Kenneth arrived in a wheelchair as one of his former students, Rubellite Johnson, chanted the name chant given him by the natives of Vahitahi on his departure from the atoll in 1930. Kenneth sat through an hour and a half of slides and speech-making before the doctor finally decided he'd had enough. As a parting gesture Kenneth gave a shrill toot on the silver whistle he had always carried on expeditions.

Probably the honor he appreciated most came in 1983 from his colleagues at the museum. In memory of the leis he had distributed for so many years, the staff planted a grove of *puakenikeni* trees in an open space along the walkway to the old stone museum building. A journalist with a calculator estimated that Kenneth had, by this time, bestowed leis on more than 40,000 women with a kiss for each, an international record in the scientific world.

When it was all over, Kenneth said, "I'd rather have a grove of *puakenikeni* named after me than a building."

Acknowledgments

For at least three decades, members of the Kenneth Emory World Wide Fan Club tried to cajole, pressure, and otherwise shame their hero into writing a book about the amazing fund of anecdotes, adventure, and detailed knowledge that he carried around in his head about Polynesia. He always said he was too busy. I was taken by surprise, therefore, when the phone rang in my office at *The Honolulu Advertiser* late in 1983 and Kenneth's weak but spritely voice came on the line. He said his friends had finally talked him into having the story of his life written and he wanted me to do it.

I was between books. Choosing which book to write next is a normally a painful, protracted decision. It determines how you will spend the next year of two of your life. Kenneth's request came as informally as an invitation to lunch, because we had been friends for twenty-five years. I spent about five seconds making up my mind. Then I said, "Okay, Kenneth, I'll do it." Three and one-half years later, I finished it.

So many people have waited so long for the book on Kenneth Emory that I felt a heavy weight of responsibility. I collected eleven thousand sheets of typewritten notes and filed them chronologically in twenty-two large loose-leaf binders that take up four feet of shelf space. Most of this material has not been published until now, and much of it has not been available in libraries. This material includes transcriptions of ninety-two tapes of interviews with people who know Kenneth or worked with him, including about fifty tapes of conversations with Kenneth and Marguerite. It also includes entries copied from his diaries kept at home, newspaper clippings, copies of the private journals he kept on expeditions, material from his published works (but not very much), copies of his correspondence, and a mass of other material on file at the Bishop Museum library. More of the same was copied from his personal files, to which I had complete access, and his large file of newspaper clippings at the Hawaii Newspaper Agency.

This abundance of unpublished material, including material that was neither indexed nor filed, created two vexing problems. First, interesting facets of the story as well as anecdotes about Kenneth's life had to be left out to hold the manuscript to manageable size. Second, fully annotating the book to reflect the amount of documentation available would have made the manuscript even more bulky.

There is no neat solution to these problems but I tried to cope with them first by citing sources in the body of the text to lessen the need for other annotation, and second by donating my workbooks to the Bishop Museum Library. From beginning to end, all material in the workbooks is arranged by date. A researcher can find documentation and additional information, probably more than he or she cares to know, about any part of the book by looking in the workbooks under the date it happened. To make the search easier, I have created a short chronology of Kenneth's life that provides dates to use as landmarks while consulting the workbooks. This chronology follows these acknowledgments.

A book as human as the biography of Kenneth Emory requires the input of humans as its basic raw material. My debt to the people who contributed to the humanity of this work is profound. While most of them are named in the book, I want to express here my thanks to those who patiently endured my questions, who gave me lessons in the science of anthropology, and who trusted me with sensitive information.

First and foremost is Kenneth himself. To make the best use of our time together I first transcribed his handwritten, line-a-day diaries for the period we were to discuss. Using the diary as a framework I prepared questions about the events I wanted to know more about. Kenneth's answers are on the tapes that are transcribed in the workbooks.

My respect for Kenneth expanded the deeper I probed. There are things in this book he would prefer had been omitted. I know this because I read the book to him as I wrote it. We read through more than half of it before a stroke robbed him of the ability to communicate. There were parts he didn't like very well, and he corrected errors—for which I am grateful. Yet his criterion of acceptance was not his own ego, but rather what actually happened. If I could produce a letter, or a journal entry, or a witness to the part he questioned, that was the end of it. I hope his personal commitment to scientific objectivity, as well as his humility and delightful sense of humor, comes through in the book. The mistakes that remain in the book are mine, not his.

Marguerite's amazing recall of personal minutia formed the counterpoint to Kenneth's complete dedication to anthropology, as we sat through some fifty taping sessions around their dining room table. Marguerite has contributed immeasurably to the book and, after Kenneth became incapacitated, it was she who pulled together their family photo albums to be culled for illustrations.

Other friends of Kenneth who added information make their homes in places scattered between Hawaii, New York, and Tahiti. I especially wish to name and thank Dick Emory, Tiare Emory, Summer Banner, the late Edwin Bryan, the late Lorrin P. Thurston, Dr. Laura Thompson, Mary Stacey Judd, Dr. Douglas Oliver, Pat Bacon, David Twigg-Smith, Dr. Harry Shapiro, Dr. Bengt Danielsson, Aurora Natua, Medford Kellum, Gladys Kellum, Marii a Teai, Alex Ata, Henry Rittmeister, Edward Dodd, Dr. Yosihiko Sinoto, Dr. Alex Spoehr, Marion Kelly, Dr. Harold St. John, Dr. Yoshio Kondo, Dr. Raymond Fosberg, Dr. Roland Force, and Maryanne Force.

The unsung heroes and heroines of every book of nonfiction are the librarians who dig up the endless recorded scraps of information that anchor the dates, spell the names right, preserve the detail of past decades, and provide a framework on which to hang the anecdotes. Therefore I express my deep appreciation to Cynthia Timerlake, Marguerite Ashford, B. J. Short, and Eiko Lynch at the Bishop Museum Library for their courtesy and assistance during the many months I worked there with the Emory Collection. I wish also to thank photo librarian Betty Kam for help in making Bishop Museum photographs available. My thanks go also to the librarians at the Hawaii State Archives, and to Beatrice Kaya and her assistants at the Hawaii Newspaper Agency Library, and to *The Honolulu Advertiser* for use of photographs. Finally, I want to acknowledge my debt to Jean Brady, editor at the University of Hawaii Press, who polished the manuscript.

> Bob Krauss
> Honolulu 1987

Chronology

1893—Walter Emory and Winifred Pike, Kenneth's parents, are married.

1897, Nov. 23—Kenneth Emory is born in Fitchburg, Massachusetts.

1898, July 7—Hawaii is annexed to the United States.

1900—The Emorys move to Hawaii.

1901-1912—Kenneth's childhood, grade school, and summer vacations; he meets Jack London in 1907; Emorys move to Bates Street.

1912-1916—Kenneth at Punahou School; actively pursues hobbies: stamp collecting, shell collecting, printing, photography, steel guitar, surfing, fascination with the South Seas; visit to Haleakala Ranch in 1913; visit to Molokai with Jack London in 1915, study of Hawaiian language with Thomas Maunupau in 1916.

1916-1920—Career at Dartmouth College: hiking, skiing, the Mandolin Club, Dartmouth Winter Carnival, first published writing, biology major, summer vacations as swimming instructor, romances.

1920—Meeting at Yale with Dr. Herbert Gregory, Jan. 10. Kenneth is hired as assistant ethnologist for Bishop Museum at $75 per month. Initial assignment is errand boy for the first Pan-Pacific Scientific Congress on July 22. Accompanies archaeologist Robert T. Aitken on the first survey of ruins in Haleakala Crater on Maui on Aug. 27. Kenneth returns in charge of an expedition to complete the Haleakala Survey on Oct. 1. Assists Louis Sullivan in measuring Hawaii school children for racial characteristics on Nov. 16. Sails for the University of California at Berkeley for a semester of anthropology study with Dr. A. L. Kroeber on Dec. 29.

1921, July 12—Begins archaeological survey of Lanai, which ends Jan. 27, 1922. The survey results in his first major scientific publication.

1922, July 22—Sails for Harvard to study under Dr. Roland D. Dixon; earns a master's degree in anthropology. Returns to Honolulu on June 11, 1923.

1923, Nov.—Assists folk music specialist Helen Roberts in research that results in the classic work, *Ancient Hawaiian Music.*

1924—Bishop Museum director Gregory gives Kenneth on May 28 a place in the expedition to Samoa on board the luxury yacht, *Kaimiloa,* owned by Medford R. Kellum. Kenneth asks Armstrong Sperry to come along. Kenneth sails July 7 on the USS *Tanager,* a minesweeper, for an archaeological survey of Nihoa and Necker islets, discovers a strange type of shrine. *Kaimiloa* sails for Tahiti from Pier 10 in Honolulu on Nov. 9. Arrives at Fanning Island on Nov. 25, Christmas Island Dec. 6, Malden Island Dec. 20, and Tongareva (Penrhyn) Dec. 24.

1925—*Kaimiloa* arrives at Papeete, Tahiti, Jan. 1. Kenneth makes first voyage by copra schooner to the Tuamotus, Feb. 6–11. Meets Marguerite Thuret at a fancy dress ball, they begin romance on Feb. 21. Armstrong Sperry and Kenneth travel to Bora-Bora via Raiatea, March 10. Kenneth explores remote island of Maupiti March 17–25. Measures *marae*s on Bora-Bora March 26 to April 5. Kenneth measures *marae*s on Raiatea May 4–23. First expedition into Papenoo Valley May 4–23. Marguerite and Kenneth are married at Poofa'i Church on Sept. 17. Honeymoon trip to Moorea Oct. 6–17. Expedition to Huahine Nov. 18 to Dec. 12.

1926—Marguerite and Kenneth sail for France in the *El Kantaru* on Mar. 25. *El Kantaru* docks at Marseille on May 15. Emorys arrive in Paris, begin visiting museums on May 22. Kenneth meets Margaret Mead in the Trocadero on June 9. Survey of museums in Italy and Switzerland June 19 to July 22. Kenneth attends British Association for the Advancement of Science Aug. 4–13. Marguerite and Kenneth embark for England on Aug. 22. Sail from Liverpool for the United States to visit his family in New England on Sept. 4. Arrive in Honolulu on Dec. 14.

1927—Emorys buy a lot in Dowsett Highlands, begin building a home on Jan. 18. First child, Tiare, is born June 9. Kenneth's salary raised to $3,500 per year, and he helps edit *Ancient Tahiti* by Teuira Henry in August. Clears Lohiau's ruins at Haena, Kauai, on Sept. 19. Emorys move into new home Oct. 9. Kenneth writes up plans for Tuamotu expedition and correspondence begins between Frank Stimson and Kenneth in December.

1928—Stimson is appointed by Gregory to work with Kenneth as linguist in the Tuamotus on Feb. 21. Final plans for Tuamotu expedition approved by Gregory on Aug. 28. Marguerite becomes U.S. citizen on Sept. 25.

1929—Emorys sail to Tahiti, Feb. 14 to March 2. Kenneth decides to build a boat for sailing among the Tuamotu atolls, and frustrating failure of Bishop Museum treasurer to send money on time begins in March. First probe of Tuamotus by Kenneth, Stimson, and Harry Shapiro, April 16 to May 15. *Mahina-i-te-Pua* is launched on July 6. Kenneth picks up Peter Buck at Raiatea in the *Mahina* and returns for hasty conference with Stimson and Shapiro on July 18. Tuamotu expedition sails from Tautira, Tahiti, in the *Mahina* on Sept. 29; at Faite Sept. 11; at Katiu Sept. 12–14; at Raroia Sept. 16–20; at Napuka Sept. 21–Oct. 4; at Fangatau, where Kenneth gets names of shrine gods from aged sage, Temiro, Oct. 4–28; at Amanu Oct. 29– Nov. 5; at Hau Nov. 5–11. Kenneth makes voyage back to Tahiti in the *Mahina* on Nov. 11–16. Stimson and Shapiro are marooned on Hao until Dec. 27.

1930—Marguerite and Kenneth visit Makatea to see her Tahitian uncle and search for artifacts Feb. 17–29. Kenneth gets a coral cut while helping a companion after fall from cliff on March 23. Second long voyage in the *Mahina* begins June 17, arrives at Vahitahi on June 29. People of Vahitahi haul the *Mahina* out of the water and Kenneth films event on July 9. *Tipara* ceremony begins on July 16 and controversy begins between Stimson and Kenneth about the meaning of Kio. Kenneth sails for Tahiti in the *Pro-Patria* on Aug. 12–25. Returns to Vahitahi and films *tipara* on Sept. 11. Kenneth and Stimson sail from Vahitahi for Tahiti on Nov. 3

1931—Kenneth reads and is concerned about Stimson's paper on Kio on Jan. 21. The Emorys sail for Honolulu via New Zealand on May 22; controversy between Stimson and Kenneth continues by letter.

1932—Gregory edits Stimson's Kio/Kiho manuscripts. Baby girl, Winifred Emory, born July 22.

1933—Raymond Firth inquires about Kiho and sparks more controversy in January. Stimson's Kiho book is in type in February. Kenneth works out theory on ancient Polynesian navigation and records the chants of Kuluwaimaka; Theodore Kelsey transcribes them in March. Marguerite and Kenneth have Jacques Yves Cousteau to dinner in April. Stimson's first publications about Kiho come out in September. Mangareva expedition takes shape during the winter.

1934—Kenneth's report on archaeology of Tahiti, *Stone Structures in the Society Islands*, is published on Feb. 23. The Mangareva expedition sails in the sampan, *Islander*, for the South Seas from Honolulu on April 15. Kenneth disembarks with newsman Clifford Gessler at Napuka on May 16. Gessler's finger becomes infected on July 21. They sail from Napuka on July 28, and arrive at Fangatau on July 29 where Kenneth learns that Stimson's Kiho chants are invented by Fareua. Stimson and Kenneth land at Tatakoto on Aug.

9. Peter Buck arrives at Tatakoto in schooner, *Moana*, and all sail to Mangareva on Sept. 5. Kenneth works with Buck at Mangareva, Sept. 12–Nov. 5. Kenneth sails in *Tiare Tahiti* to rejoin Stimson on Pinaki and they clash about Kiho on nearby Nukutavaki on Nov. 5. Kenneth sails for home on Dec. 5.

1935—Confrontation between Kenneth and Gregory about Stimson who is asked to come to Honolulu for meeting on Feb. 15. Alfred Metraux arrives with expedition on Easter Island on Feb. 22. Stimson arrives in Honolulu on June 6. Stimson and Kenneth meet with Buck and Handy to discuss tampering with chants, and Kenneth begins his own interpretation of Tuamotu chants on July 15. Bishop Museum trustees announce retirement of Gregory, appointment of Buck as director for following year on Sept. 6.

1937—Kenneth finishes his own work on *Tuamotuan Religious Beliefs*, but Buck declines publication Feb. 16. Metraux sounds alarm about Stimson Kiho material in April. Buck warns editor of *Polynesian Journal* about Stimson errors in translation of Easter Island chants on May 4. Kenneth climbs Mauna Kea on Aug. 15 to study shrines of adz makers and finds they are similar to Necker shrines. *Polynesian Journal* rejects Stimson article in the winter, accepts Kenneth's piece on Tuamotuan religion.

1938—Kenneth discovers Hawaiian burial ground on Mokapu Beach, Kaneohe, in March and begins long period of excavation. Begins writing "Flying Spray" articles in September.

1939, Jan. 13—First of "Flying Spray" articles published in Honolulu newspapers.

1940, Aug. 13—Kenneth sails for Yale to begin his doctorate.

1941—Marguerite joins Kenneth at New Haven on March 18. Kenneth takes oral exam for doctorate in anthropology and passes on May 10. The Emorys return to Honolulu in the *Lurline* on Sept. 10. Japanese war planes bomb Pearl Harbor on Dec. 7. Kenneth begins storing artifacts, microfilming rare documents on Dec. 8. He joins Businessmen's Training Corps.

1942—Dinner on Oct. 14 with Dartmouth classmate Clark Ingraham, now a naval officer, who asks for advice about survival on atolls. Kenneth's survival manual, *Castaway's Baedeker*, is published on Dec. 6, becomes museum's all-time bestseller.

1943—Kenneth begins survival demonstrations at Honolulu Academy of Arts on Jan. 6. Survival demonstrations move to Bishop Museum on Jan. 13. Kenneth flies to Espiritu Santo in the New Hebrides (Vanuatu) to give survival lectures and study Melanesians, Sept. 15–Oct. 28.

1944, Nov. 9—Kenneth and George P. Murdock talk about exploring Micronesia.

1945—Kenneth discusses Micronesia with group including Douglas Oliver in February, and meetings continue. Begins work on Ph.D. dissertation, chronology based on language of first settlement of Polynesians, on Sept. 1.

1946—Finishes Ph.D. dissertation on April 19. Attends meeting on Micronesia in Washington, D.C., continues on to Yale to receive Ph.D. in June. Gives first lecture on Sept. 24 as anthropology instructor at University of Hawaii, night classes.

1947—Kenneth sets out on July 12 with Peter Buck, Sam Elbert, and Carroll Lathrop for Kapingamarangi, Polynesian outlier in Micronesia, arrives at Kapinga on July 15. Departs from Kapinga on Oct. 15.

1948—Low pay and high living costs in Honolulu reduce Emorys to pennypinching. Kenneth asks permission to teach daytime classes at U.H. to support himself, trustees give permission.

1949—Kenneth travels to Dartmouth to be awarded honorary doctorate of science.

1950—Kenneth begins teaching a class in archaeology at the university, takes his class to dig in a shelter cave at Kuliouou in February, although accepted dogma says it is a waste of time. The class soon finds many artifacts; charcoal sample from Kuliouou cave sent to Dr. W. F. Libby at the University of Chicago for carbon dating in June. Kenneth marooned for four months on Kapingamarangi with medical doctor Ralph Miller, makes definitive study of the culture July 1–Nov. 27.

1951—First carbon date for Polynesia received (from Kuliouou Cave sample) A.D. 1004, on Feb. 19. Conservation Council formed at Iolani Palace to save historic and archaeological sites on Feb. 22; Kenneth becomes hero of site committees. Peter Buck dies, Kenneth appeals on Dec. 1 to George Murdock at Yale to help the failing museum.

1952—Murdock makes a whirlwind visit to Bishop Museum, sets in motion new era on Jan. 8. Kenneth takes his university archaeology class to Molokai to dig at Moomomi Beach in the summer. Dig supported by grant from McInerny Foundation.

1953—Dr. Alexander Spoehr arrives to be director of Bishop Museum on Jan. 23. Dig under Kenneth begins at South Point, Hawaii, on Aug. 28; through fishhooks, eventually leads to direct links to Tahiti.

1954—Kenneth and his class return to South Point. Yosihiko

Sinoto from Japan turns up at dig on July 10, becomes Kenneth's assistant.

1955—More excavation at South Point. Kenneth leads survey of South Kohala Coast. Yosi and Kenneth working on fishhooks for use as time tracers.

1957—Survey of Honaunau for National Park Service, Jan. 22–Feb. 10. Charles E. Snow, Kenneth, and Yosi investigate casket of Liloa, find iron dagger and woven *malo* on April 11.

1958—Dig at Nualolo Kai, Kauai. Frank Stimson dies.

1959—Hawaii becomes a State of the Union on March 12. Kenneth sums up what he has learned from dirt archaeology to Social Science Association on April 6. Begins twenty-year battle to save Kamehameha's old living site at Kamakahonu in Kailua, Kona, on April 22. Carbon date for South Point comes in at A.D. 124 in July. Kenneth is cautious. Hurricane Dot catches Bishop Museum expedition in Nualolo Kai valley in August.

1960, April 17–Sept. 13—Kenneth and Yosi in Tahiti to introduce dirt archaeology, disappointing results.

1961—Pacific Science Congress convenes in Honolulu on Aug. 21, plan formed for archaeological investigation of the Pacific. Spoehr resigns as director of Bishop Museum in November, Dr. Roland Force appointed. National Science Foundation grants $79,000 to fund archaeology in Polynesia and Kenneth named as principal investigator on Dec. 14.

1962—Another expedition in Tahiti begins on May 16. In Papeete, Yosi stumbles upon archaic artifacts from Maupiti on May 20. Yosi returns from Maupiti on June 19 with more archaic artifacts linking Tahiti to New Zealand and the Marquesas to Hawaii. Kenneth helps Yosi settle in at Moorea, they find fishhooks June 27–July 7. Kenneth returns to Honolulu, sums up Tahiti discoveries for *New York Times*, and explores Haleakala July 7–Aug. 1.

1963—Kenneth and Yosi return to Maupiti on May 17, supply boat capsizes and fifteen people drown. Kenneth on Bora-Bora restoring *marae*s Aug. 21–Oct. 25, returns to Honolulu on Oct. 26. At American Anthropological Association meeting in San Francisco in November, Kenneth delivers lecture summing up Bishop Museum discoveries in Tahiti.

1964–1965—Yosi conducts classic dig at Uahuka, Marquesas.

1966—Pacific Science Congress convenes in Tokyo.

1967—Kenneth turns seventy, is surprised with a dinner, a book in his honor, *Polynesian Culture History*, and is recipient of new John Ledyard Distinguished Chair in Culture History.

1970—Yosi replaces Kenneth as chairman of anthropology at Bishop Museum. Kenneth becomes senior anthropologist.

1974—Kamakahonu at Kailua, Kona, restored.

1976—*Hōkūle'a* makes first voyage to Tahiti.

1983—Kenneth receives Gregory Medal at Pacific Science Congress in New Zealand. Grove of *puakenikeni* trees planted at Bishop Museum in his honor.

1984—Receives Governor's Award for Distinguished Achievement in Culture, the Arts and Humanities.

1985—Five hundred attend dinner in Kenneth's honor, he comes in spite of heart attack.

Index